THE WORLD'S CLASSICS

A HAZARD OF NEW FORTUNES

WILLIAM DEAN HOWELLS (1837–1920) was born in Ohio, the son of a printer. Despite a scant formal education Howells read widely, and later, while a journalist on the *Ohio State Journal*, began to study languages. In 1860 he wrote a campaign biography of Lincoln, and was rewarded with the consulate in Venice, where he wrote several studies of Italian life and literature. Shortly after his return to America in 1865, he took up the subeditorship of the *Atlantic Monthly*; after five years he became its editor-in-chief and held the post for a decade. During those years he wrote several novels, including *Their Wedding Journey* (1872) and *The Lady of the Aroostook* (1879). The 1880s, after Howells had left the *Atlantic*, saw a shift in emphasis in his fiction towards realism. The major novels from this period include *A Modern Instance* (1882), *The Rise of Silas Lapham* (1885), a masterpiece on Boston society and the self-made businessman, and *Indian Summer* (1886).

In 1889 he moved from Boston to New York, to work on the staff of *Harper's* magazine. His major novel of this period, *A Hazard of New Fortunes* (1890), reflects his increasingly socialist sympathies and his interest in the problems of industrialism.

Throughout his later life Howells was considered the pre-eminent man of American letters. He continued to write prolifically, producing several volumes of literary criticism (including *Criticism and Fiction*, 1891), over thirty dramas, further novels, autobiographies, travel sketches, and many short stories. He was also enormously influential in promoting the work of other writers, including Henry James, Stephen Crane, and Mark Twain.

TONY TANNER is a Fellow of King's College, Cambridge. His books on American literature include *The Reign of Wonder*, *City of Words*, and *Scenes of Nature, Signs of Men*. For the World's Classics he has edited Melville's *Moby Dick* and another novel by Howells, *Indian Summer* (also with John Dugdale).

JOHN DUGDALE is the author of a forthcoming study of the novelist Thomas Pynchon.

THE WORLD'S CLASSICS

===

WILLIAM DEAN HOWELLS

A Hazard of New Fortunes

A Novel

===

with an Introduction by
TONY TANNER

and Explanatory Notes by
JOHN DUGDALE

Oxford   New York
OXFORD UNIVERSITY PRESS
1990

Oxford University Press, Walton Street, Oxford OX2 6DP

Oxford New York Toronto
Delhi Bombay Calcutta Madras Karachi
Petaling Jaya Singapore Hong Kong Tokyo
Nairobi Dar es Salaam Cape Town
Melbourne Auckland
and associated companies in
Berlin Ibadan

Oxford is a trade mark of Oxford University Press

Published in the United States
by Oxford University Press, New York

Introduction, Note on the Text © Oxford University Press 1965
Select Bibliography, Chronology © John Dugdale 1988
Explanatory Notes © John Dugdale 1990

First published as a World's Classics paperback 1990

Library of Congress Cataloging-in-Publication Data
Howells, William Dean, 1837–1920.
A hazard of new fortunes: a novel / William Dean Howells;
with an introduction by Tony Tanner,
and explanatory notes by John Dugdale.
p. cm. — (The World's classics)
Bibliography: p.
I. Dugdale, John. II. Title. III. Series.
PS2025.H3 1990 813'4—dc20 89-34251
ISBN 0-19-282702-2

British Library Cataloguing in Publication Data
Howells, W. D. (William Dean, 1837–1920)
A hazard of new fortunes: a novel. —
(The world's classics)
I. Title
813'.4 [F]
ISBN 0-19-282702-2

Typeset by
Eta Services (Typesetters) Ltd., Beccles, Suffolk
Printed in Great Britain by
BPCC Hazell Books Ltd
Aylesbury, Bucks

CONTENTS

INTRODUCTION

'THE most vital of my fictions', wrote Howells of *A Hazard of New Fortunes*; and certainly this book, finished in 1889 when Howells was 52, represents the peak of his achievement as a novelist. It was also the full flowering of certain changes which had come about in his life (and hence in his fiction) since 1886; and to appreciate his achievement up to that date it is useful to turn to an essay by Henry James, summing up Howells's contribution to American literature, and written in 1886, just before the changes commenced. James praises Howells's 'unerring sentiment of the American character' and notes admiringly his capacity to 'feel' and respond to the quality of contemporary American life. 'I will not say that Mr. Howells feels it all equally, for are we not perpetually conscious how vast and deep it is?—but he is an authority upon many of those parts of it which are most representative.' He then stresses the strong documentary bias in Howells's work—'I know of no English novelist of our hour whose work is so exclusively a matter of painting what he sees, and who is so sure of what he sees'—and welcomes it in these terms: 'His work is of a kind of which it is good that there should be much today—work of observation, of patient and definite notation.'

Howells's work does reveal a deep faith in a sort of positivism, a habit of scrupulous regard for the massed contingencies of one particular place at one particular time (he was indebted to both Comte and Taine), and his conviction as to the supreme value of sheer observation is responsible both for the limits and virtues of his work. 'The only secret of art is to observe with the naked eye', he wrote in 1871: he is surely wrong, for art has many more secrets than that, but it was just this singleness of concentration which enabled him to make his unique contribution to American literature. The American imagination, then as now, tended to express itself in romance, projecting its vision through symbol and myth, rarely content to limit itself to what James called 'the fatal futility of Fact'. But Howells considered facts to be far from futile, and he made them the object of his patient concern.

As a novelist he started late, and he started cautiously. Before his first novel, written when he was 35 and largely autobiographical (*Their Wedding Journey*), he had published books on Italy and a collection of *Suburban Sketches* which addressed themselves to the task of objective description of specific localities. Gradually Howells enlarged his scenes, trying to assemble, as it were, a gallery of limited but complete pictures of American life as it was then being lived. He was giving America something that Hawthorne, Melville, Poe, Cooper, even James himself did not give and probably did not care to give; something, however, which America very much needed at that time—normative images of contemporary society. When Mark Twain and Henry Adams both praised the 'photographic' quality of Howells's early work, they were not simply paying a fashionable compliment. American society had very few photographs of itself, and in post-Civil-War America, with convulsive industrial and social changes making themselves felt, Howells did invaluable work in showing Americans to themselves in the *milieu* of the moment. As James pointed out, he concentrated on the representative places and people of America— Bartley Hubbard and Silas Lapham rather than Hester Prynne and Captain Ahab—but though there is much that is merely charming and innocent in his early comedies of manners, he can occasionally be as sharply perceptive as his beloved Jane Austen; and works like *A Modern Instance* were the reverse of flattering. He was in fact attacked for being cold, sceptical, analytic, scientific, and too concerned with commonplace things and people. So Howells made one of his characters in *The Rise of Silas Lapham* counter the sort of romantic idealism which produced such criticisms with the words: 'Commonplace? The commonplace is just that light, impalpable, aërial essence which they've never got into their confounded books yet.' Emerson had indeed asserted the 'worth of the vulgar'—'I embrace the common,

I explore and sit at the feet of the familiar, the low'—but for purely philosophical or mystical motives. His transcendentalism enabled him to intuit the divine unity of all things by meditating on the most trivial fact; but 'embracing the common' was more of a religious exercise than anything else. For Howells it was a crucial tenet in an aesthetic creed which was to produce an important period of social realism in American literature. James's description of Howells's qualities as a novelist gains added force if we realize that it was a description which, at that time, could not have been applied to any other American writer.

He is animated by a love of the common, the immediate, the familiar and vulgar elements of life, and holds that in proportion as we move into the rare and strange we become vague and arbitrary; that truth of representation, in a word, can be achieved only so long as it is in our power to test and measure it. He thinks scarcely anything too paltry to be interesting, that the small and vulgar have been terribly neglected, and would rather see an exact account of a sentiment of a character he stumbles against every day than a brilliant evocation of a passion or a type he has never seen and does not even particularly believe in. He adores the real, the natural, the colloquial, the moderate, the optimistic, the domestic, and the democratic; looking askance at exceptions and perversities and superiorities, at surprising and incongruous phenomena in general.

James appreciates Howells's 'art of imparting a palpitating interest to common things and unheroic lives', and finishes with a generous and accurate prediction about Howells's future work. 'It is hard to see how it can help being more and more fruitful, for his face is turned in the right direction, and his work is fed from sources which play us no tricks.' But, in passing, James also offers a serious criticism of Howells's novels. He suggests that they reveal the innocence of American life inasmuch as they 'exhibit so constant a study of the actual and so small a perception of evil'.

It was a fair comment. But on 4 May 1886 a bomb was thrown in Haymarket Square, Chicago, killing eight policemen: eight known anarchists were arrested, regardless of alibis, and in an atmosphere of brutal mob hysteria, one subsequently committed suicide and four were hanged.

This was the turning-point in Howells's life. Hitherto he *had* thought that, on the whole, 'the more smiling aspects of life' were 'the more American'. Now, after this blatant and vicious miscarriage of justice, Howells lost his sanguine and complacent attitude towards American society, never fully to recapture it. To his father he wrote, 'the historical perspective is that this free Republic has killed five men for their opinions': to a friend, 'it's all been an atrocious piece of frenzy and cruelty, for which we must stand ashamed forever before history'. Howells himself, with real courage, defended the men and protested against the sentences passed. This availed nothing for the victims—but much for his fiction. He wrote to Hamlin Garland: 'I did not bring myself to the point of openly befriending those men who were civically murdered in Chicago for their opinions without thinking and feeling much, and my horizons have been indefinitely widened by the process.' Those widening horizons ultimately resulted in *A Hazard of New Fortunes*, the first comprehensive attempt to anatomize the new emergent urban-industrial America.

Up to 1866 Howells had mainly focused on the failings and foibles of individuals seen against the accepted stabilities of some provincial setting: manners and morals were scrutinized, but the complexities of economics and politics did not intrude. After that he tried increasingly to explore and reveal the forces at work in American society at large, for the stability of society could no longer be taken for granted—something was wrong with it, rotten in it. In *Silas Lapham* the subject is the moral rise which accompanies the financial fall of the main character. In *A Hazard of New Fortunes* the real subject is the future of America. That gives some idea of how much the horizons had widened for Howells in a mere three years.

Several other events and influences combined with Howells's anguish over the Haymarket affair to produce the widened scope and deeper seriousness of *A Hazard of New Fortunes*. Since he was a writer who relied very largely on personal experiences and feelings in his writing—to ensure that verifiable authenticity of texture which was his aim in fiction—it is not surprising that his letters provide some clear hints on the direct relationship between his life at the time and the novel. In a letter to Mrs. Achille Fréchette written in 1887 he describes his feelings about the execution of the anarchists and then goes on to ask: 'Have you read Tolstoi's heart-searching books? They're worth all the other novels ever written.' It was just at this time that Tolstoy became the major influence on Howells, not only encouraging him to attempt a new comprehensiveness in his coverage of society, but forcing him to re-examine his ideas on the relationship between individual morality and society. He wrote later: 'I can never again see life in the way I saw it before I knew him.' Tolstoy, as much as the Haymarket affair, determined the mood of the novel; a mood also influenced by the protracted illness and ultimate death in 1889 of his daughter Winifred, so that much of the sombre brooding in the book is charged with his own private sadness.

We have clues as well to the sources of some of the material used in the novel. Thus in 1887 he wrote to DeForest: 'I'm just back from my old home in Ohio, where I saw a town in full boom from the discovery of natural gas. It was a wonderful spectacle gaseously, materially and morally. I believe I shall try to write a story about it. I saw lots of character, blowing off with almost as much noise as the gas wells themselves.' This provided him with a potent image of the terrifying, possibly infernal, powers which had been unleashed over a land hitherto almost completely rural and agrarian, producing people with new powers and new problems—like Dryfoos in the novel. In 1888 he wrote to James: 'I found your letter here when I came home this morning from a house-hunt in New York. . . . I should hardly like to trust pen and ink with all the audacity of my social ideas; but after fifty years of optimistic content with "civilization" and its ability to come out all right in the end, I now abhor it, and feel that it is coming out all wrong in the end, unless it bases itself anew on a real equality. . . . But at the bottom of our wicked hearts we all like New York, and I hope to use some of its vast, gay, shapeless life in my fiction.' The move to New York provided Howells with the initial impetus for the novel—he himself was hazarding new fortunes in New York at the time—and his house hunt occupied the first fifth of the finished book. This move away from Boston was as significant as his earlier infiltration of it had been. It meant that the literary centre of America had moved, for the first time, out of Brahmin New England. In focusing on the mixed turbulence of New York—from whence Boston seemed to be 'of another planet'—Howells effectively signalled the end of an epoch in American literature. As for his new social ideas, they were coming to him thick and fast in the late eighties: Edward Bellamy, Henry George, Laurence Gronlund, William Morris, the 'Fabian Essays', as well as Tolstoy, all contributed to the socialist ideas which increasingly occupied his mind, and influenced his fiction. In *The Minister's Charge* (1887) the Rev. Sewell preaches his last sermon on the theme of 'Complicity', a concept which became of major importance to Howells after the Haymarket affair. Then in *Annie Kilburn* (1888), bearing in mind the more than 10,000 strikes that had disrupted the economy in 1886, Howells turned his attention squarely to 'the relations of capital and labour'. *A Hazard of New Fortunes*, with its wide spectrum of social philosophies opposed and juxtaposed, is the result of these years of incessant troubled thinking by Howells; it is his definitive attempt to explore and express the variety of social theories which proliferated as the faults and horrors of a capitalist *laissez-faire* society became increasingly apparent.

More immediately, a prolonged traction strike which occurred in New York while he was finishing his novel gave Howells just the sort of documentary material he most liked to work from, and its occasional ugly incidents offered a precedent for the violent climax with which he brought the issues of his book to a head. Howells believed that if the structure of society was all wrong then the best way to get at that wrongness was, almost literally, to go out into the streets and pick up the evidence as it offered itself. Many of the tours which Basil March takes round the city come straight out of Howells's own notebooks, kept while he was engaged in similar wanderings, and the scattered street incidents which shock him had shocked Howells: even the restaurant 'Maraoni's', where March meets Lindau, was 'Moretti's', where Howells used to dine with a club of literary and theatrical people. Similarly many of the characters for the novel were recruited at least partially from people Howells had known: Lindau was based on a lonely German refugee called Limbeck who taught Howells German when he was twenty, and Fulkerson owes much of his being to a wild, free-wheeling, picaresque character, known to Howells and Mark Twain, named Ralph Keeler. The Marches are of course based on the Howells family: his favourite observers, they occur in seven novels, three times as major figures. Basil March, standing by Lindau against the capitalist Dryfoos and risking his job, is, in effect, Howells writing in defence of the Haymarket anarchists—a gesture of principle which also could have put his employment in serious jeopardy. And Basil March, involved in a society which he knows is corrupt and unjust, feelingly aware of the inequalities and suffering around him, uncertain as to blame, uncertain as to cure, conscience-stricken but ineffectual— that too is Howells, 'theoretical Socialist, practical Aristocrat' as he called himself, the very image of the worried intellectual who sees many wrongs but has no solutions, who is himself concerned to maintain his high standard of living in the precarious society whose defects occupy his waking mind.

Before examining how Howells gathered these disparate materials together into a novel it will be helpful to consider some of his literary theories and economic ideas: we may then be in a better position to understand the form of the novel and the moral import of its action. Howells's realism, his love for 'the poetry that resides in facts and resides nowhere else', his stress on 'veritism' and 'the truthful treatment of material', was throughout moral. He himself contrasted the 'spiritual' realism of the Russians with the 'sensual' realism of the French, and in his own work he never attempted to emulate the unsparing and unremitting analytic candour of the French school. He thought that life should be looked at 'in the right American manner', a manner which will 'question the results with the last fineness for their meaning and value'. The moral meaning was out there in the facts if the novelist only observed honestly enough: 'Morality penetrates all things, it is the soul of things.' So he can assert, with no contradiction, first that 'the novel ends well that ends faithfully', and then that the most poisonous and mendacious of novels are those which 'imagine a world where the sins of sense are unvisited by the penalties following, swift or slow, but inexorably sure, in the real world'. His idea of objective truth never involved moral neutrality, simply because he did not believe that the truth could be morally neutral. A novelist must not be false to humanity, 'either in its facts or its duties'—the one was as apparent as the other. Similarly, he would ask of a novel: 'Is it true?—true to the motives, the impulses, the principles, that shape the life of actual men and women? This truth, which *necessarily* includes the highest morality and the highest artistry—this truth given, the book cannot be wicked and cannot be weak' (my italics). Art had a responsibility, it should help us 'to know and to understand, that we may deal justly with ourselves and one another': art which 'disdains the office of teacher is one of the last refuges of the aristocratic spirit which is disappearing from politics and society, and is now seeking to shelter itself in aesthetics'. After the Haymarket affair, as his sense of involvement and responsibility grew, he felt that art, though objective, should be committed— *engagé* as we should now say. 'Art, indeed, is beginning to find out that if it does not make friends with Need it must perish.' On the other hand realism should not be 'tendencious. It does not seek to grapple with human problems, but is richly content with portraying human experiences.' It should do justice to the insoluble complexities of real life and 'the God-given complexity of motive' in real people—

no romantic gloss, no facile superadded sermons, no 'un-reality'. He wanted to see characters as he saw them in Hardy, 'in the necessity of what they do and what they suffer', that is, 'really doing what they must while seeming to do what they will'.

This raises the complicated question of determinism. Howells thought it is 'our conditioning which determines our characters, even though it does not always determine our actions'. This is an uneasy compromise which leaves some scope for moral assessment and allows important possibilities to personal conduct: it keeps the full pessimism of naturalism at bay. On the other hand it leads to difficulties when it comes to the shaping of a novel: here Howells believed that 'the man does not result from the things he does, but the things he does result from the man, and so plot comes out of character'. That is—environment determines character, which in turn should determine the shape of the book. Believing this, Howells was consistent in his scorn for 'plot' and his lack of interest in 'novels of incident, of adventure'. A novelist should just 'put certain characters before you' and, as it were, leave the rest to them. His ideal of a novel was the 'free and simple design' of *Don Quixote*, in which 'event follows event without the fettering control of intrigue' and all 'grows naturally out of character and conditions'. He thought this 'loose, free and variable form' would be ideal for portraying the fluid life of America and, although in his own early work he favoured the economic and narrow focus of Turgenev, he moved on to wider, vaster books which could encompass the random comings and goings of many characters. As though trying to catch the very shapelessness of life itself he says: 'I don't know that you are bound to relate things strictly to each other in art, any more than they are related in life'; and he came to realize and assert that 'the more art resembles life, the less responsive it [is] to any hard and fast design.' Characters should not be constrained by a plot: the constraints of environment would suffice.

This faith that observation and ordinary life when brought

together would produce a novel led Howells to undervalue style and composition: these latter sounded aristocratic and aesthetic, and Howells wanted art to be democratic and humanitarian. James saw this trend in his work. He wrote, in 1886, that Howells was wrong to say that 'style matters less and less', and he regretted that Howells 'should appear increasingly to hold composition cheap—by which I mean, should neglect the effect that comes from alternation, distribution, relief. He has an increasing tendency to tell his story altogether in conversations.' Clearly Howells's position involves grave formal difficulties since all art must depend on some selection and arrangement and Howells leaves himself few criteria to determine these. It is as though his ideal of fiction would be to capitulate to the profuse inclusiveness of life itself. We will not embark on the theoretical problems involved in his ideas, but just point to these difficulties in relation to *A Hazard of New Fortunes*. He wants to bring a number of people together to examine their various views and several fates. But how, in the absence of a plot? He himself saw the difficulty. 'There are few places, few occasions among us, in which a novelist can get a large number of polite people together. . . . Perhaps it is for this reason that we excel in small pieces with three or four figures, or in studies of rustic communities, where there is propinquity if not society. Our grasp of more urbane life is feeble; most attempts to assemble it in our pictures are failures, possibly because it is too transitory, too intangible in its nature with us, to be truthfully represented as really existent.' So, refusing to bind his fluid material with a plot, he was left with an essentially episodic method of composition. As he said, somewhat defensively, 'a big book is necessarily a group of episodes more or less loosely connected by a thread of narrative, and there seems no reason why this thread must always be supplied'. Yet without this 'thread' he still wanted to show that all human lives are intertangled, to bear out his theory of 'complicity'—and the purely episodic book would have tended to demonstrate rather the opposite, the fragmentary unrelatedness of people. So instead of a plot he sets up a situation which will plausibly permit characters to come and go and talk to each other, even bringing them into occasional collisions and embraces. This situation is the editing of the magazine *Every Other Week* (based, of course, on his long experience as editor of the *Atlantic Monthly*). The contributors and their families can fairly be expected to come into contact with each other. But this is an external contrivance: how can he initiate any significant action? The answer is that he cannot, without having recourse to tiny bits of plot—extraordinary coincidences, unexpected meetings, sudden violence in the streets (the coming together of March and Lindau at the place of Conrad's death in the riot is a contrived and melodramatic chance beyond the bounds of pure realism): these are necessary to supplement the domestic gatherings, the office meetings, the conversational strolls which permit his characters to talk but not, really, to act. Say what he will, it is Howells who forces his characters together. Left alone, there is really nothing to combine all the people in the book; no significant action irresistibly draws them all in. They converge but never really congregate: they touch and jostle with no real engaging and relating. Their lives overlap but are in no way interlocked. When they walk out of a room, or out of a chapter, they walk out into a void: when they reappear it is Howells who has summoned them. This is perhaps part of the unintentional truth of the book; that in the new world represented by the great conglomeration of New York, people are both responsible for each other and separated from each other. Alongside Howells's entirely acceptable theory of human complicity has to be set the undeniable fact of human isolation. People lead plotless lives: the writer must provide one if art is to display values and meanings not to be discerned in the blurred continuity of everyday life.

Yet Howells did want his work to do something more than display the fortuitous configurations of the commonplaces of life. What this 'more' was can best be suggested by some of his comments on the European writers he admired. Thus: 'The great and dreadful delight of Ibsen is from his power of dispersing the conventional acceptations by which men live on easy terms with themselves and obliging them to examine the grounds of their social and moral opinions.' Like Tolstoy he made it his business 'to make us look where we are standing, and see whether our feet are solidly planted or not. What is our religion, what is our society, what is our country, what is our civilization?' He welcomed the French realists because if the house of society is in disrepair we should know it, and also because 'it is extremely valuable to have the underpinnings of sentiment and opinion examined, from time to time'. The novelist cannot offer solutions ('the longer I live the more I am persuaded that the problems of life are to be solved elsewhere, or never'), but he can 'give us pause'. That is, he can and must 'make us take thought of ourselves, and look to it whether we have in us the making of this or that wrong, whether we are hypocrites, tyrants, pretenders, shams conscious or unconscious; whether our most unselfish motives are not really secret shapes of egotism; whether our convictions are not mere brute acceptations; whether we believe what we profess'. And Tolstoy's great achievement is to 'bring us back to the gospels as the fountain of righteousness'; he teaches 'the law and life of self-sacrifice'. A good novel may be sad 'because life is mainly sad everywhere', and it should not be final since finality is beyond us: but above all it should demonstrate that 'in the vast orphanage of nature we have no resource but love and union among ourselves'. This is what Howells wanted to show in his most ambitious novel.

Clearly we have gone beyond aesthetic considerations here, because for Howells ideas about art were inseparable from social and even religious convictions. His own were in fact very simple, despite all the social theorists he was reading so avidly. He had no flair for economic analysis, and his economics no less than his aesthetics were based on ethics. The most important of his ethical ideas can be traced back to his childhood, which he spent in rural Ohio under the strong influence of a father who was a benign and intense Swedenborgian. Much of what Howells found in Tolstoy was in fact a refinding of his childhood influences. As he realized: 'Tolstoi gave me new criterions, new principles, which, after all, were those taught us in our earliest childhood, before we came to the evil wisdom of the world.' The basic idea he learned from his father was that self-concern and love of this world are damning: only honest labour and selfless love can save—egotism is the root of all evil. All his later theories rest on this conviction. The other major influence was simply being brought up in rural America 'where all had enough and few too much': 'we are a village people' he later wrote, and what he meant, like any Populist, was that life in America deteriorated and grew more corrupt as it drew further from the small rural communities he grew up in. Silas Lapham is regenerated by renewed contact with rural America: Dryfoos cannot go back, any more than America could go back, and his fall seems unredeemable.

These two influences combined to make Howells detest the ferocious competitiveness involved in urban capitalism. This new economy seemed to produce 'insuperable inequalities' which effectively prevented 'the brotherhood' which was the avowed ideal of America. Howells never really understood what was happening, economically, in America. All he could see was a vicious predatory selfishness and a cruel indifference spreading among the population as the industrial revolution grew in power. At the same time the cities grew and the land was ravenously exploited and despoiled. Howells's anatomy of society went no further than a juxtaposition of these facts. In his Utopia of *Altruria* the economy tends everywhere to simplification, and the inhabitants prefer cities to shrink. Their major achievement is to have controlled the struggle for survival and to have passed from 'a civility in which people live *upon* each other to one in which they lived *for* each other'. Howells knew there was no going back, but he had no realistic notions of how to supervise and modify the growth of the society of his age, no proper concepts of the mechanics of control. He had instead a pious mystical faith (again Swedenborgian) that the new society would somehow appear. 'I look forward to the decay of both the old parties, and the growth of a new one that will mean true equality and real freedom.' He hated all violence (hence the criticism of Lindau in the book) and was convinced that 'every drop of blood shed for a good cause helps to make a bad cause'. He still believed that the labouring class 'has the majority of votes and can *vote* the laws it wants'. He was never a party man or an active reformer (a vote for Bryan in 1896 was about the limit of his partisanship): he simply had 'faith in the grand and absolute change', a faith, be it said, which was often darkened by moods of total pessimism. Letters of 1890 contain these sentiments—'for the greater part of the time I believe in nothing, though I am afraid of everything. . . . Perhaps we can only suffer into the truth, and live along, in doubt whether it was worth the suffering. It may be an illusion, as so many things are (may be all things); but I sometimes feel that the only peace is in giving up one's own will.' There was always a mystical, quietistic side to Howells, a part of him which withdrew from the world of hard facts and brutal economics. (It is worth remembering that the next novel he wrote was *The Shadow of a Dream*, a novel that moves into the silent elusive domains of the private heart and soul.)

His economics thus appear naïve. But as a novelist he was more immediately concerned with individuals and he was able to show quite graphically the havoc and despair caused by the myriad forms of egotism and selfishness which people display. He saw America becoming a plutocracy and minced no words in proclaiming the fact; but the only remedy for social wrongs, indeed for all wrongs, as far as he could see, was 'love'. His idea that 'men are bound together so indissolubly that every advance must include the whole of society', his theory of 'complicity', his notion of 'the mystery of our human solidarity'—these are more religious than political, more Christian than Marxist. The dangers of 'selfhood', 'the distinction of self-forgetfulness', the idea that 'whenever we love, the truth is added unto us', the certainty that 'unselfish labour gives so much meaning to human life'—such beliefs have little to do with economics, but they are basic to Howells's fiction. His economic ideas, then, like his mature ideas about fiction, really come down to the one basic tenet: 'In the vast orphanage of nature we have no resource but love and union among ourselves.'

This brief summary of Howells's ideas at the time should help us to appreciate what he was trying to achieve in this novel. In it he manages to touch on most of the doubts and hesitations and worries that were bothering him, and a good deal of society, when he wrote. None of the characters is wholly right or completely evil, nor are they caricatured into mere ciphers for different theories. But they do represent the varying points of view which were shaping the America of that time. Basil March is basically the centre of consciousness, and one of his meditations about the 'frantic panorama' of New York leads up to the basic proposition of the book:

Accident and then exigency seemed the forces at work to this extraordinary effect; the play of energies as free and planless as those that force the forest from the soil to the sky; and then the fierce struggle for survival, with the stronger life persisting over the deformity, the mutilation, the destruction, the decay of the weaker. The whole at moments seemed to him lawless, godless; the absence of intelligent, comprehensive purpose in the huge disorder, and the violent struggle to subordinate the result to the greater good, penetrated with its dumb appeal the consciousness of a man who had always been too self-enwrapped to perceive *the chaos to which individual selfishness must always lead.* (my italics)

This is modern America, and Howells in the book tries to show the multiplicity of types of selfishness that are responsible, somehow, for the chaos of society; and the rarer types of selflessness which at present are helpless to redeem society—as things are, they can only die for it in the name of a better future. Conrad Dryfoos is a Tolstoyan figure of renunciation and good works, too saintly to live. Lindau, the socialist, is dismembered by the society for which he once gave a hand. He dies for his opinions, like the Haymarket anarchists, though his own theories are vitiated by the acceptance of violence and he is fatally wounded in a brawl he is actively encouraging. These two selfless extremists are foredoomed victims of a selfish society, and Howells gives them added dignity by hinting a comparison between Lindau and the Old Testament prophets, and between Conrad and Christ. Another impractical idealist is Woodburn, with his hatred of commercialism and his dream of a perfected agrarian feudal society, such as he thinks the South could have created (a prophetic touch by Howells—Woodburn's ideas live on!).

The two most selfish characters are Dryfoos and Beaton, and here Howells displays real insight. Dryfoos, the very incarnation of selfish individualism, is in many ways a victim of a change in society. In a rural community his ideals of self-help were valuable, as they had been for the pioneer: with the full release of the uncontrollable potential of the industrial revolution his old virtues become new vices, because of the terrible power at their disposal. 'His moral decay began with his perception of the opportunity of making money quickly and abundantly.' He is the supreme example of 'the men who have made money and do not yet know what money has made them'. All normal feelings dry up in him: he ends a hollow man, lost to all joy, shaken by remorse, a slightly bewildered victim of the 'dog eat dog' world in which he made his pile and lost his soul. Dryfoos is Howells's mordant parabolic representative of America itself. His wife is a more pathetic victim, utterly out of place in the world of commercial success, while his daughters represent a new type—shallow and crude but destined to be a disruptive influence in society because of the unanswerable force of their wealth. Beaton is in private what Dryfoos has been in public. (Howells suggests a link through Christine's intaglio ring—Beaton trifles with it on her hand, doubtless meditating whether to marry her for her money; while it is on Dryfoos's hand when he strikes his son—his wealth has thus soured his natural affections.) Beaton is a clever artist, and also a complete egotist, utterly insensitive to the needs and feelings of other people, a subtly drawn justification of Howells's insight that 'to do whatever one likes is finally to do nothing that one likes, even though one continues to do what one will'. Howells was acute enough to realize that 'a nature like Beaton's was chiefly a torment to itself', for Beaton is condemned to selfhood, and Howells manages to convey just what a wretched, empty life results from such a condition. Beaton finally seems to lose all volition entirely, too light and irresolute to go through with the suicide that he triflingly meditates, just as he has triflingly meditated a variety of personal relationships which he is too self-preoccupied to develop. He is a nasty and rather chilling example of the utterly selfish life, and one of Howells's most telling portraits.

Fulkerson, the gay, philistine, unscrupulous, entrepreneur type, can survive in society; while March himself starts the book as a 'self-enwrapped' man of average selfishness, who gradually learns to take a more engaged, less egotistical view of society. (Just before the end of the book he gets a new hat—in Jungian terms this indicates a new personality, but it is doubtful if Howells intended anything so symbolic.) This development reflects the metamorphosis Howells himself underwent, and is a particularly interesting comment on Howells's changing conception of the responsibilities of art. At first as March wanders round New York he sees only the 'picturesque' aspects of the various poverty-stricken 'phases of low-life' he encounters: they offer good, and profitable, copy for the magazine. It is Conrad who maintains that the city is really preaching a continual sermon and that art could serve an ethical purpose by making 'the comfortable people understand how the uncomfortable live'. When the strike is on, Fulkerson is still keen to exploit its 'aesthetic aspects' for the magazine, but March develops a broader awareness and subtler conscience and is in a position to act as a spokesman for Howells's own views. Somewhat like Howells's idol Tolstoy, he has 're-placed the artistic conscience by the human conscience'. He does very little, apart from objecting to Lindau's dismissal, but his early complacency has given way to heart-felt doubts and worries and his late musings are more social than artistic:

Some one always has you by the throat, unless you have some one else in *your* grip. I wonder if that's the attitude the Almighty intended His respectable creatures to take toward one another! . . . what I object to is this economic chance-world in which we live, and which we men seem to have created. . . . At any time of life—at every time of life—a man ought to feel that if he will keep on doing his duty he shall not suffer in himself or those who are dear to him, except through natural causes. But no man can feel this as things are now; and so we go on, pushing and pulling, climbing and crawling, thrusting aside and trampling underfoot; lying, cheating, stealing; and when we get to the end, covered with blood and dirt and sin and shame, and look back over the way we've come to a palace of our own, or the poor-house, . . . I don't think the retrospect can be pleasing.

It was in the late eighties that Howells's own art began to 'make friends with Need': more generally he felt that the American artist was not paying enough attention to the conditions and qualities of the life around him. Since, as he reiterates in this book, 'conditions *make* character', it followed that he should want American artists to turn their gifts to portraying the contemporary environment. He himself goes out of his way in this novel to include descriptions of the conditions of life all over New York: he is extremely observant about architecture and interior decorations; he devotes much time and attention to clothes and furniture; he describes with care different streets and various immigrant communities. As always he is fascinated by all means of transport (he himself was an early example of the rootless, semi-nomadic artist), and he is particularly brilliant in his evocation of the Elevated trains at night and the great railway stations of the city. Indeed, he seems to anticipate the Ash-can School of painters when he comments, reproachfully, on 'the superb spectacle' of the railway 'which in a city full of painters nightly works its unrecorded miracles'. Howells took it upon himself to record a great deal of what had hitherto been left unrecorded and, in contrast to the trivial aestheticism exemplified by Beaton, he encouraged American artists to come to grips with the surging, unexplored stuff which filled their daily lives.

Thus with its compendious variety—of character, of idea,

of scenic detail—the novel attempts, as no other novel had previously attempted, to present an inclusive image of contemporary American life. It is an impressively honest book. All the characters, except the saints, live in 'enforced complicity with rapine'; they all 'respect money' and have to sell out, more or less, to survive; they all 'truckle and trick' to some degree, though some have more principles than others. March shares Howells's mystical hope that one day, somehow, 'the order of loving kindness, which our passion or our wilfulness has disturbed, will be restored', but meanwhile, as he says, 'we go on trembling before Dryfooses and living in gimcrackeries'. The book portrays a society in which people are insecure, bewildered, often alone, submerged or elevated by forces beyond their control, living in desperate poverty or surrounded by the vulgar 'gimcrackeries' which serve as the status symbols of the currently well-to-do (Howells wrote one of the most sympathetic reviews of Veblen's *Theory of the Leisure Class* when it appeared). While behind them all is the heartless teeming anonymity of the city, the new world that Dryfoos and all he stands for was all unconsciously, all inevitably, bringing into being. It was something to tremble before; and it was a remarkable feat to produce a novel which could adequately and forcefully communicate that profound apprehension.

Howells's importance for American literature transcends his actual achievement as a novelist. By the end of his life he had become the first—and hitherto the last—American Academician. It is not too much to say that for the last quarter of the nineteenth century Howells was responsible for educating and directing American literary taste. His lifelong fight was against the falsifying unreality of base romantic literature (he respected the genuine sort of romance such as Hawthorne wrote); he wanted to gain respect and attention for 'the phrase and carriage of everyday life'. He spoke for empirical observation and against facile idealism. In a famous passage he imagined the old-fashioned idealist complaining to the modern scientist in these terms:

I see that you are looking at a grasshopper there which you have found in the grass and I suppose you intend to describe it. Now don't waste your time and sin against culture in that way. I've got a grasshopper here, which has been evolved at considerable pains and expense out of the grasshopper in general; in fact, it's a type. It's made up of wire and card-board, very prettily painted in a conventional tint, and it's perfectly indestructible. It isn't very much like a real grasshopper, but it's a great deal nicer, and it's served to represent the notion of a grasshopper ever since man emerged from barbarism. You may say that it's artificial. Well, it is artificial; but then it's ideal too; and what you want to do is to cultivate the ideal. You'll find the books full of my kind of grasshopper, and scarcely a trace of yours in any of them. The thing that you are proposing to do is commonplace; but if you say that it isn't commonplace, for the very reason that it hasn't been done before, you'll have to admit that it's photographic.

Howells made the real grasshopper his particular care and the upholders of the ideal grasshopper his particular enemies. When he wrote, in his first novel, 'Ah, poor Real Life, which I love, can I make others share the delight I find in thy foolish and insipid face' he was, in effect, announcing a programme. When he started to write, the sentimental tradition had a firm grip on American literature. These romancers (like Horace Courtenay, Caroline Lee Hentz, Rose Terry—but their name is legion) inculcated, wrote Howells, 'a varying doctrine of eager conscience, romanticized actuality, painful devotion, and bullied adoration, with auroral gleams of religious sentimentality'. However, in 1862 T. W. Higginson, in 'A Letter to the Young Contributor' (published in *Atlantic Monthly*), pleaded for an indigenous and contemporary American literature; and for the next forty years, mainly under the leadership of Howells, a school of realism grew up which was to have a lasting effect on the whole subsequent development of American literature.

Apart from his own work, which was very popular and influential in his own time (he was perhaps the first American writer to make a very good living by writing), Howells encouraged other American writers and introduced foreign authors, forcing them on the attention of his contemporaries as probably no other man could have done at that time. If ever a man tried to be in touch with the best that was being written and thought, that man was Howells: it is hard to imagine what would have happened to American taste and, indeed, American literature, without his ceaseless and untiring aid, his impassioned and judicious supervision. Here are some of the writers he either encouraged to write and first published, or effectively introduced to an American audience for the first time: Henry James, Mark Twain, John DeForest, Edward Eggleston, Sarah Orne Jewett, Mary Murfree, George Washington Cable, Bret Harte, Harold Frederic, Hamlin Garland, Frank Norris, Stephen Crane. Indeed, it was almost entirely due to Howells that by 1900 there were very few sections of America that had not been written about: he made Americans regard and respect their own land, their own kind. But he also turned their attention abroad, and with the help of the remarkable Thomas Sergeant Perry (who wrote some 427 items for Howells) he introduced or directed attention towards such people as: Gogol, Tolstoy, Dostoevsky, Turgenev, Baudelaire, Flaubert, Stendhal, Zola, Musset, the Goncourts, Mérimée, Gautier, Mistral, Bourget, Scribe, Dumas the elder, Saint-Beuve, Renan, Björnson, Ibsen, Shaw, Verga, Galdós, Valdés. As well as being a cultured editor he was a brave one: in 1881 he published a sensational exposé of big business, Henry D. Lloyd's 'The Story of a Great Monopoly', which was a telling indictment of Standard Oil and a forerunner of the Muckraking movement. This list alone reveals what a generous, sensitive, and intelligent critic Howells was. Apart from 'banging the babes of Romance about' as he called it (an activity which attracted to his work the labels 'atheism', 'poison', 'dirt'), he was, in Dreiser's words, 'the lookout on the watch tower straining for a glimpse of approaching genius'. He wrote, sincerely, 'nothing of my own which I thought fresh and true ever gave me more pleasure than I got from the like qualities in the work of some young writer revealing this power', and it was surely an open-minded critic who could start his career by encouraging the unknowns, Henry James and Mark Twain, and finish it by introducing and supporting Crane, Garland, and Norris.

By the end of his life Realism was threatened by two new movements. First, a recrudescence of romanticism. Frank Norris described it in these terms: 'Just as we had with *Lapham* and *A Modern Instance* laid the foundations of a fine, hardy literature that promised to be our very, very own . . . we commenced to build upon it a whole confused congeries of borrowed, faked, pilfered romanticisms'; while in his famous interview with Howells, Stephen Crane said: 'It seemed that realism was about to capture things, but then recently I have thought that I saw coming a sort of counter wave, a flood of the other—a reaction, in fact.' That was in 1894: by 1900 books like *The Prisoner of Zenda* were selling in millions, and in 1904 *Colliers Magazine* could announce that 'the popular novel of today is romantic—romantic in subject and effusively romantic in method. . . . All this is far removed from the minute study of commonplace people which Mr. Howells has made the basis for most of his fiction'. Howells could see what was happening. It was just after the Spanish war and, he wrote, being ashamed of our 'lust of gold and blood' we now welcomed 'the tarradiddles of the historical romancers as a relief from the facts of the odious present'. As he said to Crane, 'I suppose we shall have to wait'.

But there was another, more serious, change in fiction which he recognized without being able to adapt himself to it. He wrote with typical tolerance in 1903: 'A whole order of literature has arisen, calling itself psychological, as realism called itself scientific, and dealing with life on its mystical side . . . we have indeed, in our best fiction, gone back to mysticism, if indeed we were not always there in our best fiction, and the riddle of the painful earth is again engaging us with the old fascination.' Howells's realism was based on the premiss that the meaning of life could be gleaned from the observable surfaces of people and things: now writers were diving for private meanings dragged out from hidden depths. Howells's time was over. But not before he had done enough to earn the sort of praise lavished on him in *The Critic* in 1899. 'He is part of our literary climate. We breathe Howells, most of us. . . . We cannot untangle him from ourselves. His art belongs to us. Our common American lives are the warp and woof of all that he has brought. In his large and sane and noiseless way he may be said to have done more for the self-respect of American fiction than any other living man.'

Howells's work was admired by people as various as Mark Twain and Henry James in America, and Turgenev and Thomas Hardy abroad. When *A Hazard of New Fortunes* appeared it proved to be very popular, and it undoubtedly exerted a positive influence on the progressive thinking of the nineties. Howells's reputation reached its apogee in 1912 when President Taft made a special journey to attend his 75th birthday dinner, and praised his service to the ideals of 'refinement and morality', calling him 'a force for good'. By this time Howells had become a symbol of orthodoxy and the official culture, and as such he was soon under attack from the young writers of a new age. In 1915 he wrote to James: 'I am comparatively a dead cult with my statues cut down and the grass growing over them in the pale moonlight'; and soon he was to be jeered at as being the head of the 'sissy school' of literature. Gertrude Atherton blamed Howells for making American literature 'the most timid, the most anemic, the most lacking in individualities, the most bourgeois, that any country has ever known'. Mencken, having read almost none of Howells's work, proclaimed: 'He had nothing to say. . . . His psychology was superficial, amateurish, often nonsensical; his irony was scarcely more than a polite facetiousness; his characters simply refused to live.' Sinclair Lewis spoke of him with patronizing contempt in his Nobel Prize speech of 1930 ('he had the code of a pious old maid'), and in the same year V. L. Parrington wrote that 'in elaboration of the commonplace he evades the deeper and more tragic realities that reach to the heart of life'. All rebels and innovators need a figure to tilt at, and Howells, at least as a symbol, was all too obvious and available. Since then there has been no great renewal of interest in his work, though several discerning critics have found a lasting value in it. Lionel Trilling has made a brilliant case for him (of which more later). Newton Arvin pointed out that it was Howells who described the 'warped and stunted and perverted lives' of Americans at the turn of the century, and added that 'few writers have realised so keenly what happened to the old dogmas of self-help and self-cultivation by the time the triumph of individualism had taken its toll of them'. He found Howells's work still 'usable', particularly for its 'implicit criticism of an ego-centric culture'. Henry Steele Commager found in his novels a 'realism that does not depend upon sensationalism or violence, a style that is subtle rather than raucous, and a concern for values that are permanent rather than transient'. Other critics, like Edwin Cady and Everett Carter, have written systematic and sympathetic books on Howells and gradually a more appreciative view is being taken of his total achievement. 'Your really beautiful time will come', wrote James to Howells. It has not come yet, but we are now perhaps in a good position to assess his peculiar qualities as well as his undeniable limitations.

Again it is James who provides a fine note of just appreciation, this time in a letter written to Howells on his 75th birthday (1912). He stresses the advantages Howells reaped by staying at home: 'You have piled up your monument just by remaining at your post. For you have had the advantage, after all, of breathing an air that has suited and nourished you; of sitting up to your neck as I may say—or at least up to your waist—amid the sources of your inspiration.' This gave Howells an increasing authority of perception so that 'they make a great array, a literature in themselves, your studies of American life, so acute, so direct, so disinterested, so preoccupied but with the fine truth of the case. . . . You saw your field with a rare lucidity; you saw all it had to give in the way of the romance of the real and the interest and the thrill and the charm of the common, as one may put it;

the character and the comedy, the point, the pathos, the tragedy, the particular home-grown humanity under your eyes and your hand and with which the life all about you was closely interknitted. Your hand reached out to these things with a fondness that was in itself a literary gift. . . .' It is a touching and generous piece of praise, the more so as one feels how different were James's own fictional interests from the democratic 'documentary' notation he approved in Howells. But occasionally he managed to suggest his reservations; implying not only that Howells wrote too much, too variously, and too facilely—which he did—but that he was leaving something out. In 1884 for example he wrote: 'I don't think you go far enough, and you are haunted with romantic phantoms and a tendency to factitious glosses'; and in 1890: 'There's a whole quarter of heaven upon which, in the matter of composition, you seem con-sciously—*is* it consciously?—to turn your back.' Edith Wharton doubtless had the same thing in mind when she spoke of the 'incurable moral timidity' she felt in Howells's work. More outspokenly, Norris finally came to assert the limitations of Howells's realism, with its focus on 'the ordinary, the untroubled, the commonplace', and advocated a fiction which could reach down into 'the unplumbed depths of the human heart, and the mystery of sex, and the problems of life, and the black, unsearched penetralia of the soul of man'.

There is undeniable justice in the charges brought against Howells. There are certain passions his characters are never moved by; none of them ever get out of hand; no black energy threatens the prevailingly decorous tone of his novels. Howells tended to keep any *radical* disorder out of his work. His characters appear in low relief. There are no baffling penumbras between them, no uncertain spaces and twilight recessions behind them. His novels are decidedly not 'fraught with background'. Yet he himself was far from being the 'incurable optimist' James thought him. Here, for instance, is a letter to Mark Twain about the latter's pro-posed autobiography: 'You always rather bewildered me by your veracity, and I fancy you may tell the truth about your-self. But *all* of it? The black truth, which we all know of our-selves in our hearts, or only the whitey-brown truth of the pericardium, or the nice, whitened truth of the shirtfront? Even *you* wont tell the black heart's truth. The man who could do it would be famed to the last day the sun shone on.' If Howells kept the 'black heart's truth' out of his work it was not from ignorance.

He did practise exclusion, of course, despite his avowed reverence for all truth. He admitted that he preferred 'cleanly respectabilities' and would have no 'palpitating divans' in his own work. He responded to Whitman's work but complained: 'He has told too much . . . [the reader] goes through his book, like one in an ill-conditioned dream, perfectly naked, with his clothes over his arm.' Writers of our time have often found 'more enterprise in walking naked', but Howells had different ideals. He was writing to try and create a society in which people would be 'refined, humane, appreciative, sympathetic', and to that end 'always I strove for grace, distinctness, for light, and my soul detests obscurity still'. He believed that 'most of the good things come from the mean of life'. Not that he was unaware of the turbulent amoral life of the unconscious, the 'filmy shapes that haunt the dusk' (see for instance *Between the Dark and the Daylight*), but he preferred 'clear day'. Undoubtedly there were personal motives behind this preference: it was willed, even a little desperate. 'Man is a creature of light; tragedy is darkness. In its presence he stands before the un-known, before the night, and the result is not revelation, but impenetrable darkness.' It was better, therefore, to con-centrate on 'the normal daily round, with its endless variety of revelation of traits and formative influences, its gentle humor and gentler pathos, its ills for which it ever has its uses and its cures'. Edwin Cady has described Howells's own psychic troubles and recurrent nightmares and depres-sions, and suggests that he adopted, as a strategy for survival, what William James called the religion of healthy-minded-ness, by which 'the slaughter-houses and indecencies without end on which our life is founded are huddled out of sight and never mentioned, so that the world we recognize officially in literature and society is a poetic fiction far handsomer and cleaner and better than the world that really is'. Howells knew what he was keeping out, but it seems that there were some areas he dare not penetrate, some darknesses he dare not enter. He knew about them—after all he did admire Ibsen and Zola—but he had to hold back. He could have written, with the Goncourts, that his consuming interest was 'the passion for the study of reality', but he could not have gone on, as they did, to speak of a delight in penetrating to 'life itself, with its entrails still warm and its tripe still palpitating'. And if we do detect some failure of penetration, some slackness and thinness, some lack of real imaginative thrust in his work, it is at least partially because of our current conviction that, in William James's words, 'healthy-mindedness is inadequate as a philosophical doctrine, because the evil facts which it refuses positively to account for are a genuine portion of reality, and they may after all be the best keys to life's significance, and possibly the only openers of our eyes to the deepest levels of truth'.

About the mess and injustice of his contemporary society Howells had many penetrating things to say, but in his dealings with his characters he refused to see far beyond their conscious minds. It is the relative egotism or selflessness they exhibit in relations with other people which interests him more than their most private, most inward convulsions. As people moved towards the atypical, the excessive, the aberrational, the singular experience, Howells did not follow them. We should be cautious, however, of ascribing this simply to a failure of nerve. It was also a matter of where —for civilization's sake—he thought the emphasis of fiction could most profitably be put.

'If America means anything at all, it means the sufficiency of the common, the insufficiency of the uncommon.' Howells's words come strangely to our ears, for where his fiction tried to demonstrate this adequacy of the average, the literature we now most value tends to concentrate on departures from it. There is much less consensus of agreement about external reality now, and no available normative images of society. Our literature is drawn to the private, the isolated, the alienated, the disorderly, the violent—as though life only becomes meaningful in its extreme states. This was Trilling's point with reference to Howells. He noted that we now tend to exhibit a preoccupation with evil, chaos, and disintegration which in turn leads to a devaluation of 'moderate sentiments' and commonplace existence—a devaluation which is not only impoverishing but ultimately dangerous. It is as though we feel that ordinary life, as it stands, is too small, too trivial for art. He adds: 'When we yield to our contemporary impulse to enlarge all experience, to involve it as soon as possible in history, myth, and the oneness of spirit . . . we are in danger of making experience merely typical, formal, and *representative*, and thus of losing one term of the dialectic that goes on between the spirit and the conditioned, which is, I suppose, what we mean when we speak of man's tragic fate. We lose, that is, the actuality of the conditioned, the literality of matter, the peculiar authenticity and authority of the merely denotative.' Because we now feel that 'the mind's power of shaping is more characteristic of mind than its power of observation' our artists tend increasingly to devote themselves to the power of form, a devotion which 'is likely to be conceived in terms of hostility to matter, to matter in its sheer literalness, in its stubborn denotativeness'. Howells's strength was precisely his grasp of the denotative, the actual, the given.

Much modern art tends to solipsism, moving only in inward realms, seemingly trying to free itself from the objective world altogether. This is what Georg Lukacs means by 'the attenuation of actuality' in modern western art: we are 'exalting man's subjectivity, at the expense of the objective reality of his environment'. This tendency towards 'the negation of outward reality' carries grave dangers in its train: neglect of the outer world finally leads to the disintegration of the inner self. As Lukacs says, 'attenuation of reality and dissolution of personality are interdependent'.

Now it is just this sane belief in the existence and value of external, literal matter which is Howells's strongest virtue. He had faith in the value of objective reality simply as it was observed: it did not first have to be refracted through the imagination, reshaped by the human mind. Inevitably this simple belief led him to underestimate the importance, the indispensability of form, and this in turn prevented him from achieving any profound imaginative understanding of the reality he took so sturdily for granted. But his reverence for the commonplace gives his work a health, a humanity, an integrity which our predilection for the uncommon has led us, perhaps, to undervalue. What was it Dreiser called him?—'one of the noblemen of literature . . . a wholly honest man'. As such, he deserves better than his current neglect.

A NOTE ON THE TEXT

A Hazard of New Fortunes was first published in *Harper's Weekly* between 23 March and 16 November 1889. It was issued as a novel in paper wrappers on 27 November 1889 by Harper and Brothers, New York. It was published in two volumes, cloth-bound, on 27 January 1890. It was first published in Great Britain by David Douglas, Edinburgh, on 2 December 1889 in the two-volume edition. The text which follows is taken from the first British edition. The *Yale Bibliography of American Literature* suggests (volume 4, page 408) that 'there is a possibility that the Edinburgh (Douglas) edition, 2 volumes, was issued simultaneously with the one-volume New York edition'; and as the Douglas edition was taken from the eleven paper-covered parts which were received from America and deposited at the British Museum between 10 April and 1 November 1889 (for copyright purposes), this seems to me to be the most authentic available text.

SELECT BIBLIOGRAPHY

FICTION BY HOWELLS

Selected Edition of W. D. Howells (Bloomington, Indiana: Modern Language Association), ed. E. Cady, R. Gottesman, D. Nordloh; in several volumes, and including all the works cited below.

Novels 1875–1886 (New York: Viking Library of America, 2nd printing 1982), includes *A Foregone Conclusion, A Modern Instance, Indian Summer, The Rise of Silas Lapham*.

A Modern Instance (Harmondsworth: Penguin, 1977), introd. Edwin H. Cady.

The Rise of Silas Lapham (New York: Norton Critical Edition, 1982), ed. Don L. Cook.

—— (Harmondsworth: Penguin, 1983), introd. Kermit Vanderbilt.

LETTERS

Mildred Howells (daughter), *A Life in Letters of W. D. Howells* (New York: Doubleday, 1929), 2 vols.

Mark Twain–Howells Letters; the correspondence of S. L. Clemens and W. D. Howells 1872–1910 (Cambridge, Mass.: Belknap Press, 1967), ed. Henry Nash Smith, William Gibson, 2 vols.; the same editors also produced a one-volume selection.

BIOGRAPHY

Edwin H. Cady, *The Road to Realism; the early years, 1837–1885, of William Dean Howells* (Syracuse, New York: Syracuse University Press, 1956).

—— *The Realist at War; the mature years, 1885–1920, of William Dean Howells* (Syracuse, New York: Syracuse University Press, 1958).

Mildred Howells, as above.

Kenneth S. Lynn, *William Dean Howells: an American life* (New York: Harcourt, Brace, Jovanovich, 1971).

SELECT BIBLIOGRAPHY

CRITICISM

Critical Essays on W. D. Howells, 1866–1920 (Boston: G. K. Hall, 1983), ed. Edwin H. Cady and Norma W. Cady.

Howells; a century of criticism (Dallas: Southern Methodist University Press, 1962), ed. Kenneth Eble; includes articles on Howells by Twain, James, and Hamlin Garland.

Everett Carter, *Howells and the Age of Realism* (Philadelphia: Lippincott, 1954).

John W. Crowley, *The Black Heart's Truth: the early career of W. D. Howells* (Chapel Hill: University of North Carolina Press, 1985).

Olov Fryckstedt, *In Quest of America: a study of Howells's early development as a novelist* (Cambridge, Mass.: Harvard University Press, 1958).

Kermit Vanderbilt, *The Achievement of William Dean Howells; a reinterpretation* (Princeton, NJ: Princeton University Press, 1968).

BIBLIOGRAPHIES

William Gibson and George Arms, *A Bibliography of W. D. Howells* (New York Public Library, 1948).

American Literary Realism, Howells special number (1969), includes extensive bibliographies, with more recent material.

A CHRONOLOGY OF
WILLIAM DEAN HOWELLS

1837   Born in Martinsville, Ohio, the son of William Cooper Howells, a printer and publisher of various papers in Ohio, with Swedenborgian leanings and radical political views.

1853–60   Trained as a printer and largely self-educated, Howells works as a journalist in Cincinatti and other cities in Ohio, and publishes essays, poems, and stories in the major Eastern magazines.

1861–5   As reward for writing Lincoln's campaign biography, he is made US Consul in Venice for the duration of the Civil War. Marries Elinor Mead in 1862.

1866–70   Becomes assistant editor of the *Atlantic Monthly* in Cambridge, Mass., where he moves in literary circles which include Longfellow, Lowell, and Holmes, of the older generation, and William and Henry James. Publishes two Italian travel books.

1871   Becomes editor of the *Atlantic Monthly*, which serializes works by James and Mark Twain, and carries essays by progressive thinkers on social issues.

1872   *Their Wedding Journey* published.

1873   *A Chance Acquaintance.*

1875   *A Foregone Conclusion*; *Private Theatricals.*

1879   *The Lady of the Aroostock.*

1881   Established as a novelist, Howells resigns as editor of the *Atlantic Monthly*. Publishes *Dr. Breen's Practice*; *A Fearful Responsibility.*

1882   *A Modern Instance.*

1883   *A Woman's Reason.*

1883–4   Writes *Indian Summer* after return to Italy in 1882.

1885   *The Rise of Silas Lapham.*

1886   *Indian Summer.*

1887   Pleads publicly for the lives of Chicago anarchists wrongly convicted of murder in the Haymarket Riots.

1890   *A Hazard of New Fortunes.*

1891–1909 As a freelance writer, publishes essays on current affairs from a socialist perspective, and literary criticism in which he champions European realists such as Zola and Ibsen, and supports their American counterparts, Crane and Norris. Continues to write fiction, and also memoirs.

1910   Death of Elinor Mead Howells, and of close friend Mark Twain.

1920   Dies of pneumonia.

A HAZARD OF NEW FORTUNES

PART FIRST

I

"Now, you think this thing over, March, and let me know the last of next week," said Fulkerson. He got up from the chair which he had been sitting astride, with his face to its back, and tilting toward March on its hind-legs, and came and rapped upon his table with his thin bamboo stick. "What you want to do is to get out of the insurance business, anyway. You acknowledge that yourself. You never liked it, and now it makes you sick; in other words, it's killing you. You ain't an insurance man by nature. You're a natural-born literary man; and you've been going against the grain. Now, I offer you a chance to go *with* the grain. I don't say you're going to make your everlasting fortune, but I'll give you a living salary, and if the thing succeeds you'll share in its success. We'll all share in its success. That's the beauty of it. I tell you, March, this is the greatest idea that has been struck since——". Fulkerson stopped and searched his mind for a fit image—"since the creation of man."

He put his leg up over the corner of March's table and gave himself a sharp cut on the thigh, and leaned forward to get the full effect of his words upon his listener.

March had his hands clasped together behind his head, and he took one of them down long enough to put his inkstand and mucilage-bottle* out of Fulkerson's way. After many years' experiment of a moustache and whiskers, he now wore his grizzled beard full, but cropped close; it gave him a certain grimness, corrected by the gentleness of his eyes.

"Some people don't think much of the creation of man, nowadays. Why stop at that? Why not say since the morning stars sang together?"*

"No, sir; no, sir! I don't want to claim too much, and I draw the line at the creation of man. I'm satisfied with that. But if you want to ring the morning stars into the prospectus, all right; I won't go back on you."

"But I don't understand why you've set your mind on *me*," March said. "I haven't had any magazine experience, you know that; and I haven't seriously attempted to do anything in literature since I was married. I gave up smoking and the Muse together. I suppose I could still manage a cigar, but I don't believe I could——"

"Muse worth a cent." Fulkerson took the thought out of his mouth and put it into his own words. "I know. Well, I don't want you to. I don't care if you never write a line for the thing, though you needn't reject anything of yours, if it happens to be good, on that account. And I don't want much experience in my editor; rather not have it. You told me, didn't you, that you used to do some newspaper work before you settled down?"

"Yes; I thought my lines were permanently cast in those places once. It was more an accident than anything else that I got into the insurance business. I suppose I secretly hoped that if I made my living by something utterly different, I could come more freshly to literature proper in my leisure."

"I see; and you found the insurance business too many for you. Well, anyway, you've always had a hankering for the inkpots; and the fact that you first gave me the idea of this thing shows that you've done more or less thinking about magazines."

"Yes—less."

"Well, all right. Now don't you be troubled. I know what I want, generally speaking, and in this particular instance I want *you*. I might get a man of more experience, but I should probably get a man of more prejudice and self-conceit along with him, and a man with a following of the literary hangers-on that are sure to get round an editor sooner or later. I want to start fair; and I've found out in the syndicate business all the men that are worth having. But they know me, and they don't know you, and that's where

2

we shall have the pull on them. They won't be able to work the thing. Don't you be anxious about the experience. I've got experience enough of my own to run a dozen editors. What I want is an editor who has taste, and you've got it; and conscience, and you've got it; and horse-sense, and you've got that. And I like you because you're a Western man, and I'm another. I do cotton to a Western man when I find him off East here, holding his own with the best of 'em, and showing 'em that he's just as much civilised as they are. We both know what it is to have our bright home in the setting sun; heigh?"

"I think we Western men who've come East are apt to take ourselves a little too objectively, and to feel ourselves rather more representative than we need," March remarked.

Fulkerson was delighted. "You've hit it! We do! We are!"

"And as for holding my own, I'm not very proud of what I've done in that way; it's been very little to hold. But I know what you mean, Fulkerson, and I've felt the same thing myself; it warmed me toward you when we first met. I can't help suffusing a little to any man when I hear that he was born on the other side of the Alleghanies. It's perfectly stupid. I despise the same thing when I see it in Boston people."

Fulkerson pulled first one of his blond whiskers and then the other, and twisted the end of each into a point, which he left to untwine itself. He fixed March with his little eyes, which had a curious innocence in their cunning, and tapped the desk immediately in front of him. "What I like about you is that you're broad in your sympathies. The first time I saw you, that night on the Quebec boat, I said to myself, 'There's a man I want to know. There's a human being.' I was a little afraid of Mrs. March and the children, but I felt at home with you—thoroughly domesticated—before I passed a word with you; and when you spoke first, and opened up with a joke over that fellow's tableful of light literature and Indian moccasins and birch-bark toy canoes and stereoscopic views, I knew that we were brothers—spiritual twins. I recognised the Western style of fun, and I thought, when you said you

3

were from Boston, that it was some of the same. But I see now that it's being a cold fact, as far as the last fifteen or twenty years count, is just so much gain. You know both sections, and you can make this thing go, from ocean to ocean."

"We might ring that into the prospectus, too," March suggested, with a smile. "You might call the thing *From Sea to Sea*. By the way, what are you going to call it?"

"I haven't decided yet; that's one of the things I wanted to talk with you about. I *had* thought of *The Syndicate*; but it sounds kind of dry, and it don't seem to cover the ground exactly. I should like something that would express the co-operative character of the thing; but I don't know as I can get it."

"Might call it *The Mutual*."

"They'd think it was an insurance paper. No, that won't do. But Mutual comes pretty near the idea. If we could get something like that, it would pique curiosity; and then if we could get paragraphs afloat explaining that the contributors were to be paid according to the sales, it would be a first-rate ad."

He bent a wide, anxious, inquiring smile upon March, who suggested lazily, "You might call it *The Round-Robin*. That would express the central idea of irresponsibility. As I understand, everybody is to share the profits and be exempt from the losses. Or, if I'm wrong, and the reverse is true, you might call it *The Army of Martyrs*. Come, that sounds attractive, Fulkerson! Or what do you think of *The Fifth Wheel*? That would forestall the criticism that there are too many literary periodicals already. Or, if you want to put forward the idea of complete independence, you could call it *The Free Lance*; or——"

"Or *The Hog on Ice*—either stand up or fall down, you know," Fulkerson broke in coarsely. "But we'll leave the name of the magazine till we get the editor. I see the poison's beginning to work in you, March; and if I had time, I'd leave the result to time. But I haven't. I've got to know inside of the next week. To come down to business with you,

4

March, I shan't start this thing unless I can get you to take hold of it."

He seemed to expect some acknowledgment, and March said, "Well, that's very nice of you, Fulkerson."

"No, sir; no, sir! I've always liked you, and wanted you, ever since we met that first night. I had this thing inchoately in my mind then, when I was telling you about the newspaper syndicate business*—beautiful vision of a lot of literary fellows breaking loose from the bondage of publishers, and playing it alone——"

"You might call it *The Lone Hand*; that would be attractive," March interrupted. "The whole West would know what you meant."

Fulkerson was talking seriously, and March was listening seriously; but they both broke off and laughed. Fulkerson got down off the table, and made some turns about the room. It was growing late; the October sun had left the top of the tall windows; it was still clear day, but it would soon be twilight; they had been talking a long time. Fulkerson came and stood with his little feet wide apart, and bent his little lean, square face on March: "See here! How much do you get out of this thing here, anyway?"

"The insurance business?" March hesitated a moment, and then said, with a certain effort of reserve, "At present about three thousand." He looked up at Fulkerson with a glance, as if he had a mind to enlarge upon the fact, and then dropped his eyes without saying more.

Whether Fulkerson had not thought it so much or not, he said, "Well, I'll give you thirty-five hundred. Come! And your chances in the success."

"We won't count the chances in the success. And I don't believe thirty-five hundred would go any further in New York than three thousand in Boston."

"But you don't live on three thousand here?"

"No; my wife has a little property."

"Well, she won't lose the income if you go to New York. I suppose you pay six or seven hundred a year for your house here. You can get plenty of flats in New York for the same

5

money; and I understand you can get all sorts of provisions for less than you pay now—three or four cents on the pound. Come!"

This was by no means the first talk they had had about the matter; every three or four months during the past two years the syndicate man had dropped in upon March to air the scheme and to get his impressions of it. This had happened so often that it had come to be a sort of joke between them. But now Fulkerson clearly meant business, and March had a struggle to maintain himself in a firm poise of refusal.

"I dare say it wouldn't—or it needn't—cost so very much more, but I don't want to go to New York; or my wife doesn't. It's the same thing."

"A good deal samer," Fulkerson admitted.

March did not quite like his candour, and he went on with dignity. "It's very natural she shouldn't. She has always lived in Boston; she's attached to the place. Now, if you were going to start *The Fifth Wheel* in Boston——"

Fulkerson slowly and sadly shook his head, but decidedly. "Wouldn't do. You might as well say St. Louis or Cincinnati. There's only one city that belongs to the whole country, and that's New York."

"Yes, I know," sighed March; "and Boston belongs to the Bostonians; but they like you to make yourself at home while you're visiting."

"If you'll agree to make phrases like that, right along, and get them into *The Round-Robin* somehow, I'll say four thousand," said Fulkerson. "You think it over now, March. You *talk* it over with Mrs. March; I know you will, anyway; and I might as well make a virtue of advising you to do it. Tell her I advised you to do it, and you let me know before next Saturday what you've decided."

March shut down the rolling top of his desk in the corner of the room, and walked Fulkerson out before him. It was so late that the last of the chore-women* who washed down the marble halls and stairs of the great building had wrung out her floor-cloth and departed, leaving spotless stone and a clean damp smell in the darkening corridors behind her.

6

"Couldn't offer you such swell quarters in New York, March," Fulkerson said as he went tack-tacking down the steps with his small boot-heels. "But I've got my eye on a little house round in West Eleventh Street, that I'm going to fit up for my bachelor's hall in the third story, and adapt for *The Lone Hand* in the first and second, if this thing goes through; and I guess we'll be pretty comfortable. It's right on the Sand Strip—no malaria of *any* kind."

"I don't know that I'm going to share its salubrity with you yet," March sighed in an obvious travail which gave Fulkerson hopes.

"Oh yes, you are," he coaxed. "Now, you talk it over with your wife. You give her a fair, unprejudiced chance at the thing on its merits, and I'm very much mistaken in Mrs. March if she doesn't tell you to go in and win. We're bound to win!"

They stood on the outside steps of the vast edifice beetling like a granite crag above them, with the stone groups of an allegory of life-insurance foreshortened in the bas-relief overhead. March absently lifted his eyes to it. It was suddenly strange after so many years' familiarity, and so was the well-known street in its Saturday-evening solitude. He asked himself, with prophetic homesickness, if it were an omen of what was to be. But he only said musingly, "A fortnightly. You know that didn't work in England. *The Fortnightly* is published once a month now."

"It works in France," Fulkerson retorted. "The *Revue des Deux Mondes* is still published twice a month. I guess we can make it work in America—with illustrations."

"Going to have illustrations?"

"My dear boy! What are you giving me? Do I look like the sort of lunatic who would start a thing in the twilight of the nineteenth century *without* illustrations? *Come* off!"

"Ah, that complicates it! I don't know anything about art." March's look of discouragement confessed the hold the scheme had taken upon him.

"I don't want you to!" Fulkerson retorted. "Don't you suppose I shall have an art man?"

"And will they—the artists—work at a reduced rate too, like the writers, with the hopes of a share in the success?"

"Of course they will! And if I want any particular man, for a card, I'll pay him big money besides. But I can get plenty of first-rate sketches on my own terms. You'll see! They'll *pour* in!"

"Look here, Fulkerson," said March, "you'd better call this fortnightly of yours *The Madness of the Half-Moon*; or *Bedlam Broke Loose* wouldn't be bad! Why do you throw away all your hard earnings on such a crazy venture? Don't do it!" The kindness which March had always felt, in spite of his wife's first misgivings and reservations, for the merry, hopeful, slangy, energetic little creature trembled in his voice. They had both formed a friendship for Fulkerson during the week they were together in Quebec. When he was not working the newspapers there, he went about with them over the familiar ground they were showing their children, and was simply grateful for the chance, as well as very entertaining about it all. The children liked him, too; when they got the clew to his intention, and found that he was not quite serious in many of the things he said, they thought he was great fun. They were always glad when their father brought him home on the occasion of Fulkerson's visits to Boston; and Mrs. March, though of a charier hospitality, welcomed Fulkerson with a grateful sense of his admiration for her husband. He had a way of treating March with deference, as an older and abler man, and of qualifying the freedom he used toward every one with an implication that March tolerated it voluntarily, which she thought very sweet, and even refined.

"Ah, *now* you're talking like a man and a brother," said Fulkerson. "Why, March, old man, do you suppose I'd come on here and try to talk you into this thing if I wasn't morally, if I wasn't perfectly, *sure* of success? There isn't any if or and about it. I know my ground, every inch; and I don't stand alone on it," he added, with a significance which did not escape March. "When you've made up your mind, I can give you the proof; but I'm not at liberty now to say anything more. I tell you it's going to be a triumphal march from the word go, with coffee and lemonade for the procession along the whole line. All you've got to do is to fall in." He stretched out his hand to March. "You let me know as soon as you can."

March deferred taking his hand till he could ask, "Where are you going?"

"Parker House. Take the half-past ten for New York to-night."

"I thought I might walk your way." March looked at his watch. "But I shouldn't have time. Good-bye!"

He now let Fulkerson have his hand, and they exchanged a cordial pressure. Fulkerson started off at a quick, light pace. Half a block away he stopped, turned round, and seeing March still standing where he had left him, he called back joyously, "I've got the name!"

"What?"

"*Every Other Week.*"

"It isn't bad."

"Ta-ta!"

II

ALL the way up to the South End March prolonged his talk with Fulkerson, and at his door in Nankeen Square he closed the parley with a plump refusal to go to New York on any terms. His daughter Bella was lying in wait for him in the hall, and she threw her arms round his neck with the exuberance of her fourteen years, and with something of the histrionic intention of her sex. He pressed on, with her clinging about him, to the library, and, in the glow of his decision against Fulkerson, kissed his wife, where she sat by the study lamp reading the *Transcript** through her first pair of eyeglasses: it was agreed in the family that she looked distinguished in them, or at any rate cultivated. She took them off to give him a glance of question, and their son Tom looked up from his book for a moment; he was in his last year at the high-school, and was preparing for Harvard.

"I didn't get away from the office till half-past five," March explained to his wife's glance, "and then I walked. I suppose dinner's waiting. I'm sorry, but I won't do it any more."

At table he tried to be gay with Bella, who babbled at him with a voluble pertness, which her brother had often advised her parents to check in her, unless they wanted her to be universally despised.

"Papa," she shouted, at last, "you're not listening!"

As soon as possible his wife told the children they might be excused. Then she asked, 'What *is* it, Basil?"

"What is what?" he retorted, with a specious brightness that did not avail.

"What is on your mind?"

"How do you know there's anything?"

"Your kissing me so when you came in, for one thing."

"Don't I always kiss you when I come in?"

"Not now. I suppose it isn't necessary any more. *Cela va sans baiser.*"*

"Yes, I guess it's so; we get along without the symbolism now." He stopped, but she knew that he had not finished.

"Is it about your business? Have they done anything more?"

"No; I'm still in the dark. I don't know whether they mean to supplant me, or whether they ever did. But I wasn't thinking about that. Fulkerson has been to see me again."

"Fulkerson?" She brightened at the name, and March smiled too. "Why didn't you bring him to dinner?"

"I wanted to talk with you. Then you *do* like him?"

"What has that got to do with it, Basil?"

"Nothing! nothing! That is, he was boring away about that scheme of his again. He's got it into definite shape at last."

"What shape?"

March outlined it for her, and his wife seized its main features with the intuitive sense of affairs which makes women such good business-men, when they will let it.

"It *sounds* perfectly crazy," she said finally. "But it mayn't be. The only thing I didn't like about Mr. Fulkerson was his always wanting to chance things. But what have you got to do with it?"

"What have I got to do with it?" March toyed with the delay the question gave him; then he said, with a sort of deprecatory laugh, "It seems that Fulkerson has had his eye on me ever since we met that night on the Quebec boat. I opened up pretty freely to him, as you do to a man you never expect to see again, and when I found he was in that newspaper syndicate business, I told him about my early literary ambitions——"

"You can't say that *I* ever discouraged them, Basil," his wife put in. "I should have been willing, any time, to give up everything for them."

"Well, he says that I first suggested this brilliant idea to him. Perhaps I did; I don't remember. When he told me about his supplying literature to newspapers for simultaneous publication, he says I asked, 'Why not apply the principle of co-operation to a magazine, and run it in the interest of the contributors?' and that set him to thinking, and he thought out his plan of a periodical, which should pay authors and artists a low price outright for their work, and give them a chance of the profits in the way of a percentage. After all, it isn't so very different from the chances an author takes when he publishes a book. And Fulkerson thinks that the novelty of the thing would pique public curiosity, if it didn't arouse public sympathy. And the long and short of it is, Isabel, that he wants me to help edit it."

"To edit it?" His wife caught her breath, and she took a little time to realise the fact, while she stared hard at her husband to make sure he was not joking.

"Yes. He says he owes it all to me; that I invented the idea—the germ—the microbe."

His wife had now realised the fact, at least in a degree that excluded trifling with it. "That is very honourable of Mr. Fulkerson; and if he owes it to you, it was the least he could do." Having recognised her husband's claim to the honour done him, she began to kindle with a sense of the honour itself, and the value of the opportunity. "It's a very high compliment to *you*, Basil; a *very* high compliment. And you could give up this wretched insurance business that you've always hated so, and that's making you so unhappy now that you think they're going to take it from you. Give it up, and take Mr. Fulkerson's offer! It's a perfect interposition, coming just at this time! Why, do it! Mercy!" she suddenly arrested herself, "he wouldn't expect *you* to get along on the possible profits?" Her face expressed the awfulness of the notion.

March smiled reassuringly, and waited to give himself the pleasure of the sensation he meant to give her. "If I'll make striking phrases for it and edit it too, he'll give me four thousand dollars."

He leaned back in his chair, and stuck his hands deep into his pockets, and watched his wife's face, luminous with the emotions that flashed through her mind—doubt, joy, anxiety.

"Basil! You don't mean it! Why, *take* it! Take it *instantly*! *Oh*, what a thing to happen! *Oh*, what luck! But you deserve it, if you first suggested it. What an escape, what a triumph over all those hateful insurance people! O Basil, I'm afraid he'll change his mind! You ought to have accepted on the spot. You might have *known* I would approve, and you could *so* easily have taken it back if I didn't. Telegraph him now! Run right out with the despatch! Or we can send Tom!"

In these imperatives of Mrs. March's there was always much of the conditional. She meant that he should do what she said, if it were entirely right; and she never meant to be considered as having urged him.

"And suppose his enterprise went wrong?" her husband suggested.

"It won't *go* wrong. Hasn't he made a success of his syndicate?"

"He says so—yes."

"Very well, then, it stands to reason that he'll succeed in this, too. He wouldn't undertake it if he didn't know it would succeed; he must have capital."

"It will take a great deal to get such a thing going; and even if he's got an Angel behind him——"

She caught at the word: "An Angel?"

"It's what the theatrical people call a financial backer. He dropped a hint of something of that kind."

"Of course, he's got an Angel," said his wife, promptly adopting the word. "And even if he hadn't, still, Basil, I should be willing to have you risk it. The risk isn't so great, is it? We shouldn't be ruined if it failed altogether. With our stocks we have two thousand a year, anyway, and we could pinch through on that till you got into some other business afterward, especially if we'd saved something out of your salary while it lasted. Basil, I want you to try it! I know it will give you a new lease of life to have a congenial occupation." March laughed, but his wife persisted. "I'm all for your trying it, Basil; indeed I am. If it's an experiment, you can give it up."

"It can give me up, too."

"Oh, nonsense! I guess there's not much fear of that. Now, I want you to telegraph Mr. Fulkerson, so that he'll find the despatch waiting for him when he gets to New York. I'll take the whole responsibility, Basil, and I'll risk all the consequences."

III

MARCH'S face had sobered more and more as she followed one hopeful burst with another, and now it expressed a positive pain. But he forced a smile, and said: "There's a little condition attached. Where did you suppose it was to be published?"

"Why, in Boston, of course. Where else should it be published?"

She looked at him for the intention of his question so searchingly that he quite gave up the attempt to be gay about it. "No," he said gravely, "it's to be published in New York."

She fell back in her chair. "In New York?" She leaned

forward over the table toward him, as if to make sure that she heard aright, and said, with all the keen reproach that he could have expected, "*In New York*, Basil! Oh, how *could* you have let me go on?"

He had a sufficiently rueful face in owning, "I oughtn't to have done it, but I got started wrong. I couldn't help putting the best foot forward at first—or as long as the whole thing was in the air. I didn't know that you would take so much to the general enterprise, or else I should have mentioned the New York condition at once; but of course that puts an end to it."

"Oh, of course," she assented sadly. "We *couldn't* go to New York."

"No, I know that," he said; and with this a perverse desire to tempt her to the impossibility awoke in him, though he was really quite cold about the affair himself now. "Fulkerson thought we could get a nice flat in New York for about what the interest and taxes came to here, and provisions are cheaper. But I should rather not experiment at my time of life. If I could have been caught younger, I might have been inured to New York, but I don't believe I could stand it now."

"How I hate to have you talk that way, Basil! You are young enough to try anything—anywhere; but you know I don't like New York. I don't approve of it. It's so *big*, and *so* hideous! Of course I shouldn't mind that; but I've always lived in Boston, and the children were born and have all their friendships and associations here." She added, with the helplessness that discredited her good sense and did her injustice, "I have just got them both into the Friday afternoon class at Papanti's, and you know how difficult that is."

March could not fail to take advantage of an occasion like this. "Well, that alone ought to settle it. Under the circumstances it would be flying in the face of Providence to leave Boston. The mere fact of a brilliant opening like that offered me on *The Microbe*, and the halcyon future which Fulkerson promises if we'll come to New York, is as dust in the balance against the advantages of the Friday afternoon class."

"Basil," she appealed solemnly, "have I ever interfered with your career?"

"I never had any for you to interfere with, my dear."

"Basil! Haven't I always had faith in you? And don't you suppose that if I thought it would really be for your advancement, I would go to New York or anywhere with you?"

"No, my dear, I don't," he teased. "If it would be for my salvation, yes, perhaps; but not short of that; and I should have to prove by a cloud of witnesses that it would. I don't blame you. I wasn't born in Boston, but I understand how you feel. And really, my dear," he added, without irony, "I never seriously thought of asking you to go to New York. I *was* dazzled by Fulkerson's offer, I'll own that; but his choice of me as editor sapped my confidence in him."

"I don't like to hear you say that, Basil," she entreated.

"Well, of course there were mitigating circumstances. I could see that Fulkerson meant to keep the whip-hand himself, and that was reassuring. And besides, if the Reciprocity Life should happen not to want my services any longer, it wouldn't be quite like giving up a certainty; though, as a matter of business, I let Fulkerson get that impression; I felt rather sneaking to do it. But, if the worst comes to the worst, I can look about for something to do in Boston; and, anyhow, people don't starve on two thousand a year, though it's convenient to have five. The fact is, I'm too old to change so radically. If you don't like my saying that, then *you* are, Isabel, and so are the children. I've no right to take them from the home we've made, and to change the whole course of their lives, unless I can assure them of something, and I can't assure them of anything. Boston is big enough for us, and it's certainly prettier than New York. I always feel a little proud of hailing from Boston; my pleasure in the place mounts the further I get away from it. But I do appreciate it, my dear, I've no more desire to leave it than you have. You may be sure that if you don't want to take the children out of the Friday afternoon class, I don't want to leave my library here, and all the ways I've got set in. We'll keep on. Very likely the company won't supplant me, and if it does, and Watkins gets the place, he'll give me a sub-ordinate position of some sort. Cheer up, Isabel! I have put Satan and his angel, Fulkerson, behind me, and it's all right. Let's go in to the children."

He came round the table to Isabel, where she sat in a growing distraction, and lifted her by the waist from her chair.

She sighed deeply. "Shall we tell the children about it?"

"No. What's the use, now?"

"There wouldn't be any," she assented. When they entered the family room, where the boy and girl sat on either side of the lamp working out the lessons for Monday which they had left over from the day before, she asked, "Children, how would you like to live in New York?"

Bella made haste to get in her word first. "And give up the Friday afternoon class?" she wailed.

Tom growled from his book, without lifting his eyes, "I shouldn't want to go to Columbia. They haven't got any dormitories, and you have to board round anywhere. Are you going to New York?" He now deigned to look up at his father.

"No, Tom. You and Bella have decided me against it. Your perspective shows the affair in its true proportions. I had an offer to go to New York, but I've refused it."

IV

MARCH'S irony fell harmless from the children's pre-occupation with their own affairs, but he knew that his wife felt it, and this added to the bitterness which prompted it. He blamed her for letting her provincial narrowness prevent his accepting Fulkerson's offer quite as much as if he had otherwise entirely wished to accept it. His world, like most worlds, had been superficially a disappointment. He was no richer than at the beginning, though in marrying he had given up some tastes, some preferences, some aspirations, in the hope of indulging them later, with larger means and larger leisure. His wife had not urged him to do it; in fact, her pride, as she said, was in his fitness for the life he had renounced; but she had acquiesced, and they had been very happy together. That is to say, they made up their quarrels or ignored them.

They often accused each other of being selfish and indifferent, but she knew that he would always sacrifice himself for her and the children; and he, on his part, with many gibes and mockeries, wholly trusted in her. They had grown practically tolerant of each other's disagreeable traits; and the danger that really threatened them was that they should grow too well satisfied with themselves, if not with each other. They were not sentimental, they were rather matter-of-fact in their motives; but they had both a sort of humorous fondness for sentimentality. They liked to play with the romantic, from the safe vantage-ground of their real practicality, and to divine the poetry of the commonplace. Their peculiar point of view separated them from most other people, with whom their means of self-comparison were not so good since their marriage as before. Then they had travelled and seen much of the world, and they had formed tastes which they had not always been able to indulge, but of which they felt that the possession reflected distinction on them. It enabled them to look down upon those who were without such tastes; but they were not ill-natured, and so they did not look down so much with contempt as with amusement. In their unfashionable neighbourhood they had the fame of being not exclusive precisely, but very much wrapt up in themselves and their children.

Mrs. March was reputed to be very cultivated, and Mr. March even more so, among the simpler folk around them. Their house had some good pictures, which her aunt had brought home from Europe in more affluent days, and it abounded in books on which he spent more than he ought. They had beautified it in every way, and had unconsciously taken credit to themselves for it. They felt, with a glow almost of virtue, how perfectly it fitted their lives and their children's, and they believed that somehow it expressed their characters—that it was like them. They went out very little;

she remained shut up in its refinement, working the good of her own; and he went to his business, and hurried back to forget it, and dream his dream of intellectual achievement in the flattering atmosphere of her sympathy. He could not conceal from himself that his divided life was somewhat like Charles Lamb's,* and there were times when, as he had expressed to Fulkerson, he believed that its division was favourable to the freshness of his interest in literature. It certainly kept it a high privilege, a sacred refuge. Now and then he wrote something, and got it printed after long delays, and when they met on the St. Lawrence, Fulkerson had some of March's verses in his pocket-book, which he had cut out of a stray newspaper and carried about for years, because they pleased his fancy so much; they formed an immediate bond of union between the men when their authorship was traced and owned, and this gave a pretty colour of romance to their acquaintance. But for the most part, March was satisfied to read. He was proud of reading critically, and he kept in the current of literary interests and controversies. It all seemed to him, and to his wife at second-hand, very meritorious; he could not help contrasting his life and its inner elegance with that of other men who had no such resources. He thought that he was not arrogant about it, because he did full justice to the good qualities of those other people; he congratulated himself upon the democratic instincts which enabled him to do this; and neither he nor his wife supposed that they were selfish persons. On the contrary, they were very sympathetic; there was no good cause that they did not wish well; they had a generous scorn of all kinds of narrow-heartedness; if it had ever come into their way to sacrifice themselves for others, they thought they would have done so, but they never asked why it had not come in their way. They were very gentle and kind, even when most elusive; and they taught their children to loathe all manner of social cruelty. March was of so watchful a conscience in some respects that he denied himself the pensive pleasure of lapsing into the melancholy of unfulfilled aspirations; but he did not see that if he had abandoned them, it had been for what he held dearer; generally he felt as if he had turned from them with a high altruistic aim. The practical expression of his life was that it was enough to provide well for his family; to have cultivated tastes, and to gratify them to the extent of his means; to be rather distinguished, even in the simplification of his desires. He believed, and his wife believed, that if the time ever came when he really wished to make a sacrifice to the fulfilment of the aspirations so long postponed, she would be ready to join with heart and hand.

When he went to her room from his library, where she left him the whole evening with the children, he found her before the glass thoughtfully removing the first dismantling pin from her back hair.

"I can't help feeling," she grieved into the mirror, "that it's I who keep you from accepting that offer. I know it is! I could go West with you, or into a new country—anywhere; but New York terrifies me. I don't like New York, I never did; it disheartens and distracts me; I can't find myself in it; I shouldn't know how to shop. I know I'm foolish and narrow and provincial," she went on; "but I could never have any inner quiet in New York; I couldn't live in the spirit there. I suppose people do. It can't be that all those millions——"

"Oh, not so bad as that!" March interposed, laughing. "There aren't quite two."

"I thought there were four or five. Well, no matter. You see what I am, Basil. I'm terribly limited. I couldn't make my sympathies go round two million people; I should be wretched. I suppose I'm standing in the way of your highest interest, but I can't help it. We took each other for better or worse, and you must try to bear with me——" She broke off and began to cry.

"*Stop* it!" shouted March. "I tell you I never cared anything for Fulkerson's scheme or entertained it seriously, and I shouldn't, if he'd proposed to carry it out in Boston." This was not quite true; but in the retrospect it seemed sufficiently so for the purposes of argument. "Don't say another word about it. The thing's over now, and I don't want to think of it any more. We couldn't change its nature if we talked all night. But I want you to understand that it isn't your limitations that are in the way. It's mine. I shouldn't have the courage to take such a place; I don't think I'm fit for it; and that's the long and short of it."

"Oh, you don't know how it hurts me to have you say that, Basil."

The next morning, as they sat together at breakfast, without the children, whom they let lie late on Sunday, Mrs. March said to her husband, silent over his fish-balls and baked beans: 'We will go to New York. I've decided it."

"Well, it takes two to decide that," March retorted. "We are not going to New York."

"Yes, we are. I've thought it out. Now, listen."

"Oh, I'm willing to listen," he consented airily.

"You've always wanted to get out of the insurance business, and now with that fear of being turned out which you have, you mustn't neglect this offer. I suppose it has its risks, but it's a risk keeping on as we are; and perhaps you will make a great success of it. I do want you to try, Basil. If I could once feel that you had fairly seen what you could do in literature, I should die happy."

"Not immediately after, I hope," he suggested, taking the second cup of coffee she had been pouring out for him. "And Boston?"

"We needn't make a complete break. We can keep this place for the present, anyway; we could let it for the winter, and come back in the summer next year. It would be change enough from New York."

"Fulkerson and I hadn't got as far as to talk of a vacation."

"No matter. The children and I could come. And if you didn't like New York, or the enterprise failed, you could get into something in Boston again; and we have enough to live on till you did. Yes, Basil, I'm going."

"I can see by the way your chin trembles that nothing could stop you. *You* may go to New York if you *wish*, Isabel, but I shall stay here."

"Be serious, Basil. I'm in earnest."

"Serious? If I were any more serious I should shed tears. Come, my dear, I know what you mean, and if I had my heart set on this thing—Fulkerson always calls it 'this thing'—I would cheerfully accept any sacrifice you could make to it. But I'd rather not offer you up on a shrine I don't feel any particular faith in. I'm very comfortable where I am; that is, I know just where the pinch comes, and if it comes harder, why, I've got used to bearing that kind of pinch. I'm too old to change pinches."

"Now, that *does* decide me."

"It decides me, too."

"I will take all the responsibility, Basil," she pleaded.

"Oh yes; but you'll hand it back to me as soon as you've carried your point with it. There's nothing mean about you, Isabel, where responsibility is concerned. No; if I do this thing—Fulkerson again! I can't get away from 'this thing'; it's ominous—I must do it because I want to do it, and not because you wish that you wanted me to do it. I understand your position, Isabel, and that you're really acting from a generous impulse, but there's nothing so precarious at our time of life as a generous impulse. When we were younger we could stand it; we could give way to it and take the consequences. But now we can't bear it. We must act from cold reason even in the ardour of self-sacrifice."

"Oh, as if you did that!" his wife retorted.

"Is that any cause why you shouldn't?" She could not say that it was, and he went on triumphantly: "No, I won't take you away from the only safe place on the planet, and plunge you into the most perilous, and then have you say in your revulsion of feeling that you were all against it from the first, and you gave way because you saw I had my heart set on it." He supposed he was treating the matter humorously, but in this sort of banter between husband and wife there is always much more than the joking. March had seen some pretty feminine inconsistencies and trepidations which once charmed him in his wife hardening into traits of middle-age, which were very like those of less interesting older

21

women. The sight moved him with a kind of pathos, but he felt the result hindering and vexatious.

She now retorted that if he did not choose to take her at her word he need not, but that whatever he did she should have nothing to reproach herself with; and, at least, he could not say that she had trapped him into anything.

"What do you mean by trapping?" he demanded.

"I don't know what *you* call it," she answered; "but when you get me to commit myself to a thing by leaving out the most essential point, *I* call it trapping."

"I wonder you stop at trapping, if you think I got you to favour Fulkerson's scheme, and then sprung New York on you. I don't suppose you do, though. But I guess we won't talk about it any more."

He went out for a long walk, and she went to her room. They lunched silently together in the presence of their children, who knew that they had been quarrelling, but were easily indifferent to the fact, as children get to be in such cases; nature defends their youth, and the unhappiness which they behold does not infect them. In the evening, after the boy and girl had gone to bed, the father and mother resumed their talk. He would have liked to take it up at the point from which it wandered into hostilities, for he felt it lamentable that a matter which so seriously concerned them should be confused in the fumes of senseless anger; and he was willing to make a tacit acknowledgment of his own error by recurring to the question, but she would not be content with this, and he had to concede explicitly to her weakness that she really meant it when she had asked him to accept Fulkerson's offer. He said he knew that; and he began soberly to talk over their prospects in the event of their going to New York.

"Oh, I see you are going!" she twitted.

"I'm going to stay," he answered, "and let them turn me out of my agency here!" and in this bitterness their talk ended.

V

HIS wife made no attempt to renew their talk before March went to his business in the morning, and they parted in dry offence. Their experience was that these things always came right of themselves at last, and they usually let them. He knew that she had really tried to consent to a thing that was repugnant to her, and in his heart he gave her more credit for the effort than he had allowed her openly. She knew that she had made it with the reservation he accused her of, and that he had a right to feel sore at what she could not help. But he left her to brood over his ingratitude, and she suffered him to go heavy and unfriended to meet the chances of the day. He said to himself that if she had assented cordially to the conditions of Fulkerson's offer, he would have had the courage to take all the other risks himself, and would have had the satisfaction of resigning his place. As it was, he must wait till he was removed; and he figured with bitter pleasure the pain she would feel when he came home some day and told her he had been supplanted, after it was too late to close with Fulkerson.

He found a letter on his desk from the secretary, "Dictated," in type-writing, which briefly informed him that Mr. Hubbell, the Inspector of Agencies, would be in Boston on Wednesday, and would call at his office during the forenoon. The letter was not different in tone from many that he had formerly received; but the visit announced was out of the usual order, and March believed he read his fate in it. During the eighteen years of his connection with it—first as a subordinate in the Boston office, and finally as its general agent there—he had seen a good many changes in the Reciprocity; presidents, vice-presidents, actuaries, and general agents had come and gone, but there had always seemed to be a recognition of his efficiency, or at least sufficiency, and there had never been any manner of trouble, no question of accounts, no apparent dissatisfaction with his management, until latterly, when there had begun to come from head-quarters some suggestions of enterprise in certain ways, which gave him his first suspicions of his clerk Watkins's willingness to succeed him; they embodied some of Watkins's ideas. The things proposed seemed to March undignified, and even vulgar; he had never thought himself wanting in energy, though probably he had left the business to take its own course in the old lines more than he realised. Things had always gone so smoothly that he had sometimes fancied a peculiar regard for him in the management, which he had the weakness to attribute to an appreciation of what he occasionally did in literature, though in saner moments he felt how impossible this was. Beyond a reference from Mr. Hubbell to some piece of March's, which had happened to meet his eye, no one in the management ever gave a sign of consciousness that their service was adorned by an obscure literary man; and Mr. Hubbell himself had the effect of regarding the excursions of March's pen as a sort of joke, and of winking at them, as he might have winked if once in a way he had found him a little the gayer for dining.

March wore through the day gloomily, but he had it on his conscience not to show any resentment toward Watkins, whom he suspected of wishing to supplant him, and even of working to do so. Through this self-denial he reached a better mind concerning his wife. He determined not to make her suffer needlessly, if the worst came to the worst; she would suffer enough, at the best, and till the worst came he would spare her, and not say anything about the letter he had got.

But when they met, her first glance divined that something had happened, and her first question frustrated his generous intention. He had to tell her about the letter. She would not allow that it had any significance; but she wished him to make an end of his anxieties, and forestall whatever it might portend by resigning his place at once. She said she was quite ready to go to New York; she had been thinking it all over, and now she really wanted to go. He answered, soberly, that he had thought it over, too; and he did not wish to leave Boston, where he had lived so long, or try a new way of life if he could help it. He insisted that he was quite selfish in this; in their concessions their quarrel vanished; they agreed that whatever happened would be for the best; and the next day he went to his office fortified for any event.

His destiny, if tragical, presented itself with an aspect which he might have found comic if it had been another's destiny. Mr. Hubbell brought March's removal, softened in the guise of a promotion. The management at New York, it appeared, had acted upon a suggestion of Mr. Hubbell's, and now authorised him to offer March the editorship of the monthly paper published in the interest of the company; his office would include the authorship of circulars and leaflets, in behalf of life insurance, and would give play to the literary talent which Mr. Hubbell had brought to the attention of the management; his salary would be nearly as much as at present, but the work would not take his whole time, and in a place like New York he could get a great deal of outside writing, which they would not object to his doing.

Mr. Hubbell seemed so sure of his acceptance of a place in every way congenial to a man of literary tastes, that March was afterward sorry he dismissed the proposition with obvious irony, and had needlessly hurt Hubbell's feelings; but Mrs. March had no such regrets. She was only afraid that he had not made his rejection contemptuous enough. "And now," she said, "telegraph Mr. Fulkerson, and we will go at once."

"I suppose I could still get Watkins's former place," March suggested.

"Never!' she retorted. "Telegraph instantly!"

They were only afraid now that Fulkerson might have changed his mind, and they had a wretched day in which they heard nothing from him. It ended with his answering March's telegram in person. They were so glad of his coming, and so touched by his satisfaction with his bargain, that they laid all the facts of the case before him. He entered fully into March's sense of the joke latent in Mr. Hubbell's proposition; and he tried to make Mrs. March believe that he shared her resentment of the indignity offered her husband.

March made a show of willingness to release him in view of the changed situation, saying that he held him to nothing. Fulkerson laughed, and asked him how soon he thought he could come on to New York. He refused to reopen the question of March's fitness with him; he said they had gone into that thoroughly, but he recurred to it with Mrs. March, and confirmed her belief in his good-sense on all points. She had been from the first moment defiantly confident of her husband's ability, but till she had talked the matter over with Fulkerson, she was secretly not sure of it; or, at least, she was not sure that March was not right in distrusting himself. When she clearly understood, now, what Fulkerson intended, she had no longer a doubt. He explained how the enterprise differed from others, and how he needed for its direction a man who combined general business experience and business ideas with a love for the thing, and a natural aptness for it. He did not want a young man, and yet he wanted youth—its freshness, its zest—such as March would feel in a thing he could put his whole heart into. He would not run in ruts, like an old fellow who had got hackneyed; he would not have any hobbies; he would not have any friends nor any enemies. Besides, he would have to meet people, and March was a man that people took to; she knew that herself; he had a kind of charm. The editorial management was going to be kept in the background, as far as the public was concerned; the public was to suppose that the thing ran itself. Fulkerson did not care for a great literary reputation in his editor—he implied that March had a very pretty little one. At the same time the relations between the contributors and the management were to be much more intimate than usual. Fulkerson felt his personal disqualification for working the thing socially, and he counted upon Mr. March for that; that was to say, he counted upon Mrs. March.

She protested he must not count upon her; but it by no means disabled Fulkerson's judgment in her view that March really seemed more than anything else a fancy of his. He had been a fancy of hers; and the sort of affectionate respect with which Fulkerson spoke of him laid for ever some doubt she had of the fineness of Fulkerson's manners, and reconciled her to the graphic slanginess of his speech.

The affair was now irretrievable, but she gave her approval to it as superbly as if it were submitted in its inception. Only, Mr. Fulkerson must not suppose she should ever like New York. She would not deceive him on that point. She never should like it. She did not conceal, either, that she did not like taking the children out of the Friday afternoon class; and she did not believe that Tom would ever be reconciled to going to Columbia.* She took courage from Fulkerson's suggestion that it was possible for Tom to come to Harvard even from New York; and she heaped him with questions concerning the domiciliation of the family in that city. He tried to know something about the matter, and he succeeded in seeming interested in points necessarily indifferent to him.

VI

In the uprooting and transplanting of their home that followed, Mrs. March often trembled before distant problems and possible contingencies, but she was never troubled by present difficulties. She kept up with tireless energy; and in the moments of dejection and misgiving which harassed her husband she remained dauntless, and put heart into him when he had lost it altogether.

She arranged to leave the children in the house with the servants, while she went on with March to look up a dwelling of some sort in New York. It made him sick to think of it; and when it came to the point, he would rather have given up the whole enterprise. She had to nerve him to it, to represent more than once that now they had no choice but to make this experiment. Every detail of parting was anguish to him. He got consolation out of the notion of letting the house furnished for the winter; that implied their return to it; but it cost him pangs of the keenest misery to advertise it; and when a tenant was actually found, it was all he could do to give him the lease. He tried his wife's love and patience as a man must to whom the future is easy in the mass, but terrible as it translates itself piecemeal into the present. He experienced remorse in the presence of inanimate things he was going to leave as if they had sensibly reproached him, and an anticipative homesickness that seemed to stop his heart. Again and again his wife had to make him reflect that his depression was not prophetic. She convinced him of what he already knew; and persuaded him against his knowledge that he could be keeping an eye out for something to take hold of in Boston if they could not stand New York. She ended by telling him that it was too bad to make her comfort him in a trial that was really so much more a trial to her. She had to support him in a last access of despair on their way to the Albany depôt the morning they started to New York; but when the final details had been dealt with, the tickets bought, the trunks checked, and the hand-bags hung up in their car, and the future had massed itself again at a safe distance and was seven hours and two hundred miles away, his spirits began to rise and hers to sink. He would have been willing to celebrate the taste, the domestic refinement of the ladies' waiting-room in the depôt, where they had spent a quarter of an hour before the train started. He said he did not believe there was another station in the world where mahogany rocking-chairs were provided; that the dull red warmth of the walls was as cosey as an evening-lamp, and that he always hoped to see a fire kindled on that vast hearth, and under that æsthetic mantel, but he supposed now he never should. He said it was all very different from that tunnel, the old Albany depôt, where they had waited the morning they went to New York when they were starting on their wedding journey.

"The *morning*, Basil!" cried his wife. "We went at *night*; and we were going to take the boat, but it stormed so!" She gave him a glance of such reproach that he could not answer anything, and now she asked him whether he supposed their cook and second girl would be contented with one of those dark holes where they put girls to sleep in New York flats, and what she should do if Margaret, especially, left her. He ventured to suggest that Margaret would probably like the city; but if she left, there were plenty of other girls to be had in New York. She replied that there were none she could trust, and that she knew Margaret would not stay. He asked her why she took her, then; why she did not give her up at once; and she answered that it would be inhuman to give her up just in the edge of the winter. She had promised to keep her; and Margaret was pleased with the notion of going to New York, where she had a cousin.

"Then perhaps she'll be pleased with the notion of staying," he said.

"Oh, much you know about it!" she retorted; and in view of the hypothetical difficulty and his want of sympathy, she fell into a gloom, from which she roused herself at last by declaring that if there was nothing else in the flat they took, there should be a light kitchen and a bright sunny bedroom for Margaret. He expressed the belief that they could easily find such a flat as that, and she denounced his fatal optimism, which buoyed him up in the absence of an undertaking, and let him drop into the depths of despair in its presence.

He owned this defect of temperament, but he said that it compensated the opposite in her character. "I suppose that's one of the chief uses of marriage; people supplement each other, and form a pretty fair sort of human being together. The only drawback to the theory is that unmarried people seem each as complete and whole as a married pair."

She refused to be amused; she turned her face to the window and put her handkerchief up under her veil.

It was not till the dining-car was attached to their train that they were both able to escape for an hour into the carefree mood of their earlier travels, when they were so easily taken out of themselves. The time had been when they could have found enough in the conjectural fortunes and characters of their fellow-passengers to occupy them. This phase of their youth had lasted long, and the world was still full of novelty and interest for them; but it required all the charm of the dining-car now to lay the anxieties that beset them. It was so potent for the moment, however, that they could take an objective view at their sitting cosily down there together, as if they had only themselves in the world. They wondered what the children were doing, the children who possessed them so intensely when present, and now, by a fantastic operation of absence, seemed almost non-existent. They tried to be homesick for them, but failed; they recognised with comfortable self-abhorrence that this was terrible, but owned a fascination in being alone; at the same time they could not imagine how people felt who never had any children. They contrasted the luxury of dining that way, with every advantage except a band of music, and the old way of rushing out to snatch a fearful joy at the lunch-counters of the Worcester and Springfield and New Haven stations. They had not gone often to New York since their wedding journey, but they had gone often enough to have noted the change from the lunch-counter to the lunch-basket brought in the train, from which you could subsist with more ease and dignity, but seemed destined to a superabundance of pickles, whatever you ordered.

They thought well of themselves now that they could be both critical and tolerant of flavours not very sharply distinguished from one another in their dinner, and they lingered over their coffee and watched the autumn landscape through the windows.

"Not quite so loud a pattern of calico this year," he said, with patronising forbearance toward the painted woodlands whirling by. "Do you see how the foreground next the train rushes from us and the background keeps ahead of us, while the middle distance seems stationary? I don't think I ever noticed that effect before. There ought to be something literary in it: retreating past and advancing future, and deceitfully permanent present: something like that?"

His wife brushed some crumbs from her lap before rising. "Yes. You mustn't waste any of these ideas now."

"Oh no; it would be money out of Fulkerson's pocket."

VII

THEY went to a quiet hotel far down-town, and took a small apartment which they thought they could easily afford for the day or two they need spend in looking up a furnished flat. They were used to staying at this hotel when they came on for a little outing in New York, after some rigid winter in Boston, at the time of the spring exhibitions. They were remembered there from year to year; the coloured call-boys, who never seemed to get any older, smiled upon them, and the clerk called March by name even before he registered. He asked if Mrs. March were with him, and said then he supposed they would want their usual quarters; and in a moment they were domesticated in a far interior that seemed to have been waiting for them in a clean, quiet, patient dis-occupation ever since they left it two years before. The little parlour, with its gilt paper and ebonised furniture, was the lightest of the rooms, but it was not very light at noonday without the gas, which the bell-boy now flared up for them. The uproar of the city came to it in a soothing murmur, and they took possession of its peace and comfort with open cele-bration. After all, they agreed, there *was* no place in the world so delightful as a hotel apartment like that; the boasted charms of home were nothing to it; and then the magic of its being always there, ready for any one, every one, just as if it were for some one alone: it was like the experi-ence of an Arabian Nights hero come true for all the race.

"Oh, *why* can't we always stay here, just we two!" Mrs. March sighed to her husband, as he came out of his room rubbing his face red with the towel, while she studied a new arrangement of her bonnet and hand-bag on the mantel.

"And ignore the past? I'm willing. I've no doubt that the children could get on perfectly well without us, and could find some lot in the scheme of Providence that would really be just as well for them."

"Yes; or could contrive somehow never to have existed.

I should insist upon that. If they *are*, don't you see that we couldn't wish them *not to be*?"

"Oh yes; I see your point; it's simply incontrovertible."

She laughed, and said: "Well, at any rate, if we can't find a flat to suit us we can all crowd into these three rooms somehow, for the winter, and then browse about for meals. By the week we could get them much cheaper; and we could save on the eating, as they do in Europe. Or on something else."

"Something else, probably," said March. "But we won't take this apartment till the ideal furnished flat winks out altogether. We shall not have any trouble. We can easily find some one who is going South for the winter, and will be glad to give up their flat 'to the right party' at a nominal rent. That's my notion. That's what the Evanses did one winter when they came on here in February. All but the nominality of the rent."

"Yes, and we could pay a very good rent and still something on letting our house. You can settle yourselves in a hundred different ways in New York, that *is* one merit of the place. But if everything else fails, we can come back to this. I want you to take the refusal of it, Basil. And we'll commence looking this very evening as soon as we've had dinner. I cut a lot of things out of the *Herald* as we came on. See here!"

She took a long strip of paper out of her hand-bag with minute advertisements pinned transversely upon it, and forming the effect of some glittering nondescript vertebrate.

"Looks something like the sea-serpent," said March, drying his hands on the towel, while he glanced up and down the list. "But we shan't have any trouble. I've no doubt there are half a dozen things there that will do. You haven't gone up-town? Because we must be near the *Every Other Week* office."

"No; but I *wish* Mr. Fulkerson hadn't called it that! It always makes one think of 'jam yesterday and jam to-morrow, but never jam to-day,' in *Through the Looking-glass.* They're all in this region."

They were still at their table, beside a low window, where some sort of never-blooming shrub symmetrically balanced itself in a large pot, with a leaf to the right and a leaf to the left and a spear up the middle, when Fulkerson came stepping square-footedly over the thick dining-room carpet. He wagged in the air a gay hand of salutation at sight of them, and of repression when they offered to rise to meet him; then, with an apparent simultaneity of action he gave a hand to each, pulled up a chair from the next table, put his hat and stick on the floor beside it, and seated himself.

"Well, you've burnt your ships behind you, sure enough," he said, beaming his satisfaction upon them from eyes and teeth.

"The ships are burnt," said March, "though I'm not sure we did it alone. But here we are, looking for shelter, and a little anxious about the disposition of the natives."

"Oh, they're an awful peaceable lot," said Fulkerson. "I've been round amongst the caciques a little, and I think I've got two or three places that will just suit you, Mrs. March. How did you leave the children?"

"Oh, how kind of you! Very well, and very proud to be left in charge of the smoking wrecks."

Fulkerson naturally paid no attention to what she said, being but secondarily interested in the children at the best. "Here are some things right in this neighbourhood, within gunshot of the office, and if you want you can go and look at them to-night; the agents gave me houses where the people would be in."

"We will go and look at them instantly," said Mrs. March. "Or, as soon as you've had coffee with us."

"Never do," Fulkerson replied. He gathered up his hat and stick. "Just rushed in to say Hello, and got to run right away again. I tell you, March, things are humming. I'm after those fellows with a sharp stick all the while to keep them from loafing on my house, and at the same time I'm just bubbling over with ideas about *The Lone Hand*—wish we *could* call it that!—that I want to talk up with you."

"Well, come to breakfast," said Mrs. March cordially.

"No; the ideas will keep till you've secured your lodge in this vast wilderness. Good-bye."

"You're as nice as you can be, Mr. Fulkerson," she said, "to keep us in mind when you have so much to occupy you."

"I wouldn't have *any*thing to occupy me if I *hadn't* kept you in mind, Mrs. March," said Fulkerson, going off upon as good a speech as he could apparently hope to make.

"Why, Basil," said Mrs. March, when he was gone, "he's charming! But now we mustn't lose an instant. Let's see where the places are." She ran over the half-dozen agents' permits. "Capital—first-rate—the very thing—every one. Well, I consider ourselves settled! We can go back to the children to-morrow if we like, though I rather think I should like to stay over another day and get a little rested for the final pulling up that's got to come. But this simplifies everything enormously, and Mr. Fulkerson is as thoughtful and as sweet as he can be. I know you will get on well with him. He has such a good heart. And his attitude toward you, Basil, is beautiful always—so respectful; or not that so much as appreciative. Yes, appreciative—that's the word; I must always keep that in mind."

"It's quite important to do so," said March.

"Yes," she assented seriously, "and we must not forget just what kind of flat we are going to look for. The *sine qua nons* are an elevator and steam-heat, not above the third floor, to begin with. Then we must each have a room, and you must have your study and I must have my parlour; and the two girls must each have a room. With the kitchen and dining-room, how many does that make?"

"Ten."

"I thought eight. Well, no matter. You can work in the parlour, and run into your bedroom when anybody comes; and I can sit in mine, and the girls must put up with one, if it's large and sunny, though I've always given them two at home. And the kitchen must be sunny, so they can sit in it. And the rooms must *all* have outside light. And the rent must not be over eight hundred for the winter. We only get a thousand for our whole house, and we *must* save something

34

out of that, so as to cover the expenses of moving. Now, do you think you can remember all that?"

"Not the half of it," said March. "But *you* can; or if you forget a third of it, I can come in with my partial half, and more than make it up."

She had brought her bonnet and sack downstairs with her, and was transferring them from the hat-rack to her person while she talked. The friendly door-boy let them into the street, and the clear October evening air inspirited her so, that as she tucked her hand under her husband's arm and began to pull him along, she said, "If we find something right away—and we're just as likely to get the right flat soon as late; it's all a lottery—we'll go to the theatre somewhere."

She had a moment's panic about having left the agents' permits on the table, and after remembering that she had put them into her little shopping-bag, where she kept her money (each note crushed into a round wad), and had left that on the hat-rack, where it would certainly be stolen, she found it on her wrist. She did not think that very funny, but after a first impulse to inculpate her husband, she let him laugh, while they stopped under a lamp, and she held the permits half a yard away to read the numbers on them.

"Where are your glasses, Isabel?"

"On the mantel in our room, of course."

"Then you ought to have brought a pair of tongs."

"I wouldn't get off second-hand jokes, Basil," she said; and "Why, here!" she cried, whirling round to the door before which they had halted, "this is the very number. Well, I do believe it's a sign!"

One of those coloured men who soften the trade of janitor in many of the smaller apartment houses in New York by the sweetness of their race, let the Marches in, or, rather, welcomed them to the possession of the premises by the bow with which he acknowledged their permit. It was a large, old mansion cut up into five or six dwellings, but it had kept some traits of its former dignity, which pleased people of their sympathetic tastes. The dark mahogany trim, of sufficiently ugly design, gave a rich gloom to the hallway, which was wide, and paved with marble; the carpeted stairs curved aloft through a generous space.

"There is no elevator?" Mrs. March asked of the janitor.

He answered, "No, ma'am; only two flights up," so winningly that she said—

"Oh!" in courteous apology, and whispered her husband as she followed lightly up, "We'll take it, Basil, if it's like the rest."

"If it's like him, you mean."

"I don't wonder they wanted to own them," she hurriedly philosophised. "If I had such a creature, nothing but death should part us, and I should no more think of giving him his *freedom*!"

"No; we couldn't afford it," returned her husband.

The apartment the janitor unlocked for them, and lit up from those chandeliers and brackets of gilt brass in the form of vine bunches, leaves, and tendrils in which the early gas-fitter realised most of his conceptions of beauty, had rather more of the ugliness than the dignity of the hall. But the rooms were large, and they grouped themselves in a reminiscence of the time when they were part of a dwelling, that had its charm, its pathos, its impressiveness. Where they were cut up into smaller spaces, it had been done with the frankness with which a proud old family of fallen fortunes practises its economies. The rough pine floors showed a black border of tack-heads where carpets had been lifted and put down for generations; the white paint was yellow with age; the apartment had light at the front and at the back, and two or three rooms had glimpses of the day through small windows let into their corners; another one seemed lifting an appealing eye to heaven through a glass circle in its ceiling; the rest must darkle in perpetual twilight. Yet something pleased in it all, and Mrs. March had gone far to adapt the different rooms to the members of her family, when she suddenly thought (and for her to think was to say), "Why, but there's no steam-heat!"

"No, ma'am," the janitor admitted, "But dere's grates in most o' de rooms, and dere's furnace-heat in de halls."

"That's true," she admitted, and having placed her family in the apartments, it was hard to get them out again. "Could we manage?" she referred to her husband.

"Why, *I* shouldn't care for the steam-heat if——What is the rent?" he broke off to ask the janitor.

"Nine hundred, sir."

March concluded to his wife, "If it were furnished."

"Why, of course! What could I have been thinking of? We're looking for a furnished flat," she explained to the janitor, "and this was so pleasant and home-like, that I never thought whether it was furnished or not."

She smiled upon the janitor, and he entered into the joke and chuckled so amiably at her flattering oversight on the way downstairs that she said, as she pinched her husband's arm, "Now, if you don't give him a quarter, I'll never speak to you again, Basil!"

"I would have given half a dollar willingly to get you beyond his glamour," said March, when they were safely on the pavement outside. "If it hadn't been for my strength of character, you'd have taken an unfurnished flat without heat and with no elevator, at nine hundred a year, when you had just sworn me to steam-heat, an elevator, furniture, and eight hundred."

"Yes! How could I have lost my head so completely?" she said, with a lenient amusement in her aberration which she was not always able to feel in her husband's.

"The next time a coloured janitor opens the door to us, I'll tell him the apartment doesn't suit at the threshold. It's the only way to manage you, Isabel."

"It's true. I *am* in love with the whole race. I never saw one of them that didn't have perfectly angelic manners. I think we shall all be black in heaven—that is, black-souled."

"That isn't the usual theory," said March.

"Well, perhaps not," she assented. "Where are we going now? Oh yes, to the Xenophon!"

She pulled him gaily along again, and after they had walked a block down and half a block over, they stood before the apartment-house of that name, which was cut on the gas lamps on either side of the heavily spiked, æsthetic-hinged black door. The titter of an electric bell brought a large, fat Buttons, with a stage effect of being dressed to look small, who said he would call the janitor, and they waited in the dimly splendid, copper-coloured interior, admiring the whorls and waves into which the wall-paint was combed, till the janitor came in his gold-banded cap, like a continental *portier*.* When they said they would like to see Mrs. Grosvenor Green's apartment he owned his inability to cope with the affair, and said he must send for the Superintendent; he was either in the Herodotus or the Thucydides, and would be there in a minute. The Buttons brought him—a Yankee of browbeating presence in plain clothes—almost before they had time to exchange a frightened whisper in recognition of the fact that there could be no doubt of the steam-heat and elevator in this case. Half stifled in the one, they mounted in the other eight stories, while they tried to keep their self-respect under the gaze of the Superintendent, which they felt was classing and assessing them with unfriendly accuracy. They could not, and they faltered abashed at the threshold of Mrs. Grosvenor Green's apartment, while the Superintendent lit the gas in the gangway that he called a private hall, and in the drawing-room and the succession of chambers stretching rearward to the kitchen. Everything had been done by the architect to save space, and everything to waste it by Mrs. Grosvenor Green. She had conformed to a law for the necessity of turning round in each room, and had folding-beds in the chambers; but there her subordination had ended, and wherever you might have turned round she had put a gimcrack* so that you would knock it over if you did turn. The place was rather pretty and even imposing at first glance, and it took several joint ballots for March and his wife to make sure that with the kitchen there were only six rooms. At every door hung a portière* from large rings on a brass rod; every shelf and dressing-case and mantel was littered with gimcracks, and the corners of the tiny rooms were curtained off, and behind these portières swarmed more gimcracks. The front of the upright piano had what March called a short-skirted portière on it, and the top was covered with vases, with dragon candlesticks, and with Jap fans, which also expanded themselves bat-wise on the walls between the etchings and the water-colours. The floors were covered with filling, and then rugs, and then skins; the easy-chairs all had tidies,* Armenian and Turkish and Persian; the lounges and sofas had embroidered cushions hidden under tidies. The radiator was concealed by a Jap screen, and over the top of this some Arab scarfs were flung. There was a superabundance of clocks. China pugs guarded the hearth; a brass sunflower smiled from the top of either andiron, and a brass peacock spread its tail before them inside a high filigree fender; on one side was a coal-hod in *repoussé* brass,* and on the other a wrought-iron wood-basket. Some red Japanese bird-kites were stuck about in the necks of spelter* vases, a crimson Jap umbrella hung opened beneath the chandelier, and each globe had a shade of yellow silk.

March, when he had recovered his self-command a little in the presence of the agglomeration, comforted himself by calling the bric-á-brac Jamescracks, as if this was their full name.

The disrespect he was able to show the whole apartment by means of this joke strengthened him to say boldly to the Superintendent that it was altogether too small; then he asked carelessly what the rent was.

"Two hundred and fifty."

The Marches gave a start, and looked at each other.

"Don't you think we could make it do?" she asked him, and he could see that she had mentally saved five hundred dollars as the difference between the rent of their house and that of this flat. "It has some very pretty features, and we could manage to squeeze in, couldn't we?"

"You won't find another furnished flat like it for no two fifty a month in the whole city," the Superintendent put in.

They exchanged glances again, and March said carelessly, "It's too small."

"There's a vacant flat in the Herodotus for eighteen

hundred a year, and one in the Thucydides for fifteen," the Superintendent suggested, clicking his keys together as they sank down in the elevator; "seven rooms and a bath."

"Thank you," said March, "we're looking for a furnished flat."

They felt that the Superintendent parted from them with repressed sarcasm.

"O Basil, do you think we *really* made him think it was the smallness and not the dearness?"

"No, but we saved our self-respect in the attempt; and that's a great deal."

"Of course, I *wouldn't* have taken it, anyway, with only six rooms, and so high up. But what prices! Now, we must be very circumspect about the next place."

It was a janitress, large, fat, with her arms wound up in her apron, who received them there. Mrs. March gave her a succinct but perfect statement of their needs. She failed to grasp the nature of them, or feigned to do so. She shook her head, and said that her son would show them the flat. There was a radiator visible in the narrow hall, and Isabel tacitly compromised on steam-heat without an elevator, as the flat was only one flight up. When the son appeared from below with a small kerosene hand-lamp, it appeared that the flat was unfurnished, but there was no stopping him till he had shown it in all its impossibility. When they got safely away from it and into the street March said, "Well, have you had enough for to-night, Isabel? Shall we go to the theatre now?"

"Not on any account. I want to see the whole list of flats that Mr. Fulkerson thought would be the very thing for us." She laughed, but with a certain bitterness.

"You'll be calling him my Mr. Fulkerson next, Isabel."

"Oh no!"

The fourth address was a furnished flat without a kitchen, in a house with a general restaurant. The fifth was a furnished house. At the sixth a pathetic widow and her pretty daughter wanted to take a family to board, and would give them a private table at a rate which the Marches would have thought low in Boston.

Mrs. March came away tingling with compassion for their evident anxiety, and this pity naturally soured into a sense of injury. "Well, I must say I have completely lost confidence in Mr. Fulkerson's judgment. Anything more utterly different from what I told him we wanted I couldn't imagine. If he doesn't manage any better about his business than he has done about this, it will be a perfect failure."

"Well, well, let's hope he'll be more circumspect about that," her husband returned, with ironical propitiation. "But I don't think it's Fulkerson's fault altogether. Perhaps it's the house-agents'. They're a very illusory generation. There seems to be something in the human habitation that corrupts the natures of those who deal in it, to buy or sell it, to hire or let it. You go to an agent and tell him what kind of a house you want. He has no such house, and he sends you to look at something altogether different, upon the well-ascertained principle that if you can't get what you want, you will take what you can get. You don't suppose the 'party' that took our house in Boston was looking for any such house? He was looking for a totally different kind of house in another part of the town."

"I don't believe that!" his wife broke in.

"Well, no matter. But see what a scandalous rent you asked for it."

"We didn't get much more than half; and, besides, the agent told me to ask fourteen hundred."

"Oh, I'm not blaming you, Isabel. I'm only analysing the house-agent, and exonerating Fulkerson."

"Well, I don't believe he told them just what we wanted; and at any rate, I'm done with agents. To-morrow, I'm going entirely by advertisements."

VIII

MRS. MARCH took the vertebrate with her to the Vienna Coffee-house, where they went to breakfast next morning. She made March buy her the *Herald* and the *World*,* and she added to its spiny convolutions from them. She read the new advertisements aloud with ardour and with faith to believe that the apartments described in them were every one truthfully represented, and that any one of them was richly responsive to their needs. "Elegant, light, large, single, and outside flats" were offered with "all improvements—bath, ice-box, etc."—for $25 and $30 a month. The cheapness was amazing. The Wagram, the Esmeralda, the Jacinth, advertised them for $40 and $60, "with steam-heat and elevator," rent free till November. Others, attractive from their air of conscientious scruple, announced "first-class flats; good order; reasonable rents." The Helena asked the reader if she had seen the "cabinet finish, hard-wood floors, and frescoed ceilings" of its $50 flats; the Asteroid affirmed that such apartments, with "six light rooms and bath, porcelain wash-tubs, electric bells, and hall-boy," as it offered for $75 were unapproached by competition. There was a sameness in the jargon which tended to confusion. Mrs. March got several flats on her list which promised neither steam-heat nor elevators; she forgot herself so far as to include two or three as remote from the down-town region of her choice as Harlem. But after she had rejected these the nondescript vertebrate was still voluminous enough to sustain her buoyant hopes.

The waiter, who remembered them from year to year, had put them at a window giving a pretty good section of Broadway, and before they set out on their search they had a moment of reminiscence. They recalled the Broadway of five, of ten, of twenty years ago, swelling and roaring with a tide of gaily painted omnibuses and of picturesque traffic that the horse-cars* have now banished from it. The grind of their wheels and the clash of their harsh bells imperfectly fill the silence that the omnibuses have left, and the eye misses the tumultuous perspective of former times.

They went out and stood for a moment before Grace Church,* and looked down the stately thoroughfare, and found it no longer impressive, no longer characteristic. It is still Broadway in name, but now it is like any other street. You do not now take your life in your hand when you attempt to cross it; the Broadway policeman who supported the elbow of timorous beauty in the hollow of his cotton-gloved palm and guided its little fearful boots over the crossing, while he arrested the billowy omnibuses on either side with an imperious glance, is gone, and all that certain processional, barbaric gaiety of the place is gone.

"Palmyra, Baalbec, Timour of the Desert,"* said March, voicing their common feeling of the change.

They turned and went into the beautiful church, and found themselves in time for the matin service. Rapt far from New York, if not from earth, in the dim richness of the painted light, the hallowed music took them with solemn ecstasy; the aërial, aspiring Gothic forms seemed to lift them heavenward. They came out, reluctant, into the dazzle and bustle of the street, with a feeling that they were too good for it, which they confessed to each other with whimsical consciousness.

"But no matter how consecrated we feel now," he said, "we mustn't forget that we went into the church for precisely the same reason that we went to the Vienna Café for breakfast—to gratify an æsthetic sense, to renew the faded pleasure of travel for a moment, to get back into the Europe of our youth. It was a purely Pagan impulse, Isabel, and we'd better own it."

"I don't know," she returned. "I think we reduce ourselves to the bare bones too much. I wish we didn't always recognise the facts as we do. Sometimes I should like to blink them. I should like to think I was devouter than I am, and younger and prettier."

"Better not; you couldn't keep it up. Honesty is the best policy even in such things."

"No; I don't like it, Basil. I should rather wait till the last day for some of my motives to come to the top. I know they're always mixed, but do let me give them the benefit of a doubt sometimes."

"Well, well, have it your own way, my dear. But I prefer not to lay up so many disagreeable surprises for myself at that time."

She would not consent. "I know I am a good deal younger than I was. I feel quite in the mood of that morning when we walked down Broadway on our wedding journey.* Don't you?"

"Oh yes. But I know I'm not younger; I'm only prettier."

She laughed for pleasure in his joke, and also for unconscious joy in the gay New York weather, in which there was no *arrière pensée**of the east wind. They had crossed Broadway, and were walking over to Washington Square, in the region of which they now hoped to place themselves. The *primo tenore**statue of Garibaldi had already taken possession of the place in the name of Latin progress, and they met Italian faces, French faces, Spanish faces,* as they strolled over the asphalte walks, under the thinning shadows of the autumn-stricken sycamores. They met the familiar picturesque raggedness of southern Europe with the old kindly illusion that somehow it existed for their appreciation, and that it found adequate compensation for poverty in this. March thought he sufficiently expressed his tacit sympathy in sitting down on one of the iron benches with his wife, and letting a little Neapolitan put a superfluous shine on his boots, while their desultory comment wandered with equal esteem to the old-fashioned American respectability which keeps the north side of the square in vast mansions of red brick, and the international shabbiness which has invaded the southern border, and broken it up into lodging-houses, shops, beer gardens, and studios.

They noticed the sign of an apartment to let on the north side, and as soon as the little boot-black could be bought off they went over to look at it. The janitor met them at the door and examined them. Then he said, as if still in doubt, "It has ten rooms, and the rent is twenty-eight hundred dollars."

"It wouldn't do, then," March replied, and left him to divide the responsibility between the paucity of the rooms and the enormity of the rent as he best might. But their self-love had received a wound, and they questioned each other what it was in their appearance made him doubt their ability to pay so much.

"Of course we don't look like New-Yorkers," sighed Mrs. March, "and we've walked through the Square. That might be as if we had walked along the Park Street mall in the Common before we came out on Beacon. Do you suppose he could have seen you getting your boots blacked in that way?"

"It's useless to ask," said March. "But I never can recover from this blow."

"Oh pshaw! You know you hate such things as badly as I do. It was very impertinent of him."

"Let us go back, and *écraser l'infâme* by paying him a year's rent in advance and taking immediate possession. Nothing else can soothe my wounded feelings. *You* were not having your boots blacked: why shouldn't he have supposed you were a New-Yorker, and I a country cousin?"

"They always know. Don't you remember Mrs. Williams's going to a Fifth Avenue milliner in a Worth dress, and the woman's asking her instantly what hotel she should send her hat to?"

"Yes; these things drive one to despair. I don't wonder the bodies of so many genteel strangers are found in the waters around New York. Shall we try the south side, my dear? or had we better go back to our rooms and rest a while?"

Mrs. March had out the vertebrate, and was consulting one of its glittering ribs, and glancing up from it at a house before which they stood. "Yes, it's the number; but do they call *this* being ready October 1st?" The little area in front of the basement was heaped with a mixture of mortar, bricks, laths, and shavings from the interior; the brown-stone steps to the front door were similarly bestrewn; the doorway

45

showed the half-open rough pine carpenter's hatch of an unfinished house; the sashless windows of every story showed the activity of workmen within; the clatter of hammers and the hiss of saws came out to them from every opening.

"They may call it October 1st," said March, "because it's too late to contradict them. But they'd better not call it December 1st in *my* presence; I'll let them say January 1st, at a pinch."

"We will go in and look at it anyway," said his wife; and he admired how, when she was once within, she began provisionally to settle the family in each of the several floors with the female instinct for domiciliation which never failed her. She had the help of the landlord, who was present to urge forward the workmen apparently; he lent a hopeful fancy to the solution of all her questions. To get her from under his influence March had to represent that the place was damp from undried plastering, and that if she stayed she would probably be down with that New York pneumonia which visiting Bostonians are always dying of. Once safely on the pavement outside, she realised that the apartment was not only unfinished, but unfurnished, and had neither steam-heat nor elevator. "But I thought we had better look at everything," she explained.

"Yes, but not take everything. If I hadn't pulled you away from there by main force you'd have not only died of New York pneumonia on the spot, but you'd have had us all settled there before we knew what we were about."

"Well, that's what I can't help, Basil. It's the only way I can realise whether it will do for us. I have to dramatise the whole thing."

She got a deal of pleasure as well as excitement out of this, and he had to own that the process of setting up housekeeping in so many different places was not only entertaining, but tended, through association with their first beginnings in house-keeping, to restore the image of their early married days, and to make them young again.

It went on all day, and continued far into the night, until

46

it was too late to go to the theatre, too late to do anything but tumble into bed and simultaneously fall on sleep. They groaned over their reiterated disappointments, but they could not deny that the interest was unfailing, and that they got a great deal of fun out of it all. Nothing could abate Mrs. March's faith in her advertisements. One of them sent her to a flat of ten rooms which promised to be the solution of all their difficulties; it proved to be over a livery-stable, a liquor store, and a milliner's shop, none of the first fashion. Another led them far into old Greenwich Village to an apartment-house, which she refused to enter behind a small girl with a loaf of bread under one arm and a quart can of milk under the other.

In their search they were obliged, as March complained, to the acquisition of useless information in a degree un-equalled in their experience. They came to excel in the sad knowledge of the line at which respectability distinguishes itself from shabbiness. Flattering advertisements took them to numbers of huge apartment-houses chiefly distinguish-able from tenement-houses by the absence of fire-escapes on their façades, till Mrs. March refused to stop at any door where there were more than six bell-ratchets and speaking-tubes on either hand. Before the middle of the afternoon she decided against ratchets altogether, and confined herself to knobs, neatly set in the door-trim. Her husband was still sunk in the superstition that you can live anywhere you like in New York, and he would have paused at some places where her quicker eye caught the fatal sign of "Modes" in the ground-floor windows. She found that there was an east and west line beyond which they could not go if they wished to keep their self-respect, and that within the region to which they had restricted themselves there was a choice of streets. At first all the New York streets looked to them ill-paved, dirty, and repulsive; the general infamy imparted itself in their casual impression to streets in no wise guilty. But they began to notice that some streets were quiet and clean, and, though never so quiet and clean as Boston streets, that they wore an air of encouraging reform, and suggested a future of

47

greater and greater domesticity. Whole blocks of these down-town cross streets seemed to have been redeemed from decay, and even in the midst of squalor a dwelling here and there had been seized, painted a dull-red as to its brick-work, and a glossy black as to its wood-work, and with a bright brass bell-pull and door knob and a large brass plate for its key-hole escutcheon, had been endowed with an effect of purity and pride which removed its shabby neighbourhood far from it.

Some of these houses were quite small, and imaginably within their means; but, as March said, somebody seemed always to be living there himself, and the fact that none of them were to rent kept Mrs. March true to her ideal of a flat. Nothing prevented its realisation so much as its difference from the New York ideal of a flat, which was inflexibly seven rooms and a bath. One or two rooms might be at the front, the rest crooked and cornered backward through increasing and then decreasing darkness till they reached a light bed-room or kitchen at the rear. It might be the one or the other, but it was always the seventh room with the bath; or if, as sometimes happened, it was the eighth, it was so after having counted the bath as one. In this case the janitor said you always counted the bath as one. If the flats were advertised as having "all light rooms," he explained that any room with a window giving into the open air of a court or shaft was counted a light room.

The Marches tried to make out why it was that these flats were so much more repulsive than the apartments which every one lived in abroad; but they could only do so upon the supposition that in their European days they were too young, too happy, too full of the future, to notice whether rooms were inside or outside, light or dark, big or little, high or low. "Now we're imprisoned in the present," he said, "and we have to make the worst of it."

In their despair he had an inspiration, which she declared worthy of him: it was to take two small flats, of four or five rooms and a bath, and live in both. They tried this in a great many places; but they never could get two flats of the kind on the same floor where there was steam-heat and an elevator. At one place they almost did it. They had resigned themselves to the humility of the neighbourhood, to the prevalence of modistes and livery-stablemen (they seem to consort much in New York), to the garbage in the gutters and the litter of paper in the streets, to the faltering slats in the surrounding window-shutters and the crumbled brownstone steps and sills, when it turned out that one of the apartments had been taken between two visits they made. Then the only combination left open to them was of a ground-floor flat to the right and a third-floor flat to the left.

Still they kept this inspiration in reserve for use at the first opportunity. In the meantime there were several flats which they thought they could almost make do: notably one where they could get an extra servant's room in the basement four flights down, and another where they could get it in the roof five flights up. At the first the janitor was respectful and enthusiastic; at the second he had an effect of ironical pessimism. When they trembled on the verge of taking his apartment, he pointed out a spot in the kalsomining*of the parlour ceiling, and gratuitously said, Now such a thing as that he should not agree to put in shape unless they took the apartment for a term of years. The apartment was unfurnished, and they recurred to the fact that they wanted a furnished apartment, and made their escape. This saved them in several other extremities; but short of extremity they could not keep their different requirements in mind, and were always about to decide without regard to some one of them.

They went to several places twice without intending: once to that old-fashioned house with the pleasant coloured janitor, and wandered all over the apartment again with a haunting sense of familiarity, and then recognised the janitor and laughed; and to that house with the pathetic widow and the pretty daughter who wished to take them to board. They stayed to excuse their blunder, and easily came by the fact that the mother had taken the house that the girl might have a home while she was in New York studying art, and they hoped to pay their way by taking boarders. Her daughter was at her class now, the mother concluded; and they encouraged her to believe that it could only be a few days till the rest of her scheme was realised.

"I dare say we could be perfectly comfortable there," March suggested when they had got away. "Now if we were truly humane we would modify our desires to meet their needs and end this sickening search, wouldn't we?"

"Yes, but we're *not* truly humane," his wife answered, "or at least not in that sense. You know you hate boarding; and if we went there I should have them on my sympathies the whole time."

"I see. And then you would take it out of me."

"Then I should take it out of you. And if you are going to be so weak, Basil, and let every little thing work upon you in that way, you'd better not come to New York. You'll see enough misery here."

"Well, don't take that superior tone with me, as if I were a child that had its mind set on an undesirable toy, Isabel."

"Ah, don't you suppose it's because you *are* such a child in some respects that I like you, dear?" she demanded, without relenting.

"But I don't find so much misery in New York. I don't suppose there's any more suffering here to the population than there is in the country. And they're so gay about it all. I think the outward aspect of the place and the hilarity of the sky and air must get into the people's blood. The weather is simply unapproachable; and I don't care if it is the ugliest place in the world, as you say. I suppose it is. It shrieks and yells with ugliness here and there, but it never loses its spirits. That widow is from the country. When she's been a year in New York she'll be as gay—as gay as an L road." He celebrated a satisfaction they both had in the L roads.* "They kill the streets and avenues, but at least they partially hide them, and that is some comfort; and they do triumph over their prostrate forms with a savage exultation that is intoxicating. Those bends in the L that you get in the corner of Washington Square, or just below the Cooper Institute— they're the gayest things in the world. Perfectly atrocious, of course, but incomparably picturesque! And the whole city is so," said March, "or else the L would never have got built here. New York may be splendidly gay or squalidly gay; but, prince or pauper, it's gay always."

"Yes, gay is the word," she admitted, with a sigh. "But frantic. I can't get used to it. They forget death, Basil; they forget death in New York."

"Well, I don't know that I've ever found much advantage in remembering it."

"Don't say such a thing, dearest."

He could see that she had got to the end of her nervous strength for the present, and he proposed that they should take the Elevated road as far as it would carry them into the country, and shake off their nightmare of flat-hunting for an hour or two; but her conscience would not let her. She convicted him of levity equal to that of the New-Yorkers in proposing such a thing; and they dragged through the day. She was too tired to care for dinner, and in the night she had a dream from which she woke herself with a cry that roused him too. It was something about the children at first, whom they had talked of wistfully before falling asleep, and then it was of a hideous thing with two square eyes and a series of sections growing darker and then lighter, till the tail of the monstrous articulate was quite luminous again. She shuddered at the vague description she was able to give; but he asked, "Did it offer to bite you?"

"No. That was the most frightful thing about it; it had no mouth."

March laughed. "Why, my dear, it was nothing but a harmless New York flat—seven rooms and a bath."

"I really believe it was," she consented, recognising an architectural resemblance, and she fell asleep again, and woke renewed for the work before them.

THEIR house-hunting no longer had novelty, but it still had interest; and they varied their day by taking a coupé, by renouncing advertisements, and by reverting to agents. Some of these induced them to consider the idea of furnished houses; and Mrs. March learned tolerance for Fulkerson by accepting permits to visit flats and houses which had none of the qualifications she desired in either, and were as far beyond her means as they were out of the region to which she had geographically restricted herself. They looked at three-thousand and four-thousand dollar apartments, and rejected them for one reason or another which had nothing to do with the rent; the higher the rent was, the more critical they were of the slippery inlaid floors and the arrangement of the richly decorated rooms. They never knew whether they had deceived the janitor or not; as they came in a coupé, they hoped they had.

They drove accidentally through one street that seemed gayer in the perspective than an L road. The fire-escapes, with their light iron balconies and ladders of iron, decorated the lofty house fronts; the roadway and sidewalks and door-steps swarmed with children; women's heads seemed to show at every window. In the basements, over which flights of high stone steps led to the tenements, were greengrocers' shops abounding in cabbages, and provision stores running chiefly to bacon and sausages, and cobblers' and tinners' shops, and the like, in proportion to the small needs of a poor neighbourhood. Ash barrels lined the sidewalks, and garbage heaps filled the gutters; teams of all trades stood idly about; a peddler of cheap fruit urged his cart through the street, and mixed his cry with the joyous screams and shouts of the children and the scolding and gossiping voices of the women; the burly blue bulk of a policeman defined itself at the corner; a drunkard zigzagged down the sidewalk toward him. It was not the abode of the extremest poverty, but of a poverty as hopeless as any in the world, transmitting itself from generation to generation, and establishing conditions of permanency to which human life adjusts itself as it does to those of some incurable disease, like leprosy.

The time had been when the Marches would have taken a purely æsthetic view of the facts as they glimpsed them in this street of tenement-houses; when they would have contented themselves with saying that it was as picturesque as a street in Naples or Florence, and with wondering why nobody came to paint it; they would have thought they were sufficiently serious about it in blaming the artists for their failure to appreciate it, and going abroad for the picturesque when they had it here under their noses. It was to the nose that the street made one of its strongest appeals, and Mrs. March pulled up her window of the coupé. "Why does he take us through such a disgusting street?" she demanded, with an exasperation of which her husband divined the origin.

"This driver may be a philanthropist in disguise," he answered, with dreamy irony, "and may want us to think about the people who are not merely carried through this street in a coupé, but have to spend their whole lives in it, winter and summer, with no hopes of driving out of it, except in a hearse. I must say they don't seem to mind it. I haven't seen a jollier crowd anywhere in New York. They seem to have forgotten death a little more completely than any of their fellow-citizens, Isabel. And I wonder what they think of us, making this gorgeous progress through their midst. I suppose they think we're rich, and hate us—if they hate rich people; they don't look as if they hated anybody. Should we be as patient as they are with their discomfort? I don't believe there's steam-heat or an elevator in the whole block. Seven rooms and a bath would be more than the largest and genteelest family would know what to do with. They wouldn't know what to do with the bath anyway."

His monologue seemed to interest his wife apart from the satirical point it had for themselves. "You ought to get Mr. Fulkerson to let you work some of these New York sights up for *Every Other Week*, Basil; you could do them very nicely."

"Yes; I've thought of that. But don't let's leave the personal ground. Doesn't it make you feel rather small and otherwise unworthy when you see the kind of street these fellow-beings of yours live in, and then think how particular you are about locality and the number of bell-pulls? I don't see even ratchets and speaking-tubes at these doors." He craned his neck out of the window for a better look, and the children of discomfort cheered him, out of sheer good feeling and high spirits. "I didn't know I was so popular. Perhaps it's a recognition of my humane sentiments."

"Oh, it's very easy to have humane sentiments, and to satirise ourselves for wanting eight rooms and a bath in a good neighbourhood, when we see how these wretched creatures live," said his wife. "But if we shared all we have with them, and then settled down among them, what good would it do?"

"Not the least in the world. It might help us for the moment, but it wouldn't keep the wolf from their doors for a week; and then they would go on just as before, only they wouldn't be on such good terms with the wolf. The only way for them is to keep up an unbroken intimacy with the wolf; then they can manage him somehow. I don't know how, and I'm afraid I don't want to. Wouldn't you like to have this fellow drive us round among the halls of pride somewhere for a little while? Fifth Avenue or Madison, up-town?"

"No; we've no time to waste. I've got a place near Third Avenue, on a nice cross street, and I want him to take us there." It proved that she had several addresses near together, and it seemed best to dismiss their coupé and do the rest of their afternoon's work on foot. It came to nothing; she was not humbled in the least by what she had seen in the tenement-house street; she yielded no point in her ideal of a flat, and the flats persistently refused to lend themselves to it. She lost all patience with them.

"Oh, I don't say the flats are in the right of it," said her husband, when she denounced their stupid inadequacy to the purposes of a Christian home. "But I'm not so sure that we are either. I've been thinking about that home business ever since my sensibilities were dragged—in a coupé—through that tenement-house street. Of course no child born and brought up in such a place as that could have any conception of home. But that's because those poor people can't give character to their habitations. They have to take what they can get. But people like us—that is, of our means—do give character to the average flat. It's made to meet their tastes, or their supposed tastes; and so it's made for social show, not for family life at all. Think of a baby in a flat! It's a contradiction in terms; the flat is the negation of motherhood. The flat means society life; that is, the pretence of social life. It's made to give artificial people a society basis on a little money—too much money, of course, for what they get. So the cost of the building is put into marble halls and idiotic decoration of all kinds. I don't object to the conveniences, but none of these flats have a living-room. They have drawing-rooms to foster social pretence, and they have dining-rooms and bedrooms; but they have no room where the family can all come together and feel the sweetness of being a family. The bedrooms are black-holes mostly, with a sinful waste of space in each. If it were not for the marble halls, and the decorations, and the foolishly expensive finish, the houses could be built round a court, and the flats could be shaped something like a Pompeiian house, with small sleeping closets—only lit from the outside—and the rest of the floor thrown into two or three large cheerful halls, where all the family life could go on, and society could be transacted unpretentiously. Why, those tenements are better and humaner than those flats! There the whole family lives in the kitchen, and has its consciousness of being; but the flat abolishes the family consciousness. It's confinement without coziness; it's cluttered without being snug. You couldn't keep a self-respecting cat in a flat; you couldn't go down cellar to get cider. No: the Anglo-Saxon home, as we know it in the Anglo-Saxon house, is simply impossible in the Franco-American flat, not because it's humble, but because it's false."

"Well, then," said Mrs. March, "let's look at houses."

He had been denouncing the flat in the abstract, and he had not expected this concrete result. But he said, "We will look at houses, then."

X

NOTHING mystifies a man more than a woman's aberrations from some point at which he supposes her fixed as a star. In these unfurnished houses, without steam or elevator, March followed his wife about with patient wonder. She rather liked the worst of them best; but she made him go down into the cellars and look at the furnaces; she exacted from him a rigid inquest of the plumbing. She followed him into one of the cellars by the fitful glare of successively lighted matches, and they enjoyed a moment in which the anomaly of their presence there on that errand, so remote from all the facts of their long-stablished life in Boston, realised itself for them.

"Think how easily we might have been murdered and nobody been any the wiser!" she said when they were comfortably out-doors again.

"Yes, or made way with ourselves in an access of emotional insanity, supposed to have been induced by unavailing flat-hunting," he suggested.

She fell in with the notion. "I'm beginning to *feel* crazy. But I don't want *you* to lose your head, Basil. And I don't want you to sentimentalise any of the things you see in New York. I think you were disposed to do it in that street we drove through. I don't believe there's any *real* suffering— not real *suffering*—among those people; that is, it would be suffering from our point of view, but they've been used to it all their lives, and they don't feel their discomfort so much."

"Of course I understand that, and I don't propose to sentimentalise them. I think when people get used to a bad state of things they had better stick to it; in fact they don't usually like a better state so well, and I shall keep that firmly in mind."

She laughed with him, and they walked along the L-bestridden avenue, exhilarated by their escape from murder and suicide in that cellar, toward the nearest cross-town track, which they meant to take home to their hotel. "Now to-night we will go to the theatre," she said, "and get this whole house business out of our minds, and be perfectly fresh for a new start in the morning." Suddenly she clutched his arm. "Why, did you *see* that man?" and she signed with her head toward a decently dressed person who walked beside them, next the gutter, stooping over as if to examine it, and half halting at times.

"No. What?"

"Why, I saw him pick up a dirty bit of cracker from the pavement and cram it into his mouth and eat it down as if he were famished. And look! he's actually hunting for more in those garbage heaps!"

This was what the decent-looking man with the hard hands and broken nails of a workman was doing—like a hungry dog. They kept up with him, in the fascination of the sight, to the next corner, where he turned down the side street still searching the gutter.

They walked on a few paces. Then March said, "I must go after him," and left his wife standing.

"Are you in want—hungry?" he asked the man.

The man said he could not speak English, monsieur.

March asked his question in French.

The man shrugged a pitiful, desperate shrug, "Mais, monsieur——"

March put a coin in his hand, and then suddenly the man's face twisted up; he caught the hand of this alms-giver in both of his, and clung to it. "Monsieur! monsieur!" he gasped, and the tears rained down his face.

His benefactor pulled himself away, shocked and ashamed, as one is by such a chance, and got back to his wife, and the man lapsed back into the mystery of misery out of which he had emerged.

March felt it laid upon him to console his wife for what had happened. "Of course we might live here for years and not see another case like that; and of course there are twenty places where he could have gone for help if he had known where to find them."

"Ah, but it's the possibility of his needing the help so badly as that!" she answered. "That's what I can't bear, and I shall not come to a place where such things are possible, and we may as well stop our house-hunting here at once."

"Yes? And what part of Christendom will you live in? Such things are possible everywhere in our conditions."

"Then we must change the conditions——"

"Oh no; we must go to the theatre and forget them. We can stop at Brentano's for our tickets as we pass through Union Square."

"I am not going to the theatre, Basil. I am going home to Boston to-night. You can stay and find a flat."

He convinced her of the absurdity of her position, and even of its selfishness; but she said that her mind was quite made up irrespective of what had happened; that she had been away from the children long enough; that she ought to be at home to finish up the work of leaving it. The word brought a sigh. "Ah, I don't know why we should see nothing but sad and ugly things now. When we were young——"

"Younger," he put in. "We're still young."

"That's what we pretend, but we know better. But I was thinking how pretty and pleasant things used to be turning up all the time on our travels in the old days. Why, when we were in New York here on our wedding journey the place didn't seem half so dirty as it does now, and none of these dismal things happened."

"It was a good deal dirtier," he answered; "and I fancy worse in every way—hungrier, raggeder, more wretchedly housed. But that wasn't the period of life for us to notice it. Don't you remember, when we started to Niagara the last time, how everybody seemed middle-aged and commonplace; and when we got there there were no evident brides; nothing but elderly married people?"

"At least they weren't starving," she rebelled.

"No, you don't starve in parlour cars and first-class hotels; but if you step out of them you run your chance of seeing those who do, if you're getting on pretty well in the forties. If it's the unhappy who see unhappiness, think what misery must be revealed to people who pass their lives in the really squalid tenement-house streets—I don't mean picturesque avenues like that we passed through."

"But we are *not* unhappy," she protested, bringing the talk back to the personal base again, as women must to get any good out of talk. "We're really no unhappier than we were when we were young."

"We're more serious."

"Well, I hate it; and I wish you *wouldn't* be so serious, if that's what it brings us to."

"I will be trivial from this on," said March. "Shall we go to the *Hole in the Ground* to-night?"

"I am going to Boston."

"It's much the same thing. How do you like that for triviality? It's a little blasphemous, I'll allow."

"It's very silly," she said.

At the hotel they found a letter from the agent who had sent them the permit to see Mrs. Grosvenor Green's apartment. He wrote that she had heard they were pleased with her apartment, and that she thought she could make the terms to suit. She had taken her passage for Europe, and was very anxious to let the flat before she sailed. She would call that evening at seven.

"Mrs. Grosvenor Green!" said Mrs. March. "Which of the ten thousand flats is it, Basil?"

"The gimcrackery," he answered. "In the Xenophon, you know."

"Well, she may save herself the trouble. I shall not see her. Or yes—I must. I *couldn't* go away without seeing what sort of creature could have planned that fly-away flat. She must be a perfect——"

"Parachute," March suggested.

"No: anybody so light as that couldn't come down."

"Well, toy balloon."

"Toy balloon will do for the present," Mrs. March admitted. "But I feel that naught but herself can be her parallel for volatility."

When Mrs. Grosvenor Green's card came up they both descended to the hotel parlour, which March said looked like the saloon of a Moorish day-boat; not that he knew of any such craft, but the decorations were so Saracenic and the architecture so Hudson Riverish. They found there on the grand central divan a large lady whose vast smoothness, placidity, and plumpness set at defiance all their preconceptions of Mrs. Grosvenor Green, so that Mrs. March distinctly paused with her card in her hand before venturing even tentatively to address her. Then she was astonished at the low calm voice in which Mrs. Green acknowledged herself, and slowly proceeded to apologise for calling. It was not quite true that she had taken her passage for Europe, but she hoped soon to do so, and she confessed that in the meantime she was anxious to let her flat. She was a little worn out with the care of house-keeping—Mrs. March breathed, "Oh yes!" in the sigh with which ladies recognise one another's martyrdom—and Mr. Green had business abroad, and she was going to pursue her art studies in Paris; she drew in Mr. Ilcomb's class now, but the instruction was so much better in Paris; and as the Superintendent seemed to think the price was the only objection, she had ventured to call.

"Then we didn't deceive him in the least," thought Mrs. March, while she answered sweetly: "No; we were only afraid that it would be too small for our family. We require a good many rooms." She could not forego the opportunity of saying, "My husband is coming to New York to take charge of a literary periodical, and he will have to have a room to write in," which made Mrs. Green bow to March, and made March look sheepish. "But we did think the apartment very charming (It *was* architecturally charming," she protested to her conscience), "and we should have been so glad if we could have got into it." She followed this with some account of their house-hunting, amid soft murmurs of sympathy from Mrs. Green, who said that she had been through all that, and that if she could have shown her apartment to them she felt sure that she could have explained it so that they would have seen its capabilities better. Mrs. March assented to this, and Mrs. Green added that if they found nothing exactly suitable she would be glad to have them look at it again; and then Mrs. March said that she was going back to Boston herself, but she was leaving Mr. March to continue the search, and she had no doubt he would be only *too* glad to see the apartment by daylight. "But if you take it, Basil," she warned him, when they were alone, "I shall simply renounce you. I wouldn't live in that junk shop if you gave it to me. But who would have thought she was that kind of looking person? Though of course I might have known if I had stopped to think once. It's because the place doesn't express her at all that it's so unlike her. It couldn't be like anybody, or anything that flies in the air, or creeps upon the earth, or swims in the waters under the earth. I wonder where in the world she's from; she's no New-Yorker; even we can see that; and she's not quite a country person either; she seems like a person from some large town, where she's been an æsthetic authority. And she can't find good enough art instruction in New York, and has to go to Paris for it! Well, it's pathetic, after all, Basil. I can't help feeling sorry for a person who mistakes herself to that extent."

"I can't help feeling sorry for the husband of a person who mistakes herself to that extent. What is Mr. Grosvenor Green going to do in Paris while she's working her way into the Salon?"

"Well, you keep away from her apartment, Basil; that's all I've got to say to *you*. And yet I do like some things about her."

"I like everything about her but her apartment," said March.

"I like her going to be out of the country," said his wife. "We shouldn't be overlooked. And the place was prettily shaped, you can't deny it. And there was an elevator and steam-heat. And the location *is* very convenient. And there was a hall-boy to bring up cards. The halls and stairs were kept very clean and nice. But it wouldn't do. I could put you a folding bed in the room where you wrote, and we could even have one in the parlour——"

"Behind a portière? I couldn't stand any more portières!"

"And we could squeeze the two girls into one room, or perhaps only bring Margaret, and put out the whole of the wash. Basil!" she almost shrieked, "it isn't to be thought of!"

He retorted, "I'm not thinking of it, my dear."

Fulkerson came in just before they started for Mrs. March's train, to find out what had become of them, he said, and to see whether they had got anything to live in yet.

"Not a thing," she said. "And I'm just going back to Boston, and leaving Mr. March here to do anything he pleases about it. He has *carte blanche*."

"But freedom brings responsibility, you know, Fulkerson, and it's the same as if I'd no choice. I'm staying behind because I'm left, not because I expect to do anything."

"Is that so?" asked Fulkerson. "Well, we must see what can be done. I supposed you would be all settled by this time, or I should have humped myself to find you something. None of those places I gave you amount to anything?"

"As much as forty thousand others we've looked at," said Mrs. March. "Yes, one of them *does* amount to something. It comes so near being what we want that I've given Mr. March particular instructions not to go near it."

She told him about Mrs. Grosvenor Green and her flats, and at the end he said—

"Well, well, we must look out for that. I'll keep an eye on him, Mrs. March, and see that he doesn't do anything rash, and I won't leave him till he's found just the right thing. It exists, of course; it must in a city of eighteen hundred thousand people, and the only question is where to find it. You leave him to me, Mrs. March; I'll watch out for him."

Fulkerson showed some signs of going to the station when he found they were not driving, but she bade him a peremptory good-bye at the hotel door.

"He's very nice, Basil, and his way with you is perfectly charming. It's very sweet to see how really fond of you he is.

But I didn't want him stringing along up to Forty-second Street with us, and spoiling our last moments together."

At Third Avenue they took the Elevated, for which she confessed an infatuation. She declared it the most ideal way of getting about in the world, and was not ashamed when he reminded her of how she used to say that nothing under the sun could induce her to travel on it. She now said that the night transit was even more interesting than the day, and that the fleeting intimacy you formed with people in second and third floor interiors, while all the usual street life went on underneath, had a domestic intensity mixed with a perfect repose that was the last effect of good society with all its security and exclusiveness. He said it was better than the theatre, of which it reminded him, to see those people through their windows: a family party of work-folk at a late tea, some of the men in their shirt sleeves; a woman sewing by a lamp; a mother laying her child in its cradle; a man with his head fallen on his hands upon a table; a girl and her lover leaning over the window-sill together. What suggestion! what drama! what infinite interest! At the Forth-second Street station they stopped a minute on the bridge that crosses the track to the branch road for the Central Depôt, and looked up and down the long stretch of the Elevated to north and south. The track that found and lost itself a thousand times in the flare and tremor of the innumerable lights; the moony sheen of the electrics mixing with the reddish points and blots of gas far and near; the architectural shapes of houses and churches and towers, rescued by the obscurity from all that was ignoble in them, and the coming and going of the trains marking the stations with vivider or fainter plumes of flame-shot steam—formed an incomparable perspective. They often talked afterward of the superb spectacle, which in a city full of painters nightly works its unrecorded miracles; and they were just to the Arachne roof-spun in iron over the cross street on which they ran to the depôt; but for the present they were mostly inarticulate before it. They had another moment of rich silence when they paused in the gallery that leads from the elevated station to the waiting-rooms in the Central Depôt and looked down upon the great night trains lying on the tracks dim under the rain of gas-lights that starred without dispersing the vast darkness of the place. What forces, what fates, slept in these bulks which would soon be hurling themselves north and east and west through the night! Now they waited there like fabled monsters of Arab story ready for the magician's touch, tractable, reckless, will-less—organised lifelessness full of a strange semblance of life.

The Marches admired the impressive sight with a thrill of patriotic pride in the fact that the whole world perhaps could not afford just the like. Then they hurried down to the ticket offices, and he got her a lower berth in the Boston sleeper, and went with her to the car. They made the most of the fact that her berth was in the very middle of the car; and she promised to write as soon as she reached home. She promised also that having seen the limitations of New York in respect to flats, she would not be hard on him if he took something not quite ideal. Only he must remember that it was not to be above Twentieth Street nor below Washington Square; it must not be higher than the third floor; it must have an elevator, steam-heat, hall-boys, and a pleasant janitor. These were essentials; if he could not get them, then they must do without. But he must get them.

XI

MRS. MARCH was one of those wives who exact a more rigid adherence to their ideals from their husbands than from themselves. Early in their married life she had taken charge of him in all matters which she considered practical. She did not include the business of bread-winning in these; that was an affair that might safely be left to his absent-minded, dreamy inefficiency, and she did not interfere with him there. But in such things as rehanging the pictures, deciding on a summer boarding-place, taking a seaside cottage, repapering rooms, choosing seats at the theatre, seeing what the children ate when she was not at table, shutting the cat out at night, keeping run of calls and invitations, and seeing if the furnace was damped, he had failed her so often that she felt she could not leave him the slightest discretion in regard to a flat. Her total distrust of his judgment in the matters cited and others like them consisted with the greatest admiration of his mind and respect for his character. She often said that if he would only bring them to bear in such exigencies he would be simply perfect; but she had long given up his ever doing so. She subjected him, therefore, to an iron code, but after proclaiming it she was apt to abandon him to the native lawlessness of his temperament. She expected him in this event to do as he pleased, and she resigned herself to it with considerable comfort in holding him accountable. He learned to expect this, and after suffering keenly from her disappointment with whatever he did he waited patiently till she forgot her grievance and began to extract what consolation lurks in the irreparable. She would almost admit at moments that what he had done was a very good thing, but she reserved the right to return in full force to her original condemnation of it; and she accumulated each act of independent volition in witness and warning against him. Their mass oppressed but never deterred him. He expected to do the wrong thing when left to his own devices, and he did it without any apparent recollection of his former misdeeds and their consequences. There was a good deal of comedy in it all, and some tragedy.

He now experienced a certain expansion, such as husbands of his kind will imagine, on going back to his hotel alone. It was, perhaps, a revulsion from the pain of parting; and he toyed with the idea of Mrs. Grosvenor Green's apartment, which, in its preposterous unsuitability, had a strange attraction. He felt that he could take it with less risk than anything else they had seen, but he said he would look at all the other places in town first. He really spent the greater part of the next day in hunting up the owner of an apartment that had neither steam-heat nor an elevator, but was otherwise perfect, and trying to get him to take less than the agent asked.

By a curious psychical operation he was able, in the transaction, to work himself into quite a passionate desire for the apartment, while he held the Grosvenor Green apartment in the background of his mind as something that he could return to as altogether more suitable. He conducted some simultaneous negotiation for a furnished house, which enhanced still more the desirability of the Grosvenor Green apartment. Toward evening he went off at a tangent far uptown, so as to be able to tell his wife how utterly preposterous the best there would be as compared even with this ridiculous Grosvenor Green gimcrackery. It is hard to report the processes of his sophistication; perhaps this, again, may best be left to the marital imagination.

He rang at the last of these up-town apartments as it was falling dusk, and it was long before the janitor appeared. Then the man was very surly, and said if he looked at the flat now he would say it was too dark, like all the rest. His reluctance irritated March in proportion to his insincerity in proposing to look at it at all. He knew he did not mean to take it under any circumstances; that he was going to use his inspection of it in dishonest justification of his disobedience to his wife; but he put on an air of offended dignity. "If you don't wish to show the apartment," he said, "I don't care to see it."

The man groaned, for he was heavy, and no doubt dreaded the stairs. He scratched a match on his thigh, and led the way up. March was sorry for him, and he put his fingers on a quarter in his waistcoat-pocket to give him at parting. At the same time, he had to trump up an objection to the flat. This was easy, for it was advertised as containing ten rooms, and he found the number eked out with the bathroom and two large closets. "It's light enough," said March, "but I don't see how you make out ten rooms."

"There's ten tooms," said the man, deigning no proof.

March took his fingers off the quarter, and went downstairs and out of the door without another word. It would be wrong, it would be impossible, to give the man anything after such insolence. He reflected, with shame, that it was also cheaper to punish than forgive him.

He returned to his hotel prepared for any desperate measure, and convinced now that the Grosvenor Green apartment was not merely the only thing left for him, but was, on its own merits, the best thing in New York.

Fulkerson was waiting for him in the reading-room, and it gave March the curious thrill with which a man closes with temptation when he said: "Look here! Why don't you take that woman's flat in the Xenophon? She's been at the agents again, and they've been at me. She likes your look—or Mrs. March's—and I guess you can have it at a pretty heavy discount from the original price. I'm authorised to say you can have it for one seventy-five a month, and I don't believe it would be safe for you to offer one fifty."

March shook his head, and dropped a mask of virtuous rejection over his corrupt acquiescence. "It's too small for us—we couldn't squeeze into it."

"Why, look here!" Fulkerson persisted. "How many rooms do you people want?"

"I've got to have a place to work——"

"Of course! And you've got to have it at the *Fifth Wheel* office."

"I hadn't thought of that," March began. "I suppose I *could* do my work at the office, as there's not much writing——"

"Why, of course you can't do your work at home. You just come round with me now, and look at that flat again."

"No; I can't do it."

"Why?"

"I—I've got to dine."

"All right," said Fulkerson. "Dine with me. I want to take you round to a little Italian place that I know."

One may trace the successive steps of March's descent in this simple matter with the same edification that would attend the study of the self-delusions and obfuscations of a man tempted to crime. The process is probably not at all different, and to the philosophical mind the kind of result is unimportant; the process is everything.

Fulkerson led him down one block and half across another

to the steps of a small dwelling-house, transformed, like many others, into a restaurant of the Latin ideal, with little or no structural change from the pattern of the lower middle-class New York home. There were the corroded brown-stone steps, the mean little front door, and the cramped entry with its narrow stairs by which ladies could go up to a dining-room appointed for them on the second floor; the parlours on the first were set about with tables, where men smoked cigarettes between the courses, and a single waiter ran swiftly to and fro with plates and dishes, and exchanged unintelligible outcries with a cook beyond a slide in the back parlour. He rushed at the new-comers, brushed the soiled table-cloth before them with a towel on his arm, covered its worst stains with a napkin, and brought them, in their order, the vermicelli soup, the fried fish, the cheese-strewn spa-ghetti, the veal cutlets, the tepid roast fowl and salad, and the wizened pear and coffee which form the dinner at such places.

"Ah, this is *nice*!" said Fulkerson, after the laying of the charitable napkin, and he began to recognise acquaintances, some of whom he described to March as young literary men and artists with whom they should probably have to do; others were simply frequenters of the place, and were of all nationalities and religions apparently—at least, several were Hebrews and Cubans. "You get a pretty good slice of New York here," he said, "all except the frosting on top. That you won't find much at Maroni's, though you will occa-sionally. I don't mean the ladies ever, of course." The ladies present seemed harmless and reputable looking people enough, but certainly they were not of the first fashion, and, except in a few instances, not Americans. "It's like cutting straight down through a fruit-cake," Fulkerson went on, "or a mince-pie, when you don't know who made the pie; you get a little of everything." He ordered a small flask of Chianti with the dinner, and it came in its pretty wicker jacket. March smiled upon it with tender reminiscence, and Fulker-son laughed. "Lights you up a little. I brought old Dryfoos here one day, and he thought it was sweet-oil; that's the kind of bottle they used to have it in at the country drug-stores."

"Yes, I remember now; but I'd totally forgotten it," said March. "How far back that goes! Who's Dryfoos?"

"Dryfoos?" Fulkerson, still smiling, tore off a piece of the half-yard of French loaf which had been supplied them, with two pale, thin disks of butter, and fed it into himself. "Old Dryfoos? Well, of course! I call him old, but he ain't so very. About fifty, or along there."

"No," said March, "that isn't very old—or not so old as it used to be."

"Well, I suppose you've got to know about him, anyway," said Fulkerson thoughtfully. "And I've been wondering just how I should tell you. Can't always make out exactly how much of a Bostonian you really *are*! Ever been out in the natural gas country?"

"No," said March. "I've had a good deal of curiosity about it, but I've never been able to get away except in summer, and then we always preferred to go over the old ground, out to Niagara and back through Canada, the route we took on our wedding journey. The children like it as much as we do."

"Yes, yes," said Fulkerson. "Well, the natural gas country* is worth seeing. I don't mean the Pittsburg gas-fields, but out in Northern Ohio and Indiana around Moffitt—that's the place in the heart of the gas region that they've been booming so. Yes, you ought to see that country. If you haven't been West for a good many years, you haven't got any idea how old the country looks. You remember how the fields used to be all full of stumps?"

"I should think so."

"Well, you won't see any stumps now. All that country out around Moffitt is just as smooth as a checker-board, and looks as old as England. You know how we used to burn the stumps out; and then somebody invented a stump-extracter, and we pulled them out with a yoke of oxen. Now they just touch 'em off with a little dynamite, and they've got a cellar dug and filled up with kindling ready for house-keeping whenever you want it. Only they haven't got any use for kindling in that country—all gas. I rode along on the cars* through those level black fields at corn-planting time, and every once in a while I'd come to a place with a piece of ragged old stove-pipe stickin' up out of the ground, and blazing away like forty, and a fellow ploughing all round it and not minding it any more than if it was spring violets. Horses didn't notice it, either. Well, they've always known about the gas out there; they say there are places in the woods where it's been burning ever since the country was settled.

"But when you come in sight of Moffitt—my, oh my! Well, you come in smell of it about as soon. That gas out there ain't odourless, like the Pittsburg gas, and so it's perfectly safe; but the smell isn't bad—about as bad as the finest kind of benzine. Well, the first thing that strikes you when you come to Moffitt is the notion that there has been a good warm, growing rain, and the town's come up overnight. That's in the suburbs, the annexes, and additions. But it ain't shabby—no shanty-town business; nice brick and frame houses, some of 'em Queen Anne style, and all of 'em looking as if they had come to stay. And when you drive up from the depôt you think everybody's moving. Everything seems to be piled into the street; old houses made over, and new ones going up everywhere. You know the kind of street Main Street always used to be in our section—half plank-road and turnpike, and the rest mud-hole, and a lot of stores and doggeries* strung along with false fronts a story higher than the back, and here and there a decent building with the gable end to the public; and a court-house and jail and two taverns and three or four churches. Well, they're all there in Moffitt yet, but architecture has struck it hard, and they've got a lot of new buildings that needn't be ashamed of themselves anywhere; the new court-house is as big as St. Peter's, and the Grand Opera-house is in the highest style of the art. You can't buy a lot on that street for much less than you can buy a lot in New York—or you couldn't when the boom was on; I saw the place just when the boom was in its prime. I went out there to work the newspapers in the syndicate business, and I got one of their men to write me a real bright, snappy account of the gas; and they just took me in their arms and showed me everything. Well, it *was* wonderful, and it was beautiful, too! To see a whole community stirred up like that was—just like a big boy, all hope and high spirits, and no discount on the remotest future; nothing but perpetual boom to the end of time—I tell you it warmed your blood. Why, there were some things about it that made you think what a nice kind of world this would be if people ever took hold together, instead of each fellow fighting it out on his own hook, and devil take the hindmost. They made up their minds at Moffitt that if they wanted their town to grow they'd got to keep their gas public property. So they extended their corporation line so as to take in pretty much the whole gas region round there; and then the city took possession of every well that was put down, and held it for the common good. Anybody that's a mind to come to Moffitt and start any kind of manufacture can have all the gas he wants *free*; and for fifteen dollars a year you can have all the gas you want to heat and light your private house. The people hold on to it for themselves, and, as I say, it's a grand sight to see a whole community hanging together and working for the good of all, instead of splitting up into as many different cut-throats as there are able-bodied citizens. See that fellow?" Fulkerson broke off, and indicated with a twirl of his head a short, dark, foreign-looking man going out of the door. "They say that fellow's a Socialist. I think it's a shame they're allowed to come here. If they don't like the way we manage our affairs, let 'em stay at home," Fulkerson continued. "They do a lot of mischief, shooting off their mouths round here. I believe in free speech and all that; but I'd like to see these fellows shut up in jail and left to jaw each other to death. *We* don't want any of their poison."

March did not notice the vanishing Socialist. He was watching, with a teasing sense of familiarity, a tall, shabbily dressed, elderly man, who had just come in. He had the aquiline ·profile uncommon among Germans, and yet March recognised him at once as German. His long, soft beard and moustache had once been fair, and they kept some tone of their yellow in the gray to which they had turned. His eyes were full, and his lips and chin shaped the beard to the noble outline which shows in the beards the Italian masters liked to paint for their Last Suppers. His carriage was erect and soldierly, and March presently saw that he had lost his left hand. He took his place at a table where the overworked waiter found time to cut up his meat, and put everything in easy reach of his right hand.

"Well," Fulkerson resumed, "they took me round everywhere in Moffitt, and showed me their big wells—lit 'em up for a private view, and let me hear them purr with the soft accents of a mass-meeting of locomotives. Why, when they let one of these wells loose in a meadow that they'd piped it into temporarily, it drove the flame away forty feet from the mouth of the pipe and blew it over half an acre of ground. They say when they let one of their big wells burn away all winter before they had learned how to control it, that well kept up a little summer all around it; the grass stayed green, and the flowers bloomed all through the winter. *I* don't know whether it's so or not. But I can believe anything of natural gas. My! but it was beautiful when they turned on the full force of that well and shot a roman candle into the gas—that's the way they light it—and a plume of fire about twenty feet wide and seventy-five feet high, all red and yellow and violet, jumped into the sky, and that big roar shook the ground under your feet! You felt like saying, 'Don't trouble yourself; I'm perfectly convinced. I believe in Moffitt.' We-e-e-ll!" drawled Fulkerson, with a long breath, "that's where I met old Dryfoos."

"Oh yes!—Dryfoos," said March. He observed that the waiter had brought the old one-handed German a towering glass of beer.

"Yes," Fulkerson laughed. "We've got round to Dryfoos again. I thought I could cut a long story short, but I seem to be cutting a short story long. If you're not in a hurry, though——"

"Not in the least. Go on as long as you like."

"I met him there in the office of a real-estate man—speculator, of course; everybody was, in Moffitt; but a first-rate fellow, and public-spirited as all get-out;* and when Dryfoos left he told me about him. Dryfoos was an old Pennsylvania Dutch farmer, about three or four miles out of Moffitt, and he'd lived there pretty much all his life; father was one of the first settlers. Everybody knew he had the right stuff in him, but he was slower than molasses in January, like those Pennsylvania Dutch. He'd got together the largest and handsomest farm anywhere around there; and he was making money on it, just like he was in some business somewhere; he was a very intelligent man; he took the papers and kept himself posted; but he was awfully old-fashioned in his ideas. He hung on to the doctrines as well as the dollars of the dads;*it was a real thing with him. Well, when the boom began to come he hated it awfully, and he fought it. He used to write communications to the weekly newspaper in Moffitt—they've got three dailies there now—and throw cold water on the boom. He couldn't catch on no way. It made him sick to hear the clack that went on about the gas the whole while, and that stirred up the neighbourhood and got into his family. Whenever he'd hear of a man that had been offered a big price for his land and was going to sell out and move into town, he'd go and labour with him and try to talk him out of it, and tell him how long his fifteen or twenty thousand would last him to live on, and shake the Standard Oil Company* before him, and try to make him believe it wouldn't be five years before the Standard owned the whole region.

"Of course he couldn't do anything with them. When a man's offered a big price for his farm, he don't care whether it's by a secret emissary from the Standard Oil or not; he's going to sell and get the better of the other fellow if he can. Dryfoos couldn't keep the boom out of his own family even. His wife was with him. She thought whatever he said and did was just as right as if it had been thundered down from Sinai. But the young folks were sceptical, especially the girls that had been away to school. The boy that had been kept at

home because he couldn't be spared from helping his father
manage the farm was more like him, but they contrived to
stir the boy up with the hot end of the boom too. So when a
fellow came along one day and offered old Dryfoos a cool
hundred thousand for his farm, it was all up with Dryfoos.
He'd 'a' liked to 'a' kept the offer to himself and not done
anything about it, but his vanity wouldn't let him do that;
and when he let it out in his family the girls outvoted him.
They just *made* him sell.

"He wouldn't sell all. He kept about eighty acres that was
off in one piece by itself, but the three hundred that had the
old brick house on it, and the big barn—that went, and
Dryfoos bought him a place in Moffitt and moved into town
to live on the interest of his money. Just what he had scolded
and ridiculed everybody else for doing. Well, they say that
at first he seemed like he would go crazy. He hadn't anything
to do. He took a fancy to that land-agent, and he used to go
and set in his office and ask him what he should do. 'I hain't
got any horses, I hain't got any cows, I hain't got any pigs,
I hain't got any chickens. I hain't got anything to do from
sun up to sundown.' The fellow said the tears used to run
down the old fellow's cheeks, and if he hadn't been so busy
himself he believed he should 'a' cried too. But most o'
people thought old Dryfoos was down in the mouth because
he hadn't asked more for his farm, when he wanted to buy
it back and found they held it at a hundred and fifty thousand.
People couldn't believe he was just homesick and heart-
sick for the old place. Well, perhaps he *was* sorry he hadn't
asked more; that's human nature *too*.

"After a while something happened. That land-agent used
to tell Dryfoos to get out to Europe with his money and see
life a little, or go and live in Washington, where he could *be*
somebody; but Dryfoos wouldn't, and he kept listening to
the talk there, and all of a sudden he caught on. He came
into that fellow's one day with a plan for cutting up the
eighty acres he'd kept into town lots; and he'd got it all
plotted out so well, and had so many practical ideas about it,
that the fellow was astonished. He went right in with him,

as far as Dryfoos would let him, and glad of the chance; and they were working the thing for all it was worth when I struck Moffitt. Old Dryfoos wanted me to go out and see the Dryfoos & Hendry Addition—guess he thought may be I'd write it up; and he drove me out there himself. Well, it was funny to see a town made: streets driven through; two rows of shade-trees, hard and soft, planted; cellars dug and houses put up—regular Queen Anne style, too, with stained glass— all at once. Dryfoos apologised for the streets because they were hand-made; said they expected their street-making machine Tuesday, and then they intended to *push* things."

Fulkerson enjoyed the effect of his picture on March for a moment, and then went on: "He was mighty intelligent, too, and he questioned me up about my business as sharp as *I* ever was questioned; seemed to kind of strike his fancy; I guess he wanted to find out if there was any money in it. He was making money, hand over hand, then; and he never stopped speculating and improving, till he'd scraped together three or four hundred thousand dollars; they said a million, but they like round numbers at Moffitt, and I guess half a million would lay over it comfortably and leave a few thousands to spare, probably. Then he came on to New York."

Fulkerson struck a match against the ribbed side of the porcelain cup that held the matches in the centre of the table, and lit a cigarette, which he began to smoke, throwing his head back with a leisurely effect, as if he had got to the end of at least as much of his story as he meant to tell without prompting.

March asked him the desired question. "What in the world for?"

Fulkerson took out his cigarette and said, with a smile: "To spend his money, and get his daughters into the old Knickerbocker society. May be he thought they were all the same kind of Dutch."

"And has he succeeded?"

"Well, they're not social leaders yet. But it's only a question of time—generation or two—especially if time's

75

money, and if *Every Other Week* is the success it's bound to be."

"You don't mean to say, Fulkerson," said March, with a half-doubting, half-daunted laugh, "that *he's* your Angel?"

"That's what I mean to say," returned Fulkerson. "I ran onto him in Broadway one day last summer. If you ever saw anybody in your life, you're sure to meet him in Broadway again, sooner or later. That's the philosophy of the bunco business; country people from the same neighbourhood are sure to run up against each other the first time they come to New York. I put out my hand, and I said, 'Isn't this Mr. Dryfoos from Moffitt?' He didn't seem to have any use for my hand; he let me keep it, and he squared those old lips of his till his imperial stuck straight out. Ever see Bernhardt in *L'Étrangère*? Well, the American husband is old Dryfoos all over; no moustache, and hay-coloured chin-whiskers cut slanting from the corners of his mouth. He cocked his little gray eyes at me, and says he, 'Yes, young man. My name *is* Dryfoos, and I'm from Moffitt. But I don't want no present of Longfellow's Works, illustrated; and I don't want to taste no fine teas; but I know a policeman that does; and if you're the son of my old friend Squire Strohfeldt, you'd better get out.' 'Well, then,' said I, 'how would you like to go into the newspaper syndicate business?' He gave another look at me, and then he burst out laughing, and he grabbed my hand, and he just froze to it. I never saw anybody so glad.

"Well, the long and the short of it was that I asked him round here to Maroni's to dinner; and before we broke up for the night we had settled the financial side of the plan that's brought you to New York. I can see," said Fulkerson, who had kept his eyes fast on March's face, "that you don't more than half like the idea of Dryfoos. It ought to give you more confidence in the thing than you ever had. You needn't be afraid," he added, with some feeling, "that I talked Dryfoos into the thing for my own advantage."

"Oh, my dear Fulkerson!" March protested, all the more fervently because he was really a little guilty.

"Well, of course not! I didn't mean you were. But I just

happened to tell him what I wanted to go into when I could see my way to it, and he caught on of his own accord. The fact is," said Fulkerson, "I guess I'd better make a clean breast of it, now I'm at it. Dryfoos wanted to get something for that boy of his to do. He's in railroads himself, and he's in mines and other things, and he keeps busy, and he can't bear to have his boy hanging round the house doing nothing, like as if he was a girl. I told him that the great object of a rich man was to get his son into just that fix, but he couldn't seem to see it, and the boy hated it himself. He's got a good head, and he wanted to study for the ministry when they were all living together out on the farm; but his father had the old-fashioned ideas about that. You know they used to think that any sort of stuff was good enough to make a preacher out of; but they wanted the good timber for business; and so the old man wouldn't let him. You'll see the fellow; you'll like him; he's no fool, I can tell you; and he's going to be our publisher, nominally at first and actually when I've taught him the ropes a little."

XII

FULKERSON stopped and looked at March, whom he saw lapsing into a serious silence. Doubtless he divined his uneasiness with the facts that had been given him to digest. He pulled out his watch and glanced at it. "See here, how would you like to go up to Forty-sixth Street with me, and drop in on old Dryfoos? Now's your chance. He's going West tomorrow, and won't be back for a month or so. They'll all be glad to see you, and you'll understand things better when you've seen him and his family. I can't explain."

March reflected a moment. Then he said, with a wisdom that surprised him, for he would have liked to yield to the impulse of his curiosity: "Perhaps we'd better wait till Mrs. March comes down, and let things take the usual course. The Dryfoos ladies will want to call on her as the last-comer, and if I treated myself *en garçon* now, and paid the first visit, it might complicate matters."

"Well, perhaps you're right," said Fulkerson. "I don't know much about these things, and I don't believe Ma Dryfoos does either." He was on his legs lighting another cigarette. "I suppose the girls are getting themselves up in etiquette, though. Well, then, let's have a look at the *Every Other Week* building, and then, if you like your quarters there, you can go round and close for Mrs. Green's flat."

March's dormant allegiance to his wife's wishes had been roused by his decision in favour of good social usage. "I don't think I shall take the flat," he said.

"Well, don't reject it without giving it another look, anyway. Come on!"

He helped March on with his light overcoat, and the little stir they made for their departure caught the notice of the old German; he looked up from his beer at them. March was more than ever impressed with something familiar in his face. In compensation for his prudence in regard to the Dryfooses he now indulged an impulse. He stepped across to where the old man sat, with his bald head shining like ivory under the gas-jet, and his fine patriarchal length of bearded mask taking picturesque lights and shadows, and put out his hand to him.

"Lindau! Isn't this Mr. Lindau?"

The old man lifted himself slowly to his feet with mechanical politeness, and cautiously took March's hand. "Yes, my name is Lindau," he said slowly, while he scanned March's face. Then he broke into a long cry. "Ah-h-h-h-h, my dear poy! my yong friendt! my—my—— Idt is Passil Marge, not zo? Ah, ha, ha, ha! How gladt I am to zee you! Why, I am gladt! And you rememberdt me? You remember Schiller, and Goethe, and Uhland?*And Indianapolis? You still lif in Indianapolis? It sheers my hardt to zee you. But you are lidtle oldt too? Tventy-five years makes a difference. Ah, I am gladt! Dell me, idt is Passil Marge, not zo?"

He looked anxiously into March's face, with a gentle smile of mixed hope and doubt, and March said: "As sure as it's Berthold Lindau, and I guess it's you. And you remember the old times? You were as much of a boy as I was, Lindau. Are you living in New York? Do you recollect how you tried to teach me to fence? I don't know how to this day, Lindau. How good you were, and how patient! Do you remember how we used to sit up in the little parlour back of your printing office, and read *Die Räuber* and *Die Theilung der Erde* and *Die Glocke*? And Mrs. Lindau? Is she with——"

"Deadt—deadt long ago. Right after I got home from the war—tventy years ago.* But tell me, you are married? Children? Yes! Goodt! And how oldt are you now?"

"It makes me seventeen to see you, Lindau, but I've got a son nearly as old."

"Ah, ha, ha! Goodt! And where do you lif?"

"Well, I'm just coming to live in New York," March said, looking over at Fulkerson, who had been watching his interview with the perfunctory smile of sympathy that people put on at the meeting of old friends. "I want to introduce you to my friend Mr. Fulkerson. He and I are going into a literary enterprise here."

"Ah! zo?" said the old man, with polite interest. He took Fulkerson's proffered hand, and they all stood talking a few moments together.

Then Fulkerson said, with another look at his watch, "Well, March, we're keeping Mr. Lindau from his dinner."

"Dinner!" cried the old man. "Idt's better than breadt and meadt to see Mr. Marge!"

"I must be going, anyway," said March. "But I must see you again soon, Lindau. Where do you live? I want a long talk."

"And I. You will find me here at dinner-time," said the old man. "It is the best place;" and March fancied him reluctant to give another address.

To cover his consciousness he answered gaily, "Then, it's *auf wiedersehen* with us. Well!"

"*Also!*" The old man took his hand, and made a mechanical movement with his mutilated arm, as if he would have taken it in a double clasp. He laughed at himself. "I wanted to gif you the other handt too, but I gafe it to your gountry a goodt while ago."

"To *my* country?" asked March, with a sense of pain, and yet lightly, as if it were a joke of the old man's. "Your country too, Lindau?"

The old man turned very grave, and said, almost coldly, "What gountry hass a poor man got, Mr. Marge?"

"Well, *you* ought to have a share in the one you helped to save for us rich men, Lindau," March returned, still humouring the joke.

The old man smiled sadly, but made no answer as he sat down again.

"Seems to be a little soured," said Fulkerson, as they went down the steps. He was one of those Americans whose habitual conception of life is unalloyed prosperity. When any experience or observation of his went counter to it he suffered something like physical pain. He eagerly shrugged away the impression left upon his buoyancy by Lindau, and added to March's continued silence, "What did I tell you about meeting every man in New York that you ever knew before?"

"I never expected to meet Lindau in the world again," said March, more to himself than to Fulkerson. "I had an impression that he had been killed in the war. I almost wish he had been."

"Oh, hello, now!" cried Fulkerson.

March laughed, but went on soberly. "He was a man predestined to adversity, though. When I first knew him out in Indianapolis he was starving along with a sick wife and a sick newspaper. It was before the Germans had come over to the Republicans generally, but Lindau was fighting the anti-slavery battle just as naturally at Indianapolis in 1858 as he fought behind the barricades at Berlin in 1848. And yet he was always such a gentle soul! And so generous! He taught me German for the love of it; he wouldn't spoil his pleasure by taking a cent from me; he seemed to get enough out of my being young and enthusiastic, and out of prophesying great things for me. I wonder what the poor old fellow is doing here, with that one hand of his?"

"Not amassing a very handsome pittance, I should say," said Fulkerson, getting back some of his lightness. "There are lots of two-handed fellows in New York that are not doing much better, I guess. May be he gets some writing on the German papers."

"I hope so. He's one of the most accomplished men! He used to be a splendid musician—pianist—and knows eight or ten languages."

"Well, it's astonishing," said Fulkerson, "how much lumber those Germans can carry around in their heads all their lives, and never work it up into anything. It's a pity they couldn't do the acquiring, and let out the use of their learning to a few bright Americans. We could make things hum, if we could arrange 'em that way."

He talked on, unheeded by March, who went along half-consciously tormented by his lightness in the pensive memories the meeting with Lindau had called up. Was this all that sweet, unselfish nature could come to? What a homeless old age at that meagre Italian *table d'hôte*, with that tall glass of beer for a half-hour's oblivion! That shabby dress, that pathetic mutilation! He must have a pension, twelve dollars a month, or eighteen, from a grateful country. But what else did he eke out with?

"Well, here we are," said Fulkerson cheerily. He ran up the steps before March, and opened the carpenter's temporary valve in the door frame, and led the way into a darkness smelling sweetly of unpainted wood-work and newly dried plaster; their feet slipped on shavings and grated on sand. He scratched a match, and found a candle, and then walked about up and down stairs, and lectured on the advantages of the place. He had fitted up bachelor apartments for himself in the house, and said that he was going to have a flat to let on the top floor. "I didn't offer it to you because I supposed you'd be too proud to live over your shop; and it's too small, anyway; only five rooms."

"Yes, that's too small," said March, shirking the other point.

"Well, then, here's the room I intend for your office," said Fulkerson, showing him into a large back parlour one flight up. "You'll have it quiet from the street noises here, and you can be at home or not as you please. There'll be a boy on the stairs to find out. Now, you see, this makes the Grosvenor Green flat practicable, if you want it."

March felt the forces of fate closing about him and pushing him to a decision. He feebly fought them off till he could have another look at the flat. Then, baffled and subdued still more by the unexpected presence of Mrs. Grosvenor Green herself, who was occupying it so as to be able to show it effectively, he took it. He was aware more than ever of its absurdities; he knew that his wife would never cease to hate it; but he had suffered one of those eclipses of the imagination to which men of his temperament are subject, and in which he could see no future for his desires. He felt a comfort in irretrievably committing himself, and exchanging the burden of indecision for the burden of responsibility.

"I didn't know," said Fulkerson, as they walked back to his hotel together, "but you might fix it up with that lone widow and her pretty daughter to take part of *their* house here." He seemed to be reminded of it by the fact of passing the house, and March looked up at its dark front. He could not have told exactly why he felt a pang of remorse at the sight, and doubtless it was more regret for having taken the Grosvenor Green flat than for not having taken the widow's rooms. Still he could not forget her wistfulness when his wife and he were looking at them, and her disappointment when they decided against them. He had toyed, in his after-talk to Mrs. March, with a sort of hypothetical obligation they had to modify their plans so as to meet the widow's want of just such a family as theirs; they had both said what a blessing it would be to her, and what a pity they could not do it; but they had decided very distinctly that they could not. Now it seemed to him that they might; and he asked himself whether he had not actually departed as much from their ideal as if he had taken board with the widow. Suddenly it seemed to him that his wife asked him this too.

"I reckon," said Fulkerson, "that she could have arranged to give you your meals in your rooms, and it would have come to about the same thing as house-keeping."

"No sort of boarding can be the same as house-keeping," said March. "I want my little girl to have the run of a kitchen, and I want the whole family to have the moral effect of house-keeping. It's demoralising to board, in every way; it isn't a home, if anybody else takes the care of it off your hands."

"Well, I suppose so," Fulkerson assented; but March's words had a hollow ring to himself, and in his own mind he began to retaliate his dissatisfaction upon Fulkerson.

He parted from him on the usual terms outwardly, but he felt obscurely abused by Fulkerson in regard to the Dry-fooses, father and son. He did not know but Fulkerson had taken an advantage of him in allowing him to commit himself to their enterprise without fully and frankly telling him who and what his backer was; he perceived that with young Dryfoos as the publisher and Fulkerson as the general director of the paper there might be very little play for his own ideas of its conduct. Perhaps it was the hurt to his vanity involved by the recognition of this fact that made him forget how little choice he really had in the matter, and how, since he had not accepted the offer to edit the insurance paper, nothing remained for him but to close with Fulkerson. In this moment of suspicion and resentment he accused Fulkerson of hastening his decision in regard to the Grosve-nor Green apartment; he now refused to consider it a decision, and said to himself that if he felt disposed to do so he would send Mrs. Green a note reversing it in the morn-ing. But he put it all off till morning with his clothes, when he went to bed; he put off even thinking what his wife would say; he cast Fulkerson and his constructive treachery out of his mind too, and invited into it some pensive reveries of the past, when he still stood at the parting of the ways, and could take this path or that. In his middle life this was not possible; he must follow the path chosen long ago, wherever it led. He was not master of himself, as he once seemed, but the servant of those he loved; if he could do what he liked, perhaps he might renounce this whole New York enterprise, and go off somewhere out of the reach of care; but he could not do what he liked, that was very clear. In the pathos of this conviction he dwelt compassionately upon the thought of poor old Lindau; he resolved to make him accept a handsome sum of money—more than he could spare, something that he would feel the loss of—in payment of the lessons in German and fencing given so long ago. At the usual rate for such lessons, his debt, with interest for twenty odd years, would run very far into the hundreds. Too far, he perceived, for his wife's joyous approval; he determined not to add the interest; or he believed that Lindau would refuse the interest; he put a fine speech in his mouth, making him do so; and after that he got Lindau employment on *Every Other Week*, and took care of him till he died.

Through all his melancholy and munificence he was aware of sordid anxieties for having taken the Grosvenor Green apartment. These began to assume visible, tangible shapes as he drowsed, and to become personal entities, from which he woke, with little starts, to a realisation of their true nature, and then suddenly fell fast asleep.

In the accomplishment of the events which his reverie played with, there was much that retroactively stamped it with prophecy, but much also that was better than he forboded. He found that with regard to the Grosvenor Green apartment he had not allowed for his wife's willingness to get any sort of roof over her head again after the removal from their old home, or for the alleviations that grow up through mere custom. The practical workings of the apartment were not so bad; it had its good points, and after the first sensation of oppression in it they began to feel the convenience of its arrangement. They were at that time of life when people first turn to their children's opinion with deference, and, in the loss of keenness in their own likes and dislikes, consult the young preferences which are still so sensitive. It went far to reconcile Mrs. March to the apartment that her children were pleased with its novelty; when this wore off for them, she had herself begun to find it much more easily manageable than a house. After she had put away several barrels of gimcracks, and folded up screens and rugs and skins, and carried them all off to the little dark store-room which the flat developed, she perceived at once a roominess and coziness in it unsuspected before. Then, when people began to call, she had a pleasure, a superiority, in saying that it was a furnished apartment, and in disclaiming all responsibility for the upholstery and decoration. If March was by, she always explained that it was Mr. March's fancy, and amiably laughed it off with her callers as a mannish eccentricity. Nobody really seemed to think it otherwise than pretty; and this again was a triumph for Mrs. March, because it showed how inferior the New York taste was to the Boston taste in such matters.

March submitted silently to his punishment, and laughed with her before company at his own eccentricity. She had been so preoccupied with the adjustment of the family to its new quarters and circumstances that the time passed for laying his misgivings, if they were misgivings, about Fulkerson before her, and when an occasion came for expressing them they had themselves passed in the anxieties of getting forward the first number of *Every Other Week*. He kept these from her too, and the business that brought them to New York had apparently dropped into abeyance before the questions of domestic economy that presented and absented themselves. March knew his wife to be a woman of good mind and in perfect sympathy with him, but he understood the limitations of her perspective; and if he was not too wise, he was too experienced to intrude upon it any affairs of his till her own were reduced to the right order and proportion. It would have been folly to talk to her of Fulkerson's conjecturable uncandour while she was in doubt whether her cook would like the kitchen, or her two servants would consent to room together; and till it was decided what school Tom should go to, and whether Bella should have lessons at home or not, the relation which March was to bear to the Dryfooses, as owner and publisher, was not to be discussed with his wife. He might drag it in, but he was aware that with her mind distracted by more immediate interests he could not get from her that judgment, that reasoned divination, which he relied upon so much. She would try, she would do her best, but the result would be a view clouded and discoloured by the effort she must make.

He put the whole matter by, and gave himself to the details of the work before him. In this he found not only escape, but reassurance, for it became more and more apparent that whatever was nominally the structure of the business, a man of his qualifications and his instincts could not have an insignificant place in it. He had also the consolation of liking his work, and of getting an instant grasp of it that grew constantly firmer and closer. The joy of knowing that he had not made a mistake was great. In giving rein to ambitions long forborne he seemed to get back to the youth when he had indulged them first; and after half a lifetime passed in pursuits alien to his nature, he was feeling the serene happiness of being mated through his work to his early love. From the outside the spectacle might have had its pathos, and it is not easy to justify such an experiment as he had made at his time of life, except upon the ground where he rested from its consideration—the ground of necessity.

His work was more in his thoughts than himself, however, and as the time for the publication of the first number of his periodical came nearer, his cares all centred upon it. Without fixing any date, Fulkerson had announced it, and pushed his announcements with the shameless vigour of a born advertiser. He worked his interest with the press to the utmost, and paragraphs of a variety that did credit to his ingenuity were afloat everywhere. Some of them were speciously unfavourable in tone; they criticised and even ridiculed the principles on which the new departure in literary journalism was based. Others defended it; others yet denied that this rumoured principle was really the principle. All contributed to make talk. All proceeded from the same fertile invention.

March observed with a degree of mortification that the

talk was very little of it in the New York press; there the references to the novel enterprise were slight and cold. But Fulkerson said: "Don't mind that, old man. It's the whole country that makes or breaks a thing like this; New York has very little to do with it. Now if it were a play, it would be different. New York does make or break a play; but it doesn't make or break a book; it doesn't make or break a magazine. The great mass of the readers are outside of New York, and the rural districts are what we have got to go for. They don't read much in New York; they write, and talk about what they've written. Don't you worry."

The rumour of Fulkerson's connection with the enterprise accompanied many of the paragraphs, and he was able to stay March's thirst for employment by turning over to him from day to day heaps of the manuscripts which began to pour in from his old syndicate writers, as well as from adventurous volunteers all over the country. With these in hand March began practically to plan the first number, and to concrete a general scheme from the material and the experience they furnished. They had intended to issue the first number with the new year, and if it had been an affair of literature alone, it would have been very easy; but it was the art leg they limped on, as Fulkerson phrased it. They had not merely to deal with the question of specific illustrations for this article or that, but to decide the whole character of their illustrations, and first of all to get a design for a cover which should both ensnare the heedless and captivate the fastidious. These things did not come properly within March's province—that had been clearly understood—and for a while Fulkerson tried to run the art leg himself. The phrase was again his, but it was simpler to make the phrase than to run the leg. The difficult generation, at once stiff-backed and slippery, with which he had to do in this endeavour, reduced even so buoyant an optimist to despair, and after wasting some valuable weeks in trying to work the artists himself, he determined to get an artist to work them. But what artist? It could not be a man with fixed reputation and a following: he would be too costly, and would have too

many enemies among his brethren, even if he would consent
to undertake the job. Fulkerson had a man in mind, an
artist too, who would have been the very thing if he had
been the thing at all. He had talent enough, and his sort of
talent would reach round the whole situation, but, as
Fulkerson said, he was as many kinds of an ass as he was
kinds of an artist.

PART SECOND

I

THE evening when March closed with Mrs. Green's reduced offer, and decided to take her apartment, the widow whose lodgings he had rejected sat with her daughter in an upper room at the back of her house. In the shaded glow of the drop-light she was sewing, and the girl was drawing at the same table. From time to time, as they talked, the girl lifted her head and tilted it a little on one side so as to get some desired effect of her work.

"It's a mercy the cold weather holds off," said the mother. "We should have to light the furnace, unless we wanted to scare everybody away with a cold house; and I don't know who would take care of it, or what would become of us, every way."

"They seem to have been scared away from a house that wasn't cold," said the girl. "Perhaps they might like a cold one. But it's too early for cold yet. It's only just in the beginning of November."

"The *Messenger* says they've had a sprinkling of snow."

"Oh yes, at St. Barnaby! I don't know when they don't have sprinklings of snow there. I'm awfully glad we haven't got *that* winter before us."

The widow sighed as mothers do who feel the contrast their experience opposes to the hopeful recklessness of such talk as this. "We may have a worse winter here," she said darkly.

"Then I couldn't stand it," said the girl, "and I should go in for lighting out to Florida double-quick."

"And how would you get to Florida?" demanded her mother severely.

"Oh, by the usual conveyance—Pullman vestibuled train,"

I suppose. What makes you so blue, mamma?" The girl was all the time sketching away, rubbing out, lifting her head for the effect, and then bending it over her work again without looking at her mother.

"I am *not* blue, Alma. But I cannot endure this—this hopefulness of yours."

"Why? What harm does it do?"

"Harm?" echoed the mother.

Pending the effort she must make in saying, the girl cut in: "Yes, harm. You've kept your despair dusted off and ready for use at an instant's notice ever since we came, and what good has *it* done? I'm going to keep on hoping to the bitter end. That's what papa did."

It was what the Rev. Archibald Leighton had done with all the consumptive's buoyancy. The morning he died he told them that now he had turned the point and was really going to get well. The cheerfulness was not only in his disease, but in his temperament. Its excess was always a little against him in his church-work, and Mrs. Leighton was right enough in feeling that if it had not been for the ballast of her instinctive despondency he would have made shipwreck of such small chances of prosperity as befell him in life. It was not from him that his daughter got her talent, though he had left her his temperament intact of his widow's legal thirds. He was one of those men of whom the country people say when he is gone that the woman gets along better without him. Mrs. Leighton had long eked out their income by taking a summer boarder or two, as a great favour, into her family; and when the greater need came, she frankly gave up her house to the summer-folks (as they call them in the country), and managed it for their comfort from the small quarter of it in which she shut herself up with her daughter.

The notion of shutting up is an exigency of the rounded period. The fact is, of course, that Alma Leighton was not shut up in any sense whatever. She was the pervading light, if not force, of the house. She was a good cook, and she managed the kitchen with the help of an Irish girl, while her mother looked after the rest of the house-keeping. But she was not systematic; she had inspiration but not discipline, and her mother mourned more over the days when Alma left the whole dinner to the Irish girl than she rejoiced in those when one of Alma's great thoughts took form in a chicken-pie of incomparable savour or in a matchless pudding. The off-days came when her artistic nature was expressing itself in charcoal, for she drew to the admiration of all among the lady boarders who could not draw. The others had their reserves; they readily conceded that Alma had genius, but they were sure she needed instruction. On the other hand, they were not so radical as to agree with the old painter who came every summer to paint the elms of the St. Barnaby meadows. He contended that she needed to be a man in order to amount to anything; but in this theory he was opposed by an authority of his own sex, whom the lady sketchers believed to speak with more impartiality in a matter concerning them as much as Alma Leighton. He said that instruction would do, and he was not only younger and handsomer, but he was fresher from the schools than old Harrington, who, even the lady sketchers could see, painted in an obsolescent manner. His name was Beaton—Angus Beaton; but he was not Scotch, or not more Scotch than Mary Queen of Scots was. His father was a Scotchman, but Beaton was born in Syracuse, New York, and it had taken only three years in Paris to obliterate many traces of native and ancestral manner in him. He wore his black beard cut shorter than his moustache, and a little pointed; he stood with his shoulders well thrown back and with a lateral curve of his person when he talked about art, which would alone have carried conviction even if he had not had a thick, dark bang coming almost to the brows of his mobile grey eyes, and had not spoken English with quick, staccato impulses, so as to give it the effect of epigrammatic and sententious French. One of the ladies said that you always thought of him as having spoken French after it was over, and accused herself of wrong in not being able to feel afraid of him. None of the ladies were afraid of him, though they could not believe that he was really so deferential to their work as he seemed; and they knew, when he would not criticise Mr. Harrington's work, that he was just acting from principle.

They may or may not have known the difference with which he treated Alma's work; but the girl herself felt that his abrupt, impersonal comment recognised her as a real sister in art. He told her she ought to come to New York, and draw in the League, or get into some painter's private class; and it was the sense of duty thus appealed to which finally resulted in the hazardous experiment she and her mother were now making. There were no logical breaks in the chain of their reasoning from past success with boarders in St. Barnaby to future success with boarders in New York. Of course the outlay was much greater. The rent of the furnished house they had taken was such that if they failed their experiment would be little less than ruinous.

But they were not going to fail; that was what Alma contended, with a hardy courage that her mother sometimes felt almost invited failure, if it did not deserve it. She was one of those people who believe that if you dread harm enough it is less likely to happen. She acted on this superstition as if it were a religion.

"If it had not been for my despair, as you call it, Alma," she answered, "I don't know where we should have been now."

"I suppose we should have been in St. Barnaby," said the girl. "And if it's worse to be in New York, you see what your despair's done, mamma. But what's the use? You meant well, and I don't blame you. You can't expect even despair to come out always just the way you want it. Perhaps you've used too much of it." The girl laughed, and Mrs. Leighton laughed too. Like every one else, she was not merely a prevailing mood, as people are apt to be in books, but was an irregularly spheroidal character, with surfaces that caught the different lights of circumstance and reflected them. Alma got up and took a pose before the mirror, which she then transferred to her sketch. The room was pinned about with other sketches, which showed with fantastic indistinctness in the shaded gas-light. Alma held up the drawing. "How do you like it?"

Mrs. Leighton bent forward over her sewing to look at it. "You've got the man's face rather weak."

"Yes, that's so. Either I see all the hidden weakness that's in men's natures, and bring it to the surface in their figures, or else I put my own weakness into them. And anyway, it's a drawback to their presenting a truly manly appearance. As long as I have one of the miserable objects before me, I can draw him; but as soon as his back's turned I get to putting ladies into men's clothes. I should think you'd be scandalised, mamma, if you were a really feminine person. It must be your despair that helps you to bear up. But what's the matter with the young lady in young lady's clothes? Any dust on *her*?"

"What expressions!" said Mrs. Leighton. "Really, Alma, for a refined girl you *are* the most unrefined!"

"Go on—about the girl in the picture!" said Alma, slightly knocking her mother on the shoulder, as she stood over her.

"I don't see anything *to* her. What's she doing?"

"Oh, just being made love to, I suppose."

"She's perfectly insipid!"

"You're awfully articulate, mamma! Now, if Mr. Wetmore was to criticise that picture he'd draw a circle round it in the air, and look at it through that, and tilt his head first on one side and then on the other, and then look at you, as if you were a figure in it, and then collapse a while, and moan a little and gasp, 'Isn't your young lady a little too—too——' and then he'd try to get the word out of *you*, and groan and suffer some more; and you'd say, 'She *is*, rather,' and that would give him courage, and he'd say, 'I don't mean that she's so very——' 'Of course not.' 'You understand?' 'Perfectly. I see it myself, now.' 'Well then,'—and he'd take your pencil and begin to draw—'I should give her a little more—— Ah?' 'Yes, I see the difference.' 'You see the difference?' And he'd go off to some one else, and you'd know that you'd been doing the wishy-washiest thing in the world, though he hadn't *spoken* a word of criticism, and couldn't. But *he* wouldn't have noticed the expression at all; he'd have shown you where your drawing was bad. He doesn't care for what he calls the literature of a thing; he says that will take care of itself if the drawing's good. He doesn't like my doing these *chic* things; but I'm going to keep it up, for *I* think it's the nearest way to illustrating."

She took her sketch and pinned it up on the door.

"And has Mr. Beaton been about, yet?" asked her mother.

"No," said the girl, with her back still turned; and she added, "I believe he's in New York; Mr. Wetmore's seen him."

"It's a little strange he doesn't call."

"It would be if he were not an artist. But artists never do anything like other people. He was on his good behaviour while he was with us, and he's a great deal more conventional than most of them; but even he can't keep it up. That's what makes me really think that women can never amount to anything in art. They keep all their appointments, and fulfil all their duties just as if they didn't know anything about art. Well, most of them don't. We've got that new model to-day."

"What new model?"

"The one Mr. Wetmore was telling us about—the old German; he's splendid. He's got the most beautiful head; just like the old masters' things. He used to be Humphrey Williams's model for his biblical pieces; but since he's dead, the old man hardly gets anything to do. Mr. Wetmore says there isn't anybody in the Bible that Williams didn't paint him as. He's the Law and the Prophets in all his Old Testament pictures, and he's Joseph, Peter, Judas Iscariot, and the Scribes and Pharisees in the New."

"It's a good thing people don't know how artists work, or some of the most sacred pictures would have no influence," said Mrs. Leighton.

"Why, of course not!" cried the girl. "And the influence is the last thing a painter thinks of—or supposes he thinks of. What he knows he's anxious about is the drawing and the colour. But people will never understand how simple artists are. When I reflect what a complex and sophisticated being

94

I am, I'm afraid I can never come to anything in art. Or I should be if I hadn't genius."

"Do you think Mr. Beaton is very simple?" asked Mrs. Leighton.

"Mr. Wetmore doesn't think he's very much of an artist. He thinks he talks too well. They believe that if a man can express himself clearly he can't paint."

"And what do *you* believe?"

"Oh, *I* can express myself, *too*."

The mother seemed to be satisfied with this evasion. After a while she said, "I presume he will call when he gets settled."

The girl made no answer to this. "One of the girls says that old model is an educated man. He was in the war, and lost a hand. Doesn't it seem a pity for such a man to have to sit to a class of affected geese like us as a model? I declare it makes me sick. And we shall keep him a week, and pay him six or seven dollars for the use of his grand old head, and *then* what will he do? The last time he was regularly employed was when Mr. Mace was working at his Damascus Massacre. Then he wanted so many Arab sheiks and Christian elders that he kept old Mr. Lindau steadily employed for six months. Now he has to pick up odd jobs where he can."

"I suppose he has his pension," said Mrs. Leighton.

"No; one of the girls"—that was the way Alma always described her fellow-students—"says he has no pension. He didn't apply for it for a long time, and then there was a hitch about it, and it was somethinged—vetoed, I believe she said."

"Who vetoed it?" asked Mrs. Leighton, with some curiosity about the process, which she held in reserve.

"I don't know—whoever vetoes things. I wonder what Mr. Wetmore *does* think of us—his class. We must seem perfectly crazy. There isn't one of us really knows what she's doing it for, or what she expects to happen when she's done it. I suppose every one thinks she has genius. I know the Nebraska widow does, for she says that unless you have genius it isn't the least use. Everybody's puzzled to know what she does with her baby when she's at work—whether

95

she gives it soothing syrup. I wonder how Mr. Wetmore can keep from laughing in our faces. I know he does behind our backs."

Mrs. Leighton's mind wandered back to another point. "Then if he says Mr. Beaton can't paint, I presume he doesn't respect him very much."

"Oh, he never *said* he couldn't paint. But I know he thinks so. He says he's an excellent critic."

"Alma," her mother said, with the effect of breaking off, "what *do* you suppose is the reason he hasn't been near us?"

"Why, I don't know, mamma, except that it would have been natural for another person to come, and he's an artist— at least, artist enough for that."

"That doesn't account for it altogether. He was very nice at St. Barnaby, and seemed so interested in you—your work."

"Plenty of people were nice at St. Barnaby. That rich Mrs. Horn couldn't contain her joy when she heard we were coming to New York, but she hasn't poured in upon us a great deal since we got here."

"But that's different. She's very fashionable, and she's taken up with her own set. But Mr. Beaton's one of our kind."

"Thank you. Papa wasn't *quite* a tombstone-cutter, mamma."

"That makes it all the harder to bear. He *can't* be ashamed of us. Perhaps he doesn't know where we are."

"Do you wish to send him your card, mamma?" The girl flushed and towered in scorn of the idea.

"Why, no, Alma," returned her mother.

"Well, then," said Alma.

But Mrs. Leighton was not so easily quelled. She had got her mind on Mr. Beaton, and she could not detach it at once. Besides, she was one of those women (they are commoner than the same sort of men) whom it does not pain to take out their most intimate thoughts and examine them in the light of other people's opinions. "But I don't see how he can behave so. He must know that——"

"That *what*, mamma?" demanded the girl.

"That he influenced us a great deal in coming——"

"He *didn't*. If he dared to presume to think such a thing——"

"Now, Alma," said her mother with the clinging persistence of such natures, "you know he did. And it's no use for you to pretend that we didn't count upon him in—in every way. *You* may not have noticed his attentions, and I don't say you did, but others certainly did; and I must say that I *didn't* expect he would drop us so."

"*Drop* us!" cried Alma, in a fury. "Oh!"

"Yes, *drop* us, Alma. He must know where we are. Of *course*, Mr. Wetmore's spoken to him about you, and it's a shame that he hasn't been near us. I should have thought common gratitude, common decency, would have brought him after—after all we did for him."

"We did nothing for him—*nothing!* He paid his board, and that ended it."

"No, it didn't, Alma. You know what he used to say—about its being like home, and all that; and I must say that after his attentions to you, and all the things you told me he said, I expected something very dif——"

A sharp peal of the door-bell thrilled through the house, and as if the pull of the bell-wire had twitched her to her feet, Mrs. Leighton sprang up and grappled with her daughter in their common terror.

They both glared at the clock and made sure that it was five minutes after nine. Then they abandoned them some moments to the unrestricted play of their apprehensions.

II

"WHY, Alma," whispered the mother, "who in the world can it be at this time of night? You don't suppose he——"

"Well, I'm not going to the door anyhow, mother, I don't care who it is; and of course he wouldn't be such a goose as to come at this hour." She put on a look of miserable trepidation, and shrank back from the door, while the hum of the bell died away in the hall.

"What shall we do?" asked Mrs. Leighton helplessly.

"Let him go away—whoever they are," said Alma.

Another and more peremptory ring forbade them refuge in this simple expedient.

"Oh dear! what shall we do? Perhaps it's a despatch."

The conjecture moved Alma to no more than a rigid stare. "I shall not go," she said. A third ring more insistent than the others followed, and she said: "You go ahead, mamma, and I'll come behind to scream if it's anybody. We can look through the side-lights at the door first."

Mrs. Leighton fearfully led the way from the back chamber where they had been sitting, and slowly descended the stairs. Alma came behind and turned up the hall gas-jet with a sudden flash that made them both jump a little. The gas inside rendered it more difficult to tell who was on the threshold, but Mrs. Leighton decided from a timorous peep through the scrims that it was a lady and gentleman. Something in this distribution of sex emboldened her; she took her life in her hand, and opened the door.

The lady spoke. "Does Mrs. Leighton live heah?" she said, in a rich, throaty voice; and she feigned a reference to the agent's permit she held in her hand.

"Yes," said Mrs. Leighton; she mechanically occupied the doorway, while Alma already quivered behind her with impatience of her impoliteness.

"Oh," said the lady, who began to appear more and more a young lady, "Ah didn't know but Ah had mistaken the ho'se. Ah suppose it's rather late to see the Apawtments, and Ah most ask you to pawdon us." She put this tentatively, with a delicately growing recognition of Mrs. Leighton as the lady of the house, and a humorous intelligence of the situation in the glance she threw Alma over her mother's shoulder. "Ah'm afraid we most have frightened you."

"Oh, not at all," said Alma; and at the same time her mother said, "Will you walk in, please?"

The gentleman promptly removed his hat and made the

Leightons an inclusive bow. "You awe very kind, madam, and I am sorry for the trouble we awe giving you." He was tall and severe-looking, with a grey, trooperish moustache and iron-grey hair, and, as Alma decided, iron-grey eyes. His daughter was short, plump, and fresh-coloured, with an effect of liveliness that did not all express itself in her broad-vowelled, rather formal speech, with its odd valuations of some of the auxiliary verbs, and its total elision of the canine letter.

"We awe from the Soath," she said, "and we arrived this mawning, but we got this cyahd from the brokah just befo' dinnah, and so we awe rathah late."

"Not at all; it's only nine o'clock," said Mrs. Leighton, in condonation. She looked up from the card the young lady had given her, and explained, "We haven't got in our servants yet, and we had to answer the bell ourselves, and——"

"You *were* frightened, of coase," said the young lady caressingly.

The gentleman said they ought not to *have* come so late, and he offered some formal apologies.

"We should have been just as much scared any time after five o'clock," Alma said to the sympathetic intelligence in the girl's face.

She laughed out. "Of coase! Ah would have my hawt in my moath all day long too, if *Ah* was living in a big hoase alone."

A moment of stiffness followed; Mrs. Leighton would have liked to withdraw from the intimacy of the situation, but she did not know how. It was very well for these people to assume to be what they pretended; but, she reflected too late, she had no proof of it except the agent's permit. They were all standing in the hall together, and she prolonged the awkward pause while she examined the permit. "You are Mr. Woodburn?" she asked, in a way that Alma felt implied he might not be.

"Yes, madam; from Charlottesboag, Virginia," he answered, with the slight umbrage a man shows when the strange cashier turns his check over and questions him before cashing it.

Alma writhed internally, but outwardly remained subordinate; she examined the other girl's dress, and decided in a superficial consciousness that she had made her own bonnet.

"I shall be glad to show you my rooms," said Mrs. Leighton, with an irrelevant sigh. "You must excuse their being not just as I should wish them. We're hardly settled yet."

"Don't speak of it, madam," said the gentleman, "if you can overlook the trouble we awe giving you at such an unseasonable houah."

"Ah'm a hoase-keepah mahself," Miss Woodburn joined in, "and Ah know ho' to accyoant fo' everything."

Mrs. Leighton led the way upstairs, and the young lady decided upon the large front room and small side-room on the third story. She said she could take the small one, and the other was so large that her father could both sleep and work in it. She seemed not ashamed to ask if Mrs. Leighton's price was inflexible, but gave way laughing when her father refused to have any bargaining, with a haughty self-respect which he softened to deference for Mrs. Leighton. His impulsiveness opened the way for some confidences from her, and before the affair was arranged she was enjoying in her quality of clerical widow the balm of the Virginians' reverent sympathy. They said they were Church people themselves.

"Ah don't know what yo' mothah means by yo' hoase not being in oddah," the young lady said to Alma, as they went downstairs together. "Ah'm a great hoase-keepah mahself, and Ah mean what Ah say."

They had all turned mechanically into the room where the Leightons were sitting when the Woodburns rang. Mr. Woodburn consented to sit down, and he remained listening to Mrs. Leighton while his daughter bustled up to the sketches pinned round the room, and questioned Alma about them.

"Ah suppose you awe going to be a great awtust?" she said, in friendly banter, when Alma owned to having done the things. "Ah've a great notion to take a few lessons mahself. Who's yo' teachah?"

Alma said she was drawing in Mr. Wetmore's class, and Miss Woodburn said: "Well, it's just beautiful, Miss Leighton; it's grand. Ah suppose it's raght expensive, now? Mah goodness! we have to cyoant the coast so much nowadays, it seems to me we do nothing *but* cyoant it. Ah'd like to bah something once without askin' the price."

"Well, if you didn't ask it," said Alma, "I don't believe Mr. Wetmore would ever know what the price of his lessons was. He has to think, when you ask him."

"Why, he most be chomming," said Miss Woodburn. "Perhaps Ah maght get the lessons for nothing from him. Well, Ah believe in my soul Ah'll trah. Now ho' did you begin? and ho' do you expect to get anything oat of it?" She turned on Alma eyes brimming with a shrewd mixture of fun and earnest, and Alma made note of the fact that she had an early nineteenth-century face, round, arch, a little coquettish, but extremely sensible and unspoiled-looking, such as used to be painted a good deal in miniature at that period; a tendency of her brown hair to twine and twist at the temples helped the effect; a high comb would have completed it, Alma felt, if she had her bonnet off. It was almost a Yankee country-girl type; but perhaps it appeared so to Alma because it was, like that, pure Anglo-Saxon. Alma herself, with her dull dark skin, slender in figure, slow in speech, with aristocratic forms in her long hands, and the oval of her fine face pointed to a long chin, felt herself much more Southern in style than this blooming, bubbling, bustling Virginian.

"I don't know," she answered slowly.

"Going to take po'traits," suggested Miss Woodburn, "or just paint the ahdeal?" A demure burlesque lurked in her tone.

"I suppose I don't expect to paint at all," said Alma. "I'm going to illustrate books—if anybody will let me."

"Ah should think they'd just joamp at you," said Miss Woodburn. "Ah'll tell you what let's do, Miss Leighton:

you make some pictures, and Ah'll wrahte a book fo' them. Ah've got to do something. Ah maght as well wrahte a book. You know we Southerners have all had to go to woak. But Ah don't mand it. I tell papa I shouldn't ca' fo' the disgrace of bein' poo' if it wasn't fo' the inconvenience."

"Yes, it's inconvenient," said Alma; "but you forget it when you're at work, don't you think?"

"Mah, yes! Perhaps that's one reason why poo' people have to woak so hawd—to keep their mands off their poverty."

The girls both tittered, and turned from talking in a low tone with their backs toward their elders, and faced them.

"Well, Madison," said Mr. Woodburn, "it is time we should go. I bid you good night, madam," he bowed to Mrs. Leighton. "Good night," he bowed again to Alma.

His daughter took leave of them in formal phrase, but with a jolly cordiality of manner that deformalised it. "We shall be roand raght soon in the mawning, then," she threatened at the door.

"We shall be all ready for you," Alma called after her down the steps.

"Well, Alma?" her mother asked, when the door closed upon them.

"She doesn't know any more about *art*," said Alma, "than —nothing at all. But she's jolly and good-hearted. She praised everything that was bad in my sketches, and said she was going to take lessons herself. When a person talks about taking lessons, as if they could learn it, you know where they belong artistically."

Mrs. Leighton shook her head with a sigh. "I wish I knew where they belonged financially. We shall have to get in two girls at once. I shall have to go out the first thing in the morning, and then our troubles will begin."

"Well, didn't you want them to begin? I will stay home and help you get ready. Our prosperity couldn't begin without the troubles, if you mean boarders, and boarders mean servants. I shall be very glad to be afflicted with a cook for a while myself."

"Yes; but we don't know anything about these people, or whether they will be able to pay us. Did she talk as if they were well off?"

"She talked as if they were poor; poo' she called it."

"Yes, how queerly she pronounced," said Mrs. Leighton. "Well, I ought to have told them that I required the first week in advance."

"Mamma! If *that's* the way you're going to act——"

"Oh, of course, I couldn't, after he wouldn't let her bargain for the rooms. I didn't like that."

"*I* did. And you can see that they were perfect ladies; or at least one of them." Alma laughed at herself, but her mother did not notice.

"Their being ladies won't help if they've got no money. It'll make it all the worse."

"Very well, then; we have no money, either. We're a match for them any day there. We can show them that two can play at that game."

III

ANGUS BEATON'S studio looked at first glance like many other painters' studios. A grey wall quadrangularly vaulted to a large north light; casts of feet, hands, faces hung to nails about; prints, sketches in oil and water-colour stuck here and there lower down; a rickety table, with paint and palettes and bottles of varnish and siccative* tossed comfortlessly on it; an easel, with a strip of some faded mediæval silk trailing from it; a lay figure simpering in incomplete nakedness, with its head on one side, and a stocking on one leg, and a Japanese dress dropped before it; dusty rugs and skins kicking over the varnished floor; canvases faced to the mop-board;* an open trunk overflowing with costumes: these features one might notice anywhere. But besides there was a bookcase with an unusual number of books in it, and there was an open colonial writing-desk, claw-footed, brass-handled, and scutcheoned,* with foreign periodicals—French and English—littering its leaf, and some pages of manuscript scattered among them. Above all, there was a sculptor's revolving stand, supporting a bust which Beaton was modelling, with an eye fixed as simultaneously as possible on the clay and on the head of the old man who sat on the platform beside it.

Few men have been able to get through the world with several gifts to advantage in all; and most men seem handicapped for the race if they have more than one. But they are apparently immensely interested as well as distracted by them. When Beaton was writing, he would have agreed, up to a certain point, with any one who said literature was his proper expression; but then, when he was painting, up to a certain point, he would have maintained against the world that he was a colourist and supremely a colourist. At the certain point in either art he was apt to break away in a frenzy of disgust, and wreak himself upon some other. In these moods he sometimes designed elevations of buildings, very striking, very original, very *chic*, very everything but habitable. It was in this way that he had tried his hand on sculpture, which he had at first approached rather slightingly as a mere decorative accessory of architecture. But it had grown in his respect till he maintained that the accessory business ought to be all the other way: that temples should be raised to enshrine statues, not statues made to ornament temples; that was putting the cart before the horse with a vengeance. This was when he had carried a plastic study so far that the sculptors who saw it said that Beaton might have been an architect, but would certainly never be a sculptor. At the same time he did some hurried, nervous things that had a popular charm, and that sold in plaster reproductions, to the profit of another. Beaton justly despised the popular charm in these, as well as in the paintings he sold from time to time; he said it was flat burglary to have taken money for them, and he would have been living almost wholly upon the bounty of the old tombstone-cutter in Syracuse if it had not been for the syndicate letters which he supplied to Fulkerson for ten dollars a week.

They were very well done, but he hated doing them after the first two or three, and had to be punched up for them by Fulkerson, who did not cease to prize them, and who never failed to punch him up. Beaton being what he was, Fulkerson was his creditor as well as patron; and Fulkerson being what he was, had an enthusiastic patience with the elusive, facile, adaptable, unpractical nature of Beaton. He was very proud of his art-letters, as he called them; but then Fulkerson was proud of everything he secured for his syndicate. The fact that he had secured it gave it value; he felt as if he had written it himself.

One art trod upon another's heels with Beaton. The day before he had rushed upon canvas the conception of a picture which he said to himself was glorious, and to others (at the *table d'hôte* of Maroni) was not bad. He had worked at it in a fury till the light failed him, and he execrated the dying day. But he lit his lamp, and transferred the process of his thinking from the canvas to the opening of the syndicate letter which he knew Fulkerson would be coming for in the morning. He remained talking so long after dinner in the same strain as he had painted and written in that he could not finish his letter that night. The next morning, while he was making his tea for breakfast, the postman brought him a letter from his father enclosing a little check, and begging him with tender, almost deferential, urgence to come as lightly upon him as possible, for just now his expenses were very heavy. It brought tears of shame into Beaton's eyes— the fine smouldering, floating eyes that many ladies admired under the thick bang—and he said to himself that if he were half a man he would go home and go to work cutting gravestones in his father's shop. But he would wait, at least, to finish his picture; and as a sop to his conscience, to stay its immediate ravening, he resolved to finish that syndicate letter first, and borrow enough money from Fulkerson to be able to send his father's check back; or if not that, then to return the sum of it partly in Fulkerson's check. While he still teemed with both of these good intentions the old man from whom he was modelling his head of Judas came, and

Beaton saw that he must get through with him before he finished either the picture or the letter; he would have to pay him for the time anyway. He utilised the remorse with which he was tingling to give his Judas an expression which he found novel in the treatment of that character—a look of such touching, appealing self-abhorrence that Beaton's artistic joy in it amounted to rapture; between the breathless moments when he worked in dead silence for an effect that was trying to escape him, he sang and whistled fragments of comic opera.

In one of the hushes there came a blow on the outside of the door that made Beaton jump, and swear with a modified profanity that merged itself in apostrophic prayer. He knew it must be Fulkerson, and after roaring, "Come in!" he said to the model, "That'll do this morning, Lindau."

Fulkerson squared his feet in front of the bust, and compared it by fleeting glances with the old man as he got stiffly up, and suffered Beaton to help him on with his thin shabby overcoat.

"Can you come to-morrow, Lindau?"

"No, not to-morrow, Mr. Peaton. I haf to zit for the young ladties."

"Oh!" said Beaton. "Wetmore's class? Is Miss Leighton doing you?"

"I don't know their namess," Lindau began, when Fulkerson said——

"Hope you haven't forgotten mine, Mr. Lindau? I met you with Mr. March at Maroni's one night." Fulkerson offered him a universally shakable hand.

"Oh yes! I am gladt to zee you again, Mr. Vulkerzon. And Mr. Marge—he don't zeem to gome any more?"

"Up to his eyes in work. Been moving on from Boston and getting settled, and starting in on our enterprise. Beaton here hasn't got a very flattering likeness of you, hey? Well, good morning," he said, for Lindau appeared not to have heard him, and was escaping with a bow through the door.

Beaton lit a cigarette which he pinched nervously between

his lips before he spoke. "You've come for that letter, I suppose, Fulkerson? It isn't done."

Fulkerson turned from staring at the bust to which he had mounted. "What you fretting about that letter for? I don't want your letter."

Beaton stopped biting his cigarette, and looked at him. "Don't want my letter? Oh, very good!" he bristled up. He took his cigarette from his lips, and blew the smoke through his nostrils, and then looked at Fulkerson.

"No; *I* don't want your letter; I want *you*." Beaton disdained to ask an explanation, but he internally lowered his crest, while he continued to look at Fulkerson without changing his defiant countenance. This suited Fulkerson well enough, and he went on with relish: "I'm going out of the syndicate business, old man, and I'm on a new thing." He put his leg over the back of a chair and rested his foot on its seat, and with one hand in his pocket, he laid the scheme of *Every Other Week* before Beaton with the help of the other. The artist went about the room, meanwhile, with an effect of indifference which by no means offended Fulkerson. He took some water into his mouth from a tumbler, which he blew in a fine mist over the head of Judas, before swathing it in a dirty cotton cloth; he washed his brushes and set his palette; he put up on his easel the picture he had blocked on the day before, and stared at it with a gloomy face; then he gathered the sheets of his unfinished letter together and slid them into a drawer of his writing-desk. By the time he had finished and turned again to Fulkerson, Fulkerson was saying: "I did think we could have the first number out by New-Year's; but it will take longer than that—a month longer; but I'm not sorry, for the holidays kill everything; and by February, or the middle of February, people will get their breath again, and begin to look round and ask what's new. Then we'll reply in the language of Shakespeare and Milton, *Every Other Week*; and don't you forget it." He took down his leg and asked, "Got a pipe of 'baccy anywhere?"

Beaton nodded at a clay stem sticking out of a Japanese

vase of bronze on his mantel. "There's yours," he said; and Fulkerson said, "Thanks," and filled the pipe, and sat down and began to smoke tranquilly.

Beaton saw that he would have to speak now. "And what do you want with me?"

"You? Oh yes!" Fulkerson humorously dramatised a return to himself from a pensive absence. "Want you for the art department."

Beaton shook his head. "I'm not your man, Fulkerson," he said compassionately. "You want a more practical hand; one that's in touch with what's going. I'm getting further and further away from this century and its claptrap. I don't believe in your enterprise; I don't respect it, and I won't have anything to do with it. It would—choke me, that kind of thing."

"That's all right," said Fulkerson. He esteemed a man who was not going to let himself go cheap. "Or if it isn't, we can make it. You and March will pull together first-rate. I don't care how much ideal you put into the thing; the more the better. I can look after the other end of the schooner myself."

"You don't understand me," said Beaton. "I'm not trying to get a rise out of you. I'm in earnest. What you want is some man who can have patience with mediocrity putting on the style of genius, and with genius turning mediocrity on his hands. I haven't any luck with men; I don't get on with them; I'm not popular." Beaton recognised the fact with the satisfaction which it somehow always brings to human pride.

"So much the better!" Fulkerson was ready for him at this point. "I don't want you to work the old established racket—the reputations. When I want them I'll go to them with a pocketful of rocks—knock-down argument. But my idea is to deal with the volunteer material. Look at the way the periodicals are carried on now! Names! names! names! In a country that's just boiling over with literary and artistic ability of every kind the new fellows have no chance. The editors all engage their material. I don't believe there are fifty volunteer contributions printed in a year in all the New York magazines. It's all wrong; it's suicidal. *Every Other*

Week is going back to the good old anonymous system, the only fair system. It's worked well in literature, and it will work well in art."

"It *won't* work well in art," said Beaton. "There you have a totally different set of conditions. What you'll get by inviting volunteer illustrations will be a lot of amateur trash. And how are you going to submit your literature for illustration? It can't be done. At any rate, *I* won't undertake to do it."

"We'll get up a School of Illustration," said Fulkerson, with cynical security. "You can read the things and explain 'em, and your pupils can make their sketches under your eye. They wouldn't be much further out than most illustrations are if they never knew what they were illustrating. You might select from what comes in and make up a sort of pictorial variations to the literature without any particular reference to it. Well, I understand you to accept?"

"No, you don't."

"That is, to consent to help us with your advice and criticism. That's all I want. It won't commit you to anything; and you can be as anonymous as anybody." At the door Fulkerson added: "By the way, the new man—the fellow that's taken my old syndicate business—will want you to keep on; but I guess he's going to try to beat you down on the price of the letters. He's going in for retrenchment. I brought along a check for this one; I'm to pay for that." He offered Beaton an envelope.

"I can't take it, Fulkerson. The letter's paid for already." Fulkerson stepped forward and laid the envelope on the table among the tubes of paint.

"It isn't the letter merely. I thought you wouldn't object to a little advance on your *Every Other Week* work till you kind of got started."

Beaton remained inflexible. "It can't be done, Fulkerson. Don't I tell you I can't sell myself out to a thing I don't believe in? Can't you understand that?"

"Oh yes; I can understand that first-rate. I don't want to buy you; I want to borrow you. It's all right. See? Come round when you can; I'd like to introduce you to old March. That's going to be our address." He put a card on the table beside the envelope, and Beaton allowed him to go without making him take the check back. He had remembered his father's plea; that unnerved him, and he promised himself again to return his father's poor little check and to work on that picture and give it to Fulkerson for the check he had left and for his back debts. He resolved to go to work on the picture at once; he had set his palette for it; but first he looked at Fulkerson's check. It was for only fifty dollars, and the canny Scotch blood in Beaton rebelled; he could not let this picture go for any such money; he felt a little like a man whose generosity has been trifled with. The conflict of emotions broke him up, and he could not work.

IV

THE day wasted away in Beaton's hands; at half-past four o'clock he went out to tea at the house of a lady who was At Home that afternoon from four till seven. By this time Beaton was in possession of one of those other selves, of which we each have several about us, and was again the laconic, staccato, rather worldlified young artist whose moments of a controlled utterance and a certain distinction of manner had commended him to Mrs. Horn's fancy in the summer at St. Barnaby.

Mrs. Horn's rooms were large, and they never seemed very full, though this perhaps was because people were always so quiet. The ladies, who outnumbered the men ten to one, as they always do at a New York tea, were dressed in sympathy with the low tone every one spoke in, and with the subdued light which gave a crepuscular uncertainty to the few objects, the dim pictures, the unexcited upholstery, of the rooms. One breathed free of bric-à-brac there, and the new-comer breathed softly as one does on going into church after service has begun. This might be a suggestion from the voiceless behaviour of the man-servant who let you in, but it was also because Mrs. Horn's At Home was a ceremony, a decorum, and not festival. At far greater houses there was more gaiety, at richer houses there was more freedom; the suppression at Mrs. Horn's was a personal, not a social, effect; it was an efflux of her character, demure, silentious, vague, but very correct.

Beaton easily found his way to her around the grouped skirts and among the detached figures, and received a pressure of welcome from the hand which she momentarily relaxed from the teapot. She sat behind a table put crosswise of a remote corner, and offered tea to people whom a niece of hers received provisionally or sped finally in the outer room. They did not usually take tea, and when they did they did not usually drink it; but Beaton was feverishly glad of his cup; he took rum and lemon in it, and stood talking at Mrs. Horn's side till the next arrival should displace him: he talked in his French manner.

"I have been hoping to see you," she said. "I wanted to ask you about the Leightons. Did they really come?"

"I believe so. They are in town—yes. I haven't seen them."

"Then you don't know how they're getting on—that pretty creature, with her cleverness, and poor Mrs. Leighton? I was afraid they were venturing on a rash experiment. Do you know where they are?"

"In West Eleventh Street somewhere. Miss Leighton is in Mr. Wetmore's class."

"I must look them up. Do you know their number?"

"Not at the moment. I can find out."

"Do," said Mrs. Horn. "What courage they must have, to plunge into New York as they've done! I really didn't think they would. I wonder if they've succeeded in getting anybody into their house yet?"

"I don't know," said Beaton.

"I discouraged their coming all I could," she sighed, "and I suppose you did too. But it's quite useless trying to make people in a place like St. Barnaby understand how it is in town."

"Yes," said Beaton. He stirred his tea, while inwardly he tried to believe that he had really discouraged the Leightons from coming to New York. Perhaps the vexation of his failure made him call Mrs. Horn in his heart a fraud.

"Yes," she went on. "It is very, very hard. And when they won't understand, and rush on their doom, you feel that they are going to hold you respons——"

Mrs. Horn's eyes wandered from Beaton; her voice faltered in the faded interest of her remark, and then rose with renewed vigour in greeting a lady who came up and stretched her glove across the teacups.

Beaton got himself away and out of the house with a much briefer adieu to the niece than he had meant to make. The patronising compassion of Mrs. Horn for the Leightons filled him with indignation toward her, toward himself. There was no reason why he should not have ignored them as he had done; but there was a feeling. It was his nature to be careless, and he had been spoiled into recklessness; he neglected everybody, and only remembered them when it suited his whim or his convenience; but he fiercely resented the inattention of others toward himself. He had no scruple about breaking an engagement or failing to keep an appointment; he made promises without thinking of their fulfilment, and not because he was a faithless person, but because he was imaginative, and expected at the time to do what he said, but was fickle, and so did not. As most of his short-comings were of a society sort, no great harm was done to anybody else. He had contracted somewhat the circle of his acquaintance by what some people called his rudeness, but most people treated it as his oddity, and were patient with it. One lady said she valued his coming when he said he would come because it had the charm of the unexpected. "Only it shows that it isn't always the unexpected that happens," she explained.

It did not occur to him that his behaviour was immoral; he did not realise that it was creating a reputation if not a character for him. While we are still young we do not realise that our actions have this effect. It seems to us that people will judge us from what we think and feel. Later we find out that this is impossible; perhaps we find it out too late; some of us never find it out at all.

In spite of his shame about the Leightons Beaton had no present intention of looking them up or sending Mrs. Horn their address. As a matter of fact, he never did send it; but he happened to meet Mr. Wetmore and his wife at the restaurant where he dined, and he got it of the painter for himself. He did not ask him how Miss Leighton was getting on; but Wetmore launched out, with Alma for a tacit text, on the futility of women generally going in for art. "Even when they have talent they've got too much against them. Where a girl doesn't seem very strong, like Miss Leighton, no amount of *chic* is going to help."

His wife disputed him on behalf of her sex, as women always do.

"No, Dolly," he persisted; "she'd better be home milking the cows and leading the horse to water."

"Do you think she'd better be up till two in the morning at balls and going all day to receptions and luncheons?"

"Oh, I guess it isn't a question of that, even if she weren't drawing. You knew them at home," he said to Beaton.

"Yes."

"I remember. Her mother said you suggested me. Well, the girl has some notion of it; there's no doubt about that. But—she's a woman. The trouble with these talented girls is that they're *all* woman. If they weren't, there wouldn't be much chance for the men, Beaton. But we've got Providence on our own side from the start. I'm able to watch all their inspirations with perfect composure. I know just how soon it's going to end in nervous breakdown. Somebody ought to marry them all and put them out of their misery."

"And what will you do with your students who are married already?" his wife said. She felt that she had let him go on long enough.

"Oh, they ought to get divorced."

"You ought to be ashamed to take their money if that's what you think of them."

113

"My dear, I have a wife to support."

Beaton intervened with a question. "Do you mean that Miss Leighton isn't standing it very well?"

"How do I know? She isn't the kind that bends; she's the kind that breaks."

After a little silence Mrs. Wetmore asked, "Won't you come home with us, Mr. Beaton?"

"Thank you; no. I have an engagement."

"I don't see why that should prevent you," said Wetmore. "But you always *were* a punctilious cuss. Well!"

Beaton lingered over his cigar; but no one else whom he knew came in, and he yielded to the threefold impulse of conscience, of curiosity, of inclination, in going to call at the Leightons'. He asked for the ladies, and the maid showed him into the parlour, where he found Mrs. Leighton and Miss Woodburn.

The widow met him with a welcome neatly marked by resentment; she meant him to feel that his not coming sooner had been noticed. Miss Woodburn bubbled and gurgled on, and did what she could to mitigate his punishment, but she did not feel authorised to stay it, till Mrs. Leighton, by studied avoidance of her daughter's name, obliged Beaton to ask for her. Then Miss Woodburn caught up her work, and said, "Ah'll go and tell her, Mrs. Leighton." At the top of the stairs she found Alma, and Alma tried to make it seem as if she had not been standing there. "Mah goodness, chald! there's the handsomest young man asking for you down there you evah saw. Ah told you' mothah Ah would come up fo' you."

"What—who is it?"

"Don't you *know*? But ho' could you? He's got the most beautiful eyes, and he wea's his hai' in a bang, and he talks English like it was something else, and his name's Mr. Beaton."

"Did he—ask for me?" said Alma, with a dreamy tone. She put her hand on the stairs rail, and a little shiver ran over her.

"Didn't I tell you? Of coase he did! And you ought to go raght down if you want to save the poo' fellah's lahfe; you' mothah's just freezin' him to death."

V

"She *is?*" cried Alma. "Tchk!" She flew downstairs, and flitted swiftly into the room, and fluttered up to Beaton, and gave him a crushing hand-shake.

"How *very* kind of you to come and see us, Mr. Beaton! When did you come to New York? Don't you find it warm here? We've only just lighted the furnace, but with this mild weather it seems too early. Mamma *does* keep it so hot!" She rushed about opening doors and shutting registers, and then came back and sat facing him from the sofa with a mask of radiant cordiality. "How *have* you been since we saw you?"

"Very well," said Beaton. "I hope you're well, Miss Leighton?"

"Oh, *perfectly!* I think New York agrees with us both wonderfully. I never knew such air. And to think of our not having snow yet! I should think everybody would want to come here! Why don't *you* come, Mr. Beaton?"

Beaton lifted his eyes and looked at her. "I—I live in New York," he faltered.

"In New York *city!*" she exclaimed.

"Surely, Alma," said her mother, "you remember Mr. Beaton's telling us he lived in New York."

"But I thought you came from Rochester; or was it Syracuse? I always get those places mixed up."

"Probably I told you my father lived at Syracuse. I've been in New York ever since I came home from Paris," said Beaton, with the confusion of a man who feels himself played upon by a woman.

"From Paris!" Alma echoed, leaning forward, with her smiling mask tight on. "Wasn't it Munich, where you studied?"

"I was at Munich too. I met Wetmore there."

"Oh, *do* you know Mr. Wetmore?"

"Why, Alma," her mother interposed again, "it was Mr. Beaton who *told* you of Mr. Wetmore."

"Was it? Why, yes, to be sure. It was Mrs. Horn; she suggested Mr. Ilcomb. I remember now. I can't thank you enough for *having* sent me to Mr. Wetmore, Mr. Beaton. Isn't he delightful? Oh yes, I'm a perfect Wetmorian, I can assure you. The whole class is the same way."

"I just met him and Mrs. Wetmore at dinner," said Beaton, attempting the recovery of something that he had lost through the girl's shining ease and steely sprightliness. She seemed to him so smooth and hard, with a repellent elasticity from which he was flung off. "I hope you're not working too hard, Miss Leighton?"

"Oh no! I enjoy every minute of it, and grow stronger on it. Do I look very much wasted away?" She looked him full in the face, brilliantly smiling, and intentionally beautiful.

"No," he said, with a slow sadness; "I never saw you looking better."

"Poor Mr. Beaton!" she said, in recognition of his doleful tune. "It seems to be quite a blow."

"Oh no——"

"I remember all the good advice you used to give me about not working too hard, and probably it's that that's saved my life—that and the house-hunting. Has mamma told you of our adventures in getting settled? Some time we must. It was such fun! And didn't you think we were fortunate to get such a pretty house? You must see both our parlours."

She jumped up, and her mother followed her with a bewildered look as she ran into the back parlour and flashed up the gas.

"Come in here, Mr. Beaton. I want to show you the great feature of the house." She opened the low windows that gave upon a glazed veranda stretching across the end of the room. "Just think of this in New York! You can't see it very well at night, but when the southern sun pours in here all the afternoon——"

"Yes, I can imagine it," he said. He glanced up at the bird-cage hanging from the roof. "I suppose Gypsy enjoys it."

"You remember Gypsy?" she said; and she made a cooing, kissing little noise up at the bird, who responded drowsily. "Poor old Gypsum! Well, he *shan't* be disturbed. Yes, it's Gyp's delight, and Colonel Woodburn likes to write here in the morning. Think of us having a real live author in the house! And Miss Woodburn: I'm so glad you've seen her! They're Southern people."

"Yes, that was obvious in her case."

"From her accent? Isn't it fascinating? I didn't believe I could ever endure Southerners, but we're like one family with the Woodburns. I should think you'd want to paint Miss Woodburn. Don't you think her colouring is delicious? And such a quaint kind of eighteenth-century type of beauty! But she's perfectly lovely every way, and everything she says is so funny. The Southerners seem to be such great talkers; better than we are, don't you think?"

"I don't know," said Beaton, in pensive discouragement. He was sensible of being manipulated, operated, but he was helpless to escape from the performer or to fathom her motives. His pensiveness passed into gloom, and was degenerating into sulky resentment when he went away, after several failures to get back to the old ground he had held in relation to Alma. He retrieved something of it with Mrs. Leighton; but Alma glittered upon him to the last with a keen impenetrable candour, a childlike singleness of glance, covering unfathomable reserve.

"Well, Alma," said her mother, when the door had closed upon him.

"Well, mother." Then, after a moment, she said, with a rush: "Did you think I was going to let him suppose we were piqued at his not coming? Did you suppose I was going to let him patronise us, or think that we were in the least dependent on his favour or friendship?"

Her mother did not attempt to answer her. She merely said, "I shouldn't think he would come any more."

"Well, we have got on so far without him; perhaps we can live through the rest of the winter."

"I couldn't help feeling sorry for him. He was quite stupefied. I could see that he didn't know what to make of you."

"He's not required to make anything of me," said Alma.

"Do you think he really believed you had forgotten all those things?"

"Impossible to say, mamma."

"Well, I don't think it was quite right, Alma."

"I'll leave him to you the next time. Miss Woodburn said you were freezing him to death when I came down."

"That was quite different. But there won't be any next time, I'm afraid," sighed Mrs. Leighton.

Beaton went home feeling sure there would not. He tried to read when he got to his room; but Alma's looks, tones, gestures, whirred through and through the woof of the story like shuttles; he could not keep them out, and he fell asleep at last, not because he forgot them, but because he forgave them. He was able to say to himself that he had been justly cut off from kindness which he knew how to value in losing it. He did not expect ever to right himself in Alma's esteem; but he hoped some day to let her know that he had understood. It seemed to him that it would be a good thing if she should find it out after his death. He imagined her being touched by it under those circumstances.

VI

In the morning it seemed to Beaton that he had done himself injustice. When he uncovered his Judas and looked at it, he could not believe that the man who was capable of such work deserved the punishment Miss Leighton had inflicted upon him. He still forgave her, but in the presence of a thing like that he could not help respecting himself; he believed that if she could see it she would be sorry that she had cut herself off from his acquaintance. He carried this strain of conviction all through his syndicate letter, which he now took out of his desk and finished, with an increasing security of his opinions and a mounting severity in his judgments. He retaliated upon the general condition of art among us the pangs of wounded vanity, which Alma had made him feel, and he folded up his manuscript and put it in his pocket, almost healed of his humiliation. He had been able to escape from its sting so entirely while he was writing that the notion of making his life more and more literary commended itself to him. As it was now evident that the future was to be one of renunciation, of self-forgetting, an oblivion tinged with bitterness, he formlessly reasoned in favour of reconsidering his resolution against Fulkerson's offer. One must call it reasoning, but it was rather that swift internal dramatisation which constantly goes on in persons of excitable sensibilities, and which now seemed to sweep Beaton physically along toward the *Every Other Week* office, and carried his mind with lightning celerity on to a time when he should have given that journal such quality and authority in matters of art as had never been enjoyed by any in America before. With the prosperity which he made attend his work he changed the character of the enterprise, and with Fulkerson's enthusiastic support he gave the public an art journal of as high grade as *Les Lettres et les Arts*, and very much that sort of thing. All this involved now the unavailing regret of Alma Leighton, and now his reconciliation with her: they were married in Grace Church, because Beaton had once seen a marriage there, and had intended to paint a picture of it some time.

Nothing in these fervid fantasies prevented his responding with due dryness to Fulkerson's cheery "Hello, old man!" when he found himself in the building fitted up for the *Every Other Week* office. Fulkerson's room was back of the smaller one occupied by the book-keeper; they had been respectively the reception-room and dining-room of the little place in its dwelling-house days, and they had been simply and tastefully treated in their transformation into business purposes. The narrow old trim of the doors and windows had been kept, and the quaintly ugly marble mantels. The architect had said, Better let them stay: they expressed epoch, if not character.

"Well, have you come round to go to work? Just hang up your coat on the floor anywhere," Fulkerson went on.

"I've come to bring you that letter," said Beaton, all the more haughtily because he found that Fulkerson was not alone when he welcomed him in these free and easy terms. There was a quiet-looking man, rather stout, and a little above the middle height, with a full, close-cropped iron-grey beard, seated beyond the table where Fulkerson tilted himself back, with his knees set against it; and leaning against the mantel there was a young man with a singularly gentle face, in which the look of goodness qualified and transfigured a certain simplicity. His large blue eyes were somewhat prominent; and his rather narrow face was drawn forward in a nose a little too long perhaps, if it had not been for the full chin deeply cut below the lip, and jutting firmly forward.

"Introduce you to Mr. March, our editor, Mr. Beaton," Fulkerson said, rolling his head in the direction of the elder man; and then nodding it toward the younger, he said, "Mr. Dryfoos, Mr. Beaton." Beaton shook hands with March, and then with Mr. Dryfoos, and Fulkerson went on gaily: "We were just talking of you, Beaton—well, you know the old saying. Mr. March, as I told you, is our editor, and Mr. Dryfoos has charge of the publishing department—he's the counting-room incarnate, the source of power, the fountain of corruption, the element that prevents journalism being the high and holy thing that it would be if there were no money in it." Mr. Dryfoos turned his large mild eyes upon Beaton, and laughed with the uneasy concession which people make to a character when they do not quite approve of the character's language. "What Mr. March and I are trying to do is to carry on this thing so that there *won't* be any money in it—or very little; and we're planning to give the public a better article for the price that it's ever had before. Now here's a dummy we've had made up for *Every Other Week*, and as we've decided to adopt it, we would naturally like your opinion of it, so 's to know what opinion to have of *you*." He reached forward and pushed toward Beaton a volume a little above the size of the ordinary duodecimo book; its ivory white pebbled paper cover was prettily illustrated with a water-coloured design irregularly washed over the greater part of its surface: quite across the page at top, and narrowing from right to left as it descended. In the triangular space left blank the title of the periodical and the publisher's imprint were tastefully lettered so as to be partly covered by the background of colour.

"It's like some of those *Tartarin* books of Daudet's,'"said Beaton, looking at it with more interest than he suffered to be seen. "But it's a book, not a magazine." He opened its pages of thick mellow white paper, with uncut leaves, the first few pages experimentally printed in the type intended to be used, and illustrated with some sketches drawn into and over the text, for the sake of the effect.

"A Daniel—a Daniel come to judgment!" Sit down, Dan'el, and take it easy." Fulkerson pushed a chair toward Beaton, who dropped into it. "You're right, Dan'el; it's a book, to all practical intents and purposes. And what we propose to do with the American public is to give it twenty-four books like this a year—a complete library—for the absurd sum of six dollars. We don't intend to sell 'em—it's no name for the transaction—but to *give* 'em. And what we want to get out of you—beg, borrow, buy, or steal from you—is an opinion whether we shall make the American public this princely present in paper covers like this, or in some sort of flexible boards, so they can set them on the shelf and say no more about it. Now, Dan'el, come to judgment, as our respected friend Shylock remarked."

Beaton had got done looking at the dummy, and he dropped it on the table before Fulkerson, who pushed it away, apparently to free himself from partiality. "I don't know anything about the business side, and I can't tell about the effect of either style on the sales; but you'll spoil the whole character of the cover if you use anything thicker than that thickish paper."

"All right; very good; first-rate. The ayes have it. Paper it is. I don't mind telling you that we had decided for that paper before you came in. Mr. March wanted it, because he felt in his bones just the way you do about it, and Mr. Dryfoos wanted it, because he's the counting-room incarnate, and it's cheaper; and I wanted it, because I always like to go with the majority. Now what do you think of that little design itself?"

"The sketch?" Beaton pulled the book toward him again and looked at it again. "Rather decorative. Drawing's not remarkable. Graceful; rather nice." He pushed the book away again, and Fulkerson pulled it to his side of the table.

"Well, that's a piece of that amateur trash you despise so much. I went to a painter I know—by the way, he was guilty of suggesting you for this thing, but I told him I was ahead of him—and I got him to submit my idea to one of his class, and that's the result. Well, now, there ain't anything in this world that sells a book like a pretty cover, and we're going to have a pretty cover for *Every Other Week* every time. We've cut loose from the old traditional quarto literary newspaper size, and we've cut loose from the old two-column big page magazine size; we're going to have a duodecimo page, clear black print, and paper that'll make your mouth water; and we're going to have a fresh illustration for the cover of each number, and we ain't a-going to give the public any rest at all. Sometimes we're going to have a delicate little landscape like this, and sometimes we're going to have an indelicate little figure, or as much so as the law will allow."

The young man leaning against the mantelpiece blushed a sort of protest.

March smiled and said dryly, "Those are the numbers that Mr. Fulkerson is going to edit himself."

"Exactly. And Mr. Beaton here is going to supply the floating females, gracefully airing themselves against a sunset or something of that kind." Beaton frowned in embarrassment, while Fulkerson went on philosophically. "It's astonishing how you fellows can keep it up at this stage of the proceedings; you can paint things that your harshest critic would be ashamed to describe accurately; you're as free as the theatre. But that's neither here nor there. What I'm after is the fact that we're going to have variety in our title-pages, and we are going to have novelty in the illustrations of the body of the book. March, here, if he had his own way, wouldn't have any illustrations at all."

"Not because I don't like them, Mr. Beaton," March interposed, "but because I like them too much. I find that I look at the pictures in an illustrated article, but I don't read the article very much, and I fancy that's the case with most other people. You've got to doing them so prettily that you take our eyes off the literature, if you don't take our minds off."

"Like the society beauties on the stage: people go in for the beauty so much that they don't know what the play is. But the box office gets there all the same, and that's what Mr. Dryfoos wants." Fulkerson looked up gaily at Mr. Dryfoos, who smiled deprecatingly.

"It was different," March went on, "when the illustrations used to be bad. Then the text had some chance."

"Old legitimate drama days, when ugliness and genius combined to storm the galleries," said Fulkerson.

"We can still make them bad enough," said Beaton, ignoring Fulkerson in his remark to March.

Fulkerson took the reply upon himself. "Well, you needn't make 'em so bad as the old-style cuts; but you can make them unobtrusive, modestly retiring. We've got hold of a process something like that those French fellows gave Daudet thirty-five thousand dollars to write a novel to use with; kind of thing that begins at one side, or one corner, and spreads in a sort of dim religious style over the print till you can't tell which is which. Then we've got a notion that where the pictures don't behave quite so sociably, they can be dropped into the text, like a little casual remark, don't you know, or a comment that has some connection, or may be none at all, with what's going on in the story. Something like this." Fulkerson took away one knee from the table long enough to open the drawer, and pull from it a book that he shoved toward Beaton. "That's a Spanish book I happened to see at Brentano's, and I froze to it on account of the pictures. I guess they're pretty good."

"Do you expect to get such drawings in this country?"

asked Beaton, after a glance at the book. "Such character—such drama? You won't."

"Well, I'm not so sure," said Fulkerson, "come to get our amateurs warmed up to the work. But what I want is to get the physical effect, so to speak—get that-sized picture into our page, and set the fashion of it. I shouldn't care if the illustration was sometimes confined to an initial letter and a tail-piece."

"Couldn't be done here. We haven't the touch. We're good in some things, but this isn't in our way," said Beaton stubbornly. "I can't think of a man who could do it; that is, amongst those that would."

"Well, think of some woman, then," said Fulkerson easily. "I've got a notion that the women could help us out on this thing, come to get 'em interested. There ain't anything so popular as female fiction; why not try female art?"

"The females themselves have been supposed to have been trying it for a good while," March suggested; and Mr. Dryfoos laughed nervously; Beaton remained solemnly silent.

"Yes, I know," Fulkerson assented. "But I don't mean that kind exactly. What we want to do is to work the *ewig Weibliche* in this concern. We want to make a magazine that will go for the women's fancy every time. I don't mean with recipes for cooking and fashions and personal gossip about authors and society, but real high-tone literature that will show women triumphing in all the stories, or else suffering tremendously. We've got to recognise that women form three-fourths of the reading public in this country, and go for their tastes and their sensibilities and their sex-piety along the whole line. They do like to think that women can do things better than men; and if we can let it leak out and get around in the papers that the managers of *Every Other Week* couldn't stir a peg in the line of the illustration they wanted till they got a lot of God-gifted girls to help them, it'll make the fortunes of the thing. See?"

He looked sunnily round at the other men, and March said: "You ought to be in charge of a Siamese white elephant, Fulkerson. It's a disgrace to be connected with you."

"It seems to me," said Beaton, "that you'd better get a God-gifted girl for your art editor."

Fulkerson leaned alertly forward, and touched him on the shoulder, with a compassionate smile. "My dear boy, they haven't got the genius of organisation. It takes a very masculine man for that—a man who combines the most subtle and refined sympathies with the most forceful purposes and the most ferruginous will power. Which his name is Angus Beaton, and here he sets!"

The others laughed with Fulkerson at his gross burlesque of flattery, and Beaton frowned sheepishly. "I suppose you understand this man's style," he growled toward March.

"They do, my son," said Fulkerson. "They know that I cannot tell a lie." He pulled out his watch, and then got suddenly upon his feet.

"It's quarter of twelve, and I've got an appointment." Beaton rose too, and Fulkerson put the two books in his lax hands. "Take these along, Michelangelo Da Vinci, my friend, and put your multitudinous mind on them for about an hour, and let us hear from you to-morrow. We hang upon your decision."

"There's no deciding to be done," said Beaton. "You can't combine the two styles. They'd kill each other."

"A Dan'el, a Dan'el come to judgment! I knew you could help us out! Take 'em along, and tell us which will go the furthest with the *ewig Weibliche*. Dryfoos, I want a word with you." He led the way into the front room, flirting an airy farewell to Beaton with his hand as he went.

VII

MARCH and Beaton remained alone together for a moment, and March said: "I hope you *will* think it worth while to take hold with us, Mr. Beaton. Mr. Fulkerson puts it in his own way, of course; but we really want to make a nice thing of the magazine." He had that timidity of the elder in the presence of the younger man which the younger, pre-occupied with his own timidity in the presence of the elder, cannot imagine. Besides, March was aware of the gulf that divided him as a literary man from Beaton as an artist, and he only ventured to feel his way toward sympathy with him. "We want to make it good; we want to make it high. Fulkerson is right about aiming to please the women, but of course he caricatures the way of going about it."

For answer, Beaton flung out, "I can't go in for a thing I don't understand the plan of."

March took it for granted that he had wounded some exposed sensibility of Beaton's. He continued still more deferentially: "Mr. Fulkerson's notion—I must say the notion is his, evolved from his syndicate experience—is that we shall do best in fiction to confine ourselves to short stories, and make each number complete in itself. He found that the most successful things he could furnish his news-papers were short stories; we Americans are supposed to excel in writing them; and most people begin with them in fiction; and it's Mr. Fulkerson's idea to work unknown talent, as he says, and so he thinks he can not only get them easily, but can gradually form a school of short-story writers. I can't say I follow him altogether, but I respect his experience. We shall not despise translations of short stories, but otherwise the matter will all be original, and of course it won't all be short stories. We shall use sketches of travel, and essays, and little dramatic studies, and bits of bio-graphy and history; but all very light, and always short enough to be completed in a single number. Mr. Fulkerson believes in pictures, and most of the things would be capable of illustration."

"I see," said Beaton.

"I don't know but this is the whole affair," said March, beginning to stiffen a little at the young man's reticence.

"I understand. Thank you for taking the trouble to explain. Good morning." Beaton bowed himself off, without offering to shake hands.

Fulkerson came in after a while from the outer office, and Mr. Dryfoos followed him. "Well, what do you think of our art editor?"

"Is he our art editor?" asked March. "I wasn't quite certain when he left."

"Did he take the books?"

"Yes, he took the books."

"I guess he's all right, then." Fulkerson added, in concession to the umbrage he detected in March, "Beaton has his times of being the greatest ass in the solar system, but he usually takes it out in personal conduct. When it comes to work, he's a regular horse."

"He appears to have compromised for the present by being a perfect mule," said March.

"Well, he's in a transition state," Fulkerson allowed. "He's the man for us. He really understands what we want. You'll see; he'll catch on. That lurid glare of his will wear off in the course of time. He's really a good fellow when you take him off his guard; and he's full of ideas. He's spread out over a good deal of ground at present, and so he's pretty thin; but come to gather him up into a lump, there's a good deal of substance to him. Yes, there is. He's a first-rate critic, and he's a nice fellow with the other artists. They laugh at his universality, but they all like him. He's the best kind of a teacher when he condescends to it; and he's just the man to deal with our volunteer work. Yes, sir, he's a prize. Well, I must go now."

Fulkerson went out of the street door and then came quickly back. "By-the-by, March, I saw that old dynamiter of yours round at Beaton's room yesterday."

"What old dynamiter of mine?"

"That old one-handed Dutchman—friend of your youth —the one we saw at Maroni's——"

"Oh—Lindau!" said March, with a vague pang of self-reproach for having thought of Lindau so little after the first flood of his tender feeling toward him was past.

"Yes, our versatile friend was modelling him as Judas Iscariot. Lindau makes a first-rate Judas, and Beaton has got a big thing in that head if he works the religious people right. But what I was thinking of was this—it struck me just as I was going out of the door: Didn't you tell me Lindau knew forty or fifty different languages?"

"Four or five, yes."

"Well, we won't quarrel about the number. The question is, why not work *him* in the field of foreign literature? *You* can't go over all their reviews and magazines, and he could do the smelling for you, if you could trust his nose. Would he know a good thing?"

"I think he would," said March, on whom the scope of Fulkerson's suggestion gradually opened. "He used to have good taste, and he must know the ground. Why, it's a capital idea, Fulkerson! Lindau wrote very fair English, and he could translate, with a little revision."

"And he would probably work cheap. Well, hadn't you better see him about it? I guess it'll be quite a windfall for him."

"Yes, it will. I'll look him up. Thank you for the suggestion, Fulkerson."

"Oh, don't mention it! *I* don't mind doing *Every Other Week* a good turn now and then when it comes in my way." Fulkerson went out again, and this time March was finally left with Mr. Dryfoos.

"Mrs. March was very sorry not to be at home when your sisters called the other day. She wished me to ask if they had any afternoon in particular. There was none on your mother's card."

"No, sir," said the young man, with a flush of embarrassment that seemed habitual with him. "She has no day. She's at home almost every day. She hardly ever goes out."

"Might we come some evening?" March asked. "We should be very glad to do that, if she would excuse the informality. Then I could come *with* Mrs. March."

"Mother isn't very formal," said the young man. "She would be very glad to see you."

"Then we'll come some night this week, if you will let us. When do you expect your father back?"

"Not much before Christmas. He's trying to settle up some things at Moffitt."

"And what do you think of our art editor?" asked March, with a smile, for the change of subject.

"Oh, I don't know much about such things," said the young man, with another of his embarrassed flushes. "Mr. Fulkerson seems to feel sure that he is the one for us."

"Mr. Fulkerson seemed to think that *I* was the one for you, too," said March; and he laughed. "That's what makes me doubt his infallibility. But he couldn't do worse with Mr. Beaton."

Mr. Dryfoos reddened and looked down, as if unable or unwilling to cope with the difficulty of making a polite protest against March's self-depreciation. He said after a moment: "It's new business to all of us except Mr. Fulkerson. But I think it will succeed. I think we can do some good in it."

March asked rather absently, "Some good?" Then he added: "Oh yes; I think we can. What do you mean by good? Improve the public taste? Elevate the standard of literature? Give young authors and artists a chance?"

This was the only good that had ever been in March's mind, except the good that was to come in a material way from his success, to himself and to his family.

"I don't know," said the young man; and he looked down in a shamefaced fashion. He lifted his head and looked into March's face. "I suppose I was thinking that some time we might help along. If we were to have those sketches of yours about life in every part of New York——"

March's authorial vanity was tickled. "Fulkerson has been talking to you about them? He seemed to think they would be a card. He believes that there's no subject so fascinating to the general average of people throughout the country as life in New York City; and he liked my notion of doing these things." March hoped that Dryfoos would answer that Fulkerson was perfectly enthusiastic about his notion; but he did not need this stimulus, and at any rate he went on without it. "The fact is, it's something that struck my fancy the moment I came here; I found myself intensely interested in the place, and I began to make notes, consciously and unconsciously, at once. Yes, I believe I can get something quite attractive out of it. I don't in the least know what it will be yet, except that it will be very desultory; and I couldn't at all say when I can get at it. If we postpone the first number till February I might get a little paper into that. Yes, I think it might be a good thing for us," March said, with modest self-appreciation.

"If you can make the comfortable people understand how the uncomfortable people live, it will be a very good thing, Mr. March. Sometimes it seems to me that the only trouble is that we don't know one another well enough; and that the first thing is to do this." The young fellow spoke with the seriousness in which the beauty of his face resided. Whenever he laughed his face looked weak, even silly. It seemed to be a sense of this that made him hang his head or turn it away at such times.

"That's true," said March, from the surface only. "And then, those phases of low life are immensely picturesque. Of course we must try to get the contrasts of luxury for the sake of the full effect. That won't be so easy. You can't penetrate to the dinner-party of a millionaire under the wing of a detective as you could to a carouse in Mulberry Street, or to his children's nursery with a philanthropist as you can to a street-boy's lodging-house." March laughed, and again the young man turned his head away. "Still, something can be done in that way by tact and patience."

VIII

THAT evening March went with his wife to return the call of the Dryfoos ladies. On their way up-town in the Elevated he told her of his talk with young Dryfoos. "I confess I was a little ashamed before him afterward for having looked at the matter so entirely from the æsthetic point of view. But of course, you know, if I went to work at those things with an ethical intention explicitly in mind, I should spoil them."

"Of course," said his wife. She had always heard him say something of this kind about such things.

He went on: "But I suppose that's just the point that such a nature as young Dryfoos' can't get hold of, or keep hold of. We're a queer lot, down there, Isabel—perfect menagerie. If it hadn't been that Fulkerson got us together, and really seems to know what he did it for, I should say he was the oddest stick among us. But when I think of myself and my own crankiness for the literary department; and young Dryfoos, who ought really to be in the pulpit, or a monastery, or something, for publisher; and that young Beaton, who probably hasn't a moral fibre in his composition, for the art man, I don't know but we could give Fulkerson odds and still beat him in oddity."

His wife heaved a deep sigh of apprehension, of renunciation, of monition. "Well, I'm glad you can feel so light about it, Basil."

"Light? I feel gay! With Fulkerson at the helm, I tell you the rocks and the lee shore had better keep out of the way." He laughed with pleasure in his metaphor. "Just when you think Fulkerson has taken leave of his senses he says or does something that shows he is on the most intimate and inalienable terms with them all the time. You know how I've been worrying over those foreign periodicals, and trying to get some translation from them for the first number? Well, Fulkerson has brought his centipedal mind to bear on the subject, and he's suggested that old German friend

131

of mine I was telling you of—the one I met in the restaurant
—the friend of my youth."

"Do you think *he* could do it?" asked Mrs. March
sceptically.

"He's a perfect Babel of strange tongues; and he's the
very man for the work, and I was ashamed I hadn't thought
of him myself, for I suspect he needs the work."

"Well, be careful how you get mixed up with him, then,
Basil," said his wife, who had the natural misgiving concern-
ing the friends of her husband's youth that all wives have.
"You know the Germans *are* so unscrupulously dependent.
You don't know anything about him now."

"I'm not afraid of Lindau," said March. "He was the best
and kindest man I ever saw, the most high-minded, the
most generous. He lost a hand in the war that helped to save
us and keep us possible, and that stump of his is character
enough for me."

"Oh, you don't think I could have meant anything *against*
him!" said Mrs. March, with the tender fervour that every
woman who lived in the time of the war must feel for those
who suffered in it. "All that I meant was that I hoped you
would not get mixed up with him too much. You're so apt
to be carried away by your impulses."

"They didn't carry me very far away in the direction of
poor old Lindau, I'm ashamed to think," said March. "I
meant all sorts of fine things by him after I met him; and
then I forgot him, and I had to be reminded of him by
Fulkerson."

She did not answer him, and he fell into a remorseful
reverie, in which he rehabilitated Lindau anew, and provided handsomely for his old age. He got him buried with
military honours, and had a shaft raised over him, with a
medallion likeness by Beaton and an epitaph by himself, by
the time they reached Forty-second Street; there was no
time to write Lindau's life, however briefly, before the train
stopped.

They had to walk up four blocks and then half a block
across before they came to the indistinctive brown-stone

house where the Dryfooses lived. It was larger than some in the same block, but the next neighbourhood of a huge apartment-house dwarfed it again. March thought he recognised the very flat in which he had disciplined the surly janitor, but he did not tell his wife; he made her notice the transition character of the street, which had been mostly built up in apartment-houses, with here and there a single dwelling dropped far down beneath and beside them, to that jag-toothed effect on the sky-line so often observable in such New York streets. "I don't know exactly what the old gentleman bought here for," he said, as they waited on the steps after ringing, "unless he expects to turn it into flats by-and-by. Otherwise, I don't believe he'll get his money back."

An Irish serving-man, with a certain surprise that delayed him, said the ladies were at home, and let the Marches in, and then carried their cards upstairs. The drawing-room, where he said they could sit down while he went on this errand, was delicately decorated in white and gold, and furnished with a sort of extravagant good taste; there was nothing to object to in the satin furniture, the pale, soft, rich carpet, the pictures, and the bronze and china bric-à-brac, except that their costliness was too evident; everything in the room meant money too plainly, and too much of it. The Marches recognised this in the hoarse whispers which people cannot get their voices above when they try to talk away the interval of waiting in such circumstances; they conjectured from what they had heard of the Dryfooses that this tasteful luxury in nowise expressed their civilisation. "Though when you come to that," said March, "I don't know that Mrs. Green's gimcrackery expresses ours."

"Well, Basil, I didn't *take* the gimcrackery. That was *your*——"

The rustle of skirts on the stairs without arrested Mrs. March in the well-merited punishment which she never failed to inflict upon her husband when the question of the gimcrackery—they always called it that—came up. She rose at the entrance of a bright-looking, pretty-looking, mature, youngish lady, in black silk of a neutral implication, who put out her hand to her, and said, with a very cheery, very lady-like accent, "Mrs. March?" and then added to both of them, while she shook hands with March, and before they could get the name out of their mouths, "No, *not* Miss Dryfoos! Neither of them; nor Mrs. Dryfoos. Mrs. Mandel. The ladies will be down in a moment. Won't you throw off your sacque,* Mrs. March? I'm afraid it's rather warm here, coming from the outside."

"I will throw it back, if you'll allow me," said Mrs. March, with a sort of provisionality, as if, pending some uncertainty as to Mrs. Mandel's quality and authority, she did not feel herself justified in going further.

But if she did not know about Mrs. Mandel, Mrs. Mandel seemed to know about her. "Oh, well, do!" she said, with a sort of recognition of the propriety of her caution. "I hope you are feeling a little at home in New York. We heard so much of your trouble in getting a flat, from Mr. Fulkerson."

"Well, a true Bostonian doesn't give up quite so soon," said Mrs. March. "But I will say New York doesn't seem so far away, now we're here."

"I'm sure you'll like it. Every one does." Mrs. Mandel added to March, "It's very sharp out, isn't it?"

"Rather sharp. But after our Boston winters I don't know but I ought to repudiate the word."

"Ah, wait till you have been here through March!" said Mrs. Mandel. She began with him, but skilfully transferred the close of her remark, and the little smile of menace that went with it, to his wife.

"Yes," said Mrs. March, "or April, either. Talk about our east winds!"

"Oh, I'm sure they can't be worse than *our* winds," Mrs. Mandel returned caressingly.

"If we escape New York pneumonia," March laughed, "it will only be to fall a prey to New York malaria as soon as the frost is out of the ground."

"Oh, but you know," said Mrs. Mandel, "I think our malaria has really been slandered a little. It's more a matter of drainage—of plumbing. I don't believe it would be possible for malaria to get into *this* house, we've had it gone over so thoroughly."

Mrs. March said, while she tried to divine Mrs. Mandel's position from this statement, "It's certainly the first duty."

"If Mrs. March could have had her way, we should have had the drainage of our whole ward put in order," said her husband, "before we ventured to take a furnished apartment for the winter."

Mrs. Mandel looked discreetly at Mrs. March for permission to laugh at this, but at the same moment both ladies became preoccupied with a second rustling on the stairs.

Two tall, well-dressed young girls came in, and Mrs. Mandel introduced, "Miss Dryfoos, Mrs. March; and Miss Mela Dryfoos, Mr. March," she added, and the girls shook hands in their several ways with the Marches.

Miss Dryfoos had keen black eyes, and her hair was intensely black. Her face, but for the slight inward curve of the nose, was regular, and the smallness of her nose and of her mouth did not weaken her face, but gave it a curious effect of fierceness, of challenge. She had a large black fan in her hand, which she waved in talking, with a slow, watchful nervousness. Her sister was blonde, and had a profile like her brother's; but her chin was not so salient, and the weak look of the mouth was not corrected by the spirituality or the fervour of his eyes, though hers were of the same mottled blue. She dropped into the low seat beside Mrs. Mandel, and intertwined her fingers with those of the hand which Mrs. Mandel let her have. She smiled upon the Marches, while Miss Dryfoos watched them intensely, with her eyes first on one and then on the other, as if she did not mean to let any expression of theirs escape her.

"My mother will be down in a minute," she said to Mrs. March.

"I hope we're not disturbing her. It is so good of you to let us come in the evening," Mrs. March replied.

"Oh, not at all," said the girl. "We receive in the evening."

"When we *do* receive," Miss Mela put in. "We don't always get the chance to." She began a laugh, which she checked at a smile from Mrs. Mandel, which no one could have seen to be reproving.

Miss Dryfoos looked down at her fan, and looked up defiantly at Mrs. March. "I suppose you have hardly got settled. We were afraid we would disturb you when we called."

"Oh no! We were very sorry to miss your visit. We are quite settled in our new quarters. Of course, it's all very different from Boston."

"I hope it's more of a sociable place there," Miss Mela broke in again. "I never saw such an unsociable place as New York. We've been in this house three months, and I don't believe that if we stayed three years any of the neighbours would call."

"I fancy proximity doesn't count for much in New York," March suggested.

Mrs. Mandel said: "That's what I tell Miss Mela. But she is a very social nature, and can't reconcile herself to the fact."

"No, I can't," the girl pouted. "I think it was twice as much fun in Moffitt. I wish I was there now."

"Yes," said March, "I think there's a great deal more enjoyment in those smaller places. There's not so much going on in the way of public amusements, and so people make more of one another. There are not so many concerts, theatres, operas——"

"Oh, they've got a spendid opera-house in Moffitt. It's just grand," said Miss Mela.

"Have you been to the opera here, this winter?" Mrs. March asked of the elder girl.

She was glaring with a frown at her sister, and detached her eyes from her with an effort. "What did you say?" she demanded, with an absent bluntness. "Oh yes. Yes! We went once. Father took a box at the Metropolitan."

"Then you got a good dose of Wagner, I suppose?" said March.

"What?" asked the girl.

"I don't think Miss Dryfoos is very fond of Wagner's

music," Mrs. Mandel said. "I believe you are all great Wagnerites in Boston?"

"I'm a very bad Bostonian, Mrs. Mandel. I suspect myself of preferring Verdi," March answered.

Miss Dryfoos looked down at her fan again, and said, "I like Trovatore the best."

"It's an opera I never get tired of," said March, and Mrs. March and Mrs. Mandel exchanged a smile of compassion for his simplicity. He detected it, and added, "But I dare say I shall come down with the Wagner fever in time. I've been exposed to some malignant cases of it."

"That night we were there," said Miss Mela, "they had to turn the gas down all through one part of it, and the papers said the ladies were awful mad because they couldn't show their diamonds. I don't wonder, if they all had to pay as much for their boxes as we did. We had to pay sixty dollars." She looked at the Marches for their sensation at this expense.

March said: "Well, I think I shall take my box by the month, then. It must come cheaper, wholesale."

"Oh no, it don't," said the girl, glad to inform him. "The people that own their boxes, and that had to give fifteen or twenty thousand dollars apiece for them, have to pay sixty dollars a night whenever there's a performance, whether they go or not."

"Then I should go every night," March said.

"Most of the ladies were low neck——"

March interposed, "Well, I shouldn't go low *neck*."

The girl broke into a fondly approving laugh at his drolling. "Oh, I guess you love to train! Us girls wanted to go low neck, too; but father said we shouldn't, and mother said if we did she wouldn't come to the front of the box once. Well, she didn't, anyway. We might just as well 'a' gone low neck. She stayed back the whole time, and when they had that dance—the ballet, you know—she just shut her eyes. Well, Conrad didn't like that part much, either; but us girls and Mrs. Mandel, we brazened it out right in the front of the box. We were about the only ones there that went high neck. Conrad had to wear a swallow-tail; but father hadn't any, and he had to patch out with a white cravat. You couldn't see what he had on in the back o' the box, anyway."

Mrs. March looked at Miss Dryfoos, who was waving her fan more and more slowly up and down, and who, when she felt herself looked at, returned Mrs. March's smile, which she meant to be ingratiating and perhaps sympathetic, with a flash that made her start, and then ran her fierce eyes over March's face. "Here comes mother," she said, with a sort of breathlessness, as if speaking her thought aloud, and through the open door the Marches could see the old lady on the stairs.

She paused half-way down, and turning, called up: "Coonrod! Coonrod! You bring my shawl down with you."

Her daughter Mela called out to her, "Now, mother, Christine 'll give it to you for not sending Mike."

"Well, I don't know where he is, Mely, child," the mother answered back. "He ain't never around when he's wanted, and when he ain't, it seems like a body couldn't git shet of him, nohow."

"Well, you ought to ring for him," cried Miss Mela, enjoying the joke.

Her mother came in with a slow step; her head shook slightly as she looked about the room, perhaps from nervousness, perhaps from a touch of palsy. In either case the fact had a pathos which Mrs. March confessed in the affection with which she took her hard, dry, large, old hand when she was introduced to her, and in the sincerity which she put into the hope that she was well.

"I'm just middlin'," Mrs. Dryfoos replied. "I ain't never so well, nowadays. I tell fawther I don't believe it agrees with me very well here; but he says I'll git used to it. He's away now, out at Moffitt," she said to March, and wavered on foot a moment before she sank into a chair. She was a tall woman, who had been a beautiful girl, and her grey hair had a memory of blondeness in it like Lindau's, March noticed. She wore a simple silk gown, of a Quakerly grey, and she held a handkerchief folded square, as it had come from the laundress. Something like the Sabbath quiet of a little wooden meeting-house in thick Western woods expressed itself to him from her presence.

"Laws, mother!" said Miss Mela; "what you got that old thing on for? If I'd 'a' known you'd 'a' come down in *that*!"

"Coonrod said it was all right, Mely," said her mother.

Miss Mela explained to the Marches: "Mother was raised among the Dunkards, and she thinks it's wicked to wear anything but a grey silk even for dress up."

"You hain't never heared o' the Dunkards, I reckon," the old woman said to Mrs. March. "Some folks calls 'em the Beardy Men, because they don't never shave; and they wash feet like they do in the Testament. My uncle was one. He raised me."

"I guess pretty much everybody's a Beardy Man nowadays, if he *ain't* a Dunkard!"

Miss Mela looked round for applause of her sally, but March was saying to his wife: "It's a Pennsylvania German sect, I believe—something like the Quakers. I used to see them when I was a boy."

"Aren't they something like the Mennists?" asked Mrs. Mandel.

"They're good people," said the old woman, "and the world'd be a heap better off if there was more like 'em."

Her son came in and laid a soft shawl over her shoulders before he shook hands with the visitors. "I am glad you found your way here," he said to them.

Christine, who had been bending forward over her fan, now lifted herself up with a sigh and leaned back in her chair.

"I'm sorry my father isn't here," said the young man to Mrs. March. "He's never met you yet?"

"No; and I should like to see him. We hear a great deal about your father, you know, from Mr. Fulkerson."

"Oh, I hope you don't believe everything Mr. Fulkerson says about people," Mela cried. "He's the greatest person for carrying on when he gets going I ever saw. It makes Christine just as mad when him and mother get to talking about religion; she says she knows he don't care anything more about it than the man in the moon. I reckon he don't try it on much with father."

"Your fawther ain't ever been a perfessor," her mother interposed; "but he's always been a good church-goin' man."

"Not since we come to New York," retorted the girl.

"He's been all broke up since he come to New York," said the old woman, with an aggrieved look.

Mrs. Mandel attempted a diversion. "Have you heard any of our great New York preachers yet, Mrs. March?"

"No, I haven't," Mrs. March admitted; and she tried to imply by her candid tone that she intended to begin hearing them the very next Sunday.

"There are a great many things here," said Conrad, "to take your thoughts off the preaching that you hear in most of the churches. I think the city itself is preaching the best sermon all the time."

"I don't know that I understand you," said March.

Mela answered for him. "Oh, Conrad has got a lot of notions that nobody can understand. You ought to see the church he goes to when he does go. I'd about as lief go to a Catholic church myself; I don't see a bit o' difference. He's the greatest crony with one of their preachers; he dresses just like a priest, and he says he *is* a priest." She laughed for enjoyment of the fact, and her brother cast down his eyes.

Mrs. March, in her turn, tried to take from it the personal tone which the talk was always assuming. "Have you been to the fall exhibition?" she asked Christine; and the girl drew herself up out of the abstraction she seemed sunk in.

"The exhibition?" She looked at Mrs. Mandel.

"The pictures of the Academy, you know," Mrs. Mandel explained. "Where I wanted you to go the day you had your dress tried on."

"No; we haven't been yet. Is it good?" She had turned to Mrs. March again.

"I believe the fall exhibitions are never so good as the spring ones. But there are some good pictures."

"I don't believe I care much about pictures," said Christine. "I don't understand them."

"Ah, *that's* no excuse for not caring about them," said March lightly. "The painters themselves don't, half the time."

The girl looked at him with that glance at once defiant and appealing, insolent and anxious, which he had noticed before, especially when she stole it toward himself and his wife during her sister's babble. In the light of Fulkerson's history of the family, its origin and its ambition, he interpreted it to mean a sense of her sister's folly and an ignorant will to override his opinion of anything incongruous in themselves and their surroundings. He said to himself that she was deathly proud—too proud to try to palliate anything, but capable of anything that would put others under her feet. Her eyes seemed hopelessly to question his wife's social quality, and he fancied, with not unkindly interest, the inexperienced girl's doubt whether to treat them with much or little respect. He lost himself in fancies about her and her ideals, necessarily sordid, of her possibilities of suffering, of the triumphs and disappointments before her. Her sister would accept both with a lightness that would keep no trace of either; but in her they would sink lastingly deep. He came out of his reverie to find Mrs. Dryfoos saying to him in her hoarse voice—

"I think it's a shame, some of the pictur's a body sees in the winders. They say there's a law aginst them things; and if there is, I don't understand why the police don't take up them that paints 'em. I hear tell, since I been here, that there's women that goes to have pictur's took from them that way by men painters." The point seemed aimed at March, as if he were personally responsible for the scandal, and it fell with a silencing effect for the moment. Nobody seemed willing to take it up, and Mrs. Dryfoos went on, with an old woman's severity: "I say they ought to be all tarred and feathered and rode on a rail. They'd be drummed out of town in Moffitt."

Miss Mela said, with a crowing laugh: "I should think they would! And they wouldn't anybody go low neck to the opera-house there, either—not low neck the way they do here, anyway."

"And that pack of worthless hussies," her mother resumed, "that come out on the stage, and begun to kick——"

"Laws, mother!" the girl shouted, "I thought you said you had your eyes shut!"

All but these two simpler creatures were abashed at the indecorum of suggesting in words the common-places of the theatre and of art.

"Well, I did, Mely, as soon as I could *believe* my eyes. I don't know what they're doin' in all their churches, to let such things go on," said the old woman. "It's a sin and a shame, *I* think. Don't you, Coonrod?"

A ring at the door cut short whatever answer he was about to deliver.

"If it's going to be company, Coonrod," said his mother, making an effort to rise, "I reckon I better go upstairs."

"It's Mr. Fulkerson, I guess," said Conrad. "He thought he might come;" and at the mention of this light spirit Mrs. Dryfoos sank contentedly back in her chair, and a relaxation of their painful tension seemed to pass through the whole company. Conrad went to the door himself (the serving-man tentatively appeared some minutes later) and let in Fulkerson's cheerful voice before his cheerful person.

"Ah, how d'ye do, Conrad? Brought our friend, Mr. Beaton, with me," those within heard him say; and then, after a sound of putting off overcoats, they saw him fill the doorway, with his feet set square and his arms akimbo.

IX

"Ah! hello! hello!" Fulkerson said, in recognition of the Marches. "Regular gathering of the clans. How are you, Mrs. Dryfoos? How do you do, Mrs. Mandel, Miss Christine, Mela, Aunt Hitty, and all the folks? How you wuz?" He shook hands gaily all round, and took a chair next the old lady, whose hand he kept in his own, and left Conrad to introduce Beaton. But he would not let the shadow of Beaton's solemnity fall upon the company. He began to joke with Mrs. Dryfoos, and to match rheumatisms with her, and he included all the ladies in the range of appropriate pleasantries. "I've brought Mr. Beaton along to-night, and I want you to make him feel at home, like you do me, Mrs. Dryfoos. He hasn't got any rheumatism to speak of; but his parents live in Syracuse, and he's a kind of an orphan, and we've just adopted him down at the office. When you going to bring the young ladies down there, Mrs. Mandel, for a champagne lunch? I will have some hydro-Mela,* and Christine it, heigh? How's that for a little starter? We dropped in at your place a moment, Mrs. March, and gave the young folks a few pointers about their studies. My goodness! it does me good to see a boy like that of yours; business, from the word go; and your girl just scoops *my* youthful affections. She's a beauty, and I guess she's good too. Well, well, what a world it is! Miss Christine, won't you show Mr. Beaton that seal ring of yours? He knows about such things, and I brought him here to see it as much as anything. It's an intaglio I brought from the other side," he explained to Mrs. March, "and I guess you'll like to look at it. Tried to *give* it to the Dryfoos family, and when I couldn't, I sold it to 'em. Bound to see it on Miss Christine's hand somehow! Hold on! Let him see it where it belongs, first!"

He arrested the girl in the motion she made to take off the ring, and let her have the pleasure of showing her hand to the company with the ring on it. Then he left her to hear the painter's words about it, which he continued to deliver dissyllabically as he stood with her under a gas jet, twisting his elastic figure and bending his head over the ring.

"Well, Mely, child," Fulkerson went on, with an open travesty of her mother's habitual address, "and how are *you* getting along? Mrs. Mandel hold you up to the proprieties pretty strictly? Well, that's right. You know you'd be roaming all over the pasture if she didn't."

The girl gurgled out her pleasure in his funning, and everybody took him on his own ground of privileged character. He brought them all together in their friendliness for himself, and before the evening was over he had inspired

Mrs. Mandel to have them served with coffee, and had made both the girls feel that they had figured brilliantly in society, and that two young men had been devoted to them.

"Oh, I think he's just as lovely as he can live!" said Mela, as she stood a moment with her sister on the scene of her triumph, where the others had left them after the departure of their guests.

"Who?" asked Christine deeply. As she glanced down at her ring, her eyes burned with a softened fire. She had allowed Beaton to change it himself from the finger where she had worn it to the finger on which he said she ought to wear it. She did not know whether it was right to let him, but she was glad she had done it.

"Who? Mr. Fulkerson, goosie-poosie! Not that old stuck-up Mr. Beaton of yours!"

"He *is* proud," assented Christine, with a throb of exultation.

Beaton and Fulkerson went to the elevated station with the Marches; but the painter said he was going to walk home, and Fulkerson let him go alone.

"One way is enough for me," he explained. "When I walk up, I don't walk down. By-by, my son!" He began talking about Beaton to the Marches as they climbed the station stairs together. "That fellow puzzles me. I don't know anybody that I have such a desire to kick, and at the same time that I want to flatter up so much. Affect you that way?" he asked of March.

"Well, as far as the kicking goes, yes."

"And how is it with you, Mrs. March?"

"Oh, I want to flatter him up."

"No; really? Why?—Hold on! I've got the change."

Fulkerson pushed March away from the ticket-office window, and made them his guests, with the inexorable American hospitality, for the ride down-town. "Three!" he said to the ticket-seller; and when he had walked them before him out on the platform and dropped his tickets into the urn, he persisted in his inquiry, "Why?"

"Why, because you always want to flatter conceited

people, don't you?" Mrs. March answered, with a laugh.

"Do you? Yes, I guess you do. You think Beaton is conceited?"

"Well, *slightly*, Mr. Fulkerson."

"I guess you're partly right," said Fulkerson, with a sigh, so unaccountable in its connection that they all laughed.

"An ideal 'busted'?" March suggested.

"No, not that, exactly," said Fulkerson. "But I had a notion may be Beaton wasn't conceited all the time."

"Oh!" Mrs. March exulted, "nobody could be so conceited all the time as Mr. Beaton is most of the time. He must have moments of the direst modesty, when he'd be quite flattery-proof."

"Yes, that's what I mean. I guess that's what makes me want to kick him. He's left compliments on my hands that no decent man would."

"Oh! that's tragical," said March.

"Mr. Fulkerson," Mrs. March began, with change of subject in her voice, "who *is* Mrs. Mandel?"

"Who? What do you think of her?" he rejoined. "I'll tell you about her when we get in the cars. *Look* at that thing! Ain't it beautiful?"

They leaned over the track, and looked up at the next station, where the train, just starting, throbbed out the flame-shot steam into the white moonlight.

"The most beautiful thing in New York—the one always and certainly beautiful thing here," said March; and his wife sighed, "Yes, yes." She clung to him, and remained rapt by the sight till the train drew near, and then pulled him back in a panic.

"Well, there ain't really much to tell about her," Fulkerson resumed, when they were seated in the car. "She's an invention of mine."

"Of yours?" cried Mrs. March.

"Of course!" exclaimed her husband.

"Yes—at least in her present capacity. She sent me a story for the syndicate, back in July some time, along about the time I first met old Dryfoos here. It was a little too long for my purpose, and I thought I could explain better how I wanted it cut in a call than I could in a letter. She gave a Brooklyn address, and I went to see her. I found her," said Fulkerson, with a vague defiance, "a perfect lady. She was living with an aunt over there; and she had seen better days, when she was a girl, and worse ones afterward. I don't mean to say her husband was a bad fellow; I guess he was pretty good; he was her music-teacher; she met him in Germany, and they got married there, and got through her property before they came over here. Well, she didn't strike me like a person that could make much headway in literature. Her story was well enough, but it hadn't much sand in it; kind of—well, academic, you know. I told her so, and she understood, and cried a little; but she did the best she could with the thing, and I took it and syndicated it. She kind of stuck in my mind, and the first time I went to see the Dryfooses— they were stopping at a sort of family hotel then till they could find a house——" Fulkerson broke off altogether, and said, "I don't know as I know just how the Dryfooses struck you, Mrs. March?"

"Can't you imagine?" she answered, with a kindly smile.

"Yes; but I don't believe I could guess how they would have struck you last summer when I first saw them. My! oh my! *there* was the native earth for you. Mely is a pretty wild colt now, but you ought to have seen her before she was broken to harness. And Christine? Ever see that black leopard they got up there in the Central Park? That was Christine. Well, I saw what they wanted. They all saw it— nobody is a fool in all directions, and the Dryfooses are in their right senses a good deal of the time. Well, to cut a long story short, I got Mrs. Mandel to take 'em in hand—the old lady as well as the girls. She was a born lady, and always lived like one till she saw Mandel; and that something academic that killed her for a writer was just the very thing for them. She knows the world well enough to know just how much polish they can take on, and she don't try to put on a bit more. See?"

"Yes, I can see," said Mrs. March.

"Well, she took hold at once, as ready as a hospital-trained nurse; and there ain't anything readier on *this* planet. She runs the whole concern, socially and economically, takes all the care of house-keeping off the old lady's hands, and goes round with the girls. By-the-by, I'm going to take my meals at your widow's, March, and Conrad's going to have his lunch there. I'm sick of browsing about."

"Mr. March's *widow*?" said his wife, looking at him with provisional severity.

"I *have* no widow, Isabel," he said, "and never expect to have, till I leave you in the enjoyment of my life insurance. I suppose Fulkerson means the lady with the daughter, who wanted to take us to board."

"Oh yes. How are they getting on, I do wonder?" Mrs. March asked of Fulkerson.

"Well, they've got one family to board; but it's a small one. I guess they'll pull through. They didn't want to take any day boarders at first, the widow said; I guess they have had to come to it."

"Poor things!" sighed Mrs. March. "I hope they'll go back to the country."

"Well, I don't know. When you've once tasted New York—— You wouldn't go back to Boston, would you?"

"Instantly."

Fulkerson laughed out a tolerant incredulity.

X

BEATON lit his pipe when he found himself in his room, and sat down before the dull fire in his grate to think. It struck him there was a dull fire in his heart a great deal like it, and he worked out a fanciful analogy with the coals, still alive, and the ashes creeping over them, and the dead clay and cinders. He felt sick of himself, sick of his life and of all his works. He was angry with Fulkerson for having got him into that art department of his, for having bought him up; and he was bitter at fate because he had been obliged to use the money to pay some pressing debts, and had not been able to return the check his father had sent him. He pitied his poor old father; he ached with compassion for him; and he set his teeth and snarled with contempt through them for his own baseness. This was the kind of world it was; but he washed his hands of it. The fault was in human nature, and he reflected with pride that he had at least not invented human nature; he had not sunk so low as that yet. The notion amused him; he thought he might get a Satanic epigram out of it some way. But in the meantime that girl, that wild animal, she kept visibly, tangibly before him; if he put out his hand he might touch hers, he might pass his arm round her waist. In Paris, in a set he knew there, what an effect she would be with that look of hers, and that beauty, all out of drawing! They would recognise the flame quality in her. He imagined a joke about her being a fiery spirit, or nymph, naiad, whatever, from one of her native gas wells. He began to sketch on a bit of paper from the table at his elbow vague lines that veiled and revealed a level, dismal landscape, and a vast flame against an empty sky, and a shape out of the flame that took on a likeness, and floated detached from it. The sketch ran up the left side of the sheet and stretched across it. Beaton laughed out. Pretty good to let Fulkerson have that for the cover of his first number! In black and red it would be effective; it would catch the eye from the news stands. He made a motion to throw it on the fire, but held it back, and slid it into the table drawer, and smoked on. He saw the dummy with the other sketch in the open drawer, which he had brought away from Fulkerson's in the morning and slipped in there, and he took it out and looked at it. He made some criticisms in line with his pencil on it, correcting the drawing here and there, and then he respected it a little more, though he still smiled at the feminine quality—a young lady quality.

In spite of his experience the night he called upon the Leightons, Beaton could not believe that Alma no longer cared for him. She played at having forgotten him admirably, but he knew that a few months before she had been very mindful of him. He knew he had neglected them since they came to New York, where he had led them to expect interest, if not attention; but he was used to neglecting people, and he was somewhat less used to being punished for it—punished and forgiven. He felt that Alma had punished him so thoroughly that she ought to have been satisfied with her work and to have forgiven him in her heart afterward. He bore no resentment after the first tingling moments were past; he rather admired her for it; and he would have been ready to go back half an hour later, and accept pardon, and be on the footing of last summer again. Even now he debated with himself whether it was too late to call; but decidedly a quarter to ten seemed late. The next day he determined never to call upon the Leightons again; but he had no reason for this; it merely came into a transitory scheme of conduct, of retirement from the society of women altogether; and after dinner he went round to see them.

He asked for the ladies, and they all three received him, Alma not without a surprise that intimated itself to him, and her mother with no appreciable relenting; Miss Woodburn, with the needlework which she found easier to be voluble over than a book, expressed in her welcome a neutrality both cordial to Beaton and loyal to Alma.

"Is it snowing out-do's?" she asked briskly, after the greetings were transacted. "Mah goodness!" she said, in answer to his apparent surprise at the question. "Ah mahght as well have stayed in the Soath, for all the winter Ah have seen in New York yet."

"We don't often have snow much before New-Year's," said Beaton.

"Miss Woodburn is wild for a real Northern winter," Mrs. Leighton explained.

"The othah naght Ah woke up and looked oat of the window and saw all the roofs covered with snow, and it turned oat to be nothing but moonlaght. I was never so disappointed in mah lahfe," said Miss Woodburn.

"If you'll come to St. Barnaby next summer, you shall have all the winter you want," said Alma.

"I can't let you slander St. Barnaby in that way," said Beaton, with the air of wishing to be understood as meaning more than he said.

"Yes?" returned Alma coolly. "I didn't know you were so fond of the climate."

"I never think of it as a climate. It's a landscape. It doesn't matter whether it's hot or cold."

"With the thermometer twenty below, you'd find that it mattered," Alma persisted.

"You don't mean it goes doan to that in the summah?" Miss Woodburn interposed.

"Well, not before the Fourth of the July after," Alma admitted.

"Is that the way you feel about St. Barnaby too, Mrs. Leighton?" Beaton asked, with affected desolation.

"I shall be glad enough to go back in the summer," Mrs. Leighton conceded.

"And I should be glad to go now," said Beaton, looking at Alma. He had the dummy of *Every Other Week* in his hand, and he saw Alma's eyes wandering toward it whenever he glanced at her. "I should be glad to go anywhere to get out of a job I've undertaken," he continued, to Mrs. Leighton. "They're going to start some sort of a new illustrated magazine, and they've got me in for their art department. I'm not fit for it; I'd like to run away. Don't you want to advise me a little, Mrs. Leighton? You know how much I value your taste, and I'd like to have you look at the design for the cover of the first number: they're going to have a different one for every number. I don't know whether you'll agree with me, but I think this is rather nice."

He faced the dummy round, and then laid it on the table before Mrs. Leighton, pushing some of her work aside to make room for it, and standing over her while she bent forward to look at it.

Alma kept her place, away from the table.

"Mah goodness! Ho' exciting!" said Miss Woodburn. "May anybody look?"

"Everybody," said Beaton.

"Well, isn't it perfectly chawming!" Miss Woodburn exclaimed. "Come and look at this, Miss Leighton," she called to Alma, who reluctantly approached.

"What lines are these?" Mrs. Leighton asked, pointing to Beaton's pencil scratches.

"They're suggestions of modification," he replied.

"I don't think they improve it much. What do you think, Alma?"

"Oh, I don't know," said the girl, constraining her voice to an effect of indifference, and glancing carelessly down at the sketch. "The design might be improved; but I don't think those suggestions would do it."

"They're mine," said Beaton, fixing his eyes upon her with a beautiful sad dreaminess that he knew he could put into them; he spoke with a dreamy remoteness of tone: his wind-harp stop, Wetmore called it.

"I supposed so," said Alma calmly.

"Oh, mah goodness!" cried Miss Woodburn. "Is that the way you awtusts talk to each othah? Well, Ah'm glad Ah'm not an awtust—unless I could do all the talking."

"Artists cannot tell a fib," Alma said, "or even act one," and she laughed in Beaton's upturned face.

He did not unbend his dreamy gaze. "You're quite right. The suggestions are stupid."

Alma turned to Miss Woodburn: "You hear? Even when we speak of our own work."

"Ah nevah hoad anything lahke it!"

"And the design itself?" Beaton persisted.

"Oh, I'm not an art editor," Alma answered, with a laugh of exultant evasion.

A tall, dark, grave-looking man of fifty, with a swarthy face, and iron-grey moustache and imperial and goatee, entered the room. Beaton knew the type; he had been through Virginia sketching for one of the illustrated papers, and he had seen such men in Richmond. Miss Woodburn hardly needed to say, "May Ah introduce you to mah fathaw, Co'nel Woodburn, Mr. Beaton?"

The men shook hands, and Colonel Woodburn said, in that soft, gentle, slow Southern voice without our Northern contractions: "I am very glad to meet you, sir; happy to make yo' acquaintance. Do not move, madam," he said to Mrs. Leighton, who made a deprecatory motion to let him pass to the chair beyond her; "I can find my way." He bowed a bulk that did not lend itself readily to the devotion, and picked up the ball of yarn she had let drop out of her lap in half rising. "Yo' worsteds, madam."

"Yarn, yarn, Colonel Woodburn!" Alma shouted. "You're quite incorrigible. A spade is a spade!"

"But sometimes it is a trump, my dear young lady," said the Colonel, with unabated gallantry; "and when yo' mothah uses yarn, it is worsteds. But I respect worsteds even under the name of yarn: our ladies—my own mothah and sistahs—had to knit the socks we wore—all we could get—in the woe."

"Yes, and aftah the woe," his daughter put in. "The knitting has not stopped yet in some places. Have you been much in the Soath, Mr. Beaton?"

Beaton explained just how much.

"Well, sir," said the Colonel, "then you have seen a country making gigantic struggles to retrieve its losses, sir. The south is advancing with enormous strides, sir."

"Too fast for some of us to keep up," said Miss Woodburn, in an audible aside. "The pace in Charlottesboag is pofectly killing, and we had to drop oat into a slow place like New York."

"The progress in the South is material now," said the Colonel; "and those of us whose interests are in another direction find ourselves—isolated—isolated, sir. The intellectual centres are still in the No'th, sir; the great cities draw the mental activity of the country to them, sir. Necessarily New York is the metropolis."

"Oh, everything comes here," said Beaton, impatient of the elder's ponderosity. Another sort of man would have sympathised with the Southerner's willingness to talk of himself, and led him on to speak of his plans and ideals. But

152

the sort of man that Beaton was could not do this; he put up the dummy into the wrapper he had let drop on the floor beside him, and tied it round with string while Colonel Woodburn was talking. He got to his feet with the words he spoke, and offered Mrs. Leighton his hand.

"Must you go?" she asked, in surprise.

"I am on my way to a reception," he said. She had noticed that he was in evening dress; and now she felt the vague hurt that people invited nowhere feel in the presence of those who are going somewhere. She did not feel it for herself, but for her daughter; and she knew Alma would not have let her feel it if she could have prevented it. But Alma had left the room for a moment, and she tacitly indulged this sense of injury in her behalf.

"Please say good night to Miss Leighton for me," Beaton continued. He bowed to Miss Woodburn, "Good night, Miss Woodburn," and to her father bluntly, "Good night."

"Good night, sir," said the Colonel, with a sort of severe suavity.

"Oh, isn't he chawming!" Miss Woodburn whispered to Mrs. Leighton when Beaton left the room.

Alma spoke to him in the hall without. "You knew that was my design Mr. Beaton. Why did you bring it?"

"Why?" He looked at her in gloomy hesitation. Then he said: "You know why. I wished to talk it over with you, to serve you, please you, get back your good opinion. But I've done neither the one nor the other; I've made a mess of the whole thing."

Alma interrupted him. "Has it been accepted?"

"It will be accepted, if you will let it."

"Let it?" she laughed. "I shall be delighted." She saw him swayed a little toward her. "It's a matter of business, isn't it?"

"Purely. Good night."

When Alma returned to the room, Colonel Woodburn was saying to Mrs. Leighton: "I do not contend that it is impossible, madam, but it is very difficult in a thoroughly commercialised society, like yours, to have the feelings of a gentleman. How can a business man, whose prosperity, whose earthly salvation, necessarily lies in the adversity of some one else, be delicate and chivalrous, or even honest? If we could have had time to perfect our system at the South, to eliminate what was evil and develop what was good in it, we should have had a perfect system. But the virus of commercialism was in us too; it forbade us to make the best of a divine institution, and tempted us to make the worst. Now the curse is on the whole country; the dollar is the measure of every value, the stamp of every success. What does not sell is a failure; and what sells succeeds."

"The hobby is oat, mah deah," said Miss Woodburn, in an audible aside to Alma.

"Were you speaking of me, Colonel Woodburn?" Alma asked.

"Surely not, my dear young lady."

"But he's been saying that awtusts are just as greedy aboat money as anybody," said his daughter.

"The law of commercialism is on everything in a commercial society," the Colonel explained, softening the tone in which his convictions were presented. "The final reward of art is money, and not the pleasure of creating."

"Perhaps they would be willing to take it all oat in that, if othah people would let them pay their bills in the pleasure of creating," his daughter teased.

"They are helpless, like all the rest," said her father, with the same deference to her as to other women. "I do not blame them."

"Oh, mah goodness! Didn't you say, sir, that Mr. Beaton had bad manners?"

Alma relieved a confusion which he seemed to feel in reference to her. "Bad manners? He has no manners! That is, when he's himself. He has pretty good ones when he's somebody else."

Miss Woodburn began, "Oh, mah——" and then stopped herself. Alma's mother looked at her with distressful question, but the girl seemed perfectly cool and contented; and she gave her mind provisionally to a point suggested by Colonel Woodburn's talk.

"Still, I can't believe it was right to hold people in slavery, to whip them and sell them. It never did seem right to me," she added, in apology for her extreme sentiments to the gentleness of her adversary.

"I quite agree with you, madam," said the Colonel. "Those were the abuses of the institution. But if we had not been vitiated on the one hand and threatened on the other by the spirit of commercialism from the North—and from Europe too—those abuses could have been eliminated, and the institution developed in the direction of the mild patriarchalism of the divine intention." The Colonel hitched his chair, which figured a hobby careering upon its hind legs, a little toward Mrs. Leighton, and the girls approached their heads, and began to whisper; they fell deferentially silent when the Colonel paused in his argument, and went on again when he went on.

At last they heard Mrs. Leighton saying, "And have you heard from the publishers about your book yet?"

Then Miss Woodburn cut in, before her father could answer: "The coase of commercialism is on that too. They are trahing to fahnd oat whethah it will pay."

"And they are right—quite right," said the Colonel. "There is no longer any other criterion; and even a work that attacks the system must be submitted to the tests of the system."

"The system won't accept destruction on any othah tomes," said Miss Woodburn demurely.

XI

AT the reception, where two men in livery stood aside to let him pass up the outside steps of the house, and two more helped him off with his overcoat indoors, and a fifth miscalled his name into the drawing-room, the Syracuse stonecutter's son met the niece of Mrs. Horn, and began at once to tell her about his evening at the Dryfooses'. He was in very good spirits, for so far as he could have been elated or depressed by his parting with Alma Leighton he had been elated; she had not treated his impudence with the contempt that he felt it deserved; she must still be fond of him; and the warm sense of this, by operation of an obscure but well-recognised law of the masculine being, disposed him to be rather fond of Miss Vance. She was a slender girl, whose semi-æsthetic dress flowed about her with an accentuation of her long forms, and redeemed them from censure by the very frankness with which it confessed them; nobody could have said that Margaret Vance was too tall. Her pretty little head, which she had an effect of choosing to have little in the same spirit of judicious defiance, had a good deal of reading in it; she was proud to know literary and artistic fashions as well as society fashions. She liked being singled out by an exterior distinction so obvious as Beaton's, and she listened with sympathetic interest to his account of those people. He gave their natural history reality by drawing upon his own; he reconstructed their plebeian past from the experiences of his childhood and his youth of the pre-Parisian period; and he had a pang of suicidal joy in insulting their ignorance of the world.

"What different kinds of people you meet!" said the girl at last, with an envious sigh. Her reading had enlarged the bounds of her imagination, if not her knowledge; the novels nowadays dealt so much with very common people, and made them seem so very much more worth while than the people one met.

She said something like this to Beaton. He answered: "You can meet the people I'm talking of very easily, if you want to take the trouble. It's what they came to New York for. I fancy it's the great ambition of their lives to be met."

"Oh yes," said Miss Vance fashionably, and looked down; then she looked up and said intellectually: "Don't you think it's a great pity? How much better for them to have stayed where they were and what they were!"

"Then you could never have had any chance of meeting

them," said Beaton. "I don't suppose you intend to go out to the gas country?"

"No," said Miss Vance, amused. "Not that I shouldn't . like to go."

"What a daring spirit! You ought to be on the staff of *Every Other Week*," said Beaton.

"The staff—*Every Other Week*? What is it?"

"The missing link; the long-felt want of a tie between the Arts and the Dollars." Beaton gave her a very picturesque, a very dramatic sketch of the theory, the purpose, and the *personnel* of the new enterprise.

Miss Vance understood too little about business of any kind to know how it differed from other enterprises of its sort. She thought it was delightful; she thought Beaton must be glad to be part of it, though he had represented himself so bored, so injured, by Fulkerson's insisting upon having him. "And is it a secret? Is it a thing not to be spoken of?"

"*Tutt' altro!** Fulkerson will be enraptured to have it spoken of in society. He would pay any reasonable bill for the advertisement."

"What a delightful creature! Tell him it shall all be spent in charity."

"He would like that. He would get two paragraphs out of the fact, and your name would go into the 'Literary Notes' of all the Newspapers."

"Oh, but I shouldn't want my *name* used!" cried the girl, half horrified into fancying the situation real.

"Then you'd better not say anything about *Every Other Week*. Fulkerson is preternaturally unscrupulous."

March began to think so too, at times. He was perpetually suggesting changes in the make-up of the first number, with a view to its greater vividness of effect. One day he came in and said: "This thing isn't going to have any sort of get up and howl about it, unless you have a paper in the first number going for Bevans's novels. Better get Maxwell to do it."

"Why, I thought you liked Bevans's novels?"

"So I do; but where the good of *Every Other Week* is

concerned I am a Roman father. The popular gag is to abuse
Bevans, and Maxwell is the man to do it. There hasn't been
a new magazine started for the last three years that hasn't
had an article from Maxwell in its first number cutting
Bevans all to pieces. If people don't see it, they'll think
Every Other Week is some old thing."

March did not know whether Fulkerson was joking or not.
He suggested, "Perhaps they'll think it's an old thing if they
do see it."

"Well, get somebody else, then; or else get Maxwell to
write under an assumed name. Or—I forgot! He'll be
anonymous under our system anyway. Now there ain't a
more popular racket for us to work in that first number than
a good, swingeing attack on Bevans. People read his books
and quarrel over 'em, and the critics are all against him, and
a regular flaying, with salt and vinegar rubbed in afterward,
will tell more with people who like good old-fashioned fiction
than anything else. *I* like Bevans's things, but, dad burn it!
when it comes to that first number, I'd offer up anybody."

"What an immoral little wretch you are, Fulkerson!"
said March, with a laugh.

Fulkerson appeared not to be very strenuous about the
attack on the novelist. "Say!" he called out gaily, "what
should you think of a paper defending the late lamented
system of slavery?"

"What *do* you mean, Fulkerson?" asked March, with a
puzzled smile.

Fulkerson braced his knees against his desk, and pushed
himself back, but kept his balance to the eye by canting his
hat sharply forward. "There's an old cock over there at the
widow's that's written a book to prove that slavery was and
is the only solution of the labour problem. He's a Southerner."

"I should imagine," March assented.

"He's got it on the brain that if the South could have been
let alone by the commercial spirit and the pseudo-phil-
anthropy of the North, it would have worked out slavery
into a perfectly ideal condition for the labourer, in which he

would have been insured against want, and protected in all his personal rights by the state. He read the introduction to me last night. I didn't catch on to all the points—his daughter's an awfully pretty girl, and I was carrying that fact in my mind all the time too, you know—but that's about the gist of it."

"Seems to regard it as a lost opportunity?" said March.

"Exactly! What a mighty catchy title, heigh? Look well on the title-page."

"Well written?"

"I reckon so; I don't know. The Colonel read it mighty eloquently."

"It mightn't be such bad business," said March, in a muse. "Could you get me a sight of it without committing yourself?"

"If the Colonel hasn't sent it off to another publisher this morning. He just got it back with thanks yesterday. He likes to keep it travelling."

"Well, try it. I've a notion it might be a curious thing."

"Look here, March," said Fulkerson, with the effect of taking a fresh hold; "I *wish* you could let me have one of those New York things of yours for the first number. After all, that's going to be the great card."

"I couldn't, Fulkerson; I couldn't, really. I want to philosophise the material, and I'm too new to it all yet. I don't want to do merely superficial sketches."

"Of course! Of course! I understand that. Well, I don't want to hurry you. Seen that old fellow of yours yet? I think we ought to have that translation in the first number; don't you? We want to give 'em a notion of what we're going to do in that line."

"Yes," said March; "and I was going out to look up Lindau this morning. I've inquired at Maroni's, and he hasn't been there for several days. I've some idea perhaps he's sick. But they gave me his address, and I'm going to see."

"Well, that's right. We want the first number to be the key-note in every way."

March shook his head. "You can't make it so. The first

number is bound to be a failure always, as far as the representative character goes. It's invariably the case. Look at the first numbers of all the things you've seen started. They're experimental, almost amateurish, and necessarily so, not only because the men that are making them up are comparatively inexperienced like ourselves, but because the material sent them to deal with is more or less consciously tentative. People send their adventurous things to a new periodical because the whole thing is an adventure. I've noticed that quality in all the volunteer contributions; it's in the articles that have been done to order even. No; I've about made up my mind that if we can get one good striking paper into the first number that will take people's minds off the others, we shall be doing all we can possibly hope for. I should like," March added, less seriously, "to make up three numbers ahead, and publish the third one first."

Fulkerson dropped forward and struck his fist on the desk. "It's a first-rate idea. Why not *do* it?"

March laughed. "Fulkerson, I don't believe there's any quackish thing you wouldn't do in this cause. From time to time I'm thoroughly ashamed of being connected with such a charlatan."

Fulkerson struck his hat sharply backward. "Ah, dad burn it! To give that thing the right kind of start I'd walk up and down Broadway between two boards, with the title-page of *Every Other Week* facsimiled on one and my name and address on the——" He jumped to his feet and shouted, "March, I'll *do* it!"

"*What?*"

"I'll hire a lot of fellows to make mud-turtles of themselves, and I'll have a lot of big facsimiles of the title-page, and I'll paint the town red!"

March looked aghast at him. "Oh, come, now, Fulkerson!"

"I mean it. I was in London when a new man had taken hold of the old *Cornhill*,* and they were trying to boom it, and they had a procession of these mud-turtles that reached from Charing Cross to Temple Bar. '*Cornhill Magazine*. Sixpence. Not a dull page in it.' I said to myself then that it was the livest thing I ever saw. I respected the man that did that thing from the bottom of my heart. I wonder I ever forgot it. But it shows what a shaky thing the human mind is at its best."

"You infamous mountebank!" said March, with great amusement at Fulkerson's access; "you call that congeries of advertising instincts of yours the human mind at its best? Come, don't be so diffident, Fulkerson. Well, I'm off to find Lindau, and when I come back I hope Mr. Dryfoos will have you under control. I don't suppose you'll be quite sane again till after the first number is out. Perhaps public opinion will sober you then."

"Confound it, March! How do you think they *will* take it? I swear I'm getting so nervous I don't know half the time which end of me is up. I believe if we don't get that thing out by the first of February it'll be the death of me."

"Couldn't wait till Washington's Birthday? I was thinking it would give the day a kind of distinction, and strike the public imagination, if——"

"No, I'll be dogged if I could!" Fulkerson lapsed more and more into the parlance of his early life in this season of strong excitement. "I believe if Beaton lags any on the art-leg I'll kill him."

"Well, *I* shouldn't mind your killing Beaton," said March tranquilly, as he went out.

He went over to Third Avenue and took the Elevated down to Chatham Square. He found the variety of people in the car as unfailingly entertaining as ever. He rather preferred the east side to the west side lines, because they offered more nationalities, conditions, and characters to his inspection. They draw not only from the uptown American region, but from all the vast hive of populations swarming between them and the East River. He had found that, according to the hour, American husbands going to and from business, and American wives going to and from shopping, prevailed on the Sixth Avenue road, and that the most picturesque admixture to these familiar aspects of human nature were the brilliant eyes and complexions of the American Hebrews, who otherwise contributed to the effect of well-clad comfort and citizen-self-satisfaction of the crowd. Now and then he had found himself in a car mostly filled with Neapolitans from the constructions far up the line, where he had read how they are worked and fed and housed like beasts; and listening to the jargon of their unintelligible dialect, he had occasion for pensive question within himself as to what notion these poor animals formed of a free republic from their experience of life under its conditions; and whether they found them practically very different from those of the immemorial brigandage and enforced complicity with rapine under which they had been born. But, after all, this was an infrequent effect, however massive, of travel on the west side, whereas the east offered him continual entertainment in like sort. The sort was never quite so squalid. For short distances the lowest poverty, the hardest pressed labour, must walk; but March never entered a car without encountering some interesting shape of shabby adversity, which was almost always adversity of foreign birth. New York is still popularly supposed to be in the control of the Irish, but March noticed in these east side travels of his what must strike every observer returning to the city after a prolonged absence: the numerical subordination of the dominant race. If they do not out-vote them, the people of Germanic, of Slavonic, of Pelasgic, of Mongolian stock out-number the prepotent Celts; and March seldom found his speculation centred upon one of these. The small eyes, the high cheeks, the broad noses, the puff lips, the bare, cue-filleted* skulls, of Russians, Poles, Czechs, Chinese; the furtive glitter of Italians; the blonde dulness of Germans; the cold quiet of Scandinavians—fire under ice—were aspects that he identified, and that gave him abundant suggestion for the personal histories he constructed, and for the more public-spirited reveries in which he dealt with the future economy of our heterogeneous commonwealth. It must be owned that he did not take much trouble about this; what these poor people were thinking, hoping, fearing, enjoying, suffering; just where and how they lived; who and what they individually were—these were the matters of his waking dreams as he stared hard at them, while the train raced further into the gay ugliness—the shapeless, graceless, reckless picturesqueness of the Bowery.

There were certain signs, certain façades, certain audacities of the prevailing hideousness that always amused him in that uproar to the eye which the strident forms and colours made. He was interested in the insolence with which the railway had drawn its erasing line across the Corinthian front of an old theatre, almost grazing its fluted pillars, and flouting its dishonoured pediment. The colossal effigies of the fat women and the tuft-headed Circassian* girls of cheap museums; the vistas of shabby cross streets; the survival of an old hip-roofed house here and there at their angles; the Swiss châlet, histrionic decorativeness of the stations in prospect or retrospect; the vagaries of the lines that narrowed together or stretched apart according to the width of the avenue, but always in wanton disregard of the life that dwelt, and bought and sold, and rejoiced or sorrowed, and clattered or crawled, around, below, above—were features of the frantic panorama that perpetually touched his sense of humour and moved his sympathy. Accident and then exigency seemed the forces at work to this extraordinary effect; the play of energies as free and planless as those that force the forest from the soil to the sky; and then the fierce struggle for survival, with the stronger life persisting over the deformity, the mutilation, the destruction, the decay of the weaker. The whole at moments seemed to him lawless, godless; the absence of intelligent, comprehensive purpose in the huge disorder, and the violent struggle to subordinate the result to the greater good, penetrated with its dumb appeal the consciousness of a man who had always been too self-enwrapt to perceive the chaos to which the individual selfishness must always lead.

But there was still nothing definite, nothing better than

a vague discomfort, however poignant, in his half recognition of such facts; and he descended the station stairs at Chatham Square, with a sense of the neglected opportunities of painters in that locality. He said to himself that if one of those fellows were to see in Naples that turmoil of cars, trucks, and teams* of every sort, intershot with foot-passengers going and coming to and from the crowded pavements, under the web of the railroad tracks overhead, and amidst the spectacular approach of the streets that open into the square, he would have it down in his sketch-book at once. He decided simultaneously that his own local studies must be illustrated, and that he must come with the artist and show him just which bits to do, not knowing that the two arts can never approach the same material from the same point. He thought he would particularly like his illustrator to render the Dickensy, cockneyish quality of the shabby-genteel ballad-seller of whom he stopped to ask his way to the street where Lindau lived, and whom he instantly perceived to be, with his stock in trade, the sufficient object of an entire study by himself. He had his ballads strung singly upon a cord against the house wall, and held down in piles on the pavement with stones and blocks of wood. Their control in this way intimated a volatility which was not perceptible in their sentiment. They were mostly tragical or doleful: some of them dealt with the wrongs of the working-man; others appealed to a gay experience of the high seas; but vastly the greater part to memories and associations of an Irish origin; some still uttered the poetry of plantation life in the artless accents of the end-man.* Where they trusted themselves, with syntax that yielded promptly to any exigency of rhythmic art, to the ordinary American speech, it was to strike directly for the affections, to celebrate the domestic ties, and, above all, to embalm the memories of angel and martyr mothers, whose dissipated sons deplored their sufferings too late. March thought this not at all a bad thing in them; he smiled in patronage of their simple pathos; he paid the tribute of a laugh when the poet turned, as he sometimes did, from his conception of angel and martyr motherhood, and portrayed the mother in her more familiar phases of virtue and duty, with the retributive shingle* or slipper in her hand. He bought a pocketful of this literature, popular in a sense which the most successful book can never be, and enlisted the ballad vendor so deeply in the effort to direct him to Lindau's dwelling by the best way that he neglected another customer, till a sarcasm on his absent-mindedness stung him to retort, "I'm a-trying to answer a gentleman a civil question; that's where the absent-minded comes in."

It seemed for some reason to be a day of leisure with the Chinese dwellers in Mott Street,* which March had been advised to take first. They stood about the tops of basement stairs, and walked two and two along the dirty pavement, with their little hands tucked into their sleeves across their breasts, aloof in immaculate cleanliness from the filth around them, and scrutinising the scene with that cynical sneer of faint surprise to which all aspects of our civilisation seem to move their superiority. Their numbers gave character to the street, and rendered not them, but what was foreign to them, strange there; so that March had a sense of missionary quality in the old Catholic church, built long before their incursion was dreamt of. It seemed to have come to them there, and he fancied in the statued saint that looked down from its façade something not so much tolerant as tolerated, something propitiatory, almost deprecative. It was a fancy, of course; the street was sufficiently peopled with Christian children, at any rate, swarming and shrieking at their games; and presently a Christian mother appeared, pushed along by two policemen on a handcart, with a gelatinous tremor over the paving and a gelatinous jouncing at the curb-stones. She lay with her face to the sky, sending up an inarticulate lamentation; but the indifference of the officers forbade the notion of tragedy in her case. She was perhaps a local celebrity; the children left off their games, and ran gaily trooping after her; even the young fellow and young girl exchanging playful blows in a robust flirtation at the corner of a liquor store suspended their scuffle with a pleased interest as she passed. March understood the unwillingness of the poor to leave the worst conditions in the city for comfort and plenty in the country when he reflected upon this dramatic incident, one of many no doubt which daily occur to entertain them in such streets. A small town could rarely offer anything comparable to it, and the country never. He said that if life appeared so hopeless to him as it must to the dwellers in that neighbourhood he should not himself be willing to quit its distractions, its alleviations, for the vague promise of unknown good in the distance somewhere.

But what charm could such a man as Lindau find in such a place? It could not be that he lived there because he was too poor to live elsewhere: with a shutting of the heart, March refused to believe this as he looked round on the abounding evidences of misery, and guiltily remembered his neglect of his old friend. Lindau could probably find as cheap a lodging in some decenter part of the town; and in fact there was some amelioration of the prevailing squalor in the quieter street which he turned into from Mott.

A woman with a tied-up face of toothache opened the door for him when he pulled, with a shiver of foreboding, the bell knob, from which a yard of rusty crape dangled. But it was not Lindau who was dead, for the woman said he was at home, and sent March stumbling up the four or five dark flights of stairs that led to his tenement. It was quite at the top of the house, and when March obeyed the German-English "Komm!" that followed his knock, he found himself in a kitchen where a meagre breakfast was scattered in stale fragments on the table before the stove. The place was bare and cold; a half-empty beer bottle scarcely gave it a convivial air. On the left from this kitchen was a room with a bed in it, which seemed also to be a cobbler's shop: on the right, through a door that stood ajar, came the German-English voice again, saying this time, "Hier!"

XII

MARCH pushed the door open into a room like that on the left, but with a writing-desk instead of a cobbler's bench, and a bed, where Lindau sat propped up, with a coat over his shoulders and a skull-cap on his head, reading a book, from which he lifted his eyes to stare blankly over his spectacles at March. His hairy old breast showed through the night-shirt, which gaped apart; the stump of his left arm lay upon the book to keep it open.

"Ah, my tear yo'ng friendt! Passil! Marge! Iss it you?" he called out joyously, the next moment.

"Why, are you sick, Lindau?" March anxiously scanned his face in taking his hand.

Lindau laughed. "No; I'm all righdt. Only a lidtle lazy, and a lidtle eggonomigal. Idt's jeaper to stay in pedt sometimes as to geep a fire a-goin' all the time. Don't wandt to gome too hardt on the *brafer Mann*, you know:

'Braver Mann, er schafft mir zu essen.'

You remember? Heine? You readt Heine still? Who is your favourite boet now, Passil? You write some boetry yourself yet? No? Well, I am gladt to zee you. Brush those baperss off of that jair. Well, idt is goodt for zore eyess. How didt you findt where I lif?"

"They told me at Maroni's," said March. He tried to keep his eyes on Lindau's face, and not see the discomfort of the room, but he was aware of the shabby and frowsy bedding, the odour of stale smoke, and the pipes and tobacco shreds mixed with the books and manuscripts strewn over the leaf of the writing-desk. He laid down on the mass the pile of foreign magazines he had brought under his arm. "They gave me another address first."

"Yes. I have chust gome here," said Lindau. "Idt is not very cay, heigh?"

"It might be gayer," March admitted, with a smile.

"Still," he added soberly, "a good many people seem to live in this part of the town. Apparently they die here too, Lindau. There is crape*on your outside door. I didn't know but it was for you."

"Nodt this time," said Lindau, in the same humour. "Berhaps some other time. We geep the ondertakers bretty pusy down here."

"Well," said March, "undertakers must live, even if the rest of us have to die to let them." Lindau laughed, and March went on: "But I'm glad it isn't your funeral, Lindau. And you say you're not sick, and so I don't see why we shouldn't come to business."

"Pusiness?" Lindau lifted his eyebrows. "You gome on pusiness?"

"And pleasure combined," said March, and he went on to explain the service he desired at Lindau's hands.

The old man listened with serious attention, and with assenting nods that culminated in a spoken expression of his willingness to undertake the translations. March waited with a sort of mechanical expectation of his gratitude for the work put in his way, but nothing of the kind came from Lindau, and March was left to say, "Well, everything is understood, then; and I don't know that I need add that if you ever want any little advance on the work——"

"I will ask you," said Lindau quietly, "and I thank you for that. But I can wait; I ton't needt any money just at bresent." As if he saw some appeal for greater frankness in March's eye, he went on: "I tidn't gome here begause I was too boor to lif anywhere else, and I ton't stay in pedt begause I couldn't haf a fire to geep warm if I wanted it. I'm nodt zo padt off as Marmontel*when he went to Paris. I'm a lidtle loaxurious, that is all. If I stay in pedt it's zo I can fling money away on somethings else. Heigh?"

"But what *are* you living here for, Lindau?" March smiled at the irony lurking in Lindau's words.

"Well, you zee, I foundt I was begoming a lidtle too moch of an aristograt. I hadt a room oap in Creenvidge Willage, among dose pig pugs over on the west side, and I foundt"—

Lindau's voice lost its jesting quality, and his face darkened —"that I was beginning to forget the boor!"

"I should have thought," said March, with impartial interest, "that you might have seen poverty enough, now and then, in Greenwich Village* to remind you of its existence."

"Nodt' like here," said Lindau. "Andt you must zee it all the dtime—zee it, hear it, smell it, dtaste it—or you forget it. That is what I gome here for. I was begoming a ploated aristograt. I thought I was nodt like these beople down here, when I gome down once to look aroundt; I thought I must be somethings else, and zo I zaid I better take myself in time, and I gome here among my brothers—the beccars and the thiefs!" A noise made itself heard in the next room, as if the door were furtively opened, and a faint sound of tiptoeing and of hands clawing on a table. "Thiefs!" Lindau repeated, with a shout. "Lidtle thiefs, that gabture your breakfast. Ah! ha! ha!" A wild scurrying of feet, joyous cries and tittering, and a slamming door followed upon his explosion, and he resumed in the silence: "Idt is the children cot pack from school. They gome and steal what I leaf there on my daple. Idt's one of our lidtle chokes; we onderstand each other; that's all righdt. Once the goppler in the other room there he used to chase 'em; he couldn't onderstand their lidtle tricks. Now dot goppler's teadt, and he ton't chase 'em any more. He was a Bohemian. Gindt of grazy, I cuess."

"Well, it's a sociable existence," March suggested. "But perhaps if you let them have the things without stealing——"

"Oh no, no! Most nodt mage them too gonceitedt. They mostn't go and feel themselfs petter than those boor millionairss that hadt to steal their money."

March smiled indulgently at his old friend's violence. "Oh, there are fagots and fagots,* you know, Lindau; perhaps not all the millionaires are so guilty."

"Let us speak German," cried Lindau, in his own tongue, pushing his book aside, and thrusting his skull-cap back from his forehead. "How much money can a man honestly earn without wronging or oppressing some other man?"

"Well, if you'll let me answer in English," said March, "I should say about five thousand dollars a year. I name that figure because it's my experience that I never could earn more; but the experience of other men may be different, and if they tell me they can earn ten, or twenty, or fifty thousand a year, I'm not prepared to say they can't do it."

Lindau hardly waited for his answer. "Not the most gifted man that ever lived, in the practice of any art or science, and paid at the highest rate that exceptional genius could justly demand from those who have worked for their money, could ever earn a million dollars. It is the landlords and the merchant princes, the railroad kings and the coal barons* (the oppressors to whom you instinctively give the titles of tyrants)—it is these that *make* the millions, but no man *earns* them. What artist, what physician, what scientist, what poet was ever a millionaire?"

"I can only think of the poet Rogers,"* said March, amused by Lindau's tirade. "But he was as exceptional as the other Rogers, the martyr,* who died with warm feet." Lindau had apparently not understood his joke, and he went on, with the American ease of mind about everything: "But you must allow, Lindau, that some of those fellows don't do so badly with their guilty gains. Some of them give work to armies of poor people——"

Lindau furiously interrupted. "Yes, when they have gathered their millions together from the hunger and cold and nakedness and ruin and despair of hundreds of thousands of other men, they 'give work' to the poor! They *give* work! They allow their helpless brothers to earn enough to keep life in them! They give *work*! Who is it gives *toil*, and where will your rich men be when once the poor shall refuse to give toil? Why, you have come to give *me* work!"

March laughed outright. "Well, I'm not a millionaire, anyway, Lindau, and I hope you won't make an example of me by refusing to give toil. I dare say the millionaires deserve it, but I'd rather they wouldn't suffer in my person."

"No," returned the old man, mildly relaxing the fierce glare he had bent upon March. "No man deserves to suffer at the hands of another. I lose myself when I think of the injustice in the world. But I must not forget that I am like the worst of them."

"You might go up Fifth Avenue and live among the rich awhile, when you're in danger of that," suggested March. "At any rate," he added, by an impulse which he knew he could not justify to his wife, "I wish you'd come some day and lunch with their emissary. I've been telling Mrs. March about you, and I want her and the children to see you. Come over with these things and report." He put his hand on the magazines as he rose.

"I will come," said Lindau gently.

"Shall I give you your book?" asked March.

"No; I gidt oap bretty soon."

"And—and—can you dress yourself?"

"I vhistle, and one of those lidtle fellowss comess. We haf to dake gare of one another in a blace like this. Idt iss nodt like the worldt," said Lindau gloomily.

March thought he ought to cheer him up. "Oh, it isn't such a bad world, Lindau! After all, the average of millionaires is small in it." He added, "And I don't believe there's an American living that could look at that arm of yours and not wish to lend you a hand for the one you gave us all." March felt this to be a fine turn, and his voice trembled slightly in saying it.

Lindau smiled grimly. "You think zo?" I wouldn't moch like to drost 'em. I've driedt idt too often." He began to speak German again fiercely: "Besides, they owe me nothing. Do you think I knowingly gave my hand to save this oligarchy of traders and tricksters, this aristocracy of railroad wreckers and stock gamblers and mine-slave drivers and mill-serf owners? No; I gave it to the slave; the slave—ha! ha! ha!—whom I helped to unshackle to the common liberty of hunger and cold. And you think I would be the beneficiary of such a state of things?"

"I'm sorry to hear you talk so, Lindau," said March; "very sorry." He stopped with a look of pain, and rose to go. Lindau suddenly broke into a laugh and into English.

"Oh, well, it is only dalk, Passil, and it toes me goodt. My parg is worse than my pidte, I cuess. I pring these things roundt bretty soon. Good-bye, Passil, my tear poy. *Auf wiedersehen!*"

XIII

MARCH went away thinking of what Lindau had said, but not for the impersonal significance of his words so much as for the light they cast upon Lindau himself. He thought the words violent enough, but in connection with what he remembered of the cheery, poetic, hopeful idealist, they were even more curious than lamentable. In his own life of comfortable reverie he had never heard any one talk so before, but he had read something of the kind now and then in blatant labour newspapers which he had accidentally fallen in with, and once at a strikers' meeting he had heard rich people denounced with the same frenzy. He had made his own reflections upon the tastelessness of the rhetoric, and the obvious buncombe*of the motive, and he had not taken the matter seriously.

He could not doubt Lindau's sincerity, and he wondered how he came to that way of thinking. From his experience of himself he accounted for a prevailing literary quality in it; he decided it to be from Lindau's reading and feeling rather than his reflection. That was the notion he formed of some things he had met with in Ruskin*to much the same effect; he regarded them with amusement as the chimeras of a rhetorician run away with by his phrases.

But as to Lindau, the chief thing in his mind was a conception of the droll irony of a situation in which so fervid a hater of millionaires should be working, indirectly at least, for the prosperity of a man like Dryfoos, who, as March understood, had got his money together out of every gambler's chance in speculation, and all a schemer's thrift from the error and need of others. The situation was not more incongruous, however, than all the rest of the *Every*

Other Week affair. It seemed to him that there were no crazy fortuities that had not tended to its existence, and as time went on, and the day drew near for the issue of the first number, the sense of this intensified till the whole lost at moments the quality of a waking fact, and came to be rather a fantastic fiction of sleep.

Yet the heterogeneous forces did co-operate to a reality which March could not deny, at least in their presence, and the first number was representative of all their nebulous intentions in a tangible form. As a result, it was so respectable that March began to respect these intentions, began to respect himself for combining and embodying them in the volume which appealed to him with a novel fascination, when the first advance copy was laid upon his desk. Every detail of it was tiresomely familiar already, but the whole had a fresh interest now. He now saw how extremely fit and effective Miss Leighton's decorative design for the cover was, printed in black and brick-red on the delicate grey tone of the paper. It was at once attractive and refined, and he credited Beaton with quite all he merited in working it over to the actual shape. The touch and the taste of the art editor were present throughout the number. As Fulkerson said, Beaton had caught on with the delicacy of a humming-bird and the tenacity of a bull-dog to the virtues of their illustrative process, and had worked it for all it was worth. There were seven papers in the number, and a poem on the last page of the cover, and he had found some graphic comment for each. It was a larger proportion than would afterward be allowed, but for once in a way it was allowed. Fulkerson said they could not expect to get their money back on that first number anyway. Seven of the illustrations were Beaton's; two or three he got from practised hands; the rest were the work of unknown people which he had suggested, and then related and adapted with unfailing ingenuity to the different papers. He handled the illustrations with such sympathy as not to destroy their individual quality, and that indefinable charm which comes from good amateur work in whatever art. He rescued them from their weaknesses and errors, while he left in them the evidence of the pleasure with which a clever young man, or a sensitive girl, or a refined woman had done them. Inevitably from his manipulation, however, the art of the number acquired homogeneity, and there was nothing casual in its appearance. The result, March eagerly owned, was better than the literary result, and he foresaw that the number would be sold and praised chiefly for its pictures. Yet he was not ashamed of the literature, and he indulged his admiration of it the more freely because he had not only not written it, but in a way had not edited it. To be sure, he had chosen all the material, but he had not voluntarily put it all together for that number; it had largely put itself together, as every number of every magazine does, and as it seems more and more to do, in the experience of every editor. There had to be, of course, a story, and then a sketch of travel. There was a literary essay and a social essay; there was a dramatic trifle, very gay, very light; there was a dashing criticism on the new pictures, the new plays, the new books, the new fashions; and then there was the translation of a bit of vivid Russian realism, which the editor owed to Lindau's exploration of the foreign periodicals left with him; Lindau was himself a romanticist of the Victor Hugo sort, but he said this fragment of Dostoyevski was good of its kind. The poem was a bit of society verse, with a backward look into simpler and wholesomer experiences.

Fulkerson was extremely proud of the number; but he said it was too good—too good from every point of view. The cover was too good, and the paper was too good, and that device of rough edges, which got over the objection to uncut leaves while it secured their æsthetic effect, was a thing that he trembled for, though he rejoiced in it as a stroke of the highest genius. It had come from Beaton at the last moment, as a compromise, when the problem of the vulgar croppiness of cut leaves and the unpopularity of uncut leaves seemed to have no solution but suicide. Fulkerson was still morally crawling round on his hands and knees, as he said, in abject gratitude at Beaton's feet, though he had his qualms, his questions; and he declared that Beaton was the

most inspired ass since Balaam's.* "We're all asses, of course,"
he admitted, in semi-apology to March; "but we're no such
asses as Beaton." He said that if the tasteful decorativeness
of the thing did not kill it with the public outright, its
literary excellence would give it the finishing stroke. Perhaps
that might be overlooked in the impression of novelty which
a first number would give, but it must never happen again.
He implored March to promise that it should never happen
again; he said their only hope was in the immediate cheapen-
ing of the whole affair. It was bad enough to give the public
too much quantity for their money, but to throw in such
quality as that was simply ruinous; it must be stopped.
These were the expressions of his intimate moods; every
front that he presented to the public wore a glow of lofty,
of devout exultation. His pride in the number gushed out in
fresh bursts of rhetoric to every one whom he could get to
talk with him about it. He worked the personal kindliness of
the press to the utmost. He did not mind making himself
ridiculous or becoming a joke in the good cause, as he called
it. He joined in the applause when a humorist at the club
feigned to drop dead from his chair at Fulkerson's introduction of the topic, and he went on talking that first number into the surviving spectators. He stood treat upon all
occasions, and he lunched attachés of the press at all hours.
He especially befriended the correspondents of the newspapers of other cities, for, as he explained to March, those
fellows could give him any amount of advertising simply as
literary gossip. Many of the fellows were ladies who could
not be so summarily asked out to lunch, but Fulkerson's
ingenuity was equal to every exigency, and he contrived
somehow to make each of these feel that she had been possessed of exclusive information. There was a moment when
March conjectured a willingness in Fulkerson to work Mrs.
March into the advertising department, by means of a tea
to these ladies and their friends which she should administer
in his apartment, but he did not encourage Fulkerson to be
explicit, and the moment passed. Afterward, when he told
his wife about it, he was astonished to find that she would

not have minded doing it for Fulkerson, and he experienced
another proof of the bluntness of the feminine instincts in
some directions, and of the personal favour which Fulkerson seemed to enjoy with the whole sex. This alone was
enough to account for the willingness of these correspondents
to write about the first number, but March accused him of
sending it to their addresses with boxes of Jacqueminot
roses and Huyler candy.

Fulkerson let him enjoy his joke. He said that he would do
that or anything else for the good cause, short of marrying
the whole circle of female correspondents.

March was inclined to hope that if the first number had
been made too good for the country at large, the more enlightened taste of metropolitan journalism would invite a
compensating favour for it in New York. But first Fulkerson
and then the event proved him wrong. In spite of the quality
of the magazine, and in spite of the kindness which so many
newspaper men felt for Fulkerson, the notices in the New
York papers seemed grudging and provisional to the ardour
of the editor. A merit in the work was acknowledged, and
certain defects in it for which March had trembled were
ignored; but the critics astonished him by selecting for
censure points which he was either proud of or had never
noticed; which being now brought to his notice he still could
not feel were faults. He owned to Fulkerson that if they had
said so and so against it, he could have agreed with them,
but that to say thus and so was preposterous; and that if the
advertising had not been adjusted with such generous recognition of the claims of the different papers, he should have
known the counting-room was at the bottom of it. As it was,
he could only attribute it to perversity or stupidity. It was
certainly stupid to condemn a magazine novelty like *Every
Other Week* for being novel; and to augur that if it failed, it
would fail through its departure from the lines on which all
the other prosperous magazines had been built, was in the
last degree perverse, and it looked malicious. The fact that
it was neither exactly a book nor a magazine ought to be for it
and not against it, since it would invade no other field; it
would prosper on no ground but its own.

XIV

THE more March thought of the injustice of the New York press (which had not, however, attacked the literary quality of the number) the more bitterly he resented it; and his wife's indignation superheated his own. *Every Other Week* had become a very personal affair with the whole family; the children shared their parents' disgust; Bella was outspoken in her denunciations of a venal press. Mrs. March saw nothing but ruin ahead, and began tacitly to plan a retreat to Boston, and an establishment retrenched to the basis of two thousand a year. She shed some secret tears in anticipation of the privations which this must involve; but when Fulkerson came to see March rather late the night of the publication day, she nobly told him that if the worst came to the worst she could only have the kindliest feeling toward him, and should not regard him as in the slightest degree responsible.

"Oh, hold on, hold on!" he protested. "You don't think we've made a failure, do you?"

"Why, of course," she faltered, while March remained gloomily silent.

"Well, I guess we'll wait for the official count, first. Even New York hasn't gone against us, and I guess there's a majority coming down to Harlem River that could sweep everything before it, anyway."

"What do you mean, Fulkerson?" March demanded sternly.

"Oh, nothing! Only, the News Company has *ordered* ten thousand now; and you know we had to give them the first twenty on commission."

"What *do* you mean?" March repeated; his wife held her breath.

"I mean that the first number is a booming success already, and that it's going to a hundred thousand before it stops. That unanimity and variety of censure in the morning papers, combined with the attractiveness of the thing itself, has cleared every stand in the city, and now if the favour of the country press doesn't turn the tide against us, our fortune's made." The Marches remained dumb. "Why, look here! Didn't I tell you those criticisms would be the making of us, when they first began to turn you blue this morning, March?"

"He came home to lunch perfectly sick," said Mrs. March; "and I wouldn't let him go back again."

"Didn't I *tell* you so?" Fulkerson persisted.

March could not remember that he had, or that he had been anything but incoherently and hysterically jocose over the papers, but he said, "Yes, yes—I think so."

"I knew it from the start," said Fulkerson. "The only other person who took those criticisms in the right spirit was Mother Dryfoos—I've just been bolstering up the Dryfoos family. She had them read to her by Mrs. Mandel, and she understood them to be all the most flattering prophecies of success. Well, I didn't read between the lines to that extent, quite; but I saw that they were going to help us, if there was anything in us, more than anything that could have been done. And there was something in us! I tell you, March, that seven-shooting self-cocking donkey of a Beaton has given us the greatest start! He's caught on like a mice.* He's made the thing awfully *chic*; it's jimmy;* there's lots of dog* about it. He's managed that process so that the illustrations look as expensive as first-class wood-cuts, and they're cheaper than chromos.* He's put style into the whole thing."

"Oh yes," said March with eager meekness, "it's Beaton that's done it."

Fulkerson read jealousy of Beaton in Mrs. March's face. "Beaton has given us the start because his work appeals to the eye. There's no denying that the pictures have sold this first number; but I expect the literature of this first number to sell the pictures of the second. I've been reading it all over, nearly, since I found how the cat was jumping; I was anxious about it, and I tell you, old man, it's *good*. Yes, sir! I was afraid may be you had got it *too* good, with that Boston refinement of yours; but I reckon you haven't. I'll risk it. I don't see how you got so much variety into so few things, and all of them palpitant, all of 'em on the keen jump with actuality."

The mixture of American slang with the jargon of European criticism in Fulkerson's talk made March smile, but his wife did not seem to notice it in her exultation. "That is just what I say," she broke in. "It's perfectly wonderful. I never was anxious about it a moment, except, as you say, Mr. Fulkerson, I was afraid it might be too good."

They went on in an antiphony of praise till March said, "Really, I don't see what's left me but to strike for higher wages. I perceive that I'm indispensable."

"Why, old man, you're coming in on the divvy, you know," said Fulkerson.

They both laughed, and when Fulkerson was gone, Mrs. March asked her husband what a divvy was.

"It's a chicken before it's hatched."

"No! Truly?"

He explained, and she began to spend the divvy.

At Mrs. Leighton's Fulkerson gave Alma all the honour of the success; he told her mother that the girl's design for the cover had sold every number, and Mrs. Leighton believed him.

"Well, Ah think *Ah* maght have *some* of the glory," Miss Woodburn pouted. "Where am *Ah* comin' in?"

"You're coming in on the cover of the next number," said Fulkerson. "We're going to have your face there; Miss Leighton's going to sketch it in." He said this reckless of the fact that he had already shown them the design of the second number which was Beaton's weird bit of gas-country landscape.

"Ah don't see why *you* don't wrahte the fiction for your magazine, Mr. Fulkerson," said the girl.

This served to remind Fulkerson of something. He turned to her father. "I'll tell you what, Colonel Woodburn, I want Mr. March to see some chapters of that book of yours. I've been talking to him about it."

"I do not think it would add to the popularity of your periodical, sir," said the Colonel, with a stately pleasure in being asked. "My views of a civilisation based upon responsible slavery would hardly be acceptable to your commercialised society."

"Well, not as a practical thing, of course," Fulkerson admitted. "But as something retrospective, speculative, I believe it would make a hit. There's so much going on now about social questions; I guess people would like to read it."

"I do not know that my work is intended to amuse people," said the Colonel, with some state.

"Mah goodness! Ah only wish it *was*, then," said his daughter; and she added: "Yes, Mr. Fulkerson, the Colonel will be very glad to submit po'tions of his woak to yo' edito'. We want to have some of the honaw. Perhaps we can say we helped to stop yo' magazine, if we didn't help to stawt it."

They all laughed at her boldness, and Fulkerson said, "It'll take a good deal more than that to stop *Every Other Week*. The Colonel's whole book couldn't do it." Then he looked unhappy, for Colonel Woodburn did not seem to enjoy his reassuring words; but Miss Woodburn came to his rescue. "You maght illustrate it with the po'trait of the awthor's daughtaw, if it's too late for the covah."

"Going to have *that* in every number, Miss Woodburn," he cried.

"Oh, mah goodness!" she said, with mock humility.

Alma sat looking at her piquant head, black, unconsciously outlined against the lamp, as she sat working by the table. "Just keep still a moment!"

She got her sketch-block and pencils, and began to draw; Fulkerson tilted himself forward and looked over her shoulder; he smiled outwardly; inwardly he was divided between admiration of Miss Woodburn's arch beauty and appreciation of the skill which reproduced it; at the same time he was trying to remember whether March had authorised him to go so far as to ask for a sight of Colonel Woodburn's manuscript. He felt that he had trenched upon March's province, and he framed one apology to the editor for bringing him the manuscript, and another to the author for bringing it back.

"Most Ah hold raght still like it was a photograph?" asked Miss Woodburn. "Can Ah toak?"

"Talk all you want," said Alma, squinting her eyes. "And you needn't be either adamantine, nor yet—wooden."

"Oh, ho' very good of you! Well, if Ah can toak—go on, Mr. Fulkerson!"

"Me talk? I can't breathe till this thing is done!" sighed Fulkerson; at that point of his mental drama the Colonel was behaving rustily about the return of his manuscript, and he felt that he was looking his last on Miss Woodburn's profile.

"Is she getting it raght?" asked the girl.

"I don't know which is which," said Fulkerson.

"Oh, Ah hope *Ah* shall! I don't want to go round feelin' like a sheet of papah half the time."

"You could rattle on, just the same," suggested Alma.

"Oh, now! Jost listen to that, Mr. Fulkerson. Do you call that any way to toak to people?"

"You might know which you were by the colour," Fulkerson began, and then he broke off from the personal consideration with a business inspiration, and smacked himself on the knee: "We could *print* it in colour!"

Mrs. Leighton gathered up her sewing and held it with both hands in her lap, while she came round, and looked critically at the sketch and the model over her glasses. "It's very good, Alma," she said.

Colonel Woodburn remained restively on his side of the table. "Of course, Mr. Fulkerson, you were jesting, sir, when you spoke of printing a sketch of my daughter."

"Why, I don't know—— If you object——"

"I do, sir—decidedly," said the Colonel.

"Then that settles it, of course," said Fulkerson. "I only meant——"

"Indeed it doesn't!" cried the girl. "Who's to know who it's from? Ah'm jost set on havin' it printed! Ah'm going to appear as the head of Slavery—in opposition to the head of Liberty."

"There'll be a revolution inside of forty-eight hours, and we'll have the Colonel's system going wherever a copy of *Every Other Week* circulates," said Fulkerson.

"This sketch belongs to me," Alma interposed. "I'm not going to let it be printed."

"Oh, mah goodness!" said Miss Woodburn, laughing good-humouredly. "That's becose you were brought up to hate slavery."

"I should like Mr. Beaton to see it," said Mrs. Leighton in a sort of absent tone. She added, to Fulkerson: "I rather expected he might be in to night."

"Well, if he comes we'll leave it to Beaton," Fulkerson said, with relief in the solution, and an anxious glance at the Colonel, across the table, to see how he took that form of the joke. Miss Woodburn intercepted his glance and laughed, and Fulkerson laughed too, but rather forlornly.

Alma set her lips primly and turned her head first on one side and then on the other to look at the sketch. "I don't think we'll leave it to Mr. Beaton, even if he comes."

"We left the other design for the cover to Beaton," Fulkerson insinuated. "I guess you needn't be afraid of him."

"Is it a question of my being afraid?" Alma asked; she seemed coolly intent on her drawing.

"Miss Leighton thinks he ought to be afraid of her," Miss Woodburn explained.

"It's a question of *his* courage, then?" said Alma.

"Well, I don't think there are many young ladies that Beaton's afraid of," said Fulkerson, giving himself the respite of this purely random remark, while he interrogated the faces of Mrs. Leighton and Colonel Woodburn for some light upon the tendency of their daughters' words.

He was not helped by Mrs. Leighton's saying, with a certain anxiety, "I don't know what you mean, Mr. Fulkerson."

"Well, you're as much in the dark as I am myself, then,"

said Fulkerson. "I suppose I meant that Beaton is rather—a—favourite, you know. The women like him."

Mrs. Leighton sighed, and Colonel Woodburn rose and left the room.

XV

IN the silence that followed, Fulkerson looked from one lady to the other with dismay. "I seem to have put my foot in it, somehow," he suggested, and Miss Woodburn gave a cry of laughter.

"Poo' Mr. Fulkerson! *Poo'* Mr. Fulkerson! Papa thoat you wanted him to go."

"Wanted him to go?" repeated Fulkerson.

"We always mention Mr. Beaton when we want to get rid of papa."

"Well, it seems to me that I *have* noticed that he didn't take much interest in Beaton, as a general topic. But I don't know that I ever saw it drive him out of the room before!"

"Well, he isn't always so bad," said Miss Woodburn. "But it was a case of hate at first sight, and it seems to be growin' on papa."

"Well, I can understand that," said Fulkerson. "The impulse to destroy Beaton is something that everybody has to struggle against at the start."

"I must say, Mr. Fulkerson," said Mrs. Leighton in the tremor through which she nerved herself to differ openly with any one she liked, "I never had to struggle with anything of the kind, in regard to Mr. Beaton. He has always been most respectful and—and considerate, with *me*, whatever he has been with others."

"Well, of course, Mrs. Leighton!" Fulkerson came back in a soothing tone. "But you see you're the rule that proves the exception. I was speaking of the way *men* felt about Beaton. It's different with ladies; I just said so."

"Is it always different?" Alma asked, lifting her head and her hand from her drawing, and staring at it absently.

Fulkerson pushed his hands both through his whiskers. "Look here! Look here!" he said. "Won't somebody start some other subject? We haven't had the weather up yet, have we? Or the opera? What is the matter with a few remarks about politics?"

"Why I thoat you lahked to toak about the staff of yo' magazine," said Miss Woodburn.

"Oh, I do!" said Fulkerson. "But not always about the same member of it. He gets monotonous, when he doesn't get complicated. I've just come round from the Marches'," he added, to Mrs. Leighton.

"I suppose they've got thoroughly settled in their apartment by this time." Mrs. Leighton said something like this whenever the Marches were mentioned. At the bottom of her heart she had not forgiven them for not taking her rooms; she had liked their looks so much; and she was always hoping that they were uncomfortable or dissatisfied; she could not help wanting them punished a little.

"Well, yes; as much as they ever will be," Fulkerson answered. "The Boston style is pretty different, you know; and the Marches are old-fashioned folks, and I reckon they never went in much for bric-à-brac. They've put away nine or ten barrels of dragon candlesticks, but they keep finding new ones."

"Their landlady has just joined our class," said Alma. "Isn't her name Green? She happened to see my copy of *Every Other Week*, and said she knew the editor; and told me."

"Well, it's a little world," said Fulkerson. "You seem to be touching elbows with everybody. Just think of your having had our head translator for a model."

"Ah think that your whole publication revolves aroand the Leighton family," said Miss Woodburn.

"That's pretty much so," Fulkerson admitted. "Anyhow, the publisher seems disposed to do so."

"Are you the publisher? I thought it was Mr. Dryfoos," said Alma.

"It is."

"Oh!"

The tone and the word gave Fulkerson a discomfort which he promptly confessed. "Missed again."

The girls laughed, and he regained something of his lost spirits, and smiled upon their gaiety, which lasted beyond any apparent reason for it.

Miss Woodburn asked, "And is Mr. Dryfoos senio' anything like *ouah* Mr. Dryfoos?"

"Not the least."

"But he's jost as exemplary?"

"Yes; in his way."

"Well, Ah wish Ah could see all those pinks of puffection togethath, once."

"Why, look here! I've been thinking I'd celebrate a little, when the old gentleman gets back. Have a little supper—something of that kind. How would you like to let me have your parlours for it, Mrs. Leighton? You ladies could stand on the stairs, and have a peep at us, in the bunch."

"Oh, mah! What a privilege! And will Miss Alma be there, with the othah contributors? Ah shall jost expah of envy!"

"She won't be there in person," said Fulkerson, "but she'll be represented by the head of the art department."

"Mah goodness! And who'll the head of the publishing department represent?"

"He can represent you," said Alma.

"Well, Ah want to be represented, someho'."

"We'll have the banquet the night before you appear on the cover of our fourth number," said Fulkerson.

"Ah thoat that was doubly fo'bidden," said Miss Woodburn. "By the stern parent and the envious awtust."

"We'll get Beaton to get round them, somehow. I guess we can trust him to manage that."

Mrs. Leighton sighed her resentment of the implication.

"I always feel that Mr. Beaton doesn't do himself justice," she began.

Fulkerson could not forego the chance of a joke. "Well,

may be he would rather temper justice with mercy in a case like his." This made both the younger ladies laugh. "I judge this is my chance to get off with my life," he added, and he rose as he spoke. "Mrs. Leighton, I am about the only man of my sex who doesn't thirst for Beaton's blood most of the time. But I know him and I don't. He's more kinds of a good fellow than people generally understand. He don't wear his heart upon his sleeve—not his ulster sleeve, anyway. You can always count me on your side when it's a question of finding Beaton not guilty if he'll leave the State."

Alma set her drawing against the wall, in rising to say good night to Fulkerson. He bent over on his stick to look at it. "Well, it's beautiful," he sighed, with unconscious sincerity.

Alma made him a courtesy of mock modesty. "Thanks to Miss Woodburn."

"Oh no! All she had to do was simply to stay put."

"Don't you think Ah might have improved it if Ah had looked better?" the girl asked gravely.

"Oh, you *couldn't*!" said Fulkerson, and he went off triumphant in their applause and their cries of "Which? which?"

Mrs. Leighton sank deep into an accusing gloom when at last she found herself alone with her daughter. "I don't know what you are thinking about, Alma Leighton. If you don't like Mr. Beaton——"

"I don't."

"You don't? You know better than that. You know that you did care for him."

"Oh! that's a very different thing. That's a thing that can be got over."

"Got over!" repeated Mrs. Leighton, aghast.

"Of course, it can! Don't be romantic, mamma. People get over dozens of such fancies. They even marry for love two or three times."

"Never!" cried her mother, doing her best to feel shocked, and at last looking it.

Her looking it had no effect upon Alma. "You can easily

get over caring for people; but you can't get over liking them—if you like them because they are sweet and good. That's what lasts. I was a simple goose, and he imposed upon me because he was a sophisticated goose. Now the case is reversed."

"He *does* care for you, now. You can see it. Why do you encourage him to come here?"

"I don't," said Alma. "I will tell him to keep away if you like. But whether he comes or goes, it will be the same."

"Not to him, Alma! He is in love with you!"

"He has never said so."

"And you would really let him say so, when you intend to refuse him?"

"I can't very well refuse him till he *does* say so."

This was undeniable. Mrs. Leighton could only demand in an awful tone, "May I ask *why*—if you cared for him; and I know you care for him still—you will refuse him?"

Alma laughed. "Because—because I'm wedded to my Art, and I'm not going to commit bigamy, whatever I do."

"Alma!"

"Well, then, because I don't *like* him—that is, I don't believe in him, and don't trust him. He's fascinating, but he's false and he's fickle. He can't help it, I dare say."

"And you are perfectly hard. Is it possible that you were actually pleased to have Mr. Fulkerson tease you about Mr. Dryfoos?"

"Oh, good night, now, mamma! This is becoming personal."

187

PART THIRD

I

THE scheme of a banquet to celebrate the initial success of
Every Other Week expanded in Fulkerson's fancy into a
series. Instead of the publishing and editorial force, with
certain of the more representative artists and authors sitting
down to a modest supper in Mrs. Leighton's parlours, he
conceived of a dinner at Delmonico's, with the principal
literary and artistic people throughout the country as guests,
and an inexhaustible hospitality to reporters and correspondents, from whom paragraphs, prophetic and historic,
would flow weeks before and after the first of the series. He
said the thing was a new departure in magazines; it amounted
to something in literature as radical as the American Revolution in politics: it was the idea of self-government in the
arts; and it was this idea that had never yet been fully
developed in regard to it. That was what must be done in the
speeches at the dinner, and the speeches must be reported.
Then it would go like wildfire. He asked March whether he
thought Mr. Depew* could be got to come; Mark Twain, he
was sure would come; he was a literary man. They ought to
invite Mr. Evarts,* and the Cardinal and the leading Protestant divines. His ambition stopped at nothing, nothing
but the question of expense; there he had to wait the return
of the elder Dryfoos from the West, and Dryfoos was still
delayed at Moffitt, and Fulkerson openly confessed that he
was afraid he would stay there till his own enthusiasm
escaped in other activities, other plans.

Fulkerson was as little likely as possible to fall under a
superstitious subjection to another man; but March could
not help seeing that in this possible measure Dryfoos was
Fulkerson's fetish. He did not revere him, March decided,

because it was not in Fulkerson's nature to revere anything; he could like and dislike, but he could not respect. Apparently, however, Dryfoos daunted him somehow; and besides the homage which those who have not pay to those who have, Fulkerson rendered Dryfoos the tribute of a feeling which March could only define as a sort of bewilderment. As well as March could make out, this feeling was evoked by the spectacle of Dryfoos's unfailing luck, which Fulkerson was fond of dazzling himself with. It perfectly consisted with a keen sense of whatever was sordid and selfish in a man on whom his career must have had its inevitable effect. He liked to philosophise the case with March, to recall Dryfoos as he was when he first met him still somewhat in the sap, at Moffitt, and to study the processes by which he imagined him to have dried into the hardened speculator, without even the pretence to any advantage but his own in his ventures. He was aware of painting the character too vividly, and he warned March not to accept it exactly in those tints, but to subdue them and shade it for himself. He said that where his advantage was not concerned, there was ever so much good in Dryfoos, and that if in some things he had grown inflexible, he had expanded in others to the full measure of the vast scale on which he did business. It had seemed a little odd to March that a man should put money into such an enterprise as *Every Other Week* and go off about other affairs, not only without any sign of anxiety but without any sort of interest. But Fulkerson said that was the splendid side of Dryfoos. He had a courage, a magnanimity, that was equal to the strain of any such uncertainty. He had faced the music once for all, when he asked Fulkerson what the thing would cost in the different degrees of potential failure; and then he had gone off, leaving everything to Fulkerson and the younger Dryfoos, with the instruction simply to go ahead and not bother him about it. Fulkerson called that pretty tall for an old fellow who used to bewail the want of pigs and chickens to occupy his mind. He alleged it as another proof of the versatility of the American mind, and of the grandeur of institutions and opportunities that let every man grow to his full size, so that any man in America could run the concern if necessary. He believed that old Dryfoos could step into Bismarck's shoes, and run the German Empire at ten days' notice, or about as long as it would take him to go from New York to Berlin. But Bismarck would not know anything about Dryfoos's plans till Dryfoos got ready to show his hand. Fulkerson himself did not pretend to say what the old man had been up to, since he went West. He was at Moffitt first, and then he was at Chicago, and then he had gone out to Denver to look after some mines he had out there, and a railroad or two; and now he was at Moffitt again. He was supposed to be closing up his affairs there, but nobody could say.

Fulkerson told March the morning after Dryfoos returned that he had not only not pulled out at Moffitt, but had gone in deeper, ten times deeper than ever. He was in a royal good-humour, Fulkerson reported, and was going to drop into the office on his way up from the street (March understood Wall Street) that afternoon. He was tickled to death with *Every Other Week* so far as it had gone, and was anxious to pay his respects to the editor.

March accounted for some rhetoric in this, but let it flatter him, and prepared himself for a meeting about which he could see that Fulkerson was only less nervous than he had shown himself about the public reception of the first number. It gave March a disagreeable feeling of being owned and of being about to be inspected by his proprietor; but he fell back upon such independence as he could find in the thought of those two thousand dollars of income beyond the caprice of his owner, and maintained an outward serenity.

He was a little ashamed afterward of the resolution it had cost him to do so. It was not a question of Dryfoos's physical presence: that was rather effective than otherwise, and carried a suggestion of moneyed indifference to convention in the grey business suit of provincial cut, and the low, wide-brimmed hat of flexible black felt. He had a stick with an old-fashioned top of buck-horn worn smooth and bright by the palm of his hand, which had not lost its character in fat, and which had a history of former work in its enlarged knuckles, though it was now as soft as March's, and must once have been small even for a man of Mr. Dryfoos's stature; he was below the average size. But what struck March was the fact that Dryfoos seemed furtively conscious of being a country person, and of being aware that in their meeting he was to be tried by other tests than those which would have availed him as a shrewd speculator. He evidently had some curiosity about March, as the first of his kind whom he had encountered; some such curiosity as the country school trustee feels and tries to hide in the presence of the new schoolmaster. But the whole affair was of course on a higher plane; on one side Dryfoos was much more a man of the world than March was, and he probably divined this at once, and rested himself upon the fact in a measure. It seemed to be his preference that his son should introduce them, for he came upstairs with Conrad, and they had fairly made acquaintance before Fulkerson joined them.

Conrad offered to leave them at once, but his father made him stay. "I reckon Mr. March and I haven't got anything so private to talk about that we want to keep it from the other partners. Well, Mr. March, are you getting used to New York yet? It takes a little time."

"Oh yes. But not so much time as most places. Everybody belongs more or less in New York; nobody has to belong here altogether."

"Yes, that is so. You can try it, and go away if you don't like it a good deal easier than you could from a smaller place. Wouldn't make so much talk, would it?" He glanced at March with a jocose light in his shrewd eyes. "That is the way I feel about it all the time: just visiting. Now, it wouldn't be that way in Boston, I reckon?"

"You couldn't keep on visiting there your whole life," said March.

Dryfoos laughed, showing his lower teeth in a way that was at once simple and fierce. "Mr. Fulkerson didn't hardly know as he could get you to leave. I suppose you got used to it there. I never been in your city."

"I had got used to it; but it was hardly my city, except by marriage. My wife's a Bostonian."

"She's been a little homesick here, then," said Dryfoos, with a smile of the same quality as his laugh.

"Less than I expected," said March. "Of course she was very much attached to our old home."

"I guess my wife won't ever get used to New York," said Dryfoos, and he drew in his lower lip with a sharp sigh. "But my girls like it; they're young. You never been out our way yet, Mr. March? Out West?"

"Well, only for the purpose of being born, and brought up. I used to live in Crawfordsville, and then Indianapolis."

"Indianapolis is bound to be a great place," said Dryfoos. "I remember now, Mr. Fulkerson told me you was from our State." He went on to brag of the West, as if March were an Easterner and had to be convinced. "You ought to see all that country. It's a great country."

"Oh yes," said March, "I understand that." He expected the praise of the great West to lead up to some comment on *Every Other Week*; and there was abundant suggestion of that topic in the manuscripts, proofs of letter-press and illustrations, with advance copies of the latest number strewn over his table.

But Dryfoos apparently kept himself from looking at these things. He rolled his head about on his shoulders to take in the character of the room, and said to his son, "You didn't change the woodwork after all."

"No; the architect thought we had better let it be, unless we meant to change the whole place. He liked its being old-fashioned."

"I hope you feel comfortable here, Mr. March," the old man said, bringing his eyes to bear upon him again after their tour of inspection.

"Too comfortable for a working-man," said March, and he thought that this remark must bring them to some talk about his work, but the proprietor only smiled again.

"I guess I shan't lose much on this house," he returned, as if musing aloud. "This down-town property is coming up.

Business is getting in on all these side streets. I thought I paid a pretty good price for it, too." He went on to talk of real estate, and March began to feel a certain resentment at his continued avoidance of the only topic in which they could really have a common interest. "You live down this way somewhere, don't you?" the old man concluded.

"Yes. I wished to be near my work." March was vexed with himself for having recurred to it; but afterward he was not sure but Dryfoos shared his own diffidence in the matter, and was waiting for him to bring it openly into the talk. At times he seemed wary and masterful, and then March felt that he was being examined and tested; at others so simple that March might well have fancied that he needed encouragement, and desired it. He talked of his wife and daughters in a way that invited March to say friendly things of his family, which appeared to give the old man first an undue pleasure, and then a final distrust. At moments he turned, with an effect of finding relief in it, to his son and spoke to him across March of matters which he was unacquainted with; he did not seem aware that this was rude, but the young man must have felt it so; he always brought the conversation back, and once at some cost to himself when his father made it personal.

"I want to make a regular New York business man out of that fellow," he said to March, pointing at Conrad with his stick. "You s'pose I'm ever going to do it?"

"Well, I don't know," said March, trying to fall in with the joke. "Do you mean nothing but a business man?"

The old man laughed at whatever latent meaning he fancied in this, and said, "You think he would be a little too much for me there? Well, I've seen enough of 'em to know it don't always take a large pattern of a man to do a large business. But I want him to get the business training, and then if he wants to go into something else, he knows what the world is, anyway. Heigh?"

"Oh yes!" March assented, with some compassion for the young man reddening patiently under his father's comment.

Dryfoos went on as if his son were not in hearing. "Now that boy wanted to be a preacher. What does a preacher know about the world he preaches against, when he's been brought up a preacher? He don't know so much as a bad little boy in his Sunday-school; he knows about as much as a girl. I always told him, You be a man first, and then you be a preacher, if you want to. Heigh?"

"Precisely." March began to feel some compassion for himself in being witness of the young fellow's discomfort under his father's homily.

"When we first come to New York, I told him, Now here's your chance to see the world on a big scale. You know already what work and saving and steady habits and sense will bring a man to; you don't want to go round among the rich; you want to go among the poor, and see what laziness, and drink, and dishonesty, and foolishness will bring men to. And I guess he knows, about as well as anybody; and if he ever goes to preaching he'll know what he's preaching about." The old man smiled his fierce, simple smile, and in his sharp eyes March fancied contempt of the ambition he had balked in his son. The present scene must have been one of many between them, ending in meek submission on the part of the young man whom his father perhaps without realising his cruelty treated as a child. March took it hard that he should be made to suffer in the presence of a co-ordinate power like himself, and began to dislike the old man out of proportion to his offence, which might have been mere want of taste, or an effect of mere embarrassment before him. But evidently, whatever rebellion his daughters had carried through against him, he had kept his dominion over this gentle spirit unbroken. March did not choose to make any response, but to let him continue, if he would, entirely upon his own impulse.

II

A SILENCE followed, of rather painful length. It was broken by the cheery voice of Fulkerson, sent before him to herald Fulkerson's cheery person. "Well, I suppose you've got the glorious success of *Every Other Week* down pretty cold in your talk by this time. I should have been up sooner to join you, but I was nipping a man for the last page of the cover. I guess we'll have to let the Muse have that for an advertisement instead of a poem the next time, March. Well, the old gentleman given you boys your scolding?" The person of Fulkerson had got into the room long before he reached this question, and had planted itself astride a chair. Fulkerson looked over the chair back, now at March, and now at the elder Dryfoos as he spoke.

March answered him. "I guess we must have been waiting for you, Fulkerson. At any rate we hadn't got to the scolding yet."

"Why, I didn't suppose Mr. Dryfoos could 'a' held in so long. I understood he was awful mad at the way the thing started off, and wanted to give you a piece of his mind, when he got at you. I inferred as much from a remark that he made." March and Dryfoos looked foolish, as men do when made the subject of this sort of merry misrepresentation.

"I reckon my scolding will keep awhile yet," said the old man dryly.

"Well, then, I guess it's a good chance to give Mr. Dryfoos an idea of what we've really done—just while we're resting, as Artemus Ward says. Heigh, March?"

"I will let you blow the trumpet, Fulkerson. I think it belongs strictly to the advertising department," said March. He now distinctly resented the old man's failure to say anything to him of the magazine; he made his inference that it was from a suspicion of his readiness to presume upon a recognition of his share in the success, and he was determined to second no sort of appeal for it.

"The advertising department is the heart and soul of every business," said Fulkerson hardily, "and I like to keep my hand in with a little practice on the trumpet in private. I don't believe Mr. Dryfoos has got any idea of the extent of this thing. He's been out among those Rackensackens, where we were all born, and he's read the notices in their seven by nine dailies, and he's seen the thing selling on the cars, and he thinks he appreciates what's been done. But I should just like to take him round in this little old metropolis awhile, and show him *Every Other Week* on the centre tables of the millionaires—the Vanderbilts and the Astors—and in the homes of culture and refinement everywhere, and let him judge for himself. It's the talk of the clubs and the dinner-tables; children cry for it; it's the Castoria of literature, and the Pearline of art, the Won't-be-happy-till-he-gets-it of every enlightened man, woman, and child in this vast city. I knew we could capture the country; but, my goodness! I *didn't* expect to have New York fall into our hands at a blow. But that's just exactly what New York has done. *Every Other Week* supplies the long-felt want that's been grinding round in New York and keeping it awake nights ever since the war. It's the culmination of all the high and ennobling ideals of the past——"

"How much," asked Dryfoos, "do you expect to get out of it the first year, if it keeps the start it's got?"

"Comes right down to business, every time!" said Fulkerson, referring the characteristic to March with a delighted glance. "Well, sir, if everything works right, and we get rain enough to fill up the springs, and it isn't a grasshopper year, I expect to clear above all expenses something in the neighbourhood of twenty-five thousand dollars."

"Humph! And you are all going to work a year—editor, manager, publisher, artists, writers, printers, and the rest of 'em—to clear twenty-five thousand dollars?—I made that much in half a day in Moffitt once. I see it made in half a minute in Wall Street, sometimes." The old man presented this aspect of the case with a good-natured contempt, which included Fulkerson and his enthusiasm in an obvious liking.

His son suggested, "But when we make that money here, no one loses it."

"Can you prove that?" His father turned sharply upon him. "Whatever is won is lost. It's all a game; it don't make any difference what you bet on. Business is business, and a business man takes his risks with his eyes open."

"Ah, but the glory!" Fulkerson insinuated with impudent persiflage. "I hadn't got to the glory yet, because it's hard to estimate it; but put the glory at the lowest figure, Mr. Dryfoos, and add it to the twenty-five thousand, and you've got an annual income from *Every Other Week* of dollars enough to construct a silver railroad, double-track, from this office to the moon. I don't mention any of the sister planets because I like to keep within bounds."

Dryfoos showed his lower teeth for pleasure in Fulkerson's fooling, and said, "That's what I like about you, Mr. Fulkerson: you always keep within bounds."

"Well, I *ain't* a shrinking Boston violet, like March here. More sunflower in my style of diffidence; but I am modest, I don't deny it," said Fulkerson. "And I do hate to have a thing overstated."

"And the glory—you do really think there's something in the glory that pays?"

"Not a doubt of it! I shouldn't care for the paltry return in money," said Fulkerson, with a burlesque of generous disdain, "if it wasn't for the glory along with it."

"And how should you feel about the glory, if there was no money along with it?"

"Well, sir, I'm happy to say we haven't come to that yet."

"Now, Conrad, here," said the old man, with a sort of pathetic rancour, "would rather have the glory alone. I believe he don't even care much for your kind of glory, either, Mr. Fulkerson."

Fulkerson ran his little eyes curiously over Conrad's face and then March's, as if searching for a trace there of something gone before which would enable him to reach Dryfoos's whole meaning. He apparently resolved to launch himself upon conjecture. "Oh, well, we know how Conrad feels about the things of this world, anyway. I should like to take 'em on the plane of another sphere, too, sometimes; but I noticed a good while ago that this was the world I was born into, and so I made up my mind that I would do pretty much what I saw the rest of the folks doing here below. And I can't see but what Conrad runs the thing on business principles in his department, and I guess you'll find it so if you look into it. I consider that we're a whole team and big dog under the wagon with you to draw on for supplies, and March, here, at the head of the literary business, and Conrad in the counting-room, and me to do the heavy lying in the advertising part. Oh, and Beaton, of course, in the art. I 'most forgot Beaton—*Hamlet* with Hamlet left out."

Dryfoos looked across at his son. "Wasn't that the fellow's name that was there last night?"

"Yes," said Conrad.

The old man rose. "Well, I reckon I got to be going. You ready to go up-town, Conrad?"

"Well, not quite yet, father."

The old man shook hands with March, and went downstairs, followed by his son.

Fulkerson remained.

"He didn't jump at the chance you gave him to compliment us all round, Fulkerson," said March, with a smile not wholly of pleasure.

Fulkerson asked with as little joy, in the grin he had on, "Didn't he say anything to you before I came in?"

"Not a word."

"Dogged if *I* know what to make of it," sighed Fulkerson, "but I guess he's been having a talk with Conrad that's soured on him. I reckon may be he came back expecting to find that boy reconciled to the glory of this world, and Conrad's showed himself just as set against it as ever."

"It might have been that," March admitted pensively. "I fancied something of the kind myself from words the old man let drop."

Fulkerson made him explain, and then he said, "That's it, then; and it's all right. Conrad'll come round in time;

and all we've got to do is to have patience with the old man till he does. I know he likes *you*." Fulkerson affirmed this only interrogatively, and looked so anxiously to March for corroboration that March laughed.

"He dissembled his love," he said; but afterward in describing to his wife his interview with Mr. Dryfoos he was less amused with this fact.

When she saw that he was a little cast down by it, she began to encourage him. "He's just a common, ignorant man, and probably didn't know how to express himself. You may be perfectly sure that he's delighted with the success of the magazine, and that he understands as well as you do that he owes it all to you."

"Ah, I'm *not* so sure. I don't believe a man's any better for having made money so easily and rapidly as Dryfoos has done, and I doubt if he's any wiser. I don't know just the point he's reached in his evolution from grub to beetle, but I do know that so far as it's gone the process must have involved a bewildering change of ideals and criterions. I guess he's come to despise a great many things that he once respected, and that intellectual ability is among them— what *we* call intellectual ability. He must have undergone a moral deterioration, an atrophy of the generous instincts, and I don't see why it shouldn't have reached his mental make-up. He has sharpened, but he has narrowed; his sagacity has turned into suspicion, his caution to meanness, his courage to ferocity. That's the way I philosophise a man of Dryfoos's experience, and I am not very proud when I realise that such a man and his experience are the ideal and ambition of most Americans. I rather think they came pretty near being mine, once."

"No, dear, they never did," his wife protested.

"Well, they're not likely to be, in the future. The Dryfoos feature of *Every Other Week* is thoroughly distasteful to me."

"Why, but he hasn't really got anything to do with it, has he, beyond furnishing the money?"

"That's the impression that Fulkerson has allowed us to get. But the man that holds the purse holds the reins. He may let us guide the horse, but when he likes he can drive. If we don't like his driving, then we can get down."

Mrs. March was less interested in this figure of speech than in the personal aspects involved. "Then you think Mr. Fulkerson has deceived you?"

"Oh no!" said her husband, laughing. "But I think he has deceived himself, perhaps."

"How?" she pursued.

"He may have thought he was using Dryfoos, when Dryfoos was using him, and he may have supposed he was not afraid of him when he was very much so. His courage hadn't been put to the test, and courage is a matter of proof, like proficiency on the fiddle, you know: you can't tell whether you've got it till you try."

"Nonsense! Do you mean that he would ever sacrifice *you* to Mr. Dryfoos?"

"I hope he may not be tempted. But I'd rather be taking the chances with Fulkerson alone, than with Fulkerson and Dryfoos to back him. Dryfoos seems somehow to take the poetry and the pleasure out of the thing."

Mrs. March was a long time silent. Then she began, "Well, my dear, *I* never wanted to come to New York——"

"Neither did I," March promptly put in.

"But now that we're here," she went on, "I'm not going to have you letting every little thing discourage you. I don't see what there was in Mr. Dryfoos's manner to give you any anxiety. He's just a common, stupid, inarticulate country person, and he didn't know how to express himself, as I said in the beginning, and that's the reason he didn't say anything."

"Well, I don't deny you're right about it."

"It's dreadful," his wife continued, "to be mixed up with such a man and his family, but I don't believe he'll ever meddle with your management, and till he does, all you need do is to have as little to do with him as possible, and go quietly on your own way."

"Oh, I shall go on quietly enough," said March. "I hope I shan't begin going stealthily."

"Well, my dear," said Mrs. March, "just let me know

when you're tempted to do that. If ever you sacrifice the smallest grain of your honesty or your self-respect to Mr. Dryfoos, or anybody else, I will simply renounce you."

"In view of that I'm rather glad the management of *Every Other Week* involves tastes and not convictions" said March.

III

THAT night Dryfoos was wakened from his after-dinner nap by the sound of gay talk and nervous giggling in the drawing-room. The talk, which was Christine's, and the giggling, which was Mela's, were intershot with the heavier tones of a man's voice; and Dryfoos lay awhile on the leathern lounge in his library, trying to make out whether he knew the voice. His wife sat in a deep chair before the fire, with her eyes on his face, waiting for him to wake.

"Who is that out there?" he asked, without opening his eyes.

"Indeed, indeed I don't know, Jacob," his wife answered. "I reckon it's just some visitor of the girls."

"Was I snoring?"

"Not a bit. You was sleeping as quiet! I did hate to have 'em wake you, and I was just goin' out to shoo them. They've been playin' something, and that made them laugh."

"I didn't know but I had snored," said the old man, sitting up.

"No," said his wife. Then she asked wistfully, "Was you out at the old place, Jacob?"

"Yes."

"Did it look natural?"

"Yes; mostly. They're sinking the wells down in the woods pasture."

"And—the childern's graves?"

"They haven't touched that part. But I reckon we got to have 'em moved to the cemetery. I bought a lot."

The old woman began softly to weep. "It does seem too hard that they can't be let to rest in peace, pore little things.

I wanted you and me to lay there too, when our time come, Jacob. Just there, back o' the beehives, and under them shoomakes*—my, I can see the very place! And I don't believe I'll ever feel at home anywheres else. I woon't know where I am when the trumpet sounds. I have to think before I can tell where the east is in New York; and what if I should git faced the wrong way when I raise? Jacob, I wonder you could sell it!" Her head shook, and the fire-light shone on her tears, as she searched the folds of her dress for her pocket.

A peal of laughter came from the drawing-room, and then the sound of chords struck on the piano.

"Hush! Don't you cry 'Liz'beth!" said Dryfoos. "Here; take my handkerchief. I've got a nice lot in the cemetery, and I'm goin' to have a monument, with two lambs on it— like the one you always liked so much. It ain't the fashion, any more, to have family buryin'-grounds; they're collectin' 'em into the cemeteries, all round."

"I reckon I got to bear it," said his wife, muffling her face in his handkerchief. "And I suppose the Lord kin find me, wherever I am. But I always did want to lay just there. You mind how we used to go out and set there, after milkin', and watch the sun go down, and talk about where their angels was, and try to figger it out?"

"I remember, 'Liz'beth."

The man's voice in the drawing-room sang a snatch of French song, insolent, mocking, salient; and then Christine's attempted the same strain, and another cry of laughter from Mela followed.

"Well, I always did expect to lay there. But I reckon it's all right. It won't be a great while, now, any way. Jacob, I don't believe I'm agoin' to live very long. I know it don't agree with me here."

"Oh, I guess it does, 'Liz'beth. You're just a little pulled down with the weather. It's coming spring, and you feel it; but the doctor says you're all right. I stopped in, on the way up; and he says so."

"I reckon he don't know everything," the old woman

persisted. "I've been runnin' down ever since we left Moffitt, and I didn't feel any too well there, even. It's a very strange thing, Jacob, that the richer you git, the less you ain't able to stay where you want to, dead or alive."

"It's for the children we do it," said Dryfoos. "We got to give them their chance in the world."

"Oh, the world! They ought to bear the yoke in their youth, like we done. I know it's what Coonrod would like to do."

Dryfoos got upon his feet. "If Coonrod'll mind his own business, and do what I want him to, he'll have yoke enough to bear." He moved from his wife, without further effort to comfort her, and pottered heavily out into the dining-room. Beyond its obscurity stretched the glitter of the deep drawing-room. His feet, in their broad, flat slippers, made no sound on the dense carpet, and he came unseen upon the little group there near the piano. Mela perched upon the stool with her back to the keys, and Beaton bent over Christine, who sat with a banjo in her lap, letting him take her hands and put them in the right place on the instrument. Her face was radiant with happiness, and Mela was watching her with foolish, unselfish pleasure in her bliss.

There was nothing wrong in the affair to a man of Dryfoos's traditions and perceptions, and if it had been at home in the farm sitting-room, or even in his parlour at Moffitt, he would not have minded a young man's placing his daughter's hands on a banjo, or even holding them there; it would have seemed a proper attention from him if he was courting her. But here, in such a house as this, with the daughter of a man who had made as much money as he had, he did not know but it was a liberty. He felt the angry doubt of it which beset him in regard to so many experiences of his changed life; he wanted to show his sense of it, if it was a liberty, but he did not know how, and he did not know that it was so. Besides, he could not help a touch of the pleasure in Christine's happiness which Mela showed; and he would have gone back to the library, if he could, without being discovered.

But Beaton had seen him, and Dryfoos, with a nonchalant nod to the young man, came forward. "What you got there, Christine?"

"A banjo," said the girl, blushing in her father's presence. Mela gurgled. "Mr. Beaton is learnun' her the first position."

Beaton was not embarrassed. He was in evening dress, and his face, pointed with its brown beard, showed extremely handsome above the expanse of his broad white shirt-front. He gave back as nonchalant a nod as he had got, and without further greeting to Dryfoos, he said to Christine, "No, no. You must keep your hand and arm so." He held them in position. "There! Now strike with your right hand. See?"

"I don't believe I can ever learn," said the girl, with a fond upward look at him.

"Oh yes, you can," said Beaton.

They both ignored Dryfoos in the little play of protests which followed, and he said, half jocosely, half suspiciously, "And is the banjo the fashion, now?" He remembered it as the emblem of low-down show business, and associated it with end-men, and blackened faces, and grotesque shirt collars.

"It's all the rage," Mela shouted in answer for all. "Everybody plays it. Mr. Beaton borrowed this from a lady friend of his."

"Humph! Pity I got you a piano, then," said Dryfoos. "A banjo would have been cheaper."

Beaton so far admitted him to the conversation as to seem reminded of the piano by his mentioning it. He said to Mela, "Oh, won't you just strike those chords?" and as Mela wheeled about and beat the keys, he took the banjo from Christine and sat down with it. "This way!" He strummed it, and murmured the tune Dryfoos had heard him singing from the library, while he kept his beautiful eyes floating on Christine's. "You try that, now; it's very simple."

"Where is Mrs. Mandel?" Dryfoos demanded, trying to assert himself.

Neither of the girls seemed to have heard him at first in the chatter they broke into over what Beaton proposed. Then

Mela said absently, "Oh, she had to go out to see one of her friends that's sick," and she struck the piano keys. "Come; try it, Chris!"

Dryfoos turned about unheeded, and went back to the library. He would have liked to put Beaton out of his house, and in his heart he burned against him as a contumacious hand; he would have liked to discharge him from the art department of *Every Other Week* at once. But he was aware of not having treated Beaton with much ceremony, and if the young man had returned his behaviour in kind, with an electrical response to his own feeling, had he any right to complain? After all, there was no harm in his teaching Christine the banjo.

His wife still sat looking into the fire. "I can't see," she said, "as we've got a bit more comfort of our lives, Jacob, because we've got such piles and piles of money. I wisht to gracious we was back on the farm this minute. I wisht you had held out ag'inst the childern about sellin' it; 'twould 'a' bin the best thing fur 'em, I say. I believe in my soul they'll git spoiled here in New York. I kin see a change in 'em a'ready—in the girls."

Dryfoos stretched himself on the lounge again. "I can't see as Coonrod is much comfort, either. Why ain't he here with his sisters? What does all that work of his on the East side amount to? It seems as if he done it to cross me, as much as anything." Dryfoos complained to his wife on the basis of mere affectional habit, which in married life often survives the sense of intellectual equality. He did not expect her to reason with him, but there was help in her listening, and though she could only soothe his fretfulness with soft answers which were often wide of the purpose, he still went to her for solace. "Here, I've gone into this newspaper business, or whatever it is, on his account, and he don't seem any more satisfied than ever. I can see he hain't got his heart in it."

"The pore boy tries; I know he does, Jacob; and he wants to please you. But he give up a good deal when he give up bein' a preacher; I s'pose we ought remember that."

"A preacher!" sneered Dryfoos. "I reckon bein' a preacher wouldn't satisfy him now. He had the impudence to tell me this afternoon that he would like to be a *priest*; and he threw it up to me that he never could be, because I'd kept him from studyin'."

"He don't mean a Catholic priest—not a Roman one, Jacob," the old woman explained wistfully. "He's told me all about it. They ain't the kind o' Catholics we been used to; some sort of 'Piscopalians; and they do a heap o' good amongst the poor folks over there. He says we ain't got any idea how folks lives in them tenement-houses, hunderds of 'em in one house, and whole families in a room; and it burns in his heart to help 'em like them Fathers, as he calls 'em, that gives their lives to it. He can't be a Father, he says, because he can't git the eddication, now; but he can be a Brother; and I can't find a word to say ag'inst it, when it gits to talkin', Jacob."

"I ain't saying anything against his priests, 'Liz'beth," said Dryfoos. "They're all well enough in their way; they've given up their lives to it, and it's a matter of business with them, like any other. But what I'm talking about now is Coonrod. I don't object to his doin' all the charity he wants to, and the Lord knows I've never been stingy with him about it. He might have all the money he wants, to give round any way he pleases."

"That's what I told him once, but he says money ain't the thing—or not the only thing you got to give to them poor folks. You got to give your time, and your knowledge, and your love—I don't know what all—you got to give *yourself*, if you expect to help 'em. That's what Coonrod says."

"Well, I can tell him that charity begins at home," said Dryfoos, sitting up, in his impatience. "And he'd better give himself to *us* a little—to his old father and mother. And his sisters. What's he doin' goin' off there, to his meetings, and I don't know what all, an' leavin' them here alone?"

"Why, ain't Mr. Beaton with 'em?" asked the old woman. "I thought I heared his voice."

"Mr. Beaton! Of course, he is! And who's Mr. Beaton, anyway?"

"Why, ain't he one of the men in Coonrod's office? I thought I heared——"

"Yes, he is! But *who* is he? What's he doing round here? Is he makin' up to Christine?"

"I reckon he is. From Mely's talk, she's about crazy over the fellow. Don't you like him, Jacob?"

"I don't know him, or what he is. He hasn't got any manners. Who brought him here? How'd he come to come, in the first place?"

"Mr. Fulkerson brung him, I believe," said the old woman patiently.

"Fulkerson!" Dryfoos snorted. "Where's Mrs. Mandel, I should like to know? He brought *her*, too. Does she go trapsein' off this way, every evening?"

"No, she seems to be here pretty regular most o' the time. I don't know how we could ever git along without her, Jacob; she seems to know just what to do, and the girls would be ten times as outbreakin' without her. I hope you ain't thinkin' o' turnin' her off, Jacob?"

Dryfoos did not think it necessary to answer such a question. "It's all Fulkerson, Fulkerson, Fulkerson. It seems to me that Fulkerson about runs this family. He brought Mrs. Mandel, and he brought that Beaton, and he brought that Boston fellow! I guess I give *him* a dose, though; and I'll learn Fulkerson that he can't have everything his own way. I don't want anybody to help me spend my money. I made it, and I can manage it. I guess Mr. Fulkerson can bear a little watching, now. He's been travelling pretty free, and he's got the notion he's driving, may be. I'm agoing to look after that book a little myself."

"You'll kill yourself, Jacob," said his wife, "tryin' to do so many things. And what is it all fur? I don't see as we're better off, any, for all the money. It's just as much care as it used to be when we was all there on the farm together. I wisht we could go back, Ja——"

"We *can't* go back!" shouted the old man fiercely. "There's no farm any more to go back to. The fields is full of gas wells and oil wells and hell holes generally; the house is tore down, and the barn's goin'——"

"The *barn!*" gasped the old woman. "Oh, my!"

"If I was to give all I'm worth this minute, we couldn't go back to the farm, any more than them girls in there could go back and be little children. I don't say we're any better off, for the money. I've got more of it now than I ever had; and there's no end to the luck; it pours in. But I feel like I was tied hand and foot. I don't know which way to move; I don't know what's best to do about anything. The money don't seem to buy anything but more and more care and trouble. We got a big house that we ain't at home in; and we got a lot of hired girls round under our feet that hinder and don't help. Our children don't mind us, and we got no friends or neighbours. But it had to be. I couldn't help but sell the farm, and we can't go back to it, for it ain't there. So don't you say anything more about it, 'Liz'beth."

"Pore Jacob!" said his wife. "Well, I woon't, dear."

IV

It was clear to Beaton that Dryfoos distrusted him; and the fact heightened his pleasure in Christine's liking for him. He was as sure of this as he was of the other, though he was not so sure of any reason for his pleasure in it. She had her charm; the charm of wildness to which a certain wildness in himself responded; and there were times when his fancy contrived a common future for them, which would have a prosperity forced from the old fellow's love of the girl. Beaton liked the idea of this compulsion better than he liked the idea of the money; there was something a little repulsive in that; he imagined himself rejecting it; he almost wished he was enough in love with the girl to marry her without it; that would be fine. He was taken with her in a certain measure, in a certain way; the question was in what measure, in what way.

It was partly to escape from this question that he hurried

down town, and decided to spend with the Leightons the hour remaining on his hands before it was time to go to the reception for which he was dressed. It seemed to him important that he should see Alma Leighton. After all, it was her charm that was most abiding with him; perhaps it was to be final. He found himself very happy in his present relations with her. She had dropped that barrier of pretences and ironical surprise. It seemed to him that they had gone back to the old ground of common artistic interest which he had found so pleasant the summer before. Apparently she and her mother had both forgiven his neglect of them in the first months of their stay in New York; he was sure that Mrs. Leighton liked him as well as ever, and if there was still something a little provisional in Alma's manner at times, it was something that piqued more than it discouraged; it made him curious, not anxious.

He found the young ladies with Fulkerson when he rang. He seemed to be amusing them both, and they were both amused beyond the merit of so small a pleasantry, Beaton thought, when Fulkerson said, "Introduce myself, Mr. Beaton: Mr. Fulkerson of *Every Other Week*. Think I've met you at our place." The girls laughed, and Alma explained that her mother was not very well, and would be sorry not to see him. Then she turned, as he felt, perversely, and went on talking with Fulkerson and left him to Miss Woodburn.

She finally recognised his disappointment: "Ah don't often get a chance at you, Mr. Beaton, and Ah'm just goin' to toak yo' to death. Yo' have been Soath yo'self, and yo' know ho' we *do* toak."

"I've survived to say yes," Beaton admitted.

"Oh, now, *do* you think we toak so much mo' than you do in the No'th?" the young lady deprecated.

"I don't know. I only know you can't talk too much for me. I should like to hear you say *Soath* and *hoase* and *aboat* for the rest of my life."

"That's what Ah call raght personal, Mr. Beaton. Now Ah'm goin' to be personal, too." Miss Woodburn flung out over her lap the square of cloth she was embroidering, and asked him, "Don't you think that's beautiful? Now, as an awtust—a *great* awtust?"

"As a *great* awtust, yes," said Beaton, mimicking her accent. "If I were less than great I might have something to say about the arrangement of colours. You're as bold and original as Nature."

"Really? Oh, now, do tell me yo' favo'ite colo', Mr. Beaton."

"My favourite colour? Bless my soul, why should I prefer any? Is blue good, or red wicked? Do people have favourite colours?" Beaton found himself suddenly interested.

"Of co'se they do," answered the girl. "Don't awtusts?"

"I never heard of one that had—consciously."

"Is it possible? I supposed they all had. Now *mah* favo'ite colo' is gawnet. Don't you think it's a pretty colo'?"

"It depends upon how it's used. Do you mean in neckties?" Beaton stole a glance at the one Fulkerson was wearing.

Miss Woodburn laughed with her face bowed upon her wrist. "Ah do think you gentlemen in the No'th awe ten tahms as lahvely as the ladies."

"Strange," said Beaton. "In the South—Soath, excuse me!—I made the observation that the ladies were ten times as lively as the gentlemen. What is that you're working?"

"This?" Miss Woodburn gave it another flirt, and looked at it with a glance of dawning recognition. "Oh, this is a table-covah. Wouldn't you lahke to see where it's to go?"

"Why, certainly."

"Well, if you'll be raght good I'll let yo' give me some professional advass about putting something in the co'ners or not, when you have seen it on the table."

She rose and led the way into the other room. Beaton knew she wanted to talk with him about something else; but he waited patiently to let her play her comedy out. She spread the cover on the table, and he advised her, as he saw she wished, against putting anything in the corners; just run a line of her stitch around the edge, he said.

"Mr. Fulkerson and Ah, why, we've been having a regular faght aboat it," she commented. "But we both agreed, fahnally, to leave it to you; Mr. Fulkerson said you'd be sure to be raght. Ah'm *so* glad you took mah sahde. But he's a great admahrer of yours, Mr. Beaton," she concluded demurely, suggestively.

"Is he? Well, I'm a great admirer of Fulkerson's," said Beaton, with a capricious willingness to humour her wish to talk about Fulkerson. "He's a capital fellow; generous, magnanimous, with quite an ideal of friendship, and an eye single to the main chance all the time. He would advertise *Every Other Week* on his family vault."

Miss Woodburn laughed, and said she should tell him what Beaton had said.

"Do. But he's used to defamation from me, and he'll think you're joking."

"Ah suppose," said Miss Woodburn, "that he's quahte the tahpe of a New York business man." She added, as if it followed logically, "He's so different from what I thought a New York business man would be."

"It's your Virginia tradition to despise business," said Beaton rudely.

Miss Woodburn laughed again. "*Despahse* it? Mah goodness! we want to get *into* it, and 'woak it fo' all it's wo'th,' as Mr. Fulkerson says. That tradition is all past. You don't know what the Soath is now. Ah suppose mah fathaw despahses business, but he's a tradition himself, as Ah tell him." Beaton would have enjoyed joining the young lady in anything she might be going to say in derogation of her father, but he restrained himself, and she went on more and more as if she wished to account for her father's habitual hauteur with Beaton, if not to excuse it. "Ah tell him he don't understand the rising generation. He was brought up in the old school, and he thinks we're all just lahke he was when he was young, with all those ahdeals of chivalry and family; but mah goodness! it's money that cyoants no'adays in the Soath, just lahke it does everywhere else. Ah suppose, if we could have slavery back in the fawm mah fathaw thinks it could have been brought up to, when the commercial spirit wouldn't let it alone, it would be the best thing; but we can't have it back, and Ah tell him we had better have the commercial spirit, as the next best thing."

Miss Woodburn went on, with sufficient loyalty and piety, to expose the difference of her own and her father's ideals, but with what Beaton thought less reference to his own unsympathetic attention than to a knowledge finally of the *personnel* and *matériel* of *Every Other Week*, and Mr. Fulkerson's relation to the enterprise. "You *most* excuse my asking so many questions, Mr. Beaton. You know it's all *mah* doing that we aw heah in New York. Ah just told mah fathaw that if he was evah goin' to do anything with his wrahtings, he had got to come No'th, and Ah *made* him come. Ah believe he'd have stayed in the Soath all his lahfe. And now Mr. Fulkerson wants him to let his editor see some of his wrahtings, and Ah wanted to know something aboat the magazine. We awe a great deal excited aboat it in this hoase, you know, Mr. Beaton," she concluded, with a look that now transferred the interest from Fulkerson to Alma. She led the way back to the room where they were sitting, and went up to triumph over Fulkerson with Beaton's decision about the table-cover.

Alma was left with Beaton near the piano, and he began to talk about the Dryfooses, as he sat down on the piano stool. He said he had been giving Miss Dryfoos a lesson on the banjo; he had borrowed the banjo of Miss Vance. Then he struck the chord he had been trying to teach Christine, and played over the air he had sung.

"How do you like that?" he asked, whirling round.

"It seems rather a disrespectful little tune, somehow," said Alma placidly.

Beaton rested his elbow on the corner of the piano, and gazed dreamily at her. "Your perceptions are wonderful. It *is* disrespectful. I played it, up there, because I felt disrespectful to them."

"Do you claim that as a merit?"

"No, I state it as a fact. How can you respect such people?"

"You might respect yourself, then," said the girl. "Or perhaps that wouldn't be so easy, either."

"No, it wouldn't. I like to have you say these things to me," said Beaton impartially.

"Well, I like to say them," Alma returned.

"They do me good."

"Oh, I don't know that that was my motive."

"There is no one like you—no one," said Beaton, as if apostrophising her in her absence. "To come from that house, with its assertions of money—you can hear it chink; you can smell the foul old banknotes; it stifles you— into an atmosphere like this, is like coming into another world."

"Thank you," said Alma. "I'm glad there isn't that unpleasant odour here; but I wish there was a little more of the chinking."

"No, no! Don't say that!" he implored. "I like to think that there is one soul uncontaminated by the sense of money in this big, brutal, sordid city."

"You mean two," said Alma, with modesty. "But if you stifle at the Dryfooses', why do you go there?"

"Why do I go?" he mused. "Don't you believe in knowing all the natures, the types, you can? Those girls are a strange study: the young one is a simple, earthly creature, as common as an oat-field; and the other a sort of sylvan life: fierce, flashing, feline——"

Alma burst out into a laugh. "What apt alliteration! And do they like being studied? I should think the sylvan life might—scratch."

"No," said Beaton, with melancholy absence, "it only— purrs."

The girl felt a rising indignation. "Well, then, Mr. Beaton; I should hope it *would* scratch, and bite, too. I think you've no business to go about studying people, as you do. It's abominable."

"Go on," said the young man. "That Puritan conscience of yours! It appeals to the old Covenanter strain in me—like a voice of pre-existence. Go on——"

"Oh, if I went on I should merely say it was not only abominable, but contemptible."

"You could be my guardian angel, Alma," said the young man, making his eyes more and more slumbrous and dreamy.

"Stuff! I hope I have a soul *above* buttons!"

He smiled, as she rose, and followed her across the room. "Good night, Mr. Beaton," she said.

Miss Woodburn and Fulkerson came in from the other room. "What! You're not going, Beaton?"

"Yes; I'm going to a reception. I stopped in on my way."

"To kill time," Alma explained.

"Well," said Fulkerson gallantly, "this is the last place I should like to do it. But I guess I'd better be going too. It has sometimes occurred to me that there is such a thing as staying too late. But with Brother Beaton, here, just starting in for an evening's amusement, it does seem a little early yet. Can't you urge me to stay, somebody?"

The two girls laughed, and Miss Woodburn said, "Mr. Beaton is such a butterfly of fashion! Ah wish *Ah* was on mah way to a pawty. Ah feel quahte envious."

"But he didn't say it to *make* you," Alma explained with meek softness.

"Well, we can't all be swells. Where is your party, anyway, Beaton?" asked Fulkerson. "How do you manage to get your invitations to those things? I suppose a fellow has to keep hinting round pretty lively, heigh?"

Beaton took these mockeries serenely, and shook hands with Miss Woodburn, with the effect of having already shaken hands with Alma. She stood with hers clasped behind her.

214

BEATON went away with the smile on his face which he had kept in listening to Fulkerson, and carried it with him to the reception. He believed that Alma was vexed with him for more personal reasons than she had implied; it flattered him that she should have resented what he told her of the Dryfooses. She had scolded him in their behalf apparently; but really because he had made her jealous by his interest, of whatever kind, in some one else. What followed, had followed naturally. Unless she had been quite a simpleton she could not have met his provisional love-making on any other terms; and the reason why Beaton chiefly liked Alma Leighton was that she was not a simpleton. Even up in the country, when she was overawed by his acquaintance, at first, she was not very deeply overawed, and at times she was not overawed at all. At such times she astonished him by taking his most solemn histrionics with flippant incredulity, and even burlesquing them. But he could see, all the same, that he had caught her fancy, and he admired the skill with which she punished his neglect when they met in New York. He had really come very near forgetting the Leightons; the intangible obligations of mutual kindness which hold some men so fast, hung loosely upon him; it would not have hurt him to break from them altogether; but when he recognised them at last, he found that it strengthened them indefinitely to have Alma ignore them so completely. If she had been sentimental, or softly reproachful, that would have been the end; he could not have stood it; he would have had to drop her. But when she met him on his own ground, and obliged *him* to be sentimental, the game was in her hands. Beaton laughed, now, when he thought of that, and he said to himself that the girl had grown immensely since she had come to New York; nothing seemed to have been lost upon her; she must have kept her eyes uncommonly wide open. He noticed that especially in their talks over her work; she had profited by everything she had seen and heard; she had all of Wetmore's ideas pat; it amused Beaton to see how she seized every useful word that he dropped, too, and turned him to technical account whenever she could. He liked that; she had a great deal of talent; there was no question of that; if she were a man there could be no question of her future. He began to construct a future for her; it included provision for himself too; it was a common future, in which their lives and work were united.

He was full of the glow of its prosperity when he met Margaret Vance at the reception.

The house was one where people might chat a long time together without publicly committing themselves to an interest in each other except such as grew out of each other's ideas. Miss Vance was there because she united in her catholic sympathies or ambitions the objects of the fashionable people and of the æsthetic people who met there on common ground. It was almost the only house in New York where this happened often, and it did not happen very often there. It was a literary house, primarily, with artistic qualifications, and the frequenters of it were mostly authors and artists; Wetmore, who was always trying to fit everything with a phrase, said it was the unfrequenters who were fashionable. There was great ease there, and simplicity; and if there was not distinction, it was not for want of distinguished people, but because there seems to be some solvent in New York life that reduces all men to a common level, that touches everybody with its potent magic and brings to the surface the deeply underlying nobody. The effect for some temperaments, for consciousness, for egotism, is admirable; for curiosity, for hero-worship, it is rather baffling. It is the spirit of the street transferred to the drawing-room; indiscriminating, levelling, but doubtless finally wholesome, and witnessing the immensity of the place, if not consenting to the grandeur of reputations or presences.

Beaton now denied that this house represented a salon at all, in the old sense; and he held that the salon was impossible, even undesirable, with us, when Miss Vance sighed for it. At any rate, he said that this turmoil of coming and going, this bubble and babble, this cackling and hissing of conversation was not the expression of any such civilisation as had created the salon. Here, he owned, were the elements of intellectual delightfulness, but he said their assemblage in such quantity alone denied the salon; there was too much of a good thing. The French word implied a long evening of general talk among the guests, crowned with a little chicken at supper, ending at cock-crow. Here was tea, with milk or with lemon—baths of it—and claret cup for the hardier spirits throughout the evening. It was very nice, very pleasant, but it was not the little chicken—not the salon. In fact, he affirmed, the salon descended from above, out of the great world, and included the æsthetic world in it. But our great world—the rich people, were stupid, with no wish to be otherwise; they were not even curious about authors and artists. Beaton fancied himself speaking impartially, and so he allowed himself to speak bitterly; he said that in no other city in the world, except Vienna, perhaps, were such people so little a part of society.

"It isn't altogether the rich people's fault," said Margaret; and she spoke impartially, too. "I don't believe that the literary men and the artists would like a salon that descended to them. Madame Geoffrin,* you know, was very plebeian; her husband was a business man of some sort."

"He would have been a howling swell in New York," said Beaton, still impartially.

Wetmore came up to their corner, with a scroll of bread and butter in one hand and a cup of tea in the other. Large and fat, and clean shaven, he looked like a monk in evening dress.

"We were talking about salons," said Margaret.

"Why don't you open a salon yourself?" asked Wetmore, breathing thickly from the anxiety of getting through the crowd without spilling his tea.

"Like poor Lady Barberina Lemon?"* said the girl, with a laugh. "What a good story! That idea of a woman who

217

couldn't be interested in any of the arts because she was socially and traditionally the material of them! We can never reach that height of nonchalance in this country."

"Not if we tried seriously?" suggested the painter. "I've an idea that if the Americans ever gave their minds to that sort of thing, they could take the palm—or the cake, as Beaton here would say—just as they do in everything else. When we do have an aristocracy, it will be an aristocracy that will go ahead of anything the world has ever seen. Why don't somebody make a beginning, and go in openly for an ancestry, and a lower middle class, and an hereditary legislature, and all the rest? We've got liveries, and crests, and palaces, and caste feeling. We're all right as far as we've gone, and we've got the money to go any length."

"Like your natural-gas man, Mr. Beaton," said the girl, with a smiling glance round at him.

"Ah!" said Wetmore, stirring his tea, "has Beaton got a natural-gas man?"

"My natural-gas man," said Beaton, ignoring Wetmore's question, "doesn't know how to live in his palace yet, and I doubt if he has any caste feeling. I fancy his family believe themselves victims of it. They say—one of the young ladies does—that she never saw such an unsociable place as New York; nobody calls."

"That's good!" said Wetmore. "I suppose they're all ready for company too: good cook, furniture, servants, carriages?"

"Galore," said Beaton.

"Well, that's too bad. There's a chance for you, Miss Vance. Doesn't your philanthropy embrace the socially destitute as well as the financially? Just think of a family like that, without a friend, in a great city! I should think common charity had a duty there—not to mention the uncommon."

He distinguished that kind as Margaret's by a glance of ironical deference. She had a repute for good works which was out of proportion to the works, as it always is, but she was really active in that way, under the vague obligation, which we now all feel, to be helpful. She was of the church which seems to have found a reversion to the imposing ritual of the past the way back to the early ideals of Christian brotherhood.

"Oh, they seem to have Mr. Beaton," Margaret answered, and Beaton felt obscurely flattered by her reference to his patronage of the Dryfooses.

He explained to Wetmore, "They have me because they partly own me. Dryfoos is Fulkerson's financial backer in *Every Other Week.*"

"Is that so? Well, that's interesting too. Aren't you rather astonished, Miss Vance, to see what a pretty thing Beaton is making of that magazine of his?"

"Oh," said Margaret, "it's so very nice, every way; it makes you feel as if you *did* have a country, after all. It's as *chic*—that detestable little word!—as those new French books."

"Beaton modelled it on them. But you mustn't suppose he does everything about *Every Other Week*; he'd like you to. Beaton, you haven't come up to that cover of your first number, since. That was the design of one of my pupils, Miss Vance—a little girl that Beaton discovered down in New Hampshire last summer."

"Oh yes. And have you great hopes of her, Mr. Wetmore?"

"She seems to have more love of it and knack for it than any one of her sex I've seen yet. It really looks like a case of art for art's sake, at times. But you can't tell. They're liable to get married at any moment, you know. Look here, Beaton, when your natural-gas man gets to the picture-buying stage in his development, just remember your old friends, will you? You know, Miss Vance, those new fellows have their regular stages. They never know what to do with their money, but they find out that people buy pictures, at one point. They shut your things up in their houses where no-body comes; and after a while they overeat themselves—they don't know what else to do—and die of apoplexy, and leave your pictures to a gallery, and then they see the light. It's slow, but it's pretty sure. Well, I see Beaton isn't going to move on, as he ought to do; and so *I* must. He always *was* an unconventional creature."

Wetmore went away, but Beaton remained, and he out-stayed several other people who came up to speak to Miss Vance. She was interested in everybody, and she liked the talk of these clever literary, artistic, clerical, even theatrical people, and she liked the sort of court with which they recognised her fashion as well as her cleverness; it was very pleasant to be treated intellectually as if she were one of themselves, and socially as if she was not habitually the same, but a sort of guest in Bohemia, a distinguished stranger. If it was Arcadia rather than Bohemia, still she felt her quality of distinguished stranger. The flattery of it touched her fancy, and not her vanity; she had very little vanity. Beaton's devotion made the same sort of appeal; it was not so much that she liked him as she liked being the object of his admiration. She was a girl of genuine sympathies, intellectual rather than sentimental. In fact she was an intellectual person, whom qualities of the heart saved from being disagreeable, as they saved her on the other hand from being worldly or cruel in her fashionableness. She had read a great many books, and had ideas about them, quite courageous and original ideas; she knew about pictures—she had been in Wetmore's class; she was fond of music; she was willing to understand even politics; in Boston she might have been agnostic, but in New York she was sincerely religious; she was very accomplished, and perhaps it was her goodness that prevented her feeling what was not best in Beaton.

"Do you think," she said, after the retreat of one of the comers and goers left her alone with him again, "that those young ladies would like me to call on them?"

"Those young ladies?" Beaton echoed. "Miss Leighton and——"

"No; I have been there with my aunt's cards already."

"Oh yes," said Beaton, as if he had known of it; he admired the pluck and pride with which Alma had refrained from ever mentioning the fact to him, and had kept her mother from mentioning it, which must have been difficult.

"I mean the Miss Dryfooses. It seems really barbarous, if nobody goes near them. We do all kinds of things, and help all kinds of people in some ways, but we let strangers remain strangers unless they know how to make their way among us."

"The Dryfooses certainly wouldn't know how to make their way among you," said Beaton, with a sort of dreamy absence in his tone.

Miss Vance went on, speaking out the process of reasoning in her mind, rather than any conclusions she had reached. "We defend ourselves by trying to believe that they must have friends of their own, or that they would think us patronising, and wouldn't like being made the objects of social charity; but they needn't really suppose anything of the kind."

"I don't imagine they would," said Beaton. "I think they'd be only too happy to have you come. But you wouldn't know what to do with each other, indeed, Miss Vance."

"Perhaps we shall like each other," said the girl bravely, "and then we shall know. What church are they of?"

"I don't believe they're of any," said Beaton. "The mother was brought up a Dunkard."

"A Dunkard?"

Beaton told what he knew of the primitive sect, with its early Christian polity, its literal interpretation of Christ's ethics, and its quaint ceremonial of foot-washing; he made something picturesque of that. "The father is a Mammon-worshipper, pure and simple. I suppose the young ladies go to church, but I don't know where. They haven't tried to convert me."

"I'll tell them not to despair—after I've converted *them*," said Miss Vance. "Will you let me use you as a *point d'appui*,* Mr. Beaton?"

"Any way you like. If you're really going to see them, perhaps I'd better make a confession. I left your banjo with them, after I got it put in order."

"How very nice! Then we have a common interest already."

"Do you mean the banjo, or——?"

"The banjo, decidedly. Which of them plays?"

"Neither. But the eldest heard that the banjo was 'all the rage,' as the youngest says. Perhaps you can persuade them that good works are the rage too."

Beaton had no very lively belief that Margaret would go to see the Dryfooses; he did so few of the things he proposed that he went upon the theory that others must be as faithless. Still, he had a cruel amusement in figuring the possible encounter between Margaret Vance, with her intellectual elegance, her eager sympathies and generous ideals, and those girls with their rude past, their false and distorted perspective, their sordid and hungry selfishness, and their faith in the omnipotence of their father's wealth wounded by their experience of its present social impotence. At the bottom of his heart he sympathised with them rather than with her; he was more like them.

People had ceased coming, and some of them were going. Miss Vance said she must go too, and she was about to rise, when the host came up with March; Beaton turned away.

"Miss Vance, I want to introduce Mr. March, the editor of *Every Other Week*. You oughtn't to be restricted to the art department. We literary fellows think that arm of the service gets too much of the glory nowadays." His banter was for Beaton, but he was already beyond ear-shot, and the host went on: "Mr. March can talk with you about your favourite Boston. He's just turned his back on it."

"Oh, I hope not!" said Miss Vance. "I can't imagine anybody voluntarily leaving Boston."

"I don't say he's so bad as that," said the host, committing March to her. "He came to New York because he couldn't help it—like the rest of us. I never know whether that's a compliment to New York or not."

They talked Boston a little while, without finding that they had common acquaintance there; Miss Vance must have concluded that society was much larger in Boston than she had supposed from her visits there, or else that March did not know many people in it. But she was not a girl to care

much for the inferences that might be drawn from such conclusions; she rather prided herself upon despising them; and
she gave herself to the pleasure of being talked to as if she
were of March's own age. In the glow of her sympathetic
beauty and elegance he talked his best, and tried to amuse
her with his jokes, which he had the art of tingeing with a
little seriousness on one side. He made her laugh; and he
flattered her by making her think; in her turn she charmed
him so much by enjoying what he said that he began to brag
of his wife, as a good husband always does when another
woman charms him; and she asked, Oh, was Mrs. March
there; and would he introduce her?

She asked Mrs. March for her address, and whether she
had a day; and she said she would come to see her, if she
would let her. Mrs. March could not be so enthusiastic about
her as March was, but as they walked home together they
talked the girl over, and agreed about her beauty and her
amiability. Mrs. March said she seemed very unspoiled for
a person who must have been so much spoiled. They tried
to analyse her charm, and they succeeded in formulating it
as a combination of intellectual fashionableness and worldly
innocence. "I think," said Mrs. March, "that city girls,
brought up as she must have been, are often the most innocent of all. They never imagine the wickedness of the world,
and if they marry happily they go through life as innocent
as children. Everything combines to keep them so; the very
hollowness of society shields them. They are the loveliest of
the human race. But perhaps the rest have to pay too much
for them."

"For such an exquisite creature as Miss Vance," said
March, "we couldn't pay too much."

A wild laughing cry suddenly broke upon the air at the
street-crossing in front of them. A girl's voice called out,
"Run, run, Jen! The copper is after you." A woman's figure
rushed stumbling across the way and into the shadow of the
houses, pursued by a burly policeman.

"Ah, but if *that's* part of the price?"

They went along fallen from the gay spirit of their talk

into a silence which he broke with a sigh. "Can that poor wretch and the radiant girl we left yonder really belong to the same system of things? How impossible each makes the other seem!"

VI

MRS. HORN believed in the world and in society and its unwritten constitution devoutly, and she tolerated her niece's benevolent activities as she tolerated her æsthetic sympathies because these things, however oddly, were tolerated—even encouraged by society; and they gave Margaret a charm. They made her originality interesting. Mrs. Horn did not intend that they should ever go so far as to make her troublesome; and it was with a sense of this abeyant authority of her aunt's that the girl asked her approval of her proposed call upon the Dryfooses. She explained as well as she could the social destitution of these opulent people, and she had of course to name Beaton as the source of her knowledge concerning them.

"Did Mr. Beaton suggest your calling on them?"

"No; he rather discouraged it."

"And why do you think you ought to go in this particular instance? New York is full of people who don't know anybody."

Margaret laughed. "I suppose it's like any other charity: you reach the cases you know of. The others you say you can't help, and you try to ignore them."

"It's very romantic," said Mrs. Horn. "I hope you've counted the cost; all the possible consequences."

Margaret knew that her aunt had in mind their common experience with the Leightons, whom, to give their common conscience peace, she had called upon with her aunt's cards and excuses, and an invitation for her Thursdays, somewhat too late to make the visit seem a welcome to New York. She was so coldly received, not so much for herself as in her quality of envoy, that her aunt experienced all the comfort which vicarious penance brings. She did not perhaps consider sufficiently her niece's guiltlessness in the expiation. Margaret was not with her at St. Barnaby in the fatal fortnight she passed there, and never saw the Leightons till she went to call upon them. She never complained: the strain of asceticism, which mysteriously exists in us all, and makes us put peas, boiled or unboiled, in our shoes, gave her patience with the snub which the Leightons presented her for her aunt. But now she said with this in mind, "Nothing seems simpler than to get rid of people if you don't want them. You merely have to let them alone."

"It isn't so pleasant, letting them alone," said Mrs. Horn.

"Or having them let you alone," said Margaret; for neither Mrs. Leighton nor Alma had ever come to enjoy the belated hospitality of Mrs. Horn's Thursdays.

"Yes, or having them let you alone," Mrs. Horn courageously consented. "And all that I ask you, Margaret, is to be sure that you really want to know these people."

"I don't," said the girl seriously, "in the usual way."

"Then the question is whether you do in the unusual way. They will build a great deal upon you," said Mrs. Horn, realising how much the Leightons must have built upon her, and how much out of proportion to her desert they must now dislike her; for she seemed to have had them on her mind from the time they came, and had always meant to recognise any reasonable claim they had upon her.

"It seems very odd, very sad," Margaret returned, "that you never can act unselfishly in society affairs. If I wished to go and see those girls just to do them a pleasure, and perhaps because if they're strange and lonely, I might do them good, even—it would be impossible."

"Quite," said her aunt. "Such a thing would be Quixotic. Society doesn't rest upon any such basis. It can't; it would go to pieces, if people acted from unselfish motives."

"Then it's a painted savage!" said the girl. "All its favours are really bargains. Its gifts are for gifts back again."

"Yes, that is true," said Mrs. Horn, with no more sense of wrong in the fact than the political economist has in the fact that wages are the measure of necessity and not of merit. "You get what you pay for. It's a matter of business." She satisfied herself with this formula, which she did not invent, as fully as if it were a reason; but she did not dislike her niece's revolt against it. That was part of Margaret's originality, which pleased her aunt in proportion to her own conventionality; she was really a timid person, and she liked the show of courage which Margaret's magnanimity often reflected upon her. She had through her a repute, with people who did not know her well, for intellectual and moral qualities; she was supposed to be literary and charitable; she almost had opinions and ideals, but really fell short of their possession. She thought that she set bounds to the girl's originality because she recognised them. Margaret understood this better than her aunt, and knew that she had consulted her about going to see the Dryfooses out of deference, and with no expectation of luminous instruction. She was used to being a law to herself, but she knew what she might and might not do, so that she was rather a by-law. She was the kind of girl that might have fancies for artists and poets, but might end by marrying a prosperous broker, and leavening a vast lump of moneyed and fashionable life with her culture, generosity, and good-will. The intellectual interests were first with her, but she might be equal to sacrificing them; she had the best heart, but she might know how to harden it; if she was eccentric, her social orbit was defined; comets themselves traverse space on fixed lines. She was like every one else, a congeries of contradictions and inconsistencies, but obedient to the general expectation of what a girl of her position must and must not finally be. Provisionally, she was very much what she liked to be.

VII

MARGARET VANCE tried to give herself some reason for going to call upon the Dryfooses, but she could find none better than the wish to do a kind thing. This seemed queerer and less and less sufficient as she examined it, and she even admitted a little curiosity as a harmless element in her motive, without being very well satisfied with it. She tried to add a slight sense of social duty, and then she decided to have no motive at all, but simply to pay her visit as she would to any other eligible strangers she saw fit to call upon. She perceived that she must be very careful not to let them see that any other impulse had governed her; she determined, if possible, to let them patronise *her*; to be very modest and sincere and diffident, and, above all, not to play a part. This was easy, compared with the choice of a manner that should convey to them the fact that she was not playing a part. When the hesitating Irish serving-man had acknowledged that the ladies were at home, and had taken her card to them, she sat waiting for them in the drawing-room. Her study of its appointments, with their impersonal costliness, gave her no suggestion how to proceed; the two sisters were upon her before she had really decided, and she rose to meet them with the conviction that she was going to play a part for want of some chosen means of not doing so. She found herself, before she knew it, making her banjo a property in the little comedy, and professing so much pleasure in the fact that Miss Dryfoos was taking it up; she had herself been so much interested by it. Anything, she said, was a relief from the piano; and then, between the guitar and the banjo, one must really choose the banjo, unless one wanted to devote one's whole natural life to the violin. Of course, there was the mandolin; but Margaret asked if they did not feel that the bit of shell you struck it with interposed a distance between you and the real soul of the instrument; and then it did have such a faint, mosquitoy little tone! She made much

227

of the question, which they left her to debate alone while they gazed solemnly at her till she characterised the tone of the mandolin, when Mela broke into a large, coarse laugh.

"Well, that's just what it *does* sound like," she explained defiantly to her sister. "I always feel like it was going to settle somewhere, and I want to hit myself a slap before it begins to bite. I don't see what ever brought such a thing into fashion."

Margaret had not expected to be so powerfully seconded, and she asked, after gathering herself together, "And you are both learning the banjo?"

"My, no!" said Mela, "I've gone through enough with the piano. Christine is learning it."

"I'm so glad you are making my banjo useful at the outset, Miss Dryfoos." Both girls stared at her, but found it hard to cope with the fact that this was the lady friend whose banjo Beaton had lent them. "Mr. Beaton mentioned that he had left it here. I hope you'll keep it as long as you find it useful."

At this amiable speech even Christine could not help thanking her. "Of course," she said, "I expect to get another, right off. Mr. Beaton is going to choose it for me."

"You are very fortunate. If you haven't a teacher yet I should so like to recommend mine."

Mela broke out in her laugh again. "Oh, I guess Christine's pretty well suited with the one she's got," she said, with insinuation. Her sister gave her a frowning glance, and Margaret did not tempt her to explain.

"Then that's much better," she said. "I have a kind of superstition in such matters; I don't like to make a second choice. In a shop I like to take the first thing of the kind I'm looking for, and even if I choose further I come back to the original."

"How funny!" said Mela. "Well, now, I'm just the other way. I always take the last thing, after I've picked over all the rest. My luck always seems to be at the bottom of the heap. Now, Christine, she's more like you. I believe she could walk right up blindfolded and put her hand on the thing she wants every time."

"I'm like father," said Christine, softened a little by the celebration of her peculiarity. "He says the reason so many people don't get what they want is that they don't want it bad enough. Now, when I want a thing, it seems to me that I want it all through."

"Well, that's just like father, too," said Mela. "That's the way he done when he got that eighty-acre piece next to Moffitt that he kept when he sold the farm, and that's got some of the best gas wells on it now that there is anywhere." She addressed the explanation to her sister, to the exclusion of Margaret, who, nevertheless, listened with a smiling face and a resolutely polite air of being a party to the conversation. Mela rewarded her amiability by saying to her finally, "You never been in the natural-gas country, have you?"

"Oh no! And I should so much like to see it!" said Margaret, with a fervour that was partly voluntary.

"Would you? Well, we're kind of sick of it, but I suppose it *would* strike a stranger."

"*I* never got tired of looking at the big wells when they lit them up," said Christine. "It seems as if the world was on fire."

"Yes, and when you see the surface-gas burnun' down in the woods, like it used to by our spring-house—so still, and never spreadun' any, just like a bed of some kind of wild-flowers when you ketch sight of it a piece off."

They began to tell of the wonders of their strange land in an antiphony of reminiscences and descriptions; they unconsciously imputed a merit to themselves from the number and violence of the wells on their father's property; they bragged of the high civilisation of Moffitt, which they compared to its advantage with that of New York. They became excited by Margaret's interest in natural gas, and forgot to be suspicious and envious.

She said, as she rose, "Oh, how much I should like to see it all!" Then she made a little pause and added, "I'm so sorry my aunt's Thursdays are over; she never has them after Lent, but we're to have some people Tuesday evening at a little concert which a musical friend is going to give with

229

some other artists. There won't be any banjos, I'm afraid, but there'll be some very good singing, and my aunt would be so glad if you could come with your mother."

She put down her aunt's card on the table near her, while Mela gurgled, as if it were the best joke, "Oh, my! Mother never goes anywhere; you couldn't get her out for love or money." But she was herself overwhelmed with a simple joy at Margaret's politeness, and showed it in a sensuous way, like a child, as if she had been tickled. She came closer to Margaret and seemed about to fawn physically upon her.

"Ain't she just as lovely as she can live?" she demanded of her sister when Margaret was gone.

"I don't know," said Christine. "I guess she wanted to know who Mr. Beaton had been lending her banjo to."

"Pshaw! Do you suppose she's in love with him?" asked Mela, and then she broke into her hoarse laugh at the look her sister gave her. "Well, don't eat *me*, Christine! I wonder who she is, anyway? I'm goun' to git it out of Mr. Beaton the next time he calls. I guess she's somebody. Mrs. Mandel can tell. I wish that old friend of hers would hurry up and git well—or something. But I guess we appeared about as well as she did. I could see she was afraid of you, Christine. I reckon it's gittun' around a little about father; and when it does I don't believe we shall want for callers. Say, are you goun'? To that concert of theirs?"

"I don't know. Not till I know who they are first."

"Well, we've got to hump ourselves if we're goun' to find out before Tuesday."

As she went home Margaret felt wrought in her that most incredible of the miracles, which, nevertheless, any one may make his experience. She felt kindly to these girls because she had tried to make them happy, and she hoped that in the interest she had shown there had been none of the poison of flattery. She was aware that this was a risk she ran in such an attempt to do good. If she had escaped this effect she was willing to leave the rest with Providence.

VIII

THE notion that a girl of Margaret Vance's traditions would naturally form of girls like Christine and Mela Dryfoos would be that they were abashed in the presence of the new conditions of their lives, and that they must receive the advance she had made them with a certain grateful humility. However they received it, she had made it upon principle, from a romantic conception of duty; but this was the way she imagined they would receive it, because she thought that she would have done so if she had been as ignorant and unbred as they. Her error was in arguing their attitude from her own temperament, and endowing them, for the purposes of argument, with her perspective. They had not the means, intellectual or moral, of feeling as she fancied. If they had remained at home on the farm where they were born, Christine would have grown up that embodiment of impassioned suspicion which we find oftenest in the narrowest spheres, and Mela would always have been a good-natured simpleton; but they would never have doubted their equality with the wisest and the finest. As it was, they had not learned enough at school to doubt it, and the splendour of their father's success in making money had blinded them for ever to any possible difference against them. They had no question of themselves in the social abeyance to which they had been left in New York. They had been surprised, mystified; it was not what they had expected; there must be some mistake. They were the victims of an accident, which would be repaired as soon as the fact of their father's wealth had got around. They had been steadfast in their faith, through all their disappointment, that they were not only better than most people by virtue of his money, but as good as any; and they took Margaret's visit, so far as they investigated its motive, for a sign that at last it was beginning to get around; of course, a thing could not get around in New York so quick as it could in a small place. They were confirmed in their

231

belief by the sensation of Mrs. Mandel when she returned to duty that afternoon, and they consulted her about going to Mrs. Horn's *musicale*. If she had felt any doubt at the name—for there were Horns and Horns—the address on the card put the matter beyond question; and she tried to make her charges understand what a precious chance had befallen them. She did not succeed; they had not the premises, the experience, for a sufficient impression; and she undid her work in part by the effort to explain that Mrs. Horn's standing was independent of money; that though she was positively rich, she was comparatively poor. Christine inferred that Miss Vance had called because she wished to be the first to get in with them since it had begun to get around. This view commended itself to Mela too, but without warping her from her opinion that Miss Vance was all the same too sweet for anything. She had not so vivid a consciousness of her father's money as Christine had; but she reposed perhaps all the more confidently upon its power. She was far from thinking meanly of any one who thought highly of her for it; that seemed so natural a result as to be amiable, even admirable; she was willing that any such person should get all the good there was in such an attitude toward her.

They discussed the matter that night at dinner before their father and mother, who mostly sat silent at their meals; the father frowning absently over his plate, with his head close to it, and making play into his mouth with the back of his knife (he had got so far toward the use of his fork as to despise those who still ate from the edge of their knives), and the mother partly missing hers at times in the nervous tremor that shook her face from side to side.

After a while the subject of Mela's hoarse babble and of Christine's high-pitched, thin, sharp forays of assertion and denial in the field which her sister's voice seemed to cover, made its way into the old man's consciousness, and he perceived that they were talking with Mrs. Mandel about it, and that his wife was from time to time offering an irrelevant and mistaken comment. He agreed with Christine, and silently took her view of the affair some time before he made any sign of having listened. There had been a time in his life when other things besides his money seemed admirable to him. He had once respected himself for the hard-headed, practical common-sense which first gave him standing among his country neighbours; which made him supervisor, school trustee, justice of the peace, county commissioner, secretary of the Moffitt County Agricultural Society. In those days he had served the public with disinterested zeal and proud ability; he used to write to the *Lake Shore Farmer* on agricultural topics; he took part in opposing, through the Moffitt papers, the legislative waste of the people's money; on the question of selling a local canal to the railroad company, which killed that fine old State work, and let the dry ditch grow up to grass, he might have gone to the Legislature, but he contented himself with defeating the Moffitt member who had voted for the job. If he opposed some measures for the general good, like high-schools and school libraries, it was because he lacked perspective, in his intense individualism, and suspected all expense of being spendthrift. He believed in good district schools, and he had a fondness, crude but genuine, for some kinds of reading—history, and forensics of an elementary sort.

With his good head for figures he doubted doctors and despised preachers; he thought lawyers were all rascals, but he respected them for their ability; he was not himself litigious, but he enjoyed the intellectual encounters of a difficult lawsuit, and he often attended a sitting of the fall term of court, when he went to town, for the pleasure of hearing the speeches. He was a good citizen, and a good husband. As a good father, he was rather severe with his children, and used to whip them, especially the gentle Conrad, who somehow crossed him most, till the twins died. After that he never struck any of them; and from the sight of a blow dealt a horse he turned as if sick. It was a long time before he lifted himself up from his sorrow, and then the will of the man seemed to have been breached through his affections. He let the girls do as they pleased—the twins had been girls; he let them go away to school, and got them a piano.

233

It was they who made him sell the farm. If Conrad had only had their spirit he could have made him keep it, he felt; and he resented the want of support he might have found in a less yielding spirit than his son's.

His moral decay began with his perception of the opportunity of making money quickly and abundantly, which offered itself to him after he sold his farm. He awoke to it slowly, from a desolation in which he tasted the last bitter of homesickness, the utter misery of idleness and listlessness. When he broke down and cried for the hard-working, wholesome life he had lost, he was near the end of this season of despair, but he was also near the end of what was best in himself. He devolved upon a meaner ideal than that of conservative good citizenship, which had been his chief moral experience: the money he had already made without effort and without merit bred its unholy self-love in him; he began to honour money, especially money that had been won suddenly and in large sums; for money that had been earned, painfully, slowly, and in little amounts, he had only pity and contempt. The poison of that ambition to go somewhere and be somebody which the local speculators had instilled into him began to work in the vanity which had succeeded his somewhat scornful self-respect; he rejected Europe as the proper field for his expansion; he rejected Washington; he preferred New York, whither the men who have made money and do not yet know that money has made them, all instinctively turn. He came where he could watch his money breed more money, and bring greater increase of its kind in an hour of luck than the toil of hundreds of men could earn in a year. He called it speculation, stocks, the street; and his pride, his faith in himself, mounted with his luck. He expected, when he had sated his greed, to begin to spend, and he had formulated an intention to build a great house, to add another to the palaces of the country-bred millionaires who have come to adorn the great city. In the meantime he made little account of the things that occupied his children, except to fret at the ungrateful indifference of his son to the interests that could alone make a man of him. He did not know whether his daughters were in society or not; with people coming and going in the house he would have supposed they must be so, no matter who the people were; in some vague way he felt that he had hired society in Mrs. Mandel, at so much a year. He never met a superior himself, except now and then a man of twenty or thirty millions to his one or two, and then he felt his soul creep within him, without a sense of social inferiority; it was a question of financial inferiority; and though Dryfoos's soul bowed itself and crawled, it was with a gambler's admiration of wonderful luck. Other men said these many-millioned millionaires were smart, and got their money by sharp practices to which lesser men could not attain; but Dryfoos believed that he could compass the same ends, by the same means, with the same chances; he respected their money, not them.

When he now heard Mrs. Mandel and his daughters talking of that person, whoever she was, that Mrs. Mandel seemed to think had honoured his girls by coming to see them, his curiosity was pricked as much as his pride was galled.

"Well, anyway," said Mela, "I don't care whether Christine's goun' or not; *I* am. And you got to go with me, Mrs. Mandel."

"Well, there's a little difficulty," said Mrs. Mandel, with her unfailing dignity and politeness. "I haven't been asked, you know."

"Then what are we goun' to do?" demanded Mela, almost crossly. She was physically too amiable, she felt too well corporeally, ever to be quite cross. "She might 'a' knowed— well *known*—we couldn't 'a' come alone, in New York. I don't see why we couldn't. I don't call it much of an invitation."

"I suppose she thought you could come with your mother," Mrs. Mandel suggested.

"She didn't say anything about mother. Did she, Christine? Or, yes, she did, too. And I told her she couldn't git mother out. Don't you remember?"

"I didn't pay much attention," said Christine. "I wasn't certain we wanted to go."

"I reckon you wasn't goun' to let her see that we cared much," said Mela, half reproachful, half proud of this attitude of Christine. "Well, I don't see but what we got to stay at home." She laughed at this lame conclusion of the matter.

"Perhaps Mr. Conrad—you could very properly take him without an express invitation——" Mrs. Mandel began.

Conrad looked up in alarm and protest. "I—I don't think I could go that evening——"

"What's the reason?" his father broke in harshly. "You're not such a sheep that you're afraid to go into company with your sisters? Or are you too good to go with them?"

"If it's to be anything like that night when them hussies come out and danced that way," said Mrs. Dryfoos, "I don't blame Coonrod for not wantun' to go. I never saw the beat of it."

Mela sent a yelling laugh across the table to her mother. "Well, I wish Miss Vance could 'a' heard that! Why, mother, did you think it was like the ballet?"

"Well, I didn't know, Mely, child," said the old woman. "I didn't know *what* it was like. I hain't never been to one, and you can't be too keerful where you go, in a place like New York."

"What's the reason you can't go?" Dryfoos ignored the passage between his wife and daughter in making this demand of his son, with a sour face.

"I have an engagement that night—it's one of our meetings——"

"I reckon you can let your meeting go for one night," said Dryfoos. "It can't be so important as all that, that you must disappoint your sisters."

"I don't like to disappoint those poor creatures. They depend so much upon the meetings——"

"I reckon they can stand it for one night," said the old man. He added, "The poor ye have with you always."

"That's so, Coonrod," said his mother. "It's the Saviour's own words."

"Yes, mother. But they're not meant just as father used them."

"How do you know how they were meant? Or how I used them?" cried the father. "Now you just make your plans to go with the girls, Tuesday night. They can't go alone, and Mrs. Mandel can't go with them."

"Pshaw!" said Mela. "We don't want to take Conrad away from his meetun', do we, Chris?"

"I don't know," said Christine, in her high, fine voice. "They could get along without him for one night, as father says."

"Well, I'm not agoun' to take him," said Mela. "Now, Mrs. Mandel, just think out some other way. Say! What's the reason we couldn't get somebody else to take us just as well? Ain't that rulable?"

"It would be allowable——"

"Allowable, I *mean*," Mela corrected herself.

"But it might look a little significant, unless it was some old family friend."

"Well, let's get Mr. Fulkerson to take us. He's the oldest family friend *we* got."

"I won't go with Mr. Fulkerson," said Christine serenely.

"Why, I'm sure, Christine," her mother pleaded, "Mr. Fulkerson is a very good young man, and very nice appearun'."

Mela shouted, "He's ten times as pleasant as that old Mr. Beaton of Christine's!"

Christine made no effort to break the constraint that fell upon the table at this sally, but her father said, "Christine is right, Mela. It wouldn't do for you to go with any other young man. Conrad will go with you."

"I'm not certain I want to go, yet," said Christine.

"Well, settle that among yourselves. But if you want to go, your brother will go with you."

"Of course, Coonrod'll go, if his sisters wants him to," the old woman pleaded. "I reckon it ain't agoun' to be anything very bad; and if it is, Coonrod, why you can just git right up and come out."

"It will be all right, mother. And I will go, of course."

"There, now, I knowed you would, Coonrod. Now, fawther!" This appeal was to make the old man say something in recognition of Conrad's sacrifice.

"You'll always find," he said, "that it's those of your own household that have the first claim on you."

"That's so, Coonrod," urged his mother. "It's Bible truth. Your fawther ain't a perfesser, but he always read his Bible. Search the Scriptures. That's what it means."

"Laws!" cried Mely, "a body can see, easy enough from mother, where Conrad's wantun' to be a preacher comes from. I should 'a' thought she'd 'a' wanted to been one herself."

"Let your women keep silence in the churches,"* said the old woman solemnly.

"There you go again, mother! I guess if you was to say that to some of the lady ministers nowadays, you'd git yourself into trouble." Mela looked round for approval, and gurgled out a hoarse laugh.

IX

THE Dryfooses went late to Mrs. Horn's *musicale* in spite of Mrs. Mandel's advice. Christine made the delay, both because she wished to show Miss Vance that she was not anxious, and because she had some vague notion of the distinction of arriving late at any sort of entertainment. Mrs. Mandel insisted upon the difference between this *musicale* and an ordinary reception; but Christine rather fancied disturbing a company that had got seated, and perhaps making people rise and stand, while she found her way to her place, as she had seen them do for a tardy comer at the theatre.

Mela, whom she did not admit to her reasons or feelings always, followed her with the servile admiration she had for all that Christine did; and she took on trust as somehow successful the result of Christine's obstinacy, when they were allowed to stand against the wall at the back of the room through the whole of the long piece begun just before they came in. There had been no one to receive them; a few people, in the rear rows of chairs near them, turned their heads to glance at them, and then looked away again. Mela had her misgivings; but at the end of the piece Miss Vance came up to them at once, and then Mela knew that she had her eyes on them all the time, and that Christine must have been right. Christine said nothing about their coming late, and so Mela did not make any excuse, and Miss Vance seemed to expect none. She glanced with a sort of surprise at Conrad, when Christine introduced him; Mela did not know whether she liked their bringing him, till she shook hands with him, and said, "Oh, I am very glad indeed! Mr. Dryfoos and I have met before." Without explaining where or when, she led them to her aunt and presented them, and then said, "I'm going to put you with some friends of yours," and quickly seated them next the Marches. Mela liked that well enough; she thought she might have some joking with Mr. March, for all his wife was so stiff; but the look which Christine wore seemed to forbid, provisionally at least, any such recreation. On her part, Christine was cool with the Marches. It went through her mind that they must have told Miss Vance they knew her; and perhaps they had boasted of her intimacy. She relaxed a little toward them when she saw Beaton leaning against the wall at the end of the row next Mrs. March. Then she conjectured that he might have told Miss Vance of her acquaintance with the Marches, and she bent forward and nodded to Mrs. March across Conrad, Mela, and Mr. March. She conceived of him as a sort of hand of her father's, but she was willing to take them at their apparent social valuation for the time. She leaned back in her chair, and did not look up at Beaton after the first furtive glance, though she felt his eyes on her.

The music began again almost at once, before Mela had time to make Conrad tell her where Miss Vance had met him before. She would not have minded interrupting the music; but every one else seemed so attentive, even Christine, that she had not the courage.

The concert went on to an end without realising for her the ideal of pleasure which one ought to find in society. She was not exacting, but it seemed to her there were very few young men, and when the music was over, and their opportunity came to be sociable, they were not very sociable. They were not introduced, for one thing; but it appeared to Mela that they might have got introduced, if they had any sense; she saw them looking at her, and she was glad she had dressed so much; she was dressed more than any other lady there, and either because she was the most dressed of any person there, or because it had got around who her father was, she felt that she had made an impression on the young men. In her satisfaction with this, and from her good nature, she was contented to be served with her refreshments after the concert by Mr. March, and to remain joking with him. She was at her ease; she let her hoarse voice out in her largest laugh; she accused him, to the admiration of those near, of getting her into a perfect gale. It appeared to her, in her own pleasure, her mission to illustrate to the rather subdued people about her what a good time really was, so that they could have it if they wanted it. Her joy was crowned when March modestly professed himself unworthy to monopolise her, and explained how selfish he felt in talking to a young lady when there were so many young men dying to do so.

"Oh, pshaw dyun', yes!" cried Mela, tasting the irony. "I guess I see them!"

He asked if he might really introduce a friend of his to her, and she said, Well, yes, if he thought he could live to get to her; and March brought up a man whom he thought very young and Mela thought very old. He was a contributor to *Every Other Week*, and so March knew him; he believed himself a student of human nature in behalf of literature, and he now set about studying Mela. He tempted her to express her opinion on all points, and he laughed so amiably at the boldness and humorous vigour of her ideas that she was delighted with him. She asked him if he was a New-Yorker by birth; and she told him she pitied him, when he said he had never been West. She professed herself perfectly

sick of New York, and urged him to go to Moffitt if he wanted
to see a real live town. He wondered if it would do to put her
into literature just as she was, with all her slang and brag,
but he decided that he would have to subdue her a great
deal: he did not see how he could reconcile the facts of her
conversation with the facts of her appearance: her beauty,
her splendour of dress, her apparent right to be where she
was. These things perplexed him; he was afraid the great
American novel, if true, must be incredible. Mela said he
ought to hear her sister go on about New York when they
first came; but she reckoned that Christine was getting so
she could put up with it a little better, now. She looked
significantly across the room to the place where Christine
was now talking with Beaton; and the student of human
nature asked, Was she here? and, Would she introduce him?
Mela said she would, the first chance she got; and she added,
They would be much pleased to have him call. She felt herself to be having a beautiful time, and she got directly upon
such intimate terms with the student of human nature that
she laughed with him about some peculiarities of his, such
as his going so far about to ask things he wanted to know
from her; she said she never did believe in beating about the
bush much. She had noticed the same thing in Miss Vance
when she came to call that day; and when the young man
owned that he came rather a good deal to Mrs. Horn's house,
she asked him, Well, what sort of a girl was Miss Vance,
anyway, and where did he suppose she had met her brother?
The student of human nature could not say as to this, and
as to Miss Vance he judged it safest to treat of the non-
society side of her character, her activity in charity, her
special devotion to the work among the poor on the East
Side, which she personally engaged in.

"Oh, that's where Conrad goes, too!" Mela interrupted.
"I'll bet anything that's where she met him. I *wisht* I could
tell Christine! But I suppose she would want to kill me, if I
was to speak to her *now*."

The student of human nature said politely, "Oh, shall I
take you to her?"

Mela answered, "I guess you better *not*!" with a laugh so significant that he could not help his inferences concerning both Christine's absorption in the person she was talking with, and the habitual violence of her temper. He made note of how Mela helplessly spoke of all her family by their names, as if he were already intimate with them; he fancied that if he could get that in skilfully, it would be a valuable colour in his study; the English lord whom she should astonish with it, began to form himself out of the dramatic nebulosity in his mind, and to whirl on a definite orbit in American society. But he was puzzled to decide whether Mela's willingness to take him into her confidence on short notice was typical or personal: the trait of a daughter of the natural-gas millionaire, or a foible of her own.

Beaton talked with Christine the greater part of the evening that was left after the concert. He was very grave, and took the tone of a fatherly friend; he spoke guardedly of the people present, and moderated the severity of some of Christine's judgments of their looks and costumes. He did this out of a sort of unreasoned allegiance to Margaret, whom he was in the mood of wishing to please by being very kind and good, as she always was. He had the sense also of atoning by this behaviour for some reckless things he had said before that to Christine; he put on a sad, reproving air with her, and gave her the feeling of being held in check.

She chafed at it, and said, glancing at Margaret in talk with her brother, "I don't think Miss Vance is so very pretty, do you?"

"I never think whether she's pretty or not," said Beaton, with dreamy affectation. "She is merely perfect. Does she know your brother?"

"So *she* says. I didn't suppose Conrad ever went anywhere, except to tenement-houses."

"It might have been there," Beaton suggested. "She goes among friendless people everywhere."

"May be that's the reason she came to see *us*!" said Christine.

Beaton looked at her with his smouldering eyes, and felt

the wish to say, "Yes, it was exactly that," but he only allowed himself to deny the possibility of any such motive in that case. He added, "I am so glad you know her, Miss Dryfoos. I never met Miss Vance without feeling myself better and truer, somehow; or the wish to be so."

"And you think *we* might be improved too?" Christine retorted. "Well, I must say you're not very flattering, Mr. Beaton, anyway."

Beaton would have liked to answer her according to her cattishness, with a good clawing sarcasm that would leave its smart in her pride; but he was being good, and he could not change all at once. Besides, the girl's attitude under the social honour done her interested him. He was sure she had never been in such good company before, but he could see that she was not in the least affected by the experience. He had told her who this person and that was; and he saw she had understood that the names were of consequence; but she seemed to feel her equality with them all. Her serenity was not obviously akin to the savage stoicism in which Beaton hid his own consciousness of social inferiority; but having won his way in the world so far by his talent, his personal quality, he did not conceive the simple fact in her case. Christine was self-possessed because she felt that a knowledge of her father's fortune had got around, and she had the peace which money gives to ignorance; but Beaton attributed her poise to indifference to social values. This, while he inwardly sneered at it, avenged him upon his own too keen sense of them, and, together with his temporary allegiance to Margaret's goodness, kept him from retaliating Christine's vulgarity. He said, "I don't see how that could be," and left the question of flattery to settle itself.

The people began to go away, following each other up to take leave of Mrs. Horn. Christine watched them with unconcern, and either because she would not be governed by the general movement, or because she liked being with Beaton, gave no sign of going. Mela was still talking to the student of human nature, sending out her laugh in deep gurgles amidst the unimaginable confidences she was making him about herself, her family, the staff of *Every Other Week*, Mrs. Mandel, and the kind of life they had all led before she came to them. He was not a blind devotee of art for art's sake, and though he felt that if one could portray Mela just as she was she would be the richest possible material, he was rather ashamed to know some of the things she told him; and he kept looking anxiously about for a chance of escape. The company had reduced itself to the Dryfoos groups and some friends of Mrs. Horn's who had the right to linger, when Margaret crossed the room with Conrad to Christine and Beaton.

"I'm so glad, Miss Dryfoos, to find that I was not quite a stranger to you all when I ventured to call, the other day. Your brother and I are rather old acquaintances, though I never knew who he was before. I don't know just how to say we met where he is valued so much. I suppose I mustn't try to say how much," she added with a look of deep regard at him.

Conrad blushed and stood folding his arms tight over his breast, while his sister received Margaret's confession with the suspicion which was her first feeling in regard to any new thing. What she concluded was that this girl was trying to get in with them, for reasons of her own. She said: "Yes; it's the first *I* ever heard of his knowing you. He's so much taken up with his meetings, he didn't want to come to-night."

Margaret drew in her lip before she answered, without apparent resentment of the awkwardness or ungraciousness, whichever she found it, "I don't wonder! You become so absorbed in such work that you think nothing else is worth while. But I'm glad Mr. Dryfoos could come with you; I'm *so* glad you could all come; I knew you would enjoy the music. Do sit down——"

"No," said Christine bluntly; "we must be going. Mela!" she called out, "come!"

The last group about Mrs. Horn looked round, but Christine advanced upon them undismayed, and took the hand Mrs. Horn promptly gave her. "Well, I must bid you good night."

"Oh, good night," murmured the elder lady. "So very kind of you to come."

"I've had the best kind of a time," said Mela cordially. "I hain't laughed so much, I don't know when."

"Oh, I'm glad you enjoyed it," said Mrs. Horn in the same polite murmur she had used with Christine; but she said nothing to either sister about any future meeting.

They were apparently not troubled. Mela said over her shoulder to the student of human nature, "The next time I see you I'll *give* it to you for what you said about Moffitt."

Margaret made some entreating paces after them, but she did not succeed in covering the retreat of the sisters against critical conjecture. She could only say to Conrad, as if recurring to the subject, "I *hope* we can get our friends to play for us some night. I know it isn't any real help, but such things take the poor creatures out of themselves for the time being, don't you think?"

"Oh yes," he answered. "They're good in that way." He turned back hesitatingly to Mrs. Horn, and said, with a blush, "I thank you for a happy evening."

"Oh, I am very glad," she replied in her murmur.

One of the old friends of the house arched her eyebrows in saying good night, and offered the two young men remaining seats home in her carriage. Beaton gloomily refused, and she kept herself from asking the student of human nature, till she had got him into her carriage, "What *is* Moffitt, and what did you say about it?"

"Now you see, Margaret," said Mrs. Horn, with bated triumph, when the people were all gone.

"Yes, I see," the girl consented. "From one point of view, of course it's been a failure. I don't think we've given Miss Dryfoos a pleasure, but perhaps nobody could. And at least we've given her the opportunity of enjoying herself."

"Such people," said Mrs. Horn philosophically, "people with their money must of course be received sooner or later. You can't keep them out. Only, I believe I would rather let some one else begin with them. The Leightons didn't come?"

"I sent them cards. I *couldn't* call again."

Mrs. Horn sighed a little. "I suppose Mr. Dryfoos is one of your fellow-philanthropists?"

"He's one of the workers," said Margaret. "I met him several times at the Hall, but I only knew his first name. I think he's a great friend of Father Benedict; he seems devoted to the work. Don't you think he looks *good*?"

"Very," said Mrs. Horn, with a colour of censure in her assent. "The younger girl seemed more amiable than her sister. But what manners!"

"Dreadful!" said Margaret, with knit brows, and a pursed mouth of humorous suffering. "But she appeared to feel very much at home."

"Oh, as to that, neither of them was much abashed. Do you suppose Mr. Beaton gave the other one some hints for that quaint dress of hers? I don't imagine that black and lace is her own invention. She seems to have some sort of strange fascination for him."

"She's very picturesque," Margaret explained. "And artists see points in people that the rest of us don't."

"Could it be her money?" Mrs. Horn insinuated. "He must be very poor."

"But he isn't base," retorted the girl with a generous indignation that made her aunt smile.

"Oh no; but if he fancies her so picturesque, it doesn't follow that he would object to her being rich."

"It would with a man like Mr. Beaton!"

"You are an idealist, Margaret. I suppose your Mr. March has some disinterested motive in paying court to Miss Mela—Pamela, I suppose, is her name. He talked to her longer than her literature would have lasted."

"He seems a very kind person," said Margaret.

"And Mr. Dryfoos pays his salary?"

"I don't know anything about that. But that wouldn't make any difference with him."

Mrs. Horn laughed out at this security; but she was not displeased by the nobleness which it came from. She liked Margaret to be high-minded, and was really not distressed by any good that was in her.

The Marches walked home, both because it was not far, and because they must spare in carriage hire at any rate. As soon as they were out of the house, she applied a point of conscience to him.

"I don't see how you could talk to that girl so long, Basil, and make her laugh so."

"Why, there seemed no one else to do it, till I thought of Kendricks."

"Yes, but I kept thinking, Now he's pleasant to her because he thinks it's to his interest. If she had no relation to *Every Other Week*, he wouldn't waste his time on her."

"Isabel," March complained, "I wish you wouldn't think of me in *he, him*, and *his*: I never personalise you in my thoughts: you remain always a vague unindividualised essence, not quite without form and void, but nounless and pronounless. I call that a much more beautiful mental attitude toward the object of one's affections. But if you must *he* and *him* and *his* me in your thoughts, I wish you'd have more kindly thoughts of me."

"Do you deny that it's true, Basil?"

"Do you believe that it's true, Isabel?"

"No matter. But could you excuse it if it were?"

"Ah, I see you'd have been capable of it in my place, and you're ashamed."

"Yes," sighed the wife, "I'm afraid that I should. But tell me that *you* wouldn't, Basil!"

"I can tell you that I wasn't. But I suppose that in a real exigency, I could truckle to the proprietary Dryfooses as well as you."

"Oh no; you mustn't, dear! I'm a woman, and I'm dreadfully afraid. But you must always be a man, especially with that horrid old Mr. Dryfoos. Promise me that you'll never yield the least point to him in a matter of right and wrong!"

"Not, if he's right and I'm wrong?"

"Don't trifle, dear! You know what I mean. Will you promise?"

"I'll promise to submit the point to you, and let you do the yielding. As for me, I shall be adamant. Nothing I like better."

"They're dreadful, even that poor, good young fellow, who's so different from all the rest; he's awful, too, because you feel that he's a martyr to them."

"And I never did like martyrs a great deal," March interposed.

"I wonder how they came to be there," Mrs. March pursued, unmindful of his joke.

"That is exactly what seemed to be puzzling Miss Mela about us. She asked, and I explained as well as I could; and then she told me that Miss Vance had come to call on them and invited them; and first they didn't know how they could come till they thought of making Conrad bring them. But she didn't say why Miss Vance called on them. Mr. Dryfoos doesn't employ *her* on *Every Other Week*. But I suppose she has her own vile little motive."

"It can't be their *money*; it *can't* be!" sighed Mrs. March.

"Well, I don't know. We all respect money."

"Yes, but Miss Vance's position is so secure. She needn't pay court to those stupid, vulgar people."

"Well, let's console ourselves with the belief that she would, if she needed. Such people as the Dryfooses are the raw material of good society. It isn't made up of refined or meritorious people—professors and littérateurs, ministers and musicians, and their families. All the fashionable people there to-night were like the Dryfooses a generation or two ago. I dare say the material works up faster now, and in a season or two you won't know the Dryfooses from the other plutocrats. *They* will—a little better than they do now; they'll see a difference, but nothing radical, nothing painful. People who get up in the world by service to others—through letters, or art, or science—may have their modest little misgivings as to their social value, but people that rise by money—especially if their gains are sudden—never have.

And that's the kind of people that form our nobility; there's no use pretending that we haven't a nobility; we might as well pretend we haven't first-class cars in the presence of a vestibuled Pullman. Those girls had no more doubt of their right to be there than if they had been duchesses: *we* thought it was very nice of Miss Vance to come and ask us, but *they* didn't; they weren't afraid, or the least embarrassed; they were perfectly natural—like born aristocrats. And you may be sure that if the plutocracy that now owns the country ever sees fit to take on the outward signs of an aristocracy—titles, and arms, and ancestors—it won't falter from any inherent question of its worth. Money prizes and honours itself, and if there is anything it hasn't got, it believes it can buy it."

"Well, Basil," said his wife, "I hope you won't get infected with Lindau's ideas of rich people. Some of them are very good and kind."

"Who denies that? Not even Lindau himself. It's all right. And the great thing is that the evening's enjoyment is over. I've got my society smile off, and I'm radiantly happy. Go on with your little pessimistic diatribes, Isabel; you can't spoil *my* pleasure."

"I could see," said Mela, as she and Christine drove home together, "that she was as jealous as she could be, all the time you was talkun' to Mr. Beaton. She pretended to be talkun' to Conrad, but she kep' her eye on you pretty close, I can tell you. I bet she just got us there to see how him and you would act together. And I reckon she was satisfied. He's dead gone on you, Chris."

Christine listened with a dreamy pleasure to the flatteries with which Mela plied her in the hope of some return in kind, and not at all because she felt spitefully toward Miss Vance, or in anywise wished her ill. "Who was that fellow with you so long?" asked Christine. "I suppose you turned yourself inside out to him, like you always do."

Mela was transported by the cruel ingratitude. "It's a lie! I didn't tell him a single thing."

Conrad walked home, choosing to do so because he did not wish to hear his sisters' talk of the evening, and because there was a tumult in his spirit which he wished to let have its way. In his life with its single purpose, defeated by stronger wills than his own, and now struggling partially to fulfil itself in acts of devotion to others, the thought of women had entered scarcely more than in that of a child. His ideals were of a virginal vagueness; faces, voices, gestures had filled his fancy at times, but almost passionlessly; and the sensation that he now indulged was a kind of worship, ardent, but reverent and exalted. The brutal experiences of the world make us forget that there are such natures in it, and that they seem to come up out of the lowly earth as well as down from the high heaven. In the heart of this man well on toward thirty there had never been left the stain of a base thought; not that suggestion and conjecture had not visited him, but that he had not entertained them, or in anywise made them his. In a Catholic age and country, he would have been one of those monks who are sainted after death for the angelic purity of their lives, and whose names are invoked by believers in moments of trial, like San Luigi Gonzaga.* As he now walked along thinking, with a lover's beatified smile on his face, of how Margaret Vance had spoken and looked, he dramatised scenes in which he approved himself to her by acts of goodness and unselfishness, and died to please her for the sake of others. He made her praise him for them, to his face, when he disclaimed their merit, and after his death, when he could not. All the time he was poignantly sensible of her grace, her elegance, her style; they seemed to intoxicate him; some tones of her voice thrilled through his nerves, and some looks turned his brain with a delicious, swooning sense of her beauty; her refinement bewildered him. But all this did not admit the idea of possession, even of aspiration. At the most his worship only set her beyond the love of other men as far as beyond his own.

PART FOURTH

I

NOT long after Lent, Fulkerson set before Dryfoos one day his scheme for a dinner in celebration of the success of *Every Other Week*. Dryfoos had never meddled in any manner with the conduct of the periodical; but Fulkerson easily saw that he was proud of his relation to it, and he proceeded upon the theory that he would be willing to have this relation known. On the days when he had been lucky in stocks, he was apt to drop in at the office on Eleventh Street, on his way up-town, and listen to Fulkerson's talk. He was on good enough terms with March, who revised his first impressions of the man, but they had not much to say to each other, and it seemed to March that Dryfoos was even a little afraid of him, as of a piece of mechanism he had acquired, but did not quite understand; he left the working of it to Fulkerson, who no doubt bragged of it sufficiently. The old man seemed to have as little to say to his son; he shut himself up with Fulkerson, where the others could hear the manager begin and go on with an unstinted flow of talk about *Every Other Week*; for Fulkerson never talked of anything else if he could help it, and was always bringing the conversation back to it if it strayed.

The day he spoke of the dinner he rose and called from his door, "March, I say, come down here a minute, will you? Conrad, I want you, too."

The editor and the publisher found the manager and the proprietor seated on opposite sides of the table. "It's about those funeral baked meats, you know," Fulkerson explained, "and I was trying to give Mr. Dryfoos some idea of what we wanted to do. That is, what I wanted to do," he continued, turning from March to Dryfoos. "March, here, is opposed

251

to it, of course. *He'd* like to publish *Every Other Week* on the sly; keep it out of the papers, and off the news-stands; he's a modest Boston petunia, and he shrinks from publicity; but I am not that kind of herb myself, and I want all the publicity we can get—beg, borrow, or steal—for this thing. I say that you can't work the sacred rites of hospitality in a better cause, and what I propose is a little dinner for the purpose of recognising the hit we've made with this thing. My idea was to strike you for the necessary funds, and do the thing on a handsome scale. The term little dinner is a mere figure of speech. A little dinner wouldn't make a big talk, and what we want is the big talk, at present, if we don't lay up a cent. My notion was that pretty soon after Lent, now, when everybody is feeling just right, we should begin to send out our paragraphs, affirmative, negative, and explanatory, and along about the first of May we should sit down about a hundred strong, the most distinguished people in the country, and solemnise our triumph. There it is in a nutshell. I might expand and I might expound, but that's the sum and substance of it."

Fulkerson stopped, and ran his eyes eagerly over the faces of his three listeners, one after the other. March was a little surprised when Dryfoos turned to him, but that reference of the question seemed to give Fulkerson particular pleasure: "What do you think, Mr. March?"

The editor leaned back in his chair. "I don't pretend to have Mr. Fulkerson's genius for advertising; but it seems to me a little early yet. We might celebrate later when we've got more to celebrate. At present we're a pleasing novelty, rather than a fixed fact."

"Ah, you don't get the idea!" said Fulkerson. "What we want to do with this dinner is to fix the fact."

"Am I going to come in anywhere?" the old man interrupted.

"You're going to come in at the head of the procession! We are going to strike everything that is imaginative and romantic in the newspaper soul with you and your history and your fancy for going in for this thing. I can start you in a paragraph that will travel through all the newspapers, from Maine to Texas and from Alaska to Florida. We have had all sorts of rich men backing up literary enterprises, but the natural-gas man in literature is a new thing, and the combination of your picturesque past and your æsthetic present is something that will knock out the sympathies of the American public the first round. I feel," said Fulkerson, with a tremor of pathos in his voice, "that *Every Other Week* is at a disadvantage before the public as long as it's supposed to be *my* enterprise, *my* idea. As far as I'm known at all, I'm known simply as a syndicate man, and nobody in the press believes that I've got the money to run the thing on a grand scale; a suspicion of insolvency must attach to it sooner or later, and the fellows on the press will work up that impression, sooner or later, if we don't give them something else to work up. Now, as soon as I begin to give it away to the correspondents that *you're* in it, with your untold millions— that in fact it was your idea from the start, that you originated it to give full play to the humanitarian tendencies of Conrad here, who's always had these theories of co-operation, and longed to realise them for the benefit of our struggling young writers and artists——"

March had listened with growing amusement to the mingled burlesque and earnest of Fulkerson's self-sacrificing impudence, and with wonder as to how far Dryfoos was consenting to his preposterous proposition, when Conrad broke out, "Mr. Fulkerson, I could not allow you to do that. It would not be true; I did not wish to be here; and—and what I think—what I wish to do—that is something I will not let any one put me in a false position about. No!" The blood rushed into the young man's gentle face, and he met his father's glance with defiance.

Dryfoos turned from him to Fulkerson without speaking, and Fulkerson said caressingly, "Why, of course, Coonrod! I know how you feel, and I shouldn't let anything of that sort go out uncontradicted after*wards*. But there isn't anything in these times that would give us better standing with the public than some hint of the way you feel about such things. The public expects to be interested, and nothing would interest it more than to be told that the success of *Every Other Week* sprang from the first application of the principle of *Live and let Live* to a literary enterprise. It would look particularly well, coming from you and your father, but if you object, we can leave that part out; though if you approve of the principle I don't see why you *need* object. The main thing is to let the public know that it owes this thing to the liberal and enlightened spirit of one of the foremost capitalists of the country, and that his purposes are not likely to be betrayed in the hands of his son. I should get a little cut made from a photograph of your father, and supply it gratis with the paragraphs."

"I guess," said the old man, "we will get along without the cut."

Fulkerson laughed. "Well, well! Have it your own way. But the sight of your face in the patent outsides of the country press,* would be worth half a dozen subscribers in every school district throughout the length and breadth of this fair land."

"There was a fellow," Dryfoos explained in an aside to March, "that was getting up a history of Moffitt, and he asked me to let him put a steel engraving of me in. He said a good many prominent citizens were going to have theirs in, and his price was a hundred and fifty dollars. I told him I couldn't let mine go for less than two hundred, and when he said he could give me a splendid plate for that money, I said I should want it cash. You never saw a fellow more astonished when he got it through him that I expected *him* to pay the two hundred."

Fulkerson laughed in keen appreciation of the joke. "Well, sir, I guess *Every Other Week* will pay you that much. But if you won't sell at any price, all right; we must try to worry along without the light of your countenance on the posters, but we got to have it for the banquet."

"I don't seem to feel very hungry, yet," said the old man drily.

"Oh, *l'appétit vient en mangeant*,* as our French friends

254

say. You'll be hungry enough when you see the preliminary Little Neck clam. It's too late for oysters."

"Doesn't that fact seem to point to a postponement till they get back, sometime in October," March suggested.

"No, no!" said Fulkerson, "you don't catch on to the business end of this thing, my friends. You're proceeding on something like the old exploded idea that the demand creates the supply, when everybody knows, if he's watched the course of modern events, that it's just as apt to be the other way. I contend that we've got a real substantial success to celebrate now; but even if we hadn't, the celebration would do more than anything else to create the success, if we got it properly before the public. People will say, Those fellows are not fools; they wouldn't go and rejoice over their magazine unless they had got a big thing in it. And the state of feeling we should produce in the public mind would make a boom of perfectly unprecedented grandeur for *E. O. W.* Heigh?"

He looked sunnily from one to the other in succession. The elder Dryfoos said, with his chin on the top of his stick, "I reckon those Little Neck clams will keep."

"Well, just as you say," Fulkerson cheerfully assented. "I understand you to agree to the general principle of a little dinner?"

"The smaller the better," said the old man.

"Well, I say a little dinner because the idea of that seems to cover the case, even if we vary the plan a little. I *had* thought of a reception, may be, that would include the lady contributors and artists, and the wives and daughters of the other contributors. That would give us the chance to ring in a lot of society correspondents and get the thing written up in first-class shape. By the *way!*" cried Fulkerson, slapping himself on the leg, "why not have the dinner *and* the reception *both*?"

"I don't understand," said Dryfoos.

"Why, have a select little dinner for ten or twenty choice spirits of the male persuasion, and then about ten o'clock, throw open your palatial drawing-rooms and admit the females to champagne, salads, and ices. It is the very thing! Come!"

"What do *you* think of it, Mr. March?" asked Dryfoos, on whose social inexperience Fulkerson's words projected no very intelligible image, and who perhaps hoped for some more light.

"It's a beautiful vision," said March, "and if it will take more time to realise it I think I approve. I approve of anything that will delay Mr. Fulkerson's advertising orgie."

"Then," Fulkerson pursued, "we could have the pleasure of Miss Christine and Miss Mela's company; and may be Mrs. Dryfoos would look in on us in the course of the evening. There's no hurry, as Mr. March suggests, if we can give the thing this shape. I will cheerfully adopt the idea of my honourable colleague."

March laughed at his impudence, but at heart he was ashamed of Fulkerson for proposing to make use of Dryfoos and his house in that way. He fancied something appealing in the look that the old man turned on him, and something indignant in Conrad's flush; but probably this was only his fancy. He reflected that neither of them could feel it as people of more worldly knowledge would, and he consoled himself with the fact that Fulkerson was really not such a charlatan as he seemed. But it went through his mind that this was a strange end for all Dryfoos's money-making to come to; and he philosophically accepted the fact of his own humble fortunes when he reflected how little his money could buy for such a man. It was an honourable use that Fulkerson was putting it to in *Every Other Week*; it might be far more creditably spent on such an enterprise than on horses, or wines, or women, the usual resources of the brute rich; and if it were to be lost, it might better be lost that way than in stocks. He kept a smiling face turned to Dryfoos while these irreverent considerations occupied him, and hardened his heart against father and son and their possible emotions.

The old man rose to put an end to the interview. He only repeated, "I guess those clams will keep till fall."

But Fulkerson was apparently satisfied with the progress

he had made; and when he joined March for the stroll home-ward after office hours, he was able to detach his mind from the subject, as if content to leave it.

"This is about the best part of the year in New York," he said. In some of the areas the grass had sprouted, and the tender young foliage had loosened itself from the buds on a sidewalk tree here and there; the soft air was full of spring, and the delicate sky, far aloof, had the look it never wears at any other season. "It ain't a time of year to complain much of, anywhere; but I don't want anything better than the month of May in New York. Farther South it's too hot, and I've been in Boston in May when that east wind of yours made every nerve in my body get up and howl. I reckon the weather has a good deal to do with the local temperament. The reason a New York man takes life so easily with all his rush is that his climate don't worry him. But a Boston man must be rasped the whole while by the edge in his air. That accounts for his sharpness; and when he's lived through twenty-five or thirty Boston Mays, he gets to thinking that Providence has some particular use for him, or he wouldn't have survived, and that makes him conceited. See?"

"I see," said March. "But I don't know how you're going to work that idea into an advertisement, exactly."

"Oh, pshaw, now, March! You don't think I've got that on the brain all the time?"

"You were gradually leading up to *Every Other Week,* somehow."

"No, sir; I wasn't. I was just thinking what a different creature a Massachusetts man was from a Virginian. And yet I suppose they're both as pure English stock as you'll get anywhere in America. March, I think Colonel Wood-burn's paper is going to make a hit."

"You've got there! When it knocks down the sale about one-half, I shall know it's made a hit."

"I'm not afraid," said Fulkerson. "That thing is going to attract attention. It's well written—you can take the pomposity out of it, here and there—and it's novel. Our people like a bold strike, and it's going to shake them up tremendously to have serfdom advocated on high moral grounds as the only solution of the labour problem. You see in the first place he goes for their sympathies by the way he portrays the actual relations of capital and labour; he shows how things have got to go from bad to worse, and then he trots out his little old hobby, and proves that if slavery had not been interfered with, it would have perfected itself in the interest of humanity. He makes a pretty strong plea for it."

March threw back his head and laughed. "He's converted you! I swear, Fulkerson, if we had accepted and paid for an article advocating cannibalism as the only resource for getting rid of the superfluous poor, you'd begin to believe in it."

Fulkerson smiled in approval of the joke, and only said, "I wish you could meet the colonel in the privacy of the domestic circle, March. You'd like him. He's a splendid old fellow; regular type. Talk about spring! You ought to see the widow's little back yard these days. You know that glass gallery just beyond the dining-room? Those girls have got the pot-plants out of that, and a lot more, and they've turned the edges of that back yard, along the fence, into a regular bower; they've got sweet peas planted, and nasturtiums, and we shall be in a blaze of glory about the beginning of June. Fun to see 'em work in the garden, and the bird bossing the job in his cage under the cherry-tree. Have to keep the middle of the yard for the clothes-line, but six days in the week it's a lawn, and I go over it with a mower myself. March, there ain't anything like a home, *is* there? Dear little cot of your own, heigh? I tell you, March, when I get to pushing that mower round, and the colonel is smoking his cigar in the gallery, and those girls are pottering over the flowers, one of these soft evenings after dinner, I feel like a human being. Yes, I do. I struck it rich when I concluded to take my meals at the widow's. For eight dollars a week I get good board, refined society, and all the advantages of a Christian home. By the way, you've never had much talk with Miss Woodburn, have you, March?"

"Not so much as with Miss Woodburn's father."

"Well, he *is* rather apt to scoop the conversation. I must draw his fire, sometime, when you and Mrs. March are around, and get you a chance with Miss Woodburn."

"I should like that better, I believe," said March.

"Well, I shouldn't wonder if you did. Curious, but Miss Woodburn isn't at all your idea of a Southern girl. She's got lots of go; she's never idle a minute; she keeps the old gentleman in first-class shape, and she don't believe a bit in the slavery solution of the labour problem; says she's glad it's gone, and if it's anything like the effects of it, she's glad it went before her time. No, sir, she's as full of snap as the liveliest kind of a Northern girl. None of that sunny Southern languor you read about."

"I suppose the typical Southerner, like the typical anything else, is pretty difficult to find," said March. "But perhaps Miss Woodburn represents the new South. The modern conditions must be producing a modern type."

"Well, that's what she and the colonel both say. They say there ain't anything left of that Walter Scott dignity and chivalry in the rising generation; takes too much time. You ought to see her sketch the old-school, high-and-mighty manners, as they survive among some of the antiques in Charlottesburg. If that thing could be put upon the stage it would be a killing success. Makes the old gentleman laugh in spite of himself. But he's as proud of her as Punch, anyway. Why don't you and Mrs. March come round oftener? Look here! How would it do to have a little excursion, somewhere, after the spring fairly gets in its work?"

"Reporters present?"

"No, no! Nothing of that kind; perfectly sincere and disinterested enjoyment."

"Oh, a few handbills to be scattered around: 'Buy *Every Other Week*,' 'Look out for the next number of *Every Other Week*,' '*Every Other Week* at all the news-stands.' Well, I'll talk it over with Mrs. March. I suppose there's no great hurry."

March told his wife of the idyllic mood in which he had

left Fulkerson at the widow's door, and she said he must be in love.

"Why, of course! I wonder I didn't think of that. But Fulkerson is such an impartial admirer of the whole sex that you can't think of his liking one more than another. I don't know that he showed any unjust partiality, though, in his talk of 'those girls,' as he called them. And I always rather fancied that Mrs. Mandel—he's done so much for her, you know; and she *is* such a well-balanced, well-preserved person, and so lady-like and correct——"

"Fulkerson had the word for her: academic. She's everything that instruction and discipline can make of a woman; but I shouldn't think they could make enough of her to be in love with."

"Well, I don't know. The academic has its charm. There are moods in which I could imagine myself in love with an academic person. That regularity of line; that reasoned strictness of contour; that neatness of pose; that slightly conventional but harmonious grouping of the emotions and morals—you can see how it would have its charm, the Wedgwood in human nature? I wonder where Mrs. Mandel keeps her urn and her willow."

"I should think she might have use for them in that family, poor thing!" said Mrs. March.

"Ah, that reminds me," said her husband, "that we had another talk with the old gentleman, this afternoon, about Fulkerson's literary, artistic, and advertising orgie, and it's postponed till October."

"The later the better, I should think," said Mrs. March, who did not really think about it at all, but whom the date fixed for it caused to think of the intervening time. "We have got to consider what we will do about the summer, before long, Basil."

"Oh, not yet, not yet," he pleaded, with that man's willingness to abide in the present, which is so trying to a woman. "It's only the end of April."

"It will be the end of June before we know. And these people wanting the Boston house another year complicates it. We can't spend the summer there, as we planned."

"They oughtn't to have offered us an increased rent; they have taken an advantage of us."

"I don't know that it matters," said Mrs. March. "I had decided not to go there."

"Had you? This is a surprise."

"Everything is a surprise to you, Basil, when it happens."

"True; I keep the world fresh, that way."

"It wouldn't have been any change to go from one city to another for the summer. We might as well have stayed in New York."

"Yes, I wish we had stayed," said March, idly humouring a conception of the accomplished fact. "Mrs. Green would have let us have the gimcrackery very cheap for the summer months; and we could have made all sorts of nice little excursions and trips off, and been twice as well as if we had spent the summer away."

"Nonsense! You know we couldn't spend the summer in New York."

"I know *I* could."

"What stuff! You couldn't manage."

"Oh yes, I could. I could take my meals at Fulkerson's widow's; or at Maroni's, with poor old Lindau: he's got to dining there again. Or, I could keep house, and he could dine with me here."

There was a teasing look in March's eyes, and he broke into a laugh, at the firmness with which his wife said, "I think if there is to be any house-keeping, I will stay, too; and help to look after it. I would try not intrude upon you and your guest."

"Oh, we should be only too glad to have you join us," said March, playing with fire.

"Very well, then, I wish you would take him off to Maroni's, the next time he comes to dine here!" cried his wife.

The experiment of making March's old friend free of his house had not given her all the pleasure that so kind a thing ought to have afforded so good a woman. She received Lindau at first with robust benevolence, and the high resolve not to let any of his little peculiarities alienate her from a sense of his claim upon her sympathy and gratitude, not only as a man who had been so generously fond of her husband in his youth, but a hero who had suffered for her country. Her theory was that his mutilation must not be ignored, but must be kept in mind as a monument of his sacrifice, and she fortified Bella with this conception, so that the child bravely sat next his maimed arm at table and helped him to dishes he could not reach, and cut up his meat for him. As for Mrs. March herself, the thought of his mutilation made her a little faint; she was not without a bewildered resentment of its presence as a sort of oppression. She did not like his drinking so much of March's beer, either; it was no harm, but it was somehow unworthy, out of character with a hero of the war. But what she really could not reconcile herself to was the violence of Lindau's sentiments concerning the whole political and social fabric. She did not feel sure that he should be allowed to say such things before the children, who had been nurtured in the faith of Bunker Hill and Appomattox, as the beginning and the end of all possible progress in human rights. As a woman she was naturally an aristocrat, but as an American she was theoretically a democrat; and it astounded, it alarmed her, to hear American democracy denounced as a shuffling evasion. She had never cared much for the United States Senate, but she doubted if she ought to sit by when it was railed at as a rich man's club. It shocked her to be told that the rich and poor were not equal before the law in a country where justice must be paid for at every step in fees and costs, or where a poor man must go to war in his own person, and a rich man might hire some one to go in his. Mrs. March felt that this rebellious mind in Lindau really somehow outlawed him from sympathy, and retroactively undid his past suffering for the country: she had always particularly valued that provision of the law, because in forecasting all the possible mischances that might befall her own son, she had been comforted by the thought that if there ever was another war, and Tom were drafted, his father could buy him a substitute. Compared with such blasphemy as this, Lindau's declaration that there was not equality of opportunity in America, and that fully one-half the people were debarred their right to the pursuit of happiness by the hopeless conditions of their lives, was flattering praise. She could not listen to such things in silence, though, and it did not help matters when Lindau met her arguments with facts and reasons which she felt she was merely not sufficiently instructed to combat, and he was not quite gentlemanly to urge. "I am afraid for the effect on the children," she said to her husband. "Such perfectly distorted ideas—Tom will be ruined by them."

"Oh, let Tom find out where they're false," said March. "It will be good exercise for his faculties of research. At any rate, those things are getting said nowadays; he'll have to hear them sooner or later."

"Had he better hear them at home?" demanded his wife.

"Why, you know, as you're here to refute them, Isabel," he teased, "perhaps it's the best place. But don't mind poor old Lindau, my dear. He says himself that his parg is worse than his pidte, you know."

"Ah, it's too late now to mind him," she sighed. In a moment of rash good feeling, or perhaps an exalted conception of duty, she had herself proposed that Lindau should come every week and read German with Tom; and it had become a question first how they could get him to take pay for it, and then how they could get him to stop it. Mrs. March never ceased to wonder at herself for having brought this about, for she had warned her husband against making any engagement with Lindau which would bring him regularly to the house: the Germans stuck so, and were so unscrupulously dependent. Yet, the deed being done, she would not ignore the duty of hospitality, and it was always she who made the old man stay to their Sunday evening tea when he lingered near the hour, reading Schiller and Heine and Uhland with the boy, in the clean shirt with which he observed the day; Lindau's linen was not to be trusted during the week. She now concluded a season of mournful reflection by saying, "He will get you into trouble, somehow, Basil."

"Well, I don't know how, exactly. I regard Lindau as a political economist of an unusual type; but I shall not let him array me against the constituted authorities. Short of that, I think I am safe."

"Well, be careful, Basil; be careful. You know you are so rash."

"I suppose I may continue to pity him? He *is* such a poor, lonely old fellow. Are you really sorry he's come into our lives, my dear?"

"No, no; not that. I feel as you do about it; but I wish I felt easier about him—sure, that is, that we're not doing wrong to let him keep on talking so."

"I suspect we couldn't help it," March returned lightly. "It's one of what Lindau calls his 'brincibles' to say what he thinks."

II

THE Marches had no longer the gross appetite for novelty which urges youth to a surfeit of strange scenes, experiences, ideas; and makes travel, with all its annoyances and fatigues, an inexhaustible delight. But there is no doubt that the chief pleasure of their life in New York was from its quality of foreignness: the flavour of olives, which, once tasted, can never be forgotten. The olives may not be of the first excellence; they may be a little stale, and small and poor, to begin with, but they are still olives, and the fond palate craves them. The sort which grew in New York, on lower Sixth Avenue and in the region of Jefferson Market and on the soft exposures south of Washington Square, were none the less acceptable because they were of the commonest Italian variety.

The Marches spent a good deal of time and money in a grocery of that nationality, where they found all the patriotic comestibles and potables, and renewed their faded Italian with the friendly family in charge. Italian *table-d'hôtes* formed the adventure of the week, on the day when Mrs. March let her domestics go out, and went herself to dine abroad with her husband and children; and they became adept in the restaurants where they were served, and which they varied almost from dinner to dinner. The perfect decorum of these places, and their immunity from offence in any, emboldened the Marches to experiment in Spanish restaurants, where red pepper and beans insisted in every dinner, and where once they chanced upon a night of *olla podrida*,* with such appeals to March's memory of a boyish ambition to taste the dish that he became poetic and then pensive over its cabbage and carrots, peas and bacon. For a rare combination of international motives they prized most the *table-d'hôte* of a French lady, who had taken a Spanish husband in a second marriage, and had a Cuban negro for her cook, with a cross-eyed Alsatian for waiter, and a slim young South American for cashier. March held that something of the catholic character of these relations expressed itself in the generous and tolerant variety of the dinner, which was singularly abundant for fifty cents, without wine. At one very neat French place he got a dinner at the same price with wine, but it was not so abundant; and March inquired in fruitless speculation why the *table-d'hôte* of the Italians, a notoriously frugal and abstemious people, should be usually more than you wanted at seventy-five cents and a dollar, and that of the French rather less for half a dollar. He could not see that the frequenters were greatly different at the different places; they were mostly Americans, of subdued manners and conjecturably subdued fortunes, with here and there a table full of foreigners. There was no noise and not much smoking anywhere; March liked going to that neat French place because there Madame sat enthroned and high behind a *comptoir** at one side of the room, and everybody saluted her in going out. It was there that a gentle-looking young couple used to dine, in whom the Marches became effectlessly interested, because they thought they looked like

265

that when they were young. The wife had an æsthetic dress, and defined her pretty head by wearing her back-hair pulled up very tight under her bonnet; the husband had dreamy eyes set wide apart under a pure forehead. "They are artists, August, I think," March suggested to the waiter, when he had vainly asked about them. "Oh, hartis, cedenly," August consented; but Heaven knows whether they were, or what they were: March never learned.

This immunity from acquaintance, this touch-and-go quality in their New York sojourn, this almost loss of individuality at times, after the intense identification of their Boston life, was a relief, though Mrs. March had her misgivings, and questioned whether it were not perhaps too relaxing to the moral fibre. March refused to explore his conscience; he allowed that it might be so; but he said he liked now and then to feel his personality in that state of solution. They went and sat a good deal in the softening evenings among the infants and dotards of Latin extraction in Washington Square, safe from all who ever knew them, and enjoyed the advancing season, which thickened the foliage of the trees and flattered out of sight the churchwarden's gothic of the University Building.* The infants were sometimes cross, and cried in their weary mothers' or little sisters' arms; but they did not disturb the dotards, who slept, some with their heads fallen forward, and some with their heads fallen back; March arbitrarily distinguished those with the drooping faces as tipsy and ashamed to confront the public. The small Italian children raced up and down the asphalte paths, playing American games of tag and hide-and-whoop; larger boys passed ball, in training for potential championships. The Marches sat and mused, or quarrelled fitfully about where they should spend the summer, like sparrows, he once said, till the electric lights began to show distinctly among the leaves, and they looked round and found the infants and dotards gone and the benches filled with lovers. That was the signal for the Marches to go home. He said that the spectacle of so much courtship as the eye might take in there at a glance was not, perhaps, oppressive, but the thought that at the same hour the same thing was going on all over the country, wherever two young fools could get together, was more than he could bear; he did not deny that it was natural, and, in a measure, authorised, but he declared that it was hackneyed; and the fact that it must go on for ever, as long as the race lasted, made him tired.

At home, generally, they found that the children had not missed them, and were perfectly safe. It was one of the advantages of a flat that they could leave the children there whenever they liked without anxiety. They liked better staying there than wandering about in the evening with their parents, whose excursions seemed to them somewhat aimless, and their pleasures insipid. They studied, or read, or looked out of the window at the street sights; and their mother always came back to them with a pang for their lonesomeness. Bella knew some little girls in the house, but in a ceremonious way; Tom had formed no friendships among the boys at school such as he had left in Boston; as nearly as he could explain, the New York fellows carried canes at an age when they would have had them broken for them by the other boys at Boston; and they were both sissyish and fast. It was probably prejudice; he never could say exactly what their demerits were, and neither he nor Bella was apparently so homesick as they pretended, though they answered inquirers, the one that New York was a hole, and the other that it was horrid, and that all they lived for was to get back to Boston. In the meantime they were thrown much upon each other for society, which March said was well for both of them; he did not mind their cultivating a little gloom and the sense of a common wrong; it made them better comrades, and it was providing them with amusing reminiscences for the future. They really enjoyed Bohemianising in that harmless way: though Tom had his doubts of its respectability; he was very punctilious about his sister, and went round from his own school every day to fetch her home from hers. The whole family went to the theatre a good deal, and enjoyed themselves together in their desultory explorations of the city.

They lived near Greenwich Village, and March liked strolling through its quaintness toward the water-side on a Sunday, when a hereditary Sabbatarianism kept his wife at home; he made her observe that it even kept her at home from church. He found a lingering quality of pure Americanism in the region, and he said the very bells called to worship in a nasal tone. He liked the streets of small brick houses, with here and there one painted red, and the mortar lines picked out in white, and with now and then a fine wooden portal of fluted pillars and a bowed transom. The rear of the tenement-houses showed him the picturesqueness of clothes-lines fluttering far aloft, as in Florence; and the new apartment-houses, breaking the old sky-line with their towering stories, implied a life as alien to the American manner as anything in continental Europe. In fact, foreign faces and foreign tongues prevailed in Greenwich Village, but no longer German or even Irish tongues or faces. The eyes and ear-rings of Italians twinkled in and out of the alley-ways and basements, and they seemed to abound even in the streets, where long ranks of trucks drawn up in Sunday rest along the curb-stones suggested the presence of a race of sturdier strength than theirs. March liked the swarthy, strange visages; he found nothing menacing for the future in them; for wickedness he had to satisfy himself as he could with the sneering, insolent, clean-shaven mug of some rare American of the b'hoy* type, now almost as extinct in New York as the dodo or the volunteer fireman. When he had found his way, among the ash-barrels and the groups of decently dressed church-goers, to the docks, he experienced a sufficient excitement in the recent arrival of a French steamer, whose sheds were thronged with hacks and express-wagons, and in a tacit inquiry into the emotions of the passengers, fresh from the cleanliness of Paris, and now driving up through the filth of those streets.

Some of the streets were filthier than others; there was at least a choice; there were boxes and barrels of kitchen offal on all the sidewalks, but not everywhere manure-heaps, and in some places the stench was mixed with the more savoury smell of cooking. One Sunday morning, before the winter was quite gone, the sight of the frozen refuse melting in heaps, and particularly the loathsome edges of the rotting ice near the gutters, with the strata of waste-paper and straw litter, and egg-shells and orange-peel, potato-skins and cigar-stumps, made him unhappy. He gave a whimsical shrug for the squalor of the neighbouring houses, and said to himself rather than the boy who was with him: "It's curious, isn't it, how fond the poor people are of these unpleasant thorough-fares? You always find them living in the worst streets."

"The burden of all the wrong in the world comes on the poor," said the boy. "Every sort of fraud and swindling hurts them the worst. The city wastes the money it's paid to clean the streets with, and the poor have to suffer, for they can't afford to pay twice, like the rich."

March stopped short. "Hallo, Tom! Is that *your* wisdom?"

"It's what Mr. Lindau says," answered the boy doggedly, as if not pleased to have his ideas mocked at, even if they were second-hand.

"And you didn't tell him that the poor lived in dirty streets because they liked them, and were too lazy and worth-less to have them cleaned?"

"No; I didn't."

"I'm surprised. What do you think of Lindau, generally speaking, Tom?"

"Well, sir, I don't like the way he talks about some things. I don't suppose this country *is* perfect, but I think it's about the best there is, and it don't do any good to look at its drawbacks all the time."

"Sound, my son," said March, putting his hand on the boy's shoulder and beginning to walk on. "Well?"

"Well, then, he says that it isn't the public frauds only that the poor have to pay for, but they have to pay for all the vices of the rich; that when a speculator fails, or a bank cashier defaults, or a firm suspends, or hard times come, it's the poor who have to give up necessaries where the rich give up luxuries."

"Well, well! And then?"

"Well, then I think the crank comes in, in Mr. Lindau. He says there's no need of failures or frauds or hard times. It's ridiculous. There always have been and there always will be. But if you tell him that, it seems to make him perfectly furious."

March repeated the substance of this talk to his wife. "I'm glad to know that Tom can see through such ravings. He has lots of good common-sense."

It was the afternoon of the same Sunday, and they were sauntering up Fifth Avenue, and admiring the wide old double houses at the lower end; at one corner they got a distinct pleasure out of the gnarled elbows that a pollarded wistaria leaned upon the top of a garden wall—for its convenience in looking into the street, he said. The line of these comfortable dwellings, once so fashionable, was continually broken by the façades of shops; and March professed himself vulgarised by a want of style in the people they met in their walk to Twenty-third Street.

"Take me somewhere to meet my fellow-exclusives, Isabel," he demanded. "I pine for the society of my peers."

He hailed a passing omnibus, and made his wife get on the roof with him. "Think of our doing such a thing in Boston!" she sighed, with a little shiver of satisfaction in her immunity from recognition and comment.

"You wouldn't be afraid to do it in London or Paris?"

"No; we should be strangers there—just as we are in New York. I wonder how long one could be a stranger here."

"Oh, indefinitely, in our way of living. The place is really vast, so much larger than it used to seem, and so heterogeneous."

When they got down very far uptown, and began to walk back by Madison Avenue, they found themselves in a different population from that they dwelt among; not heterogeneous at all; very homogeneous, and almost purely American; the only qualification was American Hebrew. Such a well-dressed, well-satisfied, well-fed looking crowd poured down the broad sidewalks before the handsome, stupid houses that March could easily pretend he had got

among his fellow-plutocrats at last. Still he expressed his
doubts whether this Sunday afternoon parade, which seemed
to be a thing of custom, represented the best form among the
young people of that region; he wished he knew; he blamed
himself for becoming of a fastidious conjecture; he could
not deny the fashion and the richness and the indigeneity of
the spectacle; the promenaders looked New Yorky; they
were the sort of people whom you would know for New
Yorkers elsewhere, so well equipped and so perfectly kept
at all points. Their silk hats shone, and their boots; their
frocks had the right distension behind, and their bonnets
perfect poise and distinction.

The Marches talked of these and other facts of their appearance, and curiously questioned whether this were the
best that a great material civilisation could come to; it looked
a little dull. The men's faces were shrewd and alert, and yet
they looked dull; the women's were pretty and knowing, and
yet dull. It was, probably, the holiday expression of the vast,
prosperous commercial class, with unlimited money, and no
ideals that money could not realise; fashion and comfort were
all that they desired to compass, and the culture that
furnishes showily, that decorates and that tells; the culture,
say, of plays and operas, rather than books.

Perhaps the observers did the promenaders injustice; they
might not have been as common-minded as they looked.
"But," March said, "I understand now why the poor people
don't come up here and live in this clean, handsome, respectable quarter of the town; they would be bored to death. On
the whole, I think I should prefer Mott Street myself."

In other walks the Marches tried to find some of the streets
they had wandered through the first day of their wedding
journey in New York, so long ago. They could not make sure
of them; but once they ran down to the Battery,* and easily
made sure of that, though not in its old aspect. They recalled
the hot morning, when they sauntered over the trodden weed
that covered the sickly grass-plots there, and sentimentalised
the sweltering paupers who had crept out of the squalid tenements about for a breath of air after a sleepless night. Now

the paupers were gone, and where the old mansions that had fallen to their use once stood, there towered aloft and abroad those heights and masses of many-storied brick-work for which architecture has yet no proper form and æsthetics no name. The trees and shrubs, all in their young spring green, blew briskly over the guarded turf in the south wind that came up over the water; and in the well-paved alleys the ghosts of eighteenth-century fashion might have met each other in their old haunts, and exchanged stately congratulations upon its vastly bettered condition, and perhaps puzzled a little over the colossal lady on Bedloe's Island,* with her lifted torch, and still more over the curving tracks and châlet-stations of the Elevated road. It is an outlook of unrivalled beauty across the bay, that smokes and flashes with the innumerable stacks and sails of commerce, to the hills beyond, where the moving forest of masts halts at the shore, and roots itself in the groves of the many-villaged uplands. The Marches paid the charming prospect a willing duty, and rejoiced in it as generously as if it had been their own. Perhaps it was, they decided. He said people owned more things in common than they were apt to think; and they drew the consolations of proprietorship from the excellent management of Castle Garden, which they penetrated for a moment's glimpse of the huge rotunda, where the emigrants first set foot on our continent. It warmed their hearts, so easily moved to any cheap sympathy, to see the friendly care the nation took of these humble guests; they found it even pathetic to hear the proper authority calling out the names of such as had kin or acquaintance waiting there to meet them. No one appeared troubled or anxious; the officials had a conscientious civility; the government seemed to manage their welcome as well as a private company or corporation could have done. In fact, it was after the simple strangers had left the government care that March feared their woes might begin; and he would have liked the government to follow each of them to his home, wherever he meant to fix it within our borders. He made note of the looks of the licensed runners and touters waiting for the immigrants outside the government premises; he intended to work them up into a dramatic effect in some sketch, but they remained mere material in his memorandum-book, together with some quaint old houses on the Sixth Avenue road, which he had noticed on the way down. On the way up, these were superseded in his regard by some hip-roof structures on the Ninth Avenue, which he thought more Dutch-looking. The perspectives of the cross-streets toward the river were very lively, with their turmoil of trucks and cars and carts and hacks and foot-passengers, ending in the chimneys and masts of shipping, and final gleams of dancing water. At a very noisy corner, clangorous with some sort of iron-working, he made his wife enjoy with him the quiet sarcasm of an inn that called itself the Homelike Hotel, and he speculated at fantastic length on the gentle associations of one who should have passed his youth under its roof.

III

FIRST and last, the Marches did a good deal of travel on the Elevated roads, which, he said, gave you such glimpses of material aspects in the city as some violent invasion of others' lives might afford in human nature. Once, when the impulse of adventure was very strong in them, they went quite the length of the West side lines, and saw the city pushing its way by irregular advances into the country. Some spaces, probably held by the owners for that rise in value which the industry of others providentially gives to the land of the wise and good, it left vacant comparatively far down the road, and built up others at remoter points. It was a world of lofty apartment-houses beyond the Park, springing up in isolated blocks, with stretches of invaded rusticity between, and here and there an old country-seat standing dusty in its budding vines with the ground before it in rocky upheaval for city foundations. But wherever it went or wherever it paused, New York gave its peculiar stamp; and the adventurers were amused to find One Hundred and Twenty-fifth

Street inchoately like Twenty-third Street and Fourteenth Street in its shops and shoppers. The butchers' shops and milliners' shops on the avenue might as well have been at Tenth as at One Hundredth Street.

The adventurers were not often so adventurous. They recognised that in their willingness to let their fancy range for them, and to let speculation do the work of inquiry, they were no longer young. Their point of view was singularly unchanged, and their impressions of New York remained the same that they had been fifteen years before: huge, noisy, ugly, kindly, it seemed to them now as it seemed then. The main difference was that they saw it more now as a life, and then they only regarded it as a spectacle; and March could not release himself from a sense of complicity with it, no matter what whimsical, or alien, or critical attitude he took. A sense of the striving and the suffering deeply possessed him; and this grew the more intense as he gained some knowledge of the forces at work—forces of pity, of destruction, of perdition, or salvation. He wandered about on Sunday not only through the streets, but into this tabernacle and that, as the spirit moved him, and listened to those who dealt with Christianity as a system of economics as well as a religion. He could not get his wife to go with him; she listened to his report of what he heard, and trembled; it all seemed fantastic and menacing. She lamented the literary peace, the intellectual refinement of the life they had left behind them; and he owned it was very pretty, but he said it was not life— it was death-in-life. She liked to hear him talk in that strain of virtuous self-denunciation, but she asked him, "Which of your prophets are you going to follow?" and he answered, "All—all! And a fresh one every Sunday." And so they got their laugh out of it at last, but with some sadness at heart, and with a dim consciousness that they had got their laugh out of too many things in life.

What really occupied and compassed his activities, in spite of his strenuous reveries of work beyond it, was his editorship. On its social side it had not fulfilled all the expectations which Fulkerson's radiant sketch of its duties

and relations had caused him to form of it. Most of the contributions came from a distance; even the articles written in
New York reached him through the post, and so far from
having his valuable time, as they called it, consumed in interviews with his collaborators, he rarely saw any of them. The
boy on the stairs, who was to fence him from importunate
visitors, led a life of luxurious disoccupation, and whistled
almost uninterruptedly. When any one came, March found
himself embarrassed and a little anxious. The visitors were
usually young men, terribly respectful, but cherishing, as
he imagined, ideals and opinions chasmally different from
his; and he felt in their presence something like an anachro-
nism, something like a fraud. He tried to freshen up his
sympathies on them, to get at what they were really thinking
and feeling, and it was some time before he could understand that they were not really thinking and feeling anything
of their own concerning their art, but were necessarily, in
their quality of young, inexperienced men, mere acceptants
of older men's thoughts and feelings, whether they were
tremendously conservative, as some were, or tremendously
progressive, as others were. Certain of them called themselves realists, certain romanticists; but none of them seemed
to know what realism was, or what romanticism; they apparently supposed the difference a difference of material.
March had imagined himself taking home to lunch or dinner
the aspirants for editorial favour whom he liked, whether
he liked their work or not; but this was not an easy matter.
Those who were at all interesting seemed to have engage-
ments and preoccupations; after two or three experiments
with the bashfuller sort—those who had come up to the
metropolis with manuscripts in their hands, in the good old
literary tradition—he wondered whether he was otherwise
like them when he was young like them. He could not flatter
himself that he was not; and yet he had a hope that the world
had grown worse since his time, which his wife encouraged.

Mrs. March was not eager to pursue the hospitalities which
she had at first imagined essential to the literary prosperity
of *Every Other Week*; her family sufficed her; she would

willingly have seen no one out of it but the strangers at the
weekly *table-d'hôte* dinner, or the audiences at the theatres.
March's devotion to his work made him reluctant to delegate
it to any one; and as the summer advanced, and the question
of where to go grew more vexed, he showed a man's base
willingness to shirk it for himself by not going anywhere.
He asked his wife why she did not go somewhere with the
children, and he joined her in a search for non-malarial
regions on the map when she consented to entertain this
notion. But when it came to the point she would not go; he
offered to go with her then, and then she would not let him.
She said she knew he would be anxious about his work; he
protested that he could take it with him to any distance within a few hours, but she would not be persuaded. She would
rather he stayed; the effect would be better with Mr. Fulkerson; they could make excursions, and they could all get off
a week or two to the sea-shore near Boston—the only real
sea-shore—in August. The excursions were practically confined to a single day at Coney Island; and once they got as
far as Boston on the way to the sea-shore near Boston; that
is, Mrs. March and the children went; an editorial exigency
kept March at the last moment. The Boston streets seemed
very queer and clean and empty to the children, and the
buildings little; in the horse-cars the Boston faces seemed
to arraign their mother with a down-drawn severity that
made her feel very guilty. She knew that this was merely the
Puritan mask, the cast of a dead civilisation, which people
of very amiable and tolerant minds were doomed to wear,
and she sighed to think that less than a year of the heterogeneous gaity of New York should have made her afraid
of it. The sky seemed cold and grey; the east wind, which she
had always thought so delicious in summer, cut her to the
heart. She took her children up to the South End, and in the
pretty square where they used to live they stood before their
alienated home, and looked up at its close-shuttered windows. The tenants must have been away, but Mrs. March had
not the courage to ring and make sure, though she had always
promised herself that she would go all over the house when

she came back, and see how they had used it; she could pretend a desire for something she wished to take away. She knew she could not bear it now; and the children did not seem eager. She did not push on to the seaside; it would be forlorn there without their father; she was glad to go back to him in the immense, friendly homelessness of New York, and hold him answerable for the change, in her heart or her mind, which made its shapeless tumult a refuge and a consolation.

She found that he had been giving the cook a holiday, and dining about hither and thither with Fulkerson. Once he had dined with him at the widow's (as they always called Mrs. Leighton), and then had spent the evening there, and smoked with Fulkerson and Colonel Woodburn on the gallery overlooking the back yard. They were all spending the summer in New York. The widow had got so good an offer for her house at St. Barnaby for the summer that she could not refuse it; and the Woodburns found New York a watering-place of exemplary coolness after the burning Augusts and Septembers of Charlottesburg.

"You can stand it well enough in our climate, sir," the colonel explained, "till you come to the September heat, that sometimes runs well into October; and then you begin to lose your temper, sir. It's never quite so hot as it is in New York at times, but it's hot longer, sir." He alleged, as if something of the sort were necessary, the example of a famous South-western editor who spent all his summers in a New York hotel as the most luxurious retreat on the continent, consulting the weather forecasts, and running off on torrid days to the mountains or the sea, and then hurrying back at the promise of cooler weather. The colonel had not found it necessary to do this yet; and he had been reluctant to leave town, where he was working up a branch of the inquiry which had so long occupied him, in the libraries, and studying the great problem of labour and poverty as it continually presented itself to him in the streets. He said that he talked with all sorts of people, whom he found monstrously civil, if you took them in the right way; and he went everywhere

in the city without fear and apparently without danger.
March could not find out that he had ridden his hobby into
the homes of want which he visited, or had proposed their
enslavement to the inmates as a short and simple solution of
the great question of their lives; he appeared to have contented himself with the collection of facts for the persuasion
of the cultivated classes. It seemed to March a confirmation
of this impression that the colonel should address his deduc-
tions from these facts so unsparingly to him; he listened with
a respectful patience, for which Fulkerson afterward personally thanked him. Fulkerson said it was not often the colonel
found such a good listener; generally nobody listened but
Mrs. Leighton, who thought his ideas were shocking, but
honoured him for holding them so conscientiously. Fulkerson was glad that March, as the literary department, had
treated the old gentleman so well, because there was an open
feud between him and the art department. Beaton was out-
rageously rude, Fulkerson must say; though as for that, the
old colonel seemed quite able to take care of himself, and
gave Beaton an unqualified contempt in return for his un-
mannerliness. The worst of it was, it distressed the old lady
so; she admired Beaton as much as she respected the colonel,
and she admired Beaton, Fulkerson thought, rather more
than Miss Leighton did; he asked March if he had noticed
them together. March had noticed them, but without any
very definite impression except that Beaton seemed to give
the whole evening to the girl. Afterward he recollected that
he had fancied her rather harassed by his devotion, and it
was this point that he wished to present for his wife's
opinion.

"Girls often put on that air," she said. "It's one of their
ways of teasing. But then, if the man was really very much
in love, and she was only enough in love to be uncertain of
herself, she might very well seem troubled. It would be a
very serious question. Girls often don't know what to do in
such a case."

"Yes," said March, "I've often been glad that I was not
a girl, on that account. But I guess that on general principles

Beaton is not more in love than she is. I couldn't imagine that young man being more in love with anybody, unless it was himself. He might be more in love with himself than any one else was."

"Well, he doesn't interest me a great deal, and I can't say Miss Leighton does either. I think she can take care of herself. She has herself very well in hand."

"Why so censorious?" pleaded March. "I don't defend her for having herself in hand; but is it a fault?"

Mrs. March did not say. She asked, "And how does Mr. Fulkerson's affair get on?"

"His affair? You really think it *is* one? Well, I've fancied so myself, and I've had an idea of some time asking him; Fulkerson strikes one as truly domesticable, conjugable at heart; but I've waited for him to speak."

"I should think so."

"Yes. He's never opened on the subject yet. Do you know, I think Fulkerson has his moments of delicacy."

"Moments! He's *all* delicacy in regard to women."

"Well, perhaps so. There is nothing in them to rouse his advertising instincts."

IV

THE Dryfoos family stayed in town till August. Then the father went West again to look after his interests; and Mrs. Mandel took the two girls to one of the great hotels in Saratoga.* Fulkerson said that he had never seen anything like Saratoga for fashion, and Mrs. Mandel remembered that in her own young ladyhood this was so for at least some weeks of the year. She had been too far withdrawn from fashion since her marriage to know whether it was still so or not. In this, as in so many other matters, the Dryfoos family helplessly relied upon Fulkerson, in spite of Dryfoos's angry determination that he should not run the family, and in spite of Christine's doubt of his omniscience; if he did not know everything, she was aware that he knew more than herself.

She thought that they had a right to have him go with them to Saratoga, or at least go up and engage their rooms beforehand; but Fulkerson did not offer to do either, and she did not quite see her way to commanding his services. The young ladies took what Mela called splendid dresses with them; they sat in the park of tall, slim trees which the hotel's quadrangle enclosed, and listened to the music in the morning, or on the long piazza in the afternoon and looked at the driving in the street, or in the vast parlours by night, where all the other ladies were, and they felt that they were of the best there. But they knew nobody, and Mrs. Mandel was so particular that Mela was prevented from continuing the acquaintance even of the few young men who danced with her at the Saturday-night hops. They drove about, but they went to places without knowing why, except that the carriage man took them, and they had all the privileges of a proud exclusivism without desiring them. Once a motherly matron seemed to perceive their isolation, and made overtures to them, but then desisted, as if repelled by Christine's suspicion, or by Mela's too instant and hilarious good-fellowship, which expressed itself in hoarse laughter and in a flow of talk full of topical and syntactical freedom. From time to time she offered to bet Christine that if Mr. Fulkerson was only there they would have a good time; she wondered what they were all doing in New York, where she wished herself; she rallied her sister about Beaton, and asked her why she did not write and tell him to come up there.

Mela knew that Christine had expected Beaton to follow them. Some banter had passed between them to this effect; he said he should take them in on his way home to Syracuse. Christine would not have hesitated to write to him and remind him of his promise; but she had learned to distrust her literature with Beaton since he had laughed at the spelling in a scrap of writing which dropped out of her music-book one night. She believed that he would not have laughed if he had known it was hers; but she felt that she could hide better the deficiencies which were not committed to paper; she could manage with him in talking; she was too ignorant of her ignorance to recognise the mistakes she made then. Through her own passion she perceived that she had some kind of fascination for him; she was graceful, and she thought it must be that; she did not understand that there was a kind of beauty in her small, irregular features that piqued and haunted his artistic sense, and a look in her black eyes beyond her intelligence and intention. Once he sketched her as they sat together, and flattered the portrait without getting what he wanted in it; he said he must try her some time in colour; and he said things which, when she made Mela repeat them, could only mean that he admired her more than anybody else. He came fitfully, but he came often, and she rested content in a girl's indefiniteness concerning the affair; if her thought went beyond love-making to marriage, she believed that she could have him if she wanted him. Her father's money counted in this; she divined that Beaton was poor; but that made no difference; she would have enough for both; the money would have counted as an irresistible attraction if there had been no other.

The affair had gone on in spite of the sidelong looks of restless dislike with which Dryfoos regarded it; but now when Beaton did not come to Saratoga it necessarily dropped, and Christine's content with it. She bore the trial as long as she could; she used pride and resentment against it; but at last she could not bear it, and with Mela's help she wrote a letter, bantering Beaton on his stay in New York, and playfully boasting of Saratoga. It seemed to them both that it was a very bright letter, and would be sure to bring him; they would have had no scruple about sending it but for the doubt they had whether they had got some of the words right. Mela offered to bet Christine anything she dared that they were right, and she said, Send it anyway; it was no difference if they *were* wrong. But Christine could not endure to think of that laugh of Beaton's, and there remained only Mrs. Mandel as authority on the spelling. Christine dreaded her authority on other points, but Mela said she knew she would not interfere, and she undertook to get round her. Mrs. Mandel pronounced the spelling bad, and the taste worse; she forbade them to send the letter; and Mela failed to get round her, though she threatened, if Mrs. Mandel would not tell her how to spell the wrong words, that she would send the letter as it was; then Mrs. Mandel said that if Mr. Beaton appeared in Saratoga she would instantly take them both home. When Mela reported this result, Christine accused her of having mismanaged the whole business; she quarrelled with her, and they called each other names. Christine declared that she would not stay in Saratoga, and that if Mrs. Mandel did not go back to New York with her she should go alone. They returned the first week in September; but by that time Beaton had gone to see his people in Syracuse.

Conrad Dryfoos remained at home with his mother after his father went West. He had already taken such a vacation as he had been willing to allow himself, and had spent it on a charity farm near the city, where the fathers with whom he worked among the poor on the East side in the winter had sent some of their wards for the summer. It was not possible to keep his recreation a secret at the office, and Fulkerson found a pleasure in figuring the jolly time Brother Conrad must have teaching farm work among those paupers and potential reprobates. He invented details of his experience among them, and March could not always help joining in the laugh at Conrad's humourless helplessness under Fulkerson's burlesque denunciation of a summer outing spent in such dissipation.

They had time for a great deal of joking at the office during the season of leisure which penetrates in August to the very heart of business, and they all got on terms of greater intimacy if not greater friendliness than before. Fulkerson had not had so long to do with the advertising side of human nature without developing a vein of cynicism, of no great depth, perhaps, but broad, and underlying his whole point of view; he made light of Beaton's solemnity, as he made light of Conrad's humanity. The art editor, with abundant sarcasm, had no more humour than the publisher, and was an easy prey in the manager's hands; but when he had been led on by Fulkerson's flatteries to make some betrayal of egotism, he brooded over it till he had thought how to revenge himself in elaborate insult. For Beaton's talent Fulkerson never lost his admiration; but his joke was to encourage him to give himself airs of being the sole source of the magazine's prosperity. No bait of this sort was too obvious for Beaton to swallow; he could be caught with it as often as Fulkerson chose; though he was ordinarily suspicious as to the motives of people in saying things. With March he got on no better than at first. He seemed to be lying in wait for some encroachment of the literary department on the art department, and he met it now and then with anticipative reprisal. After these rebuffs, the editor delivered him over to the manager, who could turn Beaton's contrary-mindedness to account by asking the reverse of what he really wanted done. This was what Fulkerson said; the fact was that he did get on with Beaton; and March contented himself with musing upon the contradictions of a character at once so vain and so offensive, so fickle and so sullen, so conscious and so simple.

After the first jarring contact with Dryfoos, the editor ceased to feel the disagreeable fact of the old man's mastery of the financial situation. None of the chances which might have made it painful occurred; the control of the whole affair remained in Fulkerson's hands; before he went West again, Dryfoos had ceased to come about the office, as if, having once worn off the novelty of the sense of owning a literary periodical, he was no longer interested in it.

Yet it was a relief, somehow, when he left town, which he did not do without coming to take a formal leave of the editor at his office. He seemed willing to leave March with a better impression than he had hitherto troubled himself to make; he even said some civil things about the magazine, as if its success pleased him; and he spoke openly to March of his hope that his son would finally become interested in it to the exclusion of the hopes and purposes which divided them. It seemed to March that in the old man's warped and toughened heart he perceived a disappointed love for his son greater

283

than for his other children; but this might have been fancy. Lindau came in with some copy while Dryfoos was there, and March introduced them. When Lindau went out, March explained to Dryfoos that he had lost his hand in the war; and he told him something of Lindau's career as he had known it. Dryfoos appeared greatly pleased that *Every Other Week* was giving Lindau work. He said that he had helped to enlist a good many fellows for the war, and had paid money to fill up the Moffitt County quota under the later calls for troops. He had never been an Abolitionist, but he had joined the Anti-Nebraska party in '55, and he had voted for Fremont and for every Republican President since then.

At his own house March saw more of Lindau than of any other contributor, but the old man seemed to think that he must transact all his business with March at his place of business. The transaction had some peculiarities which perhaps made this necessary. Lindau always expected to receive his money when he brought his copy, as an acknowledgment of the immediate right of the labourer to his hire; and he would not take it in a cheque because he did not approve of banks, and regarded the whole system of banking as the capitalistic manipulation of the people's money. He would receive his pay only from March's hand, because he wished to be understood as working for him, and honestly earning money honestly earned; and sometimes March inwardly winced a little at letting the old man share the increase of capital won by such speculation as Dryfoos's, but he shook off the feeling. As the summer advanced, and the artists and classes that employed Lindau as a model left town one after another, he gave largely of his increasing leisure to the people in the office of *Every Other Week*. It was pleasant for March to see the respect with which Conrad Dryfoos always used him, for the sake of his wound and his grey beard. There was something delicate and fine in it, and there was nothing unkindly on Fulkerson's part in the hostilities which usually passed between him and Lindau. Fulkerson bore himself reverently at times too, but it was not in him to keep that up, especially when Lindau appeared with more beer aboard than, as Fulkerson said, he could manage ship-shape. On these occasions Fulkerson always tried to start him on the theme of the unduly rich; he made himself the champion of monopolies, and enjoyed the invectives which Lindau heaped upon him as a slave of capital; he said that it did him good.

One day, with the usual show of writhing under Lindau's scorn, he said, "Well, I understand that although you despise me now, Lindau——"

"I ton't desbise you," the old man broke in, his nostrils swelling and his eyes flaming with excitement, "I bity you."

"Well, it seems to come to the same thing in the end," said Fulkerson. "What I understand is that you pity me now as the slave of capital, but you would pity me a great deal more if I was the master of it."

"How you mean?"

"If I was rich."

"That would tebendt," said Lindau, trying to control himself. "If you hat inheritedt your money, you might pe innocent; but if you hat *mate* it, efery man that resbectedt himself would haf to ask *how* you mate it, and if you hat mate moch, he would know——"

"Hold on; hold on, now, Lindau! Ain't that rather un-American doctrine? We're all brought up, ain't we, to honour the man that made his money, and look down—or try to look down; sometimes it's difficult—on the fellow that his father left it to?"

The old man rose and struck his breast. "On-Amerigan!" he roared, and, as he went on, his accent grew more and more uncertain. "What iss Amerigan? Dere *iss* no Ameriga any more! You start here free and brafe, and you glaim for efery man de righdt to life, liperty, and de bursuit of habbiness. And where haf you entedt? No man that vorks vith his handts among you hass the liperty to bursue his habbiness. He iss the slafe of some richer man, some gompany, some gorporation, dat crindts him down to the least he can lif on, and that rops him of the marchin of his earnings that he might pe habby on. Oh, you Amerigans, you haf cot it down

goldt, as you say! You ton't puy foters; you puy lechisla-
tures and goncressmen; you puy gourts; you puy gombeti-
tors; you pay infentors not to infent; you *atfertise*, and the
gounting-room sees dat de etitorial-room toesn't tink."

"Yes, we've got a little arrangement of that sort with
March here," said Fulkerson.

"Oh, I am sawry," said the old man contritely, "I meant
noting bersonal. I ton't tink we are all cuilty or gorrubt, and
efen among the rich there are goodt men. But gabidal"—his
passion rose again—"where you find gabidal, millions of
money that a man hass cot togeder in fife, ten, tventy years,
you findt the smell of tears and ploodt! Dat iss what I say.
And you cot to loog oudt for yourself when you meet a rich
man whether you meet an honest man."

"Well," said Fulkerson, "I wish I was a subject of suspicion with you, Lindau. By the way," he added, "I understand that you think capital was at the bottom of the veto of
that pension of yours."

"What bension? What feto?" The old man flamed up
again. "No bension of mine was efer fetoedt. I renounce my
bension, begause I would sgorn to dake money from a
gofernment that I ton't peliefe in any more. Where you hear
that story?"

"Well, I don't know," said Fulkerson, rather embarrassed. "It's common talk."

"It's a gommon lie, then! When the time gome dat dis
iss a free gountry again, then I dake a bension again for my
woundts; but I would *sdarfe* before I dake a bension now
from a rebublic dat is bought oap by monobolies, and ron by
drusts and gompanies, and railroadts andt oil gompanies.

"Look out, Lindau," said Fulkerson. "You bite yourself
mit dat dog some day." But when the old man, with a ferocious gesture of renunciation, whirled out of the place, he
added: "I guess I went a little too far that time. I touched
him on a sore place; I didn't mean to; I heard some talk
about his pension being vetoed from Miss Leighton." He
addressed these exculpations to March's grave face, and to
the pitying deprecation in the eyes of Conrad Dryfoos, whom

Lindau's roaring wrath had summoned to the door. "But I'll make it all right with him the next time he comes. I didn't know he was loaded, or I wouldn't have monkeyed with him."

"Lindau does himself injustice when he gets to talking in that way," said March. "I hate to hear him. He's as good an American as any of us; and it's only because he has too high an ideal of us——"

"Oh, go on! Rub it in—rub it in!" cried Fulkerson, clutching his hair in suffering, which was not altogether burlesque. "How did I know he had renounced his 'bension'? Why didn't you tell me?"

"I didn't know it myself. I only knew that he had none, and I didn't ask, for I had a notion that it might be a painful subject."

Fulkerson tried to turn it off lightly. "Well, he's a noble old fellow; pity he drinks." March would not smile, and Fulkerson broke out: "Dog on it! I'll make it up to the old fool the next time he comes. I don't like that dynamite talk of his; but any man that's given his hand to the country has got mine in his grip for good. Why, March! You don't suppose I wanted to hurt his feelings, do you?"

"Why, of course not, Fulkerson."

But they could not get away from a certain ruefulness for that time, and in the evening Fulkerson came round to March's to say that he had got Lindau's address from Conrad, and had looked him up at his lodgings.

"Well, there isn't so much bric-à-brac there, quite, as Mrs. Green left you; but I've made it all right with Lindau, as far as I'm concerned. I told him I didn't know when I spoke that way, and I honoured him for sticking to his 'brincibles'; *I* don't believe in his brincibles; and we wept on each other's necks—at least, he did. Dogged if he didn't kiss me before I knew what he was up to. He said I was his chenerous yong friendt, and he begged my barton if he had said anything to wound me. I tell you it was an affecting scene, March; and rats enough round in that old barracks where he lives to fit out a first-class case of *delirium tremens*. What does he stay there for? He's not obliged to?"

Lindau's reasons, as March repeated them, affected Fulkerson as deliciously comical; but after that he confined his pleasantries at the office to Beaton and Conrad Dryfoos, or, as he said, he spent the rest of the summer in keeping Lindau smoothed up.

It is doubtful if Lindau altogether liked this as well. Perhaps he missed the occasions Fulkerson used to give him of bursting out against the millionaires; and he could not well go on denouncing as the slafe of gabidal a man who had behaved to him as Fulkerson had done, though Fulkerson's servile relations to capital had been in nowise changed by his nople gonduct.

Their relations continued to wear this irksome character of mutual forbearance; and when Dryfoos returned in October and Fulkerson revived the question of that dinner in celebration of the success of *Every Other Week*, he carried his complaisance to an extreme that alarmed March for the consequences.

V

"You see," Fulkerson explained, "I find that the old man has got an idea of his own about that banquet, and I guess there's some sense in it. He wants to have a preliminary little dinner, where we can talk the thing up first—half a dozen of us; and he wants to give us the dinner at his house. Well, that's no harm. I don't believe the old man ever gave a dinner, and he'd like to show off a little; there's a good deal of human nature in the old man, after all. He thought of you, of course, and Colonel Woodburn, and Beaton, and me at the foot of the table; and Conrad; and I suggested Kendricks: he's such a nice little chap; and the old man himself brought up the idea of Lindau. He said you told him something about him, and he asked why couldn't we have him, too; and I jumped at it."

"Have Lindau to dinner?" asked March.

"Certainly; why not? Father Dryfoos has a notion of

288

paying the old fellow a compliment for what he done for the country. There won't be any trouble about it. You can sit alongside of him, and cut up his meat for him, and help him to things——"

"Yes, but it won't *do*, Fulkerson! I don't believe Lindau ever had on a dress-coat in his life, and I don't believe his 'brincibles' would let him wear one."

"Well, neither had Dryfoos, for the matter of that. He's as high-principled as old Pan-Electric himself, when it comes to a dress-coat," said Fulkerson. "We're all going to go in business dress; the old man stipulated for that."

"It isn't the dress-coat alone," March resumed. "Lindau and Dryfoos wouldn't get on. You know they're opposite poles in everything. You mustn't do it. Dryfoos will be sure to say something to outrage Lindau's 'brincibles,' and there'll be an explosion. It's all well enough for Dryfoos to feel grateful to Lindau, and his wish to honour him does him credit; but to have Lindau to dinner isn't the way. At the best, the old fellow would be very unhappy in such a house; he would have a bad conscience; and I should be sorry to have him feel that he'd been recreant to his 'brincibles'; they're about all he's got, and whatever we think of them, we're bound to respect his fidelity to them." March warmed toward Lindau in taking this view of him. "I should feel ashamed if I didn't protest against his being put in a false position. After all, he's my old friend, and I shouldn't like to have him do himself injustice if he *is* a crank."

"Of course," said Fulkerson, with some trouble in his face. "I appreciate your feeling. But there ain't any danger," he added buoyantly. "Anyhow, you spoke too late, as the Irishman said to the chicken when he swallowed him in a fresh egg. I've asked Lindau, and he's accepted with blayzure; that's what he says."

March made no other comment than a shrug.

"You'll see," Fulkerson continued, "it'll go off all right. I'll engage to make it, and I won't hold anybody else responsible."

In the course of his married life March had learned not to censure the irretrievable; but this was just what his wife had not learned; and she poured out so much astonishment at what Fulkerson had done, and so much disapproval, that March began to palliate the situation a little.

"After all, it isn't a question of life and death; and, if it were, I don't see how it's to be helped now."

"Oh, it's not to be helped *now*. But I *am* surprised at Mr. Fulkerson."

"Well, Fulkerson has his moments of being merely human, too."

Mrs. March would not deign a direct defence of her favourite. "Well, I'm glad there are not to be ladies."

"I don't know. Dryfoos thought of having ladies, but it seems your infallible Fulkerson overruled him. Their presence might have kept Lindau and our host in bounds."

It had become part of the Marches' conjugal joke for him to pretend that she could allow nothing wrong in Fulkerson, and he now laughed with a mocking air of having expected it when she said: "Well, then, if Mr. Fulkerson says he will see that it all comes out right, I suppose you must trust his tact. I wouldn't trust yours, Basil. The first wrong step was taken when Mr. Lindau was asked to help on the magazine."

"Well, it was your infallible Fulkerson that took the step, or at least suggested it. I'm happy to say *I* had totally forgotten my early friend."

Mrs. March was daunted and silenced for a moment. Then she said: "Oh, pshaw! You know well enough he did it to please you."

"I'm very glad he didn't do it to please *you*, Isabel," said her husband, with affected seriousness. "Though perhaps he did."

He began to look at the humorous aspect of the affair, which it certainly had, and to comment on the singular incongruities which *Every Other Week* was destined to involve at every moment of its career. "I wonder if I'm mistaken in supposing that no other periodical was ever like it. Perhaps all periodicals are like it. But I don't believe there's another publication in New York that could bring together, in honour of itself, a fraternity and equality crank like poor old Lindau, and a belated sociological crank like Woodburn, and a truculent speculator like old Dryfoos, and a humanitarian dreamer like young Dryfoos, and a sentimentalist like me, and a nondescript like Beaton, and a pure advertising essence like Fulkerson, and a society spirit like Kendricks. If we could only allow one another to talk uninterruptedly all the time, the dinner would be the greatest success in the world, and we should come home full of the highest mutual respect. But I suspect we can't manage that—even your infallible Fulkerson couldn't work it—and I'm afraid that there'll be some listening that'll spoil the pleasure of the time."

March was so well pleased with this view of the case that he suggested the idea involved to Fulkerson. Fulkerson was too good a fellow not to laugh at another man's joke, but he laughed a little ruefully, and he seemed worn with more than one kind of care in the interval that passed between the present time and the night of the dinner.

Dryfoos necessarily depended upon him for advice concerning the scope and nature of the dinner, but he received the advice suspiciously, and contested points of obvious propriety with pertinacious stupidity. Fulkerson said that when it came to the point he would rather have had the thing, as he called it, at Delmonico's or some other restaurant; but when he found that Dryfoos's pride was bound up in having it at his own house, he gave way to him. Dryfoos also wanted his woman-cook to prepare the dinner, but Fulkerson persuaded him that this would not do; he must have it from a caterer. Then Dryfoos wanted his maids to wait at table, but Fulkerson convinced him that this would be incongruous at a man's dinner. It was decided that the dinner should be sent in from Frescobaldi's, and Dryfoos went with Fulkerson to discuss it with the caterer. He insisted upon having everything explained to him, and the reason for having it, and not something else in its place; and he treated Fulkerson and Frescobaldi as if they were in league to impose upon him. There were moments when Fulkerson saw the varnish of professional politeness cracking on the Neapolitan's volcanic surface, and caught a glimpse of the lava fires of the cook's nature beneath; he trembled for Dryfoos, who was walking rough-shod over him in the security of an American who had known how to make his money, and must know how to spend it; but he got him safely away at last, and gave Frescobaldi a wink of sympathy for his shrug of exhaustion as they turned to leave him.

It was at first a relief and then an anxiety with Fulkerson that Lindau did not come about after accepting the invitation to dinner, until he appeared at Dryfoos's house, prompt to the hour. There was, to be sure, nothing to bring him; but Fulkerson was uneasily aware that Dryfoos expected to meet him at the office, and perhaps receive some verbal acknowledgment of the honour done him. Dryfoos, he could see, thought he was doing all his invited guests a favour; and while he stood in a certain awe of them as people of much greater social experience than himself, regarded them with a kind of contempt, as people who were going to have a better dinner at his house than they could ever afford to have at their own. He had finally not spared expense upon it; after pushing Frescobaldi to the point of eruption with his misgivings and suspicions at the first interview, he had gone to him a second time alone, and told him not to let the money stand between him and anything he would like to do. In the absence of Frescobaldi's fellow-conspirator he restored himself in the caterer's esteem by adding whatever he suggested; and Fulkerson, after trembling for the old man's niggardliness, was now afraid of a fantastic profusion in the feast. Dryfoos had reduced the scale of the banquet as regarded the number of guests, but a confusing remembrance of what Fulkerson had wished to do remained with him in part, and up to the day of the dinner he dropped in at Frescobaldi's and ordered more dishes and more of them. He impressed the Italian as an American original of a novel kind; and when he asked Fulkerson how Dryfoos had made his money, and learned that it was primarily in natural gas, he made note of some of his eccentric tastes as peculiarities that were to be caressed in any future natural-gas millionaire who might fall into his hands. He did not begrudge the time he had to give in explaining to Dryfoos the relation of the different wines to the different dishes; Dryfoos was apt to substitute a costlier wine where he could for a cheaper one, and he gave Frescobaldi *carte blanche* for the decoration of the table with pieces of artistic confectionery. Among these the caterer designed one for a surprise to his patron and a delicate recognition of the source of his wealth, which he found Dryfoos very willing to talk about, when he intimated that he knew what it was.

Dryfoos left it to Fulkerson to invite the guests, and he found ready acceptance of his politeness from Kendricks, who rightly regarded the dinner as a part of the *Every Other Week* business, and was too sweet and kind-hearted, anyway, not to seem very glad to come. March was a matter of course; but in Colonel Woodburn Fulkerson encountered a reluctance which embarrassed him the more because he was conscious of having, for motives of his own, rather strained a point in suggesting the colonel to Dryfoos as a fit subject for invitation. There had been only one of the colonel's articles printed as yet, and though it had made a sensation in its way, and started the talk about that number, still it did not fairly constitute him a member of the staff, or even entitle him to recognition as a regular contributor. Fulkerson felt so sure of pleasing him with Dryfoos's message that he delivered it in full family council at the widow's. His daughter received it with all the enthusiasm that Fulkerson had hoped for, but the colonel said stiffly, "I have not the pleasure of knowing Mr. Dryfoos." Miss Woodburn appeared ready to fall upon him at this, but controlled herself, as if aware that filial authority had its limits, and pressed her lips together without saying anything.

"Yes, I know," Fulkerson admitted. "But it isn't a usual case. Mr. Dryfoos don't go in much for the conventionalities; I reckon he don't know much about 'em, come to boil it down; and he hoped"—here Fulkerson felt the necessity of

inventing a little—"that you would excuse any want of ceremony; it's to be such an informal affair, anyway; we're all
going in business dress, and there ain't going to be any ladies.
He'd have come himself to ask you, but he's a kind of a bash-
ful old fellow. It's all right, Colonel Woodburn."

"I take it that it is, sir," said the colonel courteously, but
with unabated state, "coming from you. But in these matters
we have no right to burden our friends with our decisions."

"Of course, of course," said Fulkerson, feeling that he had
been delicately told to mind his own business.

"I understand," the colonel went on, "the relation that Mr.
Dryfoos bears to the periodical in which you have done me
the hono' to print my papah, but this is a question of passing
the bounds of a purely business connection, and of eating the
salt of a man whom you do not definitely know to be a
gentleman."

"Mah goodness!" his daughter broke in. "If you bah
your own salt with his money——"

"It is supposed that I earn his money before I buy my
salt with it," returned her father severely. "And in these
times, when money is got in heaps, through the natural decay
of our nefarious commercialism, it behooves a gentleman to
be scrupulous that the hospitality offered him is not the profusion of a thief with his booty. I don't say that Mr. Dryfoos's
good-fortune is not honest. I simply say that I know nothing
about it, and that I should prefer to know something before
I sat down at his board."

"You're all right, colonel," said Fulkerson, "and so is Mr.
Dryfoos. I give you my word that there are no flies on his
personal integrity, if that's what you mean. He's hard, and
he'd push an advantage, but I don't believe he would take
an unfair one. He's speculated and made money every time,
but I never heard of his wrecking a railroad or belonging to
any swindling company or any grinding monopoly. He does
chance it in stocks, but he's always played on the square, if
you call stocks gambling."

"May I think this over till morning?" asked the
colonel.

"Oh, certainly, certainly," said Fulkerson eagerly. "I don't know as there's any hurry."

Miss Woodburn found a chance to murmur to him before he went: "He'll come. And Ah'm *so* much oblahged, Mr. Fulkerson. Ah jost know it's all you' doing, and it will give papa a chance to toak to some new people, and get away from us evahlastin' women for once."

"I don't see why any one should want to do that," said Fulkerson, with grateful gallantry. "But I'll be dogged," he said to March when he told him about this odd experience, "if I ever expected to find Colonel Woodburn on old Lindau's ground. He did come round handsomely this morning at breakfast and apologised for taking time to think the invitation over before he accepted. 'You understand,' he says, 'that if it had been to the table of some friend not so prosperous as Mr. Dryfoos—your friend Mr. March, for instance —it would have been sufficient to know that he was your friend. But in these days it is a duty that a gentleman owes himself to consider whether he wishes to know a rich man or not. The chances of making money disreputably are so great that the chances are against a man who has made money if he's made a great deal of it.'"

March listened with a face of ironical insinuation. "That was very good; and he seems to have had a good deal of confidence in your patience and in your sense of his importance to the occasion——"

"No, no," Fulkerson protested, "there's none of that kind of thing about the colonel. I *told* him to take time to think it over; he's the simplest-hearted old fellow in the world."

"I should say so. After all, he didn't give any reason he had for accepting. But perhaps the young lady had the reason."

"Pshaw, March!" said Fulkerson.

So far as the Dryfoos family was concerned, the dinner might as well have been given at Frescobaldi's rooms. None of the ladies appeared. Mrs. Dryfoos was glad to escape to her own chamber, where she sat before an autumnal fire, shaking her head and talking to herself at times, with the foreboding of evil which old women like her make part of their religion. The girls stood just out of sight at the head of the stairs, and disputed which guest it was at each arrival; Mrs. Mandel had gone to her room to write letters, after beseeching them not to stand there. When Kendricks came, Christine gave Mela a little pinch, equivalent to a little mocking shriek; for, on the ground of his long talk with Mela at Mrs. Horn's, in the absence of any other admirer, they based a superstition of his interest in her; when Beaton came, Mela returned the pinch, but awkwardly, so that it hurt, and then Christine involuntarily struck her.

Frescobaldi's men were in possession everywhere: they had turned the cook out of her kitchen and the waitress out of her pantry; the reluctant Irishman at the door was supplemented by a vivid Italian, who spoke French with the guests, and said, "*Bien, Monsieur,*" and "*Toute suite,*" and "*Merci!*" to all, as he took their hats and coats, and effused a hospitality that needed no language but the gleam of his eyes and teeth and the play of his eloquent hands. From his professional dress-coat, lustrous with the grease spotted on it at former dinners and parties, they passed to the frocks of the elder and younger Dryfoos in the drawing-room, which assumed informality for the affair, but did not put their wearers wholly at their ease. The father's coat was of black broadcloth, and he wore it unbuttoned; the skirts were long, and the sleeves came down to his knuckles; he shook hands with his guests, and the same dryness seemed to be in his palm and throat, as he huskily asked each to take a chair. Conrad's coat was of modern texture and cut, and was buttoned about him as if it concealed a bad conscience within its lapels; he met March with his entreating smile, and he seemed no more capable of coping with the situation than his father. They both waited for Fulkerson, who went about and did his best to keep life in the party during the half-hour that passed before they sat down at dinner. Beaton stood gloomily aloof, as if waiting to be approached on the right basis before yielding an inch of his ground; Colonel Woodburn, awaiting the moment when he could sally out on his hobby, kept himself intrenched within the dignity of a gentleman, and examined askance the figure of old Lindau as he stared about the room, with his fine head up, and his empty sleeve dangling over his wrist. March felt obliged to him for wearing a new coat in the midst of that hostile luxury, and he was glad to see Dryfoos make up to him and begin to talk with him, as if he wished to show him particular respect, though it might have been because he was less afraid of him than of the others. He heard Lindau saying, "Boat, the name is Choarman?" and Dryfoos beginning to explain his Pennsylvania Dutch origin, and he suffered himself, with a sigh of relief, to fall into talk with Kendricks, who was always pleasant; he was willing to talk about something besides himself, and had no opinions that he was not ready to hold in abeyance for the time being out of kindness to others. In that group of impassioned individualities, March felt him a refuge and comfort—with his harmless dilettante intention of some day writing a novel, and his belief that he was meantime collecting material for it.

Fulkerson, while breaking the ice for the whole company, was mainly engaged in keeping Colonel Woodburn thawed out. He took Kendricks away from March and presented him to the Colonel as a person who, like himself, was looking into social conditions; he put one hand on Kendricks' shoulder, and one on the colonel's, and made some flattering joke, apparently at the expense of the young fellow, and then left them. March heard Kendricks protest in vain, and the colonel say gravely: "I do not wonder, sir, that these things interest you. They constitute a problem which society must solve or which will dissolve society," and he knew from that formula, which the colonel had once used with him, that he was laying out a road for the exhibition of the hobby's paces later.

Fulkerson came back to March, who had turned toward Conrad Dryfoos, and said, "If we don't get this thing going pretty soon, it'll be the death of me," and just then Frescobaldi's butler came in and announced to Dryfoos that dinner was served. The old man looked toward Fulkerson with a troubled glance, as if he did not know what to do; he made a gesture to touch Lindau's elbow. Fulkerson called out, "*Here's* Colonel Woodburn, Mr. Dryfoos," as if Dryfoos were looking for him; and he set the example of what he was to do by taking Lindau's arm himself. "Mr. Lindau is going to sit at my end of the table, alongside of March. Stand not upon the order of your going, gentlemen, but fall in at once." He contrived to get Dryfoos and the colonel before him, and he let March follow with Kendricks. Conrad came last with Beaton, who had been turning over the music at the piano, and chafing inwardly at the whole affair. At the table Colonel Woodburn was placed on Dryfoos's right, and March on his left. March sat on Fulkerson's right, with Lindau next him; and the young men occupied the other seats.

"Put you next to March, Mr. Lindau," said Fulkerson, "so you can begin to put Apollinaris in his champagne-glass at the right moment; you know his little weakness of old; sorry to say it's grown on him."

March laughed with kindly acquiescence in Fulkerson's wish to start the gaiety, and Lindau patted him on the shoulder. "I know hiss veakness. If he liges a class of vine, it iss begause his loaf ingludes efen hiss enemy, as Shakespeare galled it."

"Ah, but Shakespeare couldn't have been thinking of champagne," said Kendricks.

"I suppose, sir," Colonel Woodburn interposed with lofty courtesy, "champagne could hardly have been known in his day."

"I suppose not, colonel," returned the younger man deferentially. "He seemed to think that sack and sugar might be a fault; but he didn't mention champagne."

"Perhaps he felt there was no question about that," suggested Beaton, who then felt that he had not done himself justice in the sally.

"I wonder just when champagne did come in," said March.

"I know when it ought to come in," said Fulkerson. "Before the soup!"

They all laughed, and gave themselves the air of drinking champagne out of tumblers every day, as men like to do. Dryfoos listened uneasily; he did not quite understand the allusions, though he knew what Shakespeare was, well enough; Conrad's face expressed a gentle deprecation of joking on such a subject, but he said nothing.

The talk ran on briskly through the dinner. The young men tossed the ball back and forth; they made some wild shots, but they kept it going, and they laughed when they were hit. The wine loosed Colonel Woodburn's tongue; he became very companionable with the young fellows; with the feeling that a literary dinner ought to have a didactic scope, he praised Scott and Addison as the only authors fit to form the minds of gentlemen.

Kendricks agreed with him, but wished to add the name of Flaubert as a master of style. "Style, you know," he added, "is the man."

"Very true, sir; you are quite right, sir," the colonel assented; he wondered who Flaubert was.

Beaton praised Baudelaire and Maupassant; he said these were the masters. He recited some lurid verses from Baudelaire; Lindau pronounced them a disgrace to human nature, and gave a passage from Victor Hugo on Louis Napoleon, with his heavy German accent, and then he quoted Schiller. "Ach, boat that iss peaudifool! Not zo?" he demanded of March.

"Yes, beautiful; but, of course, you know I think there's nobody like Heine!"

Lindau threw back his great old head and laughed, showing a want of teeth under his moustache. He put his hand on March's back. "This poy—he wass a poy den—wass so

gracy to pekin reading Heine that he gommence with the
tictionary bevore he knows any crammar, and ve bick it out
vort by vort togeder."

"He was a pretty cay poy in those days, heigh, Lindau?"
asked Fulkerson, burlesquing the old man's accent, with an
impudent wink that made Lindau himself laugh. "Back in
the dark ages, I mean, there in Indianapolis. Just how long
ago did you old codgers meet there, anyway?" Fulkerson saw
the restiveness in Dryfoos's eye at the purely literary course
the talk had taken; he had intended it to lead up that way to
business, to *Every Other Week*; but he saw that it was leaving
Dryfoos too far out, and he wished to get it on the personal
ground, where everybody is at home.

"Ledt me zee," mused Lindau. "Wass it in fifty-nine or
zixty, Passil? Idt wass a year or dwo pefore the war proke
oudt, anyway."

"Those were exciting times," said Dryfoos, making his
first entry into the general talk. "I went down to Indianapolis
with the first company from our place, and I saw the red-
shirts pouring in everywhere. They had a song—

"Oh, never mind the weather, but git over double trouble,
    For we're bound for the land of Canaan."

The fellows locked arms and went singin' it up and down
four or five abreast in the moonlight; crowded everybody
else off the sidewalk."

"I rememper, I rememper," said Lindau, nodding his
head slowly up and down. "A coodt many off them nefer
gome pack from that landt of Ganaan, Mr. Dryfoos?"

"You're right, Mr. Lindau. But I reckon it was worth it—
the country we've got now. Here, young man!" He caught the
arm of the waiter who was going round with the champagne
bottle. "Fill up Mr. Lindau's glass, there. I want to drink
the health of those old times with him. Here's to your empty
sleeve, Mr. Lindau. God bless it! No offence to *you*, Colonel
Woodburn," said Dryfoos, turning to him before he drank.

"Not at all, sir, not at all," said the colonel. "I will drink
with you, if you will permit me."

"We'll all drink—standing," cried Fulkerson. "Help March to get up, somebody! Fill high the bowl with Samian Apollinaris for Coonrod! Now, then, hurrah for Lindau!"

They cheered, and hammered on the table with the butts of their knife-handles. Lindau remained seated. The tears came into his eyes; he said, "I thank you, chendlemen," and hiccoughed.

"I'd 'a' went into the war myself," said Dryfoos, "but I was raisin' a family of young children, and I didn't see how I could leave my farm. But I helped to fill up the quota at every call, and when the volunteering stopped I went round with the subscription paper myself; and we offered as good bounties as any in the State. My substitute was killed in one of the last skirmishes—in fact, after Lee's surrender—and I've took care of his family, more or less, ever since."

"By the way, March," said Fulkerson, "what sort of an idea would it be to have a good war-story—might be a serial —in the magazine? The war has never fully panned out in fiction yet. It was used a good deal just after it was over, and then it was dropped. I think it's time to take it up again. I believe it would be a card."

It was running in March's mind that Dryfoos had an old rankling shame in his heart for not having gone into the war, and that he had often made that explanation of his course without having ever been satisfied with it. He felt sorry for him; the fact seemed pathetic; it suggested a dormant nobleness in the man.

Beaton was saying to Fulkerson, "You might get a series of sketches by substitutes; the substitutes haven't been much heard from in the war literature. How would 'The Autobiography of a Substitute' do? You might follow him up to the moment he was killed in the other man's place, and inquire whether he had any right to the feelings of a hero when he was only hired in the place of one. Might call it 'The Career of a Deputy Hero.'"

"I fancy," said March, "that there was a great deal of mixed motive in the men who went into the war as well as in those who kept out of it. We canonised all that died or suffered in it, but some of them must have been self-seeking and low-minded, like men in other vocations." He found himself saying this in Dryfoos's behalf; the old man looked at him gratefully at first, he thought, and then suspiciously.

Lindau turned his head toward him and said: "You are righdt, Passil; you are righdt. I haf zeen on the fieldt of pattle the voarst eggsipitions of human paseness—chelousy, fanity, ecodistic bridte. I haf zeen men in the face off death itself gofferned by motifes as low as—as pusiness motifes."

"Well," said Fulkerson, "it would be a grand thing for *Every Other Week* if we could get some of those ideas worked up into a series. It would make a lot of talk."

Colonel Woodburn ignored him in saying, "I think, Major Lindau——"

"High brifate; prefet gorporal," the old man interrupted, in rejection of the title.

Kendricks laughed and said, with a glance of appreciation at Lindau, "Brevet corporal is good."

Colonel Woodburn frowned a little, and passed over the joke. "I think Mr. Lindau is right. Such exhibitions were common to both sides, though if you gentlemen will pardon me for saying so, I think they were less frequent on ours. We were fighting more immediately for existence; we were fewer than you were, and we knew it; we felt more intensely that if each were not for all, then none was for any."

The colonel's words made their impression. Dryfoos said with authority, "That is so."

"Colonel Woodburn," Fulkerson called out, "if you'll work up those ideas into a short paper—say three thousand words—I'll engage to make March take it."

The colonel went on without replying: "But Mr. Lindau is right in characterising some of the motives that led men to the cannon's mouth as no higher than business motives, and his comparison is the most forcible that he could have used. I was very much struck by it."

The hobby was out, the colonel was in the saddle with so firm a seat that no effort sufficed to dislodge him. The dinner went on from course to course with barbaric profusion, and from time to time Fulkerson tried to bring the talk back to *Every Other Week*. But perhaps because that was only the ostensible and not the real object of the dinner, which was to bring a number of men together under Dryfoos's roof, and make them the witnesses of his splendour, make them feel the power of his wealth, Fulkerson's attempts failed. The colonel showed how commercialism was the poison at the heart of our national life; how we began as a simple, agricultural people, who had fled to these shores with the instinct, divinely implanted, of building a State such as the sun never shone upon before; how we had conquered the wilderness and the savage; how we had flung off, in our struggle with the mother-country, the trammels of tradition and precedent, and had settled down, a free nation, to the practice of the arts of peace; how the spirit of commercialism had stolen insidiously upon us, and the infernal impulse of competition had embroiled us in a perpetual warfare of interests, developing the worst passions of our nature, and teaching us to trick and betray and destroy one another in the strife for money, till now that impulse had exhausted itself, and we found competition gone and the whole economic problem in the hands of monopolies—the Standard Oil Company, the Sugar Trust, the Rubber Trust, and what not. And now what was the next thing? Affairs could not remain as they were; it was impossible; and what was the next thing?

The company listened for the main part silently. Dryfoos tried to grasp the idea of commercialism as the colonel seemed to hold it; he conceived of it as something like the dry-goods business on a vast scale, and he knew he had never been in that. He did not like to hear competition called infernal; he had always supposed it was something sacred; but he approved of what Colonel Woodburn said of the Standard Oil Company; it was all true; the Standard Oil had squeezed Dryfoos once, and made him sell it a lot of oil-wells by putting down the price of oil so low in that region that he lost money on every barrel he pumped.

All the rest listened silently, except Lindau; at every point the colonel made against the present condition of things he said more and more fiercely, "You are righdt, you are righdt." His eyes glowed, his hand played with his knife-hilt. When the colonel demanded, "And what is the next thing?" he threw himself forward, and repeated, "Yes, sir! What is the next thing?"

"Natural gas, by thunder!" shouted Fulkerson.

One of the waiters had profited by Lindau's posture to lean over him and put down in the middle of the table a structure in white sugar. It expressed Frescobaldi's conception of a derrick, and a touch of nature had been added in the flame of brandy, which burned luridly up from a small pit in the centre of the base, and represented the gas in combustion as it issued from the ground. Fulkerson burst into a roar of laughter with the words that recognised Frescobaldi's personal tribute to Dryfoos. Everybody rose and peered over at the thing, while he explained the work of sinking a gas-well, as he had already explained it to Frescobaldi. In the midst of his lecture he caught sight of the caterer himself, where he stood in the pantry doorway, smiling with an artist's anxiety for the effect of his masterpiece.

"Come in, come in, Frescobaldi! We want to congratulate you," Fulkerson called to him. "Here, gentlemen! Here's Frescobaldi's health."

They all drank; and Frescobaldi, smiling brilliantly and rubbing his hands as he bowed right and left, permitted himself to say to Dryfoos, "You are please; no? You like?"

"First-rate, first-rate!" said the old man; but when the Italian had bowed himself out and his guests had sunk into their seats again, he said dryly to Fulkerson, "I reckon they didn't have to torpedo that well, or the derrick wouldn't look quite so nice and clean."

"Yes," Fulkerson answered, "and that ain't quite the style—that little wiggly-waggly blue flame—that the gas acts when you touch off a good vein of it. This might do for weak-gas;" and he went on to explain: "They call it weak-gas when they tap it two or three hundred feet down; and anybody can sink a well in his backyard and get enough gas to light and heat his house. I remember one fellow that had it blazing up from a pipe through a flower-bed, just like a jet of water from a fountain. My, my, my! You fel—you gentlemen—ought to go out and see that country, all of you. Wish we *could* torpedo this well, Mr. Dryfoos, and let 'em see how it works! Mind that one you torpedoed for me? You know, when they sink a well," he went on to the company, "they can't always most generally sometimes tell whether they're goin' to get gas or oil or salt-water. Why, when they first began to bore for salt-water out on the Kanawha, back about the beginning of the century, they used to get gas now and then, and then they considered it a failure; they called a gas-well a blower, and give it up in disgust; the time wasn't ripe for gas yet. Now they bore away sometimes till they get half-way to China, and don't seem to strike anything worth speaking of. Then they put a dynamite torpedo down in the well and explode it. They have a little bar of iron that they call a Go-devil, and they just drop it down on the business end of the torpedo, and then stand from under, if *you* please! You hear a noise, and in about half a minute you begin to *see* one, and it begins to rain oil and mud and salt-water and rocks and pitchforks and adoptive citizens; and when it clears up the derrick's painted—got a coat on that'll wear in any climate. That's what our honoured host meant. Generally get some visiting lady, when there's one round, to drop the Go-devil. But that day we had to put up with Conrad here. They offered to let me drop it, but I declined. I told 'em I hadn't much practice with Go-devils in the newspaper syndicate business, and I wasn't very well myself, anyway. Astonishing," Fulkerson continued, with the air of relieving his explanation by an anecdote, "how reckless they get using dynamite when they're torpedoing wells. We stopped at one place where a fellow was handling the cartridges pretty freely, and Mr. Dryfoos happened to caution him a little, and that ass came up with one of 'em in his hand, and began to pound it on the buggy-wheel to show us how safe it was. I turned green, I was so scared; but Mr. Dryfoos kept his colour, and kind of coaxed the fellow till he quit. You could see he was the fool kind, that if you tried to stop him he'd keep on hammering that cartridge, just to show that it wouldn't explode, till he blew you into Kingdom Come. When we got him to go away, Mr. Dryfoos drove up to his foreman. 'Pay Sheney off, and discharge him on the spot,' says he. 'He's too safe a man to have round; he knows too much about dynamite.' I never saw anybody so cool."

Dryfoos modestly dropped his head under Fulkerson's flattery and, without lifting it, turned his eyes toward Colonel Woodburn. "I had all sorts of men to deal with in developing my property out there, but I had very little trouble with them, generally speaking."

"Ah, ah! you foundt the labouring-man reasonable—dractable—tocile?" Lindau put in.

"Yes, generally speaking," Dryfoos answered. "They mostly knew which side of their bread was buttered. I did have one little difficulty at one time. It happened to be when Mr. Fulkerson was out there. Some of the men tried to form a union——"*

"No, no!" cried Fulkerson. "Let *me* tell that! I know you wouldn't do yourself justice, Mr. Dryfoos, and I want 'em to know how a strike can be managed, if you take it in time. You see, some of those fellows got a notion that there ought to be a union among the working-men to keep up wages, and dictate to the employers, and Mr. Dryfoos's foreman was the ringleader in the business. They understood pretty well that as soon as he found it out that foreman would walk the plank, and so they watched out till they thought they had Mr. Dryfoos just where they wanted him—everything on the keen jump, and every man worth his weight in diamonds—and then they come to him, and told him to sign a promise to keep that foreman to the end of the season, or till he was through with the work on the Dryfoos and Hendry Addition, under penalty of having them all knock off. Mr. Dryfoos smelt a mice, but he couldn't tell where the mice was; he saw that they did have him, and he signed, of course. There wasn't anything really against the fellow, anyway; he was a first-rate man, and he did his duty every time; only he'd got some of those ideas into his head, and they turned it. Mr. Dryfoos signed, and then he laid low."

March saw Lindau listening with a mounting intensity, and heard him murmur in German, "Shameful! shameful!"

Fulkerson went on: "Well, it wasn't long before they began to show their hand, but Mr. Dryfoos kept dark. He agreed to everything; there never was such an obliging capitalist before; there wasn't a thing they asked of him that he didn't do, with the greatest of pleasure, and all went merry as a marriage-bell till one morning a whole gang of fresh men marched into the Dryfoos and Hendry Addition, under the escort of a dozen Pinkertons* with repeating rifles at half-cock, and about fifty fellows found themselves out of a job. You never saw such a mad set."

"Pretty neat," said Kendricks, who looked at the affair purely from an æsthetic point of view. "Such a *coup* as that would tell tremendously in a play."

"That was vile treason," said Lindau in German to March. "He's an infamous traitor! I cannot stay here. I must go."

He struggled to rise, while March held him by the coat, and implored him under his voice, "For Heaven's sake, don't, Lindau! You owe it to yourself not to make a scene, if you come here." Something in it all affected him comically; he could not help laughing.

The others were discussing the matter, and seemed not to have noticed Lindau, who controlled himself and sighed: "You are right. I must have patience."

Beaton was saying to Dryfoos, "Pity your Pinkertons couldn't have given them a few shots before they left."

"No, that wasn't necessary," said Dryfoos. "I succeeded in breaking up the union. I entered into an agreement with other parties not to employ any man who would not swear that he was non-union. If they had attempted violence, of course they could have been shot. But there was no fear of that. Those fellows can always be depended upon to cut each other's throats in the long-run."

"But sometimes," said Colonel Woodburn, who had been watching throughout for a chance to mount his hobby again, "they make a good deal of trouble first. How was it in the great railroad strike of '77?"*

"Well, I guess there was a little trouble that time, colonel," said Fulkerson. "But the men that undertake to override the laws and paralyse the industries of a country like this generally get left in the end."

"Yes, sir, generally; and up to a certain point, always. But it's the exceptional that is apt to happen, as well as the unexpected. And a little reflection will convince any gentleman here that there is always a danger of the exceptional in your system. The fact is, those fellows have the game in their own hands already. A strike of the whole body of the Brotherhood of Engineers alone would starve out the entire Atlantic seaboard in a week; labour insurrection could make head at a dozen given points, and your government couldn't move a man over the roads without the help of the engineers."

"That is so," said Kendricks, struck by the dramatic character of the conjecture. He imagined a fiction dealing with the situation as something already accomplished.

"Why don't some fellow do the *Battle of Dorking**act with that thing?" said Fulkerson. "It would be a card."

"Exactly what I was thinking, Mr. Fulkerson," said Kendricks.

Fulkerson laughed. "Telepathy—clear case of mind-transference. Better see March, here, about it. *I'd* like to have it in *Every Other Week*. It would make talk."

"Perhaps it might set your people to thinking as well as talking," said the colonel.

"Well, sir," said Dryfoos, setting his lips so tightly together that his imperial stuck straight outward, "if I had my way, there wouldn't *be* any Brotherhood of Engineers, nor any other kind of labour union in the whole country."

"What!" shouted Lindau. "You would sobbress the unionss of the voarking-men?"

"Yes, I would."

"And what would you do with the unionss of the gabidalists—the drosts—and gompines, and boolss? Would you dake the righdt from one and gif it to the odder?"

"Yes, sir, I would," said Dryfoos, with a wicked look at him.

Lindau was about to roar back at him with some furious protest, but March put his hand on his shoulder imploringly, and Lindau turned to him to say in German, "But it is infamous—infamous! What kind of man is this? Who is he? He has the heart of a tyrant."

Colonel Woodburn cut in. "You couldn't do that, Mr. Dryfoos, under your system. And if you attempted it, with your conspiracy laws, and that kind of thing, it might bring the climax sooner than you expected. Your commercialised society has built its house on the sands. It will have to go. But I should be sorry if it went before its time."

"You are righdt, sir," said Lindau. "It would be a bity. I hobe it will last till it feelss its rottenness, like Herodt. Boat, when its hour gomes, when it trops to bieces with the veight off its own gorrubtion—what then?"

"It's not to be supposed that a system of things like this can drop to pieces of its own accord, like the old Republic of Venice," said the colonel. "But when the last vestige of commercial society is gone, then we can begin to build anew; and we shall build upon the central idea, not of the false liberty you now worship, but of responsibility—responsibility. The enlightened, the moneyed, the cultivated class shall be responsible to the central authority—emperor, duke, president; the name does not matter—for the national expense and the national defence, and it shall be responsible to the working-classes of all kinds for homes and lands and implements, and the opportunity to labour at all times. The working-classes shall be responsible to the leisure class for the support of its dignity in peace, and shall be subject to its command in war. The rich shall warrant the poor against planless production and the ruin that now follows, against danger from without and famine from within, and the poor——"

"No, no, no!" shouted Lindau. "The State shall do that—the whole beople. The men who voark shall have and shall eat; and the men that will not voark, they shall sdarfe. But no man need sdarfe. He will go to the State, and the State will see that he haf voark, and that he haf foodt. All the roadts and mills and mines and landts shall be the beople's and be ron *by* the beople *for* the beople. There shall be no rich and no boor; and there shall not be war any more, for what bower wouldt dare to addack a beople bound togeder in a broder-hood like that?"

"Lion and lamb act," said Fulkerson, not well knowing, after so much champagne, what words he was using.

No one noticed him, and Colonel Woodburn said coldly to Lindau, "You are talking paternalism, sir."

"And *you* are dalking *feutalism*!" retorted the old man.

The Colonel did not reply. A silence ensued, which no one broke till Fulkerson said: "Well, now, look here. If either one of these millenniums was brought about, by force of arms, or otherwise, what would become of *Every Other Week*? Who would want March for an editor? How would Beaton sell his pictures? Who would print Mr. Kendricks' little society verses and short stories? What would become of Conrad and his good works?" Those named grinned in sup-port of Fulkerson's diversion, but Lindau and the colonel did not speak; Dryfoos looked down at his plate, frowning. A waiter came round with cigars, and Fulkerson took one. "Ah," he said, as he bit off the end, and leaned over to the emblematic masterpiece, where the brandy was still feebly flickering, "I wonder if there's enough natural gas left to light my cigar." His effort put the flame out and knocked the derrick over; it broke in fragments on the table. Fulker-son cackled over the ruin: "I wonder if all Moffitt will look that way after labour and capital have fought it out together. I hope this ain't ominous of anything personal, Dryfoos?"

"I'll take the risk of it," said the old man harshly.

He rose mechanically, and Fulkerson said to Fresco-baldi's man, "You can bring us the coffee in the library."

The talk did not recover itself there. Lindau would not sit down; he refused coffee, and dismissed himself with a haughty bow to the company; Colonel Woodburn shook hands elaborately all round, when he had smoked his cigar; the others followed him. It seemed to March that his own good-night from Dryfoos was dry and cold.

VII

MARCH met Fulkerson on the steps of the office next morning, when he arrived rather later than his wont. Fulkerson did not show any of the signs of suffering from the last night's pleasure which painted themselves in March's face. He flirted his hand gaily in the air, and said, "How's your poor head?" and broke into a knowing laugh. "You don't seem to have got up with the lark this morning. The old gentleman is in there with Conrad, as bright as a biscuit; he's beat you down. Well, we did have a good time, didn't we? And old Lindau and the colonel, didn't *they* have a good time? I don't suppose they ever had a chance before to give their theories quite so much air. Oh my, how they did ride over us! I'm just going down to see Beaton about the cover of the Christmas number. I think we ought to try it in three or four colours, if we are going to observe the day at all." He was off before March could pull himself together to ask what Dryfoos wanted at the office at that hour of the morning; he always came in the afternoon on his way up-town.

The fact of his presence renewed the sinister misgivings with which March had parted from him the night before, but Fulkerson's cheerfulness seemed to gainsay them; afterwards March did not know whether to attribute this mood to the slipperiness that he was aware of at times in Fulkerson, or to a cynical amusement he might have felt at leaving him alone to the old man, who mounted to his room shortly after March had reached it.

A sort of dumb anger showed itself in his face; his jaw was set so firmly that he did not seem able at once to open it. He asked, without the ceremonies of greeting, "What does that one-armed Dutchman do on this book?"

"What does he do?" March echoed, as people are apt to do with a question that is mandatory and offensive.

"Yes, sir, what does he do? Does he write for it?"

"I suppose you mean Lindau," said March. He saw no reason for refusing to answer Dryfoos's demand, and he decided to ignore its terms. "No, he doesn't write for it in the usual way. He translates for it; he examines the foreign magazines, and draws my attention to anything he thinks of interest. But I told you about this before——"

"I know what you told me, well enough. And I know what he is: He is a red-mouthed labour-agitator. He's one of those foreigners that come here from places where they've never had a decent meal's victuals in their lives, and as soon as they get their stomachs full, they begin to make trouble between our people and their hands. There's where the strikes come from, and the unions and the secret societies. They come here and break our Sabbath, and teach their atheism. They ought to be hung! Let 'em go back if they don't like it over here. They want to ruin the country."

March could not help smiling a little at the words, which came fast enough now in the hoarse staccato of Dryfoos's passion. "I don't know whom you mean by *they*, generally speaking; but I had the impression that poor old Lindau had once done his best to save the country. I don't always like his way of talking, but I know that he is one of the truest and kindest souls in the world; and he is no more an atheist than I am. He is my friend, and I can't allow him to be misunderstood."

"I don't care *what* he is," Dryfoos broke out, "I won't have him round. He can't have any more work from this office. I want you to stop it. I want you to turn him off."

March was standing at his desk, as he had risen to receive Dryfoos when he entered. He now sat down, and began to open his letters.

"Do you hear?" the old man roared at him. "I want you to turn him off."

"Excuse me, Mr. Dryfoos," said March, succeeding in an effort to speak calmly, "I don't know you, in such a matter as this. My arrangements as editor of *Every Other Week* were made with Mr. Fulkerson. I have always listened to any suggestion he has had to make."

"I don't care for Mr. Fulkerson! He has nothing to do with it," retorted Dryfoos; but he seemed a little daunted by March's position.

"He has everything to do with it as far as I am concerned," March answered, with a steadiness that he did not feel. "I know that you are the owner of the periodical, but I can't receive any suggestion from you, for the reason that I have given. Nobody but Mr. Fulkerson has any right to talk with me about its management."

Dryfoos glared at him for a moment, and demanded threateningly: "Then you say you won't turn that old loafer off? You say that I have got to keep on paying my money out to buy beer for a man that would cut my throat if he got the chance?"

"I say nothing at all, Mr. Dryfoos," March answered. The blood came into his face, and he added: "But I *will* say that if you speak again of Mr. Lindau in those terms, one of us must leave this room. I will not hear you."

Dryfoos looked at him with astonishment; then he struck his hat down on his head, and stamped out of the room and down the stairs; and a vague pity came into March's heart that was not altogether for himself. He might be the greater sufferer in the end, but he was sorry to have got the better of that old man for the moment; and he felt ashamed of the anger into which Dryfoos's anger had surprised him. He knew he could not say too much in defence of Lindau's generosity and unselfishness, and he had not attempted to defend him as a political economist. He could not have taken any ground in relation to Dryfoos but that which he held, and he felt satisfied that he was right in refusing to receive instructions or commands from him. Yet somehow he was not satisfied with the whole affair, and not merely because his present triumph threatened his final advantage, but because he felt that in his heat he had hardly done justice to Dryfoos's rights in the matter; it did not quite console him to reflect that Dryfoos had himself made it impossible. He was tempted to go home and tell his wife what had happened, and begin his preparations for the future at once. But he resisted this weakness and kept mechanically about his work, opening the letters and the manuscripts before him with that curious double action of the mind common in men of vivid imaginations. It was a relief when Conrad Dryfoos, having apparently waited to make sure that his father would not return, came up from the counting-room and looked in on March with a troubled face.

"Mr. March," he began, "I hope father hasn't been saying anything to you that you can't overlook. I know he was very much excited, and when he is excited he is apt to say things that he is sorry for."

The apologetic attitude taken for Dryfoos, so different from any attitude the peremptory old man would have conceivably taken for himself, made March smile. "Oh no. I fancy the boot is on the other leg. I suspect I've said some things your father can't overlook, Conrad." He called the young man by his Christian name partly to distinguish him from his father, partly from the infection of Fulkerson's habit, and partly from a kindness for him that seemed naturally to express itself in that way.

"I know he didn't sleep last night, after you all went away," Conrad pursued, "and of course that made him more irritable; and he was tried a good deal by some of the things that Mr. Lindau said."

"I was tried a good deal myself," said March. "Lindau ought never to have been there."

"No." Conrad seemed only partially to assent.

"I told Mr. Fulkerson so. I warned him that Lindau would be apt to break out in some way. It wasn't just to him, and it wasn't just to your father, to ask him."

"Mr. Fulkerson had a good motive," Conrad gently urged. "He did it because he hurt his feelings that day about the pension."

"Yes, but it was a mistake. He knew that Lindau was inflexible about his principles, as he calls them, and that one of his first principles is to denounce the rich in season and out of season. I don't remember just what he said last night; and I really thought I'd kept him from breaking out in the most offensive way. But your father seems very much incensed."

"Yes, I know," said Conrad.

"Of course, I don't agree with Lindau. I think there are as many good, kind, just people among the rich as there are among the poor, and that they are as generous and helpful. But Lindau has got hold of one of those partial truths that hurt worse than the whole truth, and——"

"Partial truth!" the young man interrupted. "Didn't the Saviour himself say, 'How hardly shall they that have riches enter into the kingdom of God'?"

"Why, bless my soul!" cried March. "Do *you* agree with Lindau?"

"I agree with the Lord Jesus Christ," said the young man solemnly, and a strange light of fanaticism, of exaltation, came into his wide blue eyes. "And I believe he meant the kingdom of heaven upon this earth, as well as in the skies."

March threw himself back in his chair and looked at him with a kind of stupefaction, in which his eye wandered to the doorway, where he saw Fulkerson standing, it seemed to him a long time, before he heard him saying, "Hello, hello! What's the row? Conrad pitching into you on old Lindau's account, too?"

The young man turned, and after a glance at Fulkerson's light, smiling face, went out, as if in his present mood he could not bear the contact of that persiflant spirit.

March felt himself getting provisionally very angry again. "Excuse me, Fulkerson, but did you know when you went out what Mr. Dryfoos wanted to see me for?"

"Well, no, I didn't exactly," said Fulkerson, taking his usual seat on a chair, and looking over the back of it at March. "I saw he was on his ear about something, and I thought I'd better not monkey with him much. I supposed he was going to bring you to book about old Lindau, some-how." Fulkerson broke into a laugh.

March remained serious. "Mr. Dryfoos," he said, willing to let the simple statement have its own weight with Fulkerson, and nothing more, "came in here and ordered me to discharge Lindau from his employment on the magazine—to turn him off, as he put it."

"Did he?" asked Fulkerson, with unbroken cheerfulness. "The old man is business, every time. Well, I suppose you can easily get somebody else to do Lindau's work for you. This town is just running over with half-starved linguists. What did you say?"

"What did I say?" March echoed. "Look here, Fulkerson; you may regard this as a joke, but *I* don't. I'm not used to being spoken to as if I were the foreman of a shop, and told to discharge a sensitive and cultivated man like Lindau, as if he were a drunken mechanic; and if that's your idea of me——"

"Oh, hello, now, March! You mustn't mind the old man's way. He don't mean anything by it—he don't *know* any better, if you come to that."

"Then *I* know better," said March. "I refused to receive any instructions from Mr. Dryfoos, whom I don't know in my relations with *Every Other Week*, and I referred him to you."

"You did?" Fulkerson whistled. "He owns the thing!"

"I don't care who owns the thing," said March. "My negotiations were with you alone from the beginning, and I leave this matter with you. What do you wish done about Lindau?"

"Oh, better let the old fool drop," said Fulkerson. "He'll light on his feet somehow, and it will save a lot of rumpus."

"And if I decline to let him drop?"

"Oh, come, now, March; don't do that," Fulkerson began.

"If I decline to let him drop," March repeated, "what will you do?"

"I'll be dogged if I know *what* I'll do," said Fulkerson. "I hope you won't take that stand. If the old man went so far as to speak to you about it, his mind is made up, and we might as well knock under first as last."

316

"And do you mean to say that you would not stand by me in what I considered my duty—in a matter of principle?"

"Why, of course, March," said Fulkerson coaxingly, "I mean to do the right thing. But Dryfoos owns the magazine——"

"He doesn't own *me*," said March, rising. "He has made the little mistake of speaking to me as if he did; and when"— March put on his hat and took his overcoat down from its nail—"when you bring me his apologies, or come to say that, having failed to make him understand they were necessary, you are prepared to stand by me, I will come back to this desk. Otherwise my resignation is at your service."

He started toward the door, and Fulkerson intercepted him. "Ah, now, look here, March! Don't do that! Hang it all, don't you see where it leaves *me*? Now, you just sit down a minute, and talk it over. I can make you see—I can show you——. Why, confound the old Dutch beer-buzzer! Twenty of him wouldn't be worth the trouble he's makin'. Let him go, and the old man'll come round in time."

"I don't think we've understood each other exactly, Mr. Fulkerson," said March, very haughtily. "Perhaps we never can; but I'll leave you to think it out."

He pushed on, and Fulkerson stood aside to let him pass, with a dazed look and a mechanical movement. There was something comic in his rueful bewilderment to March, who was tempted to smile, but he said to himself that he had as much reason to be unhappy as Fulkerson, and he did not smile. His indignation kept him hot in his purpose to suffer any consequence rather than submit to the dictation of a man like Dryfoos; he felt keenly the degradation of his connection with him, and all his resentment of Fulkerson's original uncandour returned; at the same time his heart ached with foreboding. It was not merely the work in which he had constantly grown happier that he saw taken from him; but he felt the misery of the man who stakes the security and plenty and peace of home upon some cast, and knows that losing will sweep from him most that most men find sweet and pleasant in life. He faced the fact, which no good man can front without terror, that he was risking the support of his family, and for a point of pride, of honour, which perhaps he had no right to consider in view of the possible adversity. He realised, as every hireling must, no matter how skilfully or gracefully the tie is contrived for his wearing, that he belongs to another, whose will is his law. His indignation was shot with abject impulses to go back and tell Fulkerson that it was all right, and that he gave up. To end the anguish of his struggle he quickened his steps, so that he found he was reaching home almost at a run.

VIII

HE must have made more clatter than he supposed with his key at the apartment door, for his wife had come to let him in when he flung it open. "Why, Basil," she said, "what's brought you back? Are you sick? You're all pale. Well, no wonder! This is the last of Mr. Fulkerson's dinners you shall go to. You're not strong enough for it, and your stomach will be all out of order for a week. How hot you are! and in a drip of perspiration! Now you'll be sick." She took his hat away, which hung dangling in his hand, and pushed him into a chair with tender impatience. "What *is* the matter? Has anything happened?"

"Everything has happened," he said, getting his voice after one or two husky endeavours for it; and then he poured out a confused and huddled statement of the case, from which she only got at the situation by prolonged cross-questioning.

At the end she said, "I knew Lindau would get you into trouble."

This cut March to the heart. "Isabel!" he cried reproachfully.

"Oh, I know," she retorted, and the tears began to come. "I don't wonder you didn't want to say much to me about that dinner at breakfast. I noticed it; but I thought you were just dull, and so I didn't insist. I wish I had, now. If you had told me what Lindau had said, I should have known what would have come of it, and I could have advised you———"

"Would you have advised me," March demanded curiously, "to submit to bullying like that, and meekly consent to commit an act of cruelty against a man who had once been such a friend to me?"

"It was an unlucky day when you met him. I suppose we shall have to go. And just when we had got used to New York, and begun to like it. I don't know where we shall go now; Boston isn't like home any more; and we couldn't live on two thousand there; I should be ashamed to try. I'm sure I don't know where we *can* live on it. I suppose in some country village, where there are no schools, or anything for the children. I don't know what they'll say when we tell them, poor things."

Every word was a stab in March's heart, so weakly tender to his own; his wife's tears, after so much experience of the comparative lightness of the griefs that weep themselves out in women, always seemed wrung from his own soul; if his children suffered in the least through him, he felt like a murderer. It was far worse than he could have imagined, the way his wife took the affair, though he had imagined certain words, or perhaps only looks, from her that were bad enough. He had allowed for trouble, but trouble on *his* account: a sympathy that might burden and embarrass him; but he had not dreamt of this merely domestic, this petty, this sordid view of their potential calamity, which left him wholly out of the question, and embraced only what was most crushing and desolating in the prospect. He could not bear it. He caught up his hat again, and with some hope that his wife would try to keep him, rushed out of the house. He wandered aimlessly about, thinking the same exhausting thoughts over and over, till he found himself horribly hungry; then he went into a restaurant for his lunch, and when he paid, he tried to imagine how he should feel if that were really his last dollar.

He went home toward the middle of the afternoon, basely hoping that Fulkerson had sent him some conciliatory message, or perhaps was waiting there for him to talk it over; March was quite willing to talk it over now. But it was his wife who again met him at the door, though it seemed another woman than the one he had left weeping in the morning.

"I told the children," she said, in smiling explanation of his absence from lunch, "that perhaps you were detained by business. I didn't know but you had gone back to the office."

"Did you think I would go back there, Isabel?" asked March, with a haggard look. "Well, if you say so, I will go back, and do what Dryfoos ordered me to do. I'm sufficiently cowed between him and you, I can assure you."

"Nonsense," she said. "I approve of everything you did. But sit down, now, and don't keep walking that way, and let me see if I understand it perfectly. Of course I had to have my say out."

She made him go all over his talk with Dryfoos again, and report his own language precisely. From time to time, as she got his points, she said, "That was splendid," "Good enough for him!" And "Oh, I'm so *glad* you said that to him!" At the end she said, "Well, now, let's look at it from his point of view. Let's be perfectly just to him before we take another step forward."

"Or backward," March suggested ruefully. "The case is simply this: he owns the magazine."

"Of course."

"And he has a right to expect that I will consider his pecuniary interests——"

"Oh, those detestable pecuniary interests! Don't you wish there wasn't any money in the world?"

"Yes; or else that there was a great deal more of it.—And I was perfectly willing to do that. I have always kept that in mind as one of my duties to him, ever since I understood what his relation to the magazine was."

"Yes, I can bear witness to that in any court of justice. You've done it a great deal more than I could, Basil. And it was just the same way with those horrible insurance people."

"I know," March went on, trying to be proof against her flatteries, or at least to look as if he did not deserve praise; "I know that what Lindau said was offensive to him, and I can understand how he felt that he had a right to punish it. All I say is that he had no right to punish it through me."

"Yes," said Mrs. March askingly.

"If it had been a question of making *Every Other Week* the vehicle of Lindau's peculiar opinions—though they're not so very peculiar; he might have got the most of them out of Ruskin—I shouldn't have had any ground to stand on, or at least then I should have had to ask myself whether his opinions would be injurious to the magazine or not."

"I don't see," Mrs. March interpolated, "how they could hurt it much worse than Colonel Woodburn's article crying up slavery."

"Well," said March impartially, "we could print a dozen articles praising the slavery it's impossible to have back, and it wouldn't hurt us. But if we printed one paper against the slavery which Lindau claims still exists, some people would call us bad names, and the counting-room would begin to feel it. But that isn't the point. Lindau's connection with *Every Other Week* is almost purely mechanical; he's merely a translator of such stories and sketches as he first submits to me, and it isn't at all a question of his opinions hurting us, but of my becoming an agent to punish him for his opinions. That is what I wouldn't do; that's what I never will do."

"If you did," said his wife, "I should perfectly despise you. I didn't understand how it was before. I thought you were just holding out against Dryfoos because he took a dictatorial tone with you, and because you wouldn't recognise his authority. But now I'm with you, Basil, every time, as that horrid little Fulkerson says. But who would have ever supposed he would be so base as to side against you?"

"I don't know," said March thoughtfully, "that we had a right to expect anything else. Fulkerson's standards are low; they're merely business standards, and the good that's in him is incidental, and something quite apart from his morals and methods. He's naturally a generous and right-minded creature, but life has taught him to truckle and trick, like the rest of us."

"It hasn't taught *you* that, Basil."

"Don't be so sure. Perhaps it's only that I'm a poor scholar. But I don't know, really, that I despise Fulkerson so much for his course this morning as for his gross and fulsome flatteries of Dryfoos last night. I could hardly stomach it."

His wife made him tell her what they were, and then she said, "Yes, that was loathsome; I couldn't have believed it of Mr. Fulkerson."

"Perhaps he only did it to keep the talk going, and to give the old man a chance to say something," March leniently suggested. "It was a worse effect because he didn't or couldn't follow up Fulkerson's lead."

"It was loathsome, all the same," his wife insisted. "It's the end of Mr. Fulkerson, as far as I'm concerned."

"I didn't tell you before," March resumed, after a moment, "of my little interview with Conrad Dryfoos after his father left," and now he went on to repeat what had passed between him and the young man.

"I suspect that he and his father had been having some words before the old man came up to talk with me, and that it was that made him so furious."

"Yes, but what a strange position for the son of such a man to take! Do you suppose he says such things to his father?"

"I don't know; but I suspect that in his meek way Conrad would say what he believed to anybody. I suppose we must regard him as a kind of crank."

"Poor young fellow! He always makes me feel sad somehow. He has such a pathetic face. I don't believe I ever saw him look quite happy, except that night at Mrs. Horn's, when he was talking with Miss Vance; and then he made me feel sadder than ever."

"I don't envy him the life he leads at home, with those convictions of his. I don't see why it wouldn't be as tolerable there for old Lindau himself."

"Well, now," said Mrs. March, "let us put them all out of our minds and see what we are going to do ourselves."

They began to consider their ways and means, and how and where they should live, in view of March's severance of his relations with *Every Other Week*. They had not saved anything from the first year's salary; they had only prepared to save; and they had nothing solid but their two thousand to count upon. But they built a future in which they easily lived on that and on what March earned with his pen. He became a free lance, and fought in whatever cause he thought just; he had no ties, no chains. They went back to Boston with the heroic will to do what was most distasteful; they would have returned to their own house if they had not rented it again; but, any rate, Mrs. March helped out by taking boarders, or perhaps only letting rooms to lodgers. They had some hard struggles, but they succeeded.

"The great thing," she said, "is to be right. I'm ten times as happy as if you had come home and told me that you had consented to do what Dryfoos asked, and he had doubled your salary."

"I don't think that would have happened in any event," said March dryly.

"Well, no matter. I just used it for an example."

They both experienced a buoyant relief, such as seems to come to people who begin life anew on whatever terms. "I hope we are young enough *yet*, Basil," she said, and she would not have it when he said they had once been younger.

They heard the children's knock on the door; they knocked when they came home from school so that their mother might let them in. "Shall we tell them at once?" she asked, and ran to open for them before March could answer.

They were not alone. Fulkerson, smiling from ear to ear, was with them. "Is March in?" he asked.

"Mr. March is at home, yes," she said very haughtily. "He's in his study," and she led the way there, while the children went to their rooms.

"Well, March," Fulkerson called out at sight of him, "it's all right! The old man has come down."

"I suppose if you gentlemen are going to talk busi- ness——" Mrs. March began.

"Oh, we don't want you to go away," said Fulkerson. "I reckon March has told you, anyway."

"Yes, I've told her," said March. "Don't go, Isabel. What do you mean, Fulkerson?"

"He's just gone on up home, and he sent me round with his apologies. He sees now that he had no business to speak to you as he did, and he withdraws everything. He'd 'a' come round himself if I'd said so, but I told him I could make it all right."

Fulkerson looked so happy in having the whole affair put right, and the Marches knew him to be so kindly affected toward them that they could not refuse for the moment to share his mood. They felt themselves slipping down from the moral height which they had gained, and March made a clutch to stay himself with the question, "And Lindau?"

"Well," said Fulkerson, "he's going to leave Lindau to me. You won't have anything to do with it. I'll let the old fellow down easy."

"Do you mean," asked March, "that Mr. Dryfoos insists on his being dismissed?"

"Why, there isn't any dismissing about it," Fulkerson argued. "If you don't send him any more work, he won't do any more, that's all. Or if he comes round you can—— He's to be referred to me."

March shook his head, and his wife, with a sigh, felt her- self plucked up from the soft circumstance of their lives, which she had sunk back into so quickly, and set beside him on that cold peak of principle again. "It won't do, Fulkerson. It's very good of you and all that, but it comes to the same thing in the end. I could have gone on without any apology from Mr. Dryfoos; he transcended his authority, but that's a minor matter. I could have excused it to his ignorance of life among gentlemen; but I can't consent to Lindau's dis- missal—it comes to that, whether you do it or I do it, and whether it's a positive or a negative thing—because he holds this opinion or that."

"But don't you see," said Fulkerson, "that it's just Lindau's opinions the old man can't stand? He hasn't got anything against him personally. I don't suppose there's anybody that appreciates Lindau in some ways more than the old man does."

"I understand. He wants to punish him for his opinions. Well, I can't consent to that, directly or indirectly. We don't print his opinions, and he has a perfect right to hold them, whether Mr. Dryfoos agrees with them or not."

Mrs. March had judged it decorous for her to say nothing, but she now went and sat down in the chair next her husband.

"Ah, dog on it!" cried Fulkerson, rumpling his hair with both his hands. "What am I to do? The old man says he's got to go."

"And I don't consent to his going," said March.

"And you won't stay if he goes?"

"I won't stay if he goes."

Fulkerson rose. "Well, well! I've got to see about it. I'm afraid the old man won't stand it, March; I am, indeed. I wish you'd reconsider. I—I'd take it as a personal favour if you would. It leaves me in a fix. You see I've got to side with one or the other."

March made no reply to this, except to say, "Yes, you must stand by him, or you must stand by me."

"Well, well! Hold on a while! I'll see you in the morning. Don't take any steps——"

"Oh, there are no steps to take," said March, with a melancholy smile. "The steps are stopped; that's all." He sank back into his chair when Fulkerson was gone, and drew a long breath. "This is pretty rough. I thought we had got through it."

"No," said his wife. "It seems as if I had to make the fight all over again."

"Well, it's a good thing it's a holy war."

"I can't bear the suspense. Why didn't you tell him outright you wouldn't go back on any terms?"

"I might as well, and got the glory. He'll never move Dryfoos. I suppose we both would like to go back, if we could."

"Oh, I suppose so."

They could not regain their lost exaltation, their lost dignity. At dinner Mrs. March asked the children how they would like to go back to Boston to live.

"Why, we're not going, are we?" asked Tom without enthusiasm.

"I was just wondering how you felt about it, now," she said, with an underlook at her husband.

"Well, if we go back," said Bella, "I want to live on the Back Bay. It's awfully Micky*at the South End."

"I suppose I should go to Harvard," said Tom, "and I'd room out at Cambridge. It would be easier to get at you on the Back Bay."

The parents smiled ruefully at each other, and in view of these grand expectations of his children, March resolved to go as far as he could in meeting Dryfoos's wishes. He proposed the theatre as a distraction from the anxieties that he knew were pressing equally on his wife. "We might go to the Old Homestead,'"he suggested, with a sad irony, which only his wife felt.

"Oh yes, let's!" cried Bella.

While they were getting ready, some one rang, and Bella went to the door, and then came to tell her father that it was Mr. Lindau. "He says he wants to see you just a moment. He's in the parlour, and he won't sit down, or anything."

"What can he want?" groaned Mrs. March, from their common dismay.

March apprehended a storm in the old man's face. But he only stood in the middle of the room, looking very sad and grave. "You are coing oudt," he said. "I won't geep you long. I haf gome to pring pack dose macassines, and dis mawney. I can't do any more voark for you; and I can't geep the mawney you haf baid me a'ready. It iss not hawnest mawney —that hass been oarned py voark; it iss mawney that hass peen *mate* py sbeculation, and the obbression off lapour, and the necessity of the boor, py a man——. Here it is, efery tollar, efery zent. Dake it; I feel as if dere vas ploodt on it."

"Why, Lindau," March began, but the old man interrupted him.

"Ton't dalk to me, Passil! I could not haf believedt it of you. When you know how I feel about dose tings, why tidn't you dell me *whose* mawney you bay oudt to me? Ach, I ton't plame you—I ton't rebroach you. You haf nefer thought of it; boat I—*I* have thought, and I should be cuilty, I must share that man's cuilt, if I gept hiss mawney. If you hat toldt me at the peginning—if you hat peen frank with me—boat it iss all righdt; you can go on; you ton't see dese tings as I see them; and you haf cot a family, and I am a free man. I voark to myself, and when I don't voark, I sdarfe to myself. But I geep my handts glean, voark or sdarfe. Gif him hiss mawney pack! I am sawry for him; I would not hoart hiss feelings, boat I could not pear to douch him, and hiss mawney iss like boison!"

March tried to reason with Lindau, to show him the folly, the injustice, the absurdity of his course; it ended in their both getting angry, and in Lindau's going away in a whirl of German that included Basil in the guilt of the man whom Lindau called his master.

"Well," said Mrs. March. "He is a crank, and I think you're well rid of him. Now you have no quarrel with that horrid old Dryfoos, and you can keep right on."

"Yes," said March, "I wish it didn't make me feel so sneaking. What a long day it's been! It seems like a century since I got up."

"Yes, a thousand years. Is there anything else left to happen?"

"I hope not. I'd like to go to bed."

"Why, aren't you going to the theatre?" wailed Bella, coming in upon her father's desperate expression.

"The theatre? Oh yes, certainly! I meant after we got home," and March amused himself at the puzzled countenance of the child. "Come on! Is Tom ready?"

IX

FULKERSON parted with the Marches in such trouble of
mind that he did not feel able to meet that night the people
whom he usually kept so gay at Mrs. Leighton's table. He
went to Maroni's for his dinner, for this reason, and for
others more obscure. He could not expect to do anything
more with Dryfoos at once; he knew that Dryfoos must feel
that he had already made an extreme concession to March,
and he believed that if he was to get anything more from him
it must be after Dryfoos had dined. But he was not without
the hope, vague and indefinite as it might be, that he should
find Lindau at Maroni's, and perhaps should get some concession from him, some word of regret or apology which he
could report to Dryfoos, and at least make the means of re-
opening the affair with him; perhaps Lindau, when he knew
how matters stood, would back down altogether, and for
March's sake would withdraw from all connection with
Every Other Week himself, and so leave everything serene.
Fulkerson felt capable, in his desperation, of delicately suggesting such a course to Lindau, or even of plainly advising
it: he did not care for Lindau a great deal, and he did care a
great deal for the magazine.

But he did not find Lindau at Maroni's; he only found
Beaton. He sat looking at the doorway as Fulkerson entered,
and Fulkerson naturally came and took a place at his
table. Something in Beaton's large-eyed solemnity of
aspect invited Fulkerson to confidence, and he said, as
he pulled his napkin open and strung it, still a little damp
(as the scanty, often-washed linen at Maroni's was apt
to be), across his knees, "I was looking for you this morning, to talk with you about the Christmas number, and
I was a good deal worked up because I couldn't find you;
but I guess I might as well have spared myself my emotions."

"Why?" asked Beaton briefly.

"Well, I don't know as there's going to be any Christmas number."

"Why?" Beaton asked again.

"Row between the financial angel and the literary editor about the chief translator and polyglot smeller."

"Lindau?"

"Lindau is his name."

"What does the literary editor expect after Lindau's expression of his views last night?"

"I don't know what he expected, but the ground he took with the old man was that as Lindau's opinions didn't characterise his work on the magazine he would not be made the instrument of punishing him for them: the old man wanted him turned off, as he calls it."

"Seems to be pretty good ground," said Beaton impartially, while he speculated, with a dull trouble at heart, on the effect the row would have on his own fortunes. His late visit home had made him feel that the claim of his family upon him for some repayment of help given could not be much longer delayed; with his mother sick and his father growing old, he must begin to do something for them, but up to this time he had spent his salary even faster than he had earned it: when Fulkerson came in he was wondering whether he could get him to increase it, if he threatened to give up his work, and he wished that he was enough in love with Margaret Vance, or even Christine Dryfoos, to marry her, only to end in the sorrowful conviction that he was really in love with Alma Leighton, who had no money, and who had apparently no wish to be married for love, even. "And what are you going to do about it?" he asked listlessly.

"Be dogged if I know *what* I'm going to do about it," said Fulkerson. "I've been round all day, trying to pick up the pieces—row began right after breakfast this morning—and one time I thought I'd got the thing all put together again. I got the old man to say that he had spoken to March a little too authoritatively about Lindau; that in fact he ought to have communicated his wishes through me; and that he was willing to have me get rid of Lindau, and March needn't have anything to do with it. I thought that was pretty white, but March says the apologies and regrets are all well enough in their way, but they leave the main question where they found it."

"What is the main question?" Beaton asked, pouring himself out some Chianti; as he set the flask down he made the reflection that if he would drink water instead of Chianti he could send his father three dollars a week, on his back debts, and he resolved to do it.

"The main question, as March looks at it, is the question of punishing Lindau for his private opinions; he says that if he consents to *my* bouncing the old fellow it's the same as if *he* bounced him."

"It might have that complexion in some lights," said Beaton. He drank off his Chianti, and thought he would have it twice a week, or make Maroni keep the half-bottles over for him, and send his father two dollars. "And what are you going to do now?"

"That's what I don't know," said Fulkerson ruefully. After a moment he said desperately, "Beaton, you've got a pretty good head; why don't you suggest something?"

"Why don't you let March go?" Beaton suggested.

"Ah, I couldn't," said Fulkerson. "I got him to break-up in Boston and come here; I like him; nobody else could get the hang of the thing like he has; he's—a friend." Fulkerson said this with the nearest approach he could make to seriousness, which was a kind of unhappiness.

Beaton shrugged. "Oh, if you can afford to have ideals, I congratulate you. They're too expensive for *me*. Then, suppose you get rid of Dryfoos?"

Fulkerson laughed forlornly. "Go on, Bildad.' Like to sprinkle a few ashes over my boils? Don't mind *me*!"

They both sat silent a little while, and then Beaton said, "I suppose you haven't seen Dryfoos the second time?"

"No. I came in here to gird up my loins with a little dinner before I tackled him. But something seems to be the matter with Maroni's cook. *I* don't want anything to eat."

"The cooking's about as bad as usual," said Beaton. After

a moment, he added ironically, for he found Fulkerson's misery a kind of relief from his own, and was willing to protract it as long as it was amusing: "Why not try an envoy extraordinary and minister plenipotentiary?"

"What do you mean?"

"Get that other old fool to go to Dryfoos for you!"

"Which other old fool? The old fools seem to be as thick as flies."

"That Southern one."

"Colonel Woodburn?"

"Mmmmm."

"He *did* seem to rather take to the colonel!" Fulkerson mused aloud.

"Of course he did. Woodburn, with his idiotic talk about patriarchal slavery, is the man on horseback* to Dryfoos's muddy imagination. He'd listen to him abjectly, and he'd do whatever Woodburn told him to do." Beaton smiled cynically.

Fulkerson got up and reached for his coat and hat. "You've struck it, old man." The waiter came up to help him on with his coat; Fulkerson slipped a dollar in his hand. "Never mind the coat; you can give the rest of my dinner to the poor, Paolo. Beaton, shake! You've saved my life, little boy, though I don't think you meant it." He took Beaton's hand and solemnly pressed it, and then almost ran out of the door.

They had just reached coffee at Mrs. Leighton's when he arrived, and sat down with them, and began to put some of the life of his new hope into them. His appetite revived, and after protesting that he would not take anything but coffee, he went back and ate some of the earlier courses. But with the pressure of his purpose driving him forward, he did not conceal from Miss Woodburn, at least, that he was eager to get her apart from the rest for some reason. When he accomplished this, it seemed as if he had contrived it all himself, but perhaps he had not wholly contrived it.

"I'm so glad to get a chance to speak to you alone," he said at once; and while she waited for the next word he made a pause, and then said desperately, "I want you to

331

help me; and if you can't help me, there's no help for me."

"Mah goodness," she said, "is the case so bad as that? What in the woald is the trouble?"

"Yes, it's a bad case," said Fulkerson. "I want your father to help me."

"Oh, I thoat you said *me*!"

"Yes; I want you to help me with your father. I suppose I ought to go to him at once, but I'm a little afraid of him."

"And you awe not afraid of *me*? I don't think that's very flattering, Mr. Fulkerson. You ought to think Ah'm twahce as awful as papa."

"Oh, I do! You see, I'm quite paralysed before you, and so I don't feel anything."

"Well, it's a pretty lahvely kyand of paralysis. But— go on."

"I will—I will. If I can only begin."

"Pohaps Ah maght begin fo.' you."

"No, you can't. Lord knows, I'd like to let you. Well, it's like this."

Fulkerson made a clutch at his hair, and then, after another hesitation, he abruptly laid the whole affair before her. He did not think it necessary to state the exact nature of the offence Lindau had given Dryfoos, for he doubted if she could grasp it, and he was profuse of his excuses for troubling her with the matter, and of wonder at himself for having done so. In the rapture of his concern at having perhaps made a fool of himself, he forgot why he had told her; but she seemed to like having been confided in, and she said, "Well, Ah don't see what you can do with you' ahdeals of friendship, except stand bah' Mr. Mawch."

"My ideals of friendship? What do you mean?"

"Oh, don't you suppose we know? Mr. Beaton said you we' a pofect Bahyard*in friendship, and you would sacrifice anything to it."

"Is that so?" said Fulkerson, thinking how easily he could sacrifice Lindau in this case. He had never supposed before that he was so chivalrous in such matters, but he now began to see it in that light, and he wondered that he could ever have entertained for a moment the idea of throwing March over.

"But, Ah most *say*," Miss Woodburn went on, "Ah don't envy you you' next interview with Mr. Dryfoos. Ah suppose you'll have to see him at once aboat it."

The conjecture recalled Fulkerson to the object of his confidences. "Ah, there's where your help comes in. I've exhausted all the influence *I* have with Dryfoos——"

"Good gracious, you don't expect *Ah* could have any!"

They both laughed at the comic dismay with which she conveyed the preposterous notion; and Fulkerson said, "If I judged from myself, I should expect you to bring him round instantly."

"O, *thank* you, Mr. Fulkerson," she said, with mock-meekness.

"Not at all. But it isn't Dryfoos I want you to help me with; it's your father. I want your father to interview Dryfoos for me, and I—I'm afraid to ask him."

"Poo' Mr. Fulkerson!" she said, and she insinuated something through her burlesque compassion that lifted him to the skies. He swore in his heart that the woman never lived who was so witty, so wise, so beautiful, and so good. "Come raght with me this minute, if the cyoast's clea'." She went to the door of the dining-room and looked in across its gloom to the little gallery where her father sat beside a lamp reading his evening paper; Mrs. Leighton could be heard in colloquy with the cook below, and Alma had gone to her room. She beckoned Fulkerson with the hand outstretched behind her, and said, "Go and ask him."

"Alone!" he palpitated.

"Oh, what a cyowahd!" she cried, and went with him. "Ah suppose you'll want me to tell him aboat it."

"Well, I wish you'd begin, Miss Woodburn," he said. "The fact is, you know, I've been over it so much I'm kind of sick of the thing."

Miss Woodburn advanced, and put her hand on her father's shoulder. "Look heah, papa! Mr. Fulkerson wants

333

to ask you something, and he wants me to do it fo' him."

The colonel looked up through his glasses with the sort of ferocity elderly men sometimes have to put on in order to keep their glasses from falling off. His daughter continued:—

"He's got into an awful difficulty with his edito' and his proprieto', and he wants you to pacify them."

"I do not know whethah I understand the case exactly," said the colonel, "but Mr. Fulkerson may command me to the extent of my ability."

"You don't understand it aftah what Ah've said?" cried the girl. "Then Ah don't see but what you'll have to explain it you'self, Mr. Fulkerson."

"Well, Miss Woodburn has been so luminous about it, colonel," said Fulkerson, glad of the joking shape she had given the affair, "that I can only throw in a little side light here and there."

The colonel listened, as Fulkerson went on, with a grave diplomatic satisfaction. He felt gratified, honoured, even, he said, by Mr. Fulkerson's appeal to him; and probably it gave him something of the high joy that an affair of honour would have brought him in the days when he had arranged for meetings between gentlemen. Next to bearing a challenge, this work of composing a difficulty must have been grateful. But he gave no outward sign of his satisfaction in making a *résumé* of the case so as to get the points clearly in his mind.

"I was afraid, sir," he said, with the state due to the serious nature of the facts, "that Mr. Lindau had given Mr. Dryfoos offence by some of his questions at the dinner-table last night."

"Perfect red rag to a bull," Fulkerson put in; and then he wanted to withdraw his words at the colonel's look of displeasure.

"I have no reflections to make upon Mr. Lindau," Colonel Woodburn continued, and Fulkerson felt grateful to him for going on; "I do not agree with Mr. Lindau; I totally disagree with him on sociological points; but the course of the conversation had invited him to the expression of his convictions, and he had a right to express them, so far as they had no personal bearing."

"Of course," said Fulkerson, while Miss Woodburn perched on the arm of her father's chair.

"At the same time, sir, I think that if Mr. Dryfoos felt a personal censure in Mr. Lindau's questions concerning his suppression of the strike among his workmen, he had a right to resent it."

"Exactly," Fulkerson assented.

"But it must be evident to you, sir, that a high-spirited gentleman like Mr. March—I confess that my feelings are with him very warmly in the matter—could not submit to dictation of the nature you describe."

"Yes, I see," said Fulkerson; and with that strange duplex action of the human mind, he wished that it was *his* hair, and not her father's, that Miss Woodburn was poking apart with the corner of her fan.

"Mr. Lindau," the colonel concluded, "was right from his point of view, and Mr. Dryfoos was equally right. The position of Mr. March is perfectly correct——"

His daughter dropped to her feet from his chair arm. "Mah goodness! If nobody's in the wrong, ho' awe you evah going to get the mattah straight?"

"Yes, you see," Fulkerson added, "nobody can give in."

"Pardon me," said the colonel, "the case is one in which all can give in."

"I don't know which'll begin," said Fulkerson.

The colonel rose. "Mr. Lindau must begin, sir. *We* must begin by seeing Mr. Lindau, and securing from him the assurance that in the expression of his peculiar views he had no intention of offering any personal offence to Mr. Dryfoos. If I have formed a correct estimate of Mr. Lindau, this will be perfectly simple."

Fulkerson shook his head. "But it wouldn't help. Dryfoos don't care a rap whether Lindau meant any personal offence or not. As far as that is concerned, he's got a hide like a hippopotamus. But what he hates is Lindau's opinions, and what

335

he says is that no man who holds such opinions shall have any work from him. And what March says is that no man shall be punished through him for his opinions, he don't care what they are."

The colonel stood a moment in silence. "And what do you expect me to do under the circumstances?"

"I came to you for advice—I thought you might suggest——"

"Do you wish me to see Mr. Dryfoos?"

"Well, that's about the size of it," Fulkerson admitted. "You see, colonel," he hastened on, "I know that you have a great deal of influence with him; that article of yours is about the only thing he's ever read in *Every Other Week*, and he's proud of your acquaintance. Well, you know," and here Fulkerson brought in the figure that struck him so much in Beaton's phrase, and had been on his tongue ever since, "you're the man on horseback to him; and he'd be more apt to do what you say than if anybody else said it."

"You are very good, sir," said the colonel, trying to be proof against the flattery, "but I am afraid you overrate my influence." Fulkerson let him ponder it silently, and his daughter governed her impatience by holding her fan against her lips. Whatever the process was in the colonel's mind, he said at last: "I see no good reason for declining to act for you, Mr. Fulkerson, and I shall be very happy if I can be of service to you. But"—he stopped Fulkerson from cutting in with precipitate thanks—"I think I have a right, sir, to ask what your course will be in the event of failure?"

"Failure?" Fulkerson repeated, in dismay.

"Yes, sir. I will not conceal from you that this mission is one not wholly agreeable to my feelings."

"Oh, I understand that, colonel, and I assure you that I appreciate, I——"

"There is no use trying to blink the fact, sir, that there are certain aspects of Mr. Dryfoos's character in which he is not a gentleman. We have alluded to this fact before, and I need not dwell upon it now. I may say, however, that my misgivings were not wholly removed last night."

"No," Fulkerson assented; though in his heart he thought the old man had behaved very well.

"What I wish to say now is that I cannot consent to act for you, in this matter, merely as an intermediary whose failure would leave the affair *in statu quo*."

"I see," said Fulkerson.

"And I should like some intimation, some assurance, as to which party your own feelings are with in the difference."

The colonel bent his eyes sharply on Fulkerson; Miss Woodburn let hers fall; Fulkerson felt that he was being tested, and he said, to gain time, "As between Lindau and Dryfoos?" though he knew this was not the point.

"As between Mr. Dryfoos and Mr. March," said the colonel.

Fulkerson drew a long breath, and took his courage in both hands. "There can't be any choice for me in such a case. I'm for March, every time."

The colonel seized his hand, and Miss Woodburn said, "If there had been any choice fo' you in such a case, I should never have let papa sti' a step with you."

"Why, in regard to that," said the colonel, with a literal application of the idea, "was it your intention that we should both go?"

"Well, I don't know; I suppose it was."

"I think it will be better for me to go alone," said the colonel; and, with a colour from his experience in affairs of honour, he added: "In these matters a principal cannot appear without compromising his dignity. I believe I have all the points clearly in mind, and I think I should act more freely in meeting Mr. Dryfoos alone."

Fulkerson tried to hide the eagerness with which he met these agreeable views. He felt himself exalted in some sort to the level of the colonel's sentiments, though it would not be easy to say whether this was through the desperation bred of having committed himself to March's side, or through the buoyant hope he had that the colonel would succeed in his mission. "I'm not afraid to talk with Dryfoos about it," he said.

"There is no question of courage," said the colonel. "It is a question of dignity—of personal dignity."

"Well, don't let that delay you, papa," said his daughter, following him to the door, where she found him his hat, and Fulkerson helped him on with his overcoat. "Ah shall be jost wald to know ho' it's toned oat."

"Won't you let me go up to the house with you?" Fulkerson began. "I needn't go in——"

"I prefer to go alone," said the colonel. "I wish to turn the points over in my mind, and I am afraid you would find me rather dull company."

He went out, and Fulkerson returned with Miss Woodburn to the drawing-room, where she said the Leightons were. They were not there, but she did not seem disappointed.

"Well, Mr. Fulkerson," she said, "you *have* got an ahdeal of friendship, su' enough."

"Me?" said Fulkerson. "Oh, my Lord! Don't you see I couldn't do anything else? And I'm scared half to death, anyway. If the colonel don't bring the old man round, I reckon it's all up with me. But he'll fetch him. And I'm just prostrated with gratitude to you, Miss Woodburn."

She waved his thanks aside with her fan. "What do you mean by its being all up with you?"

"Why, if the old man sticks to his position, and I stick to March, we've both got to go overboard together. Dryfoos owns the magazine; he can stop it, or he can stop us, which amounts to the same thing, as far as we're concerned."

"And then what?" the girl pursued.

"And then, nothing—till we pick ourselves up."

"Do you mean that Mr. Dryfoos will put you both oat of your places?"

"He may."

"And Mr. Mawch takes the risk of that jost fo' a principle?"

"I reckon."

"And you do it, jost fo' an ahdeal?"

"It won't do to own it. I must have my little axe to grind, somewhere."

"Well, men *awe* splendid," sighed the girl. "Ah will *say* it."

"Oh, they're not so much better than women," said Fulkerson, with a nervous jocosity. "I guess March would have backed down if it hadn't been for his wife. She was as hot as pepper about it, and you could see that she would have sacrificed all her husband's relations sooner than let him back down an inch from the stand he had taken. It's pretty easy for a man to stick to a principle if he has a woman to stand by him. But when you come to play it alone——"

"Mr. Fulkerson," said the girl solemnly, "*Ah* will stand bah you in this, if all the woald tones against you." The tears came into her eyes, and she put out her hand to him.

"You *will*?" he shouted, in a rapture. "In every way—and always—as long as you live? Do you mean it?" He had caught her hand to his breast and was grappling it tight there, and drawing her to him.

The changing emotions chased each other through her heart and over her face: dismay, shame, pride, tenderness. "You don't *believe*," she said hoarsely, "that I meant *that*?"

"No, but I hope you *do* mean it; for if you don't, nothing else means anything."

There was no space, there was only a point of wavering. "Ah *do* mean it."

When they lifted their eyes from each other again it was half-past ten. "No' you most go," she said.

"But the colonel—our fate?"

"The co'nel is often oat late, and Ah'm not afraid of any fate, no' that we've taken it into ouah own hands." She looked at him with dewy eyes of trust, of inspiration.

"Oh, it's going to come out all right," he said. "It can't come out wrong now, no matter what happens. But who'd have thought it, when I came into this house, in such a state of sin and misery, half an hour ago——"

"Three houahs and a half ago!" she said. "No' you most jost go. Ah'm tahed to death. Good night. You can come in the mawning to see—papa." She opened the door, and pushed him out with enrapturing violence, and he ran laughing down the steps into her father's arms.

"Why, colonel! I was just going up to meet you." He really thought he would walk off his exultation in that direction.

"I am very sorry to say, Mr. Fulkerson," the colonel began gravely, "that Mr. Dryfoos adheres to his position."

"Oh, all right," said Fulkerson, with unabated joy. "It's what I expected. Well, my course is clear; I shall stand by March, and I guess the world won't come to an end if he bounces us both. But I'm everlasting obliged to *you*, Colonel Woodburn, and I don't know what to say to you. I—I won't detain you now; it's so late. I'll see you in the morning. Good ni——"

Fulkerson did not realise that it takes two to part. The colonel laid hold of his arm and turned away with him. "I will walk toward your place with you. I can understand why you should be anxious to know the particulars of my interview with Mr. Dryfoos;" and in the statement which followed he did not spare him the smallest. It outlasted their walk, and detained them long on the steps of the *Every Other Week* building. But at the end, Fulkerson let himself in with his key as light of heart as if he had been listening to the gayest promises that fortune could make.

By the time he met March at the office next morning, a little, but only a very little, misgiving saddened his golden heaven. He took March's hand with high courage, and said, "Well, the old man sticks to his point, March." He added, with the sense of saying it before Miss Woodburn, "And *I* stick by *you*. I've thought it all over, and I'd rather be right with you than wrong with him."

"Well, I appreciate your motive, Fulkerson," said March. "But perhaps—perhaps we can save over our heroics for another occasion. Lindau seems to have got in with his, for the present."

He told him of Lindau's last visit, and they stood a moment looking at each other rather queerly. Fulkerson was the first to recover his spirits. "Well," he said cheerily, "that let's us out."

"Does it? I'm not sure it lets *me* out," said March; but he said this in tribute to his crippled self-respect rather than as a forecast of any action in the matter.

"Why, what are you going to do?" Fulkerson asked. "If Lindau won't work for Dryfoos you can't make him."

March sighed. "What are you going to do with this money?" He glanced at the heap of bills he had flung on the table between them.

Fulkerson scratched his head. "Ah, dogged if *I* know. Can't we give it to the deserving poor, somehow, if we can find 'em?"

"I suppose we've no right to use it in any way. You must give it to Dryfoos."

"To the deserving rich? Well, you can always find *them*. I reckon you don't want to appear in the transaction; *I* don't, either; but I guess I must." Fulkerson gathered up the money and carried it to Conrad. He directed him to account for it in his books as conscience-money, and he enjoyed the joke more than Conrad seemed to do when he was told where it came from.

Fulkerson was able to wear off the disagreeable impression the affair left during the course of the forenoon, and he met Miss Woodburn with all a lover's buoyancy when he went to lunch. She was as happy as he when he told her how fortunately the whole thing had ended, and he took her view that it was a reward of his courage in having dared the worst. They both felt, as the newly plighted always do, that they were in the best relations with the beneficent powers, and that their felicity had been especially looked to in the disposition of events. They were in a glow of rapturous content with themselves and radiant worship of each other; she was sure that he merited the bright future opening to them both, as much as if he owed it directly to some noble action of his own; he felt that he was indebted for the favour of Heaven entirely to the still incredible accident of her preference of him over other men.

Colonel Woodburn, who was not yet in the secret of their love, perhaps failed for this reason to share their satisfaction

with a result so unexpectedly brought about. The blessing
on their hopes seemed to his ignorance to involve certain
sacrifices of personal feeling at which he hinted in suggesting
that Dryfoos should now be asked to make some abstract
concessions and acknowledgments; his daughter hastened
to deny that these were at all necessary; and Fulkerson easily
explained why. The thing was over; what was the use of
opening it up again?

"Perhaps none," the colonel admitted. But he added, "I
should like the opportunity of taking Mr. Lindau's hand in
the presence of Mr. Dryfoos, and assuring him that I considered him a man of principle and a man of honour; a
gentleman, sir, whom I was proud and happy to have
known."

"Well, Ah've no doabt," said his daughter demurely,
"that you'll have the chance some day; and we would all
lahke to join you. But at the same tahme, I think Mr.
Fulkerson is well oat of it fo' the present."

PART FIFTH

I

SUPERFICIALLY, the affairs of *Every Other Week* settled into their wonted form again, and for Fulkerson they seemed thoroughly reinstated. But March had a feeling of impermanency from what had happened, mixed with a fantastic sense of shame toward Lindau. He did not sympathise with Lindau's opinions, he thought his remedy for existing evils as wildly impracticable as Colonel Woodburn's. But while he thought this, and while he could justly blame Fulkerson for Lindau's presence at Dryfoos's dinner, which his zeal had brought about in spite of March's protests, still he could not rid himself of the reproach of uncandour with Lindau. He ought to have told him frankly about the ownership of the magazine, and what manner of man the man was whose money he was taking. But he said that he never could have imagined that he was serious in his preposterous attitude in regard to a class of men who embody half the prosperity of the country; and he had moments of revolt against his own humiliation before Lindau, in which he found it monstrous that he should return Dryfoos's money as if it had been the spoil of a robber. His wife agreed with him in these moments, and said it was a great relief not to have that tiresome old German coming about. They had to account for his absence evasively to the children, whom they could not very well tell that their father was living on money that Lindau disdained to take, even though Lindau was wrong and their father was right. This heightened Mrs. March's resentment toward both Lindau and Dryfoos, who between them had placed her husband in a false position. If anything, she resented Dryfoos's conduct more than Lindau's. He had never spoken to March about the affair since Lindau had

343

renounced his work, or added to the apologetic messages he had sent by Fulkerson. So far as March knew, Dryfoos had been left to suppose that Lindau had simply stopped for some reason that did not personally affect him. They never spoke of him, and March was too proud to ask either Fulkerson or Conrad whether the old man knew that Lindau had returned his money. He avoided talking to Conrad, from a feeling that if he did, he should involuntarily lead him on to speak of his differences with his father. Between himself and Fulkerson, even, he was uneasily aware of a want of their old perfect friendliness. Fulkerson had finally behaved with honour and courage; but his provisional reluctance had given March the measure of Fulkerson's character in one direction, and he could not ignore the fact that it was smaller than he could have wished.

He could not make out whether Fulkerson shared his discomfort or not. It certainly wore away, even with March, as time passed, and with Fulkerson, in the bliss of his fortunate love, it was probably far more transient, if it existed at all. He advanced into the winter as radiantly as if to meet the spring, and he said that if there were any pleasanter month of the year than November, it was December, especially when the weather was good and wet and muddy most of the time, so that you had to keep indoors a long while after you called anywhere.

Colonel Woodburn had the anxiety, in view of his daughter's engagement, when she asked his consent to it, that such a dreamer must have in regard to any reality that threatens to affect the course of his reveries. He had not perhaps taken her marriage into account, except as a remote contingency; and certainly Fulkerson was not the kind of son-in-law that he had imagined in dealing with that abstraction. But because he had nothing of the sort definitely in mind, he could not oppose the selection of Fulkerson with success; he really knew nothing against him, and he knew many things in his favour; Fulkerson inspired him with the liking that every one felt for him in a measure; he amused him, he cheered him; and the Colonel had been so much used to leaving action of all kinds to his daughter that when he came to close quarters with the question of a son-in-law, he felt helpless to decide it, and he let her decide it, as if it were still to be decided when it was submitted to him. She was competent to treat it in all its phases: not merely those of personal interest, but those of duty to the broken Southern past, sentimentally dear to him, and practically absurd to her. No such South as he remembered had ever existed to her knowledge, and no such civilisation as he imagined would ever exist, to her belief, anywhere. She took the world as she found it, and made the best of it. She trusted in Fulkerson; she had proved his magnanimity in a serious emergency; and in small things she was willing fearlessly to chance it with him. She was not a sentimentalist, and there was nothing fantastic in her expectations; she was a girl of good sense and right mind, and she liked the immediate practicality as well as the final honour of Fulkerson. She did not idealise him, but in the highest effect she realised him; she did him justice, and she would not have believed that she did him more than justice if she had sometimes known him to do himself less.

Their engagement was a fact to which the Leighton household adjusted itself almost as simply as the lovers themselves; Miss Woodburn told the ladies at once, and it was not a thing that Fulkerson could keep from March very long. He sent word of it to Mrs. March by her husband; and his engagement perhaps did more than anything else to confirm the confidence in him which had been shaken by his early behaviour in the Lindau episode, and not wholly restored by his tardy fidelity to March. But now she felt that a man who wished to get married so obviously and entirely for love was full of all kinds of the best instincts, and only needed the guidance of a wife to become very noble. She interested herself intensely in balancing the respective merits of the engaged couple, and after her call upon Miss Woodburn in her new character she prided herself upon recognising the worth of some strictly Southern qualities in her, while maintaining the general average of New England superiority.

She could not reconcile herself to the Virginian custom illustrated in her having been christened with the surname of Madison; and she said that its pet form of Mad, which Fulkerson promptly invented, only made it more ridiculous.

Fulkerson was slower in telling Beaton. He was afraid, somehow, of Beaton's taking the matter in the cynical way; Miss Woodburn said she would break off the engagement if Beaton was left to guess it or find it out by accident, and then Fulkerson plucked up his courage. Beaton received the news with gravity, and with a sort of melancholy meekness that strongly moved Fulkerson's sympathy, and made him wish that Beaton was engaged too.

It made Beaton feel very old; it somehow left him behind and forgotten; in a manner, it made him feel trifled with. Something of the unfriendliness of fate seemed to overcast his resentment, and he allowed the sadness of his conviction that he had not the means to marry on to tinge his recognition of the fact that Alma Leighton would not have wanted him to marry her if he had. He was now often in that martyr mood in which he wished to help his father; not only to deny himself Chianti, but to forego a fur-lined overcoat which he intended to get for the winter. He postponed the moment of actual sacrifice as regarded the Chianti, and he bought the overcoat in an anguish of self-reproach. He wore it the first evening after he got it in going to call upon the Leightons, and it seemed to him a piece of ghastly irony when Alma complimented his picturesqueness in it, and asked him to let her sketch him.

"Oh, you can *sketch* me," he said, with so much gloom that it made her laugh.

"If you think it's so serious, I'd rather not."

"No, no! Go ahead! How do you want me?"

"Oh, fling yourself down on a chair in one of your attitudes of studied negligence; and twist one corner of your moustache with affected absence of mind."

"And you think I'm always studied, always affected?"

"I didn't *say* so."

"I didn't ask you what you *said*."

346

"And I won't tell you what I think."

"Ah, I know what you think."

"What made you ask, then?" The girl laughed again with the satisfaction of her sex in cornering a man.

Beaton made a show of not deigning to reply, and put himself in the pose she suggested frowning.

"Ah, that's it. But a little more animation.

> " 'As when a great thought strikes along the brain,
> And flushes all the cheek.' "*

She put her forehead down on the back of her hand and laughed again. "You ought to be photographed. You look as if you were sitting for it."

Beaton said: "That's because I know I am being photographed, in one way. I don't think you ought to call me affected. I never am so with you; I know it wouldn't be of any use."

"Oh, Mr. Beaton, you flatter."

"No, I never flatter you."

"I meant you flattered yourself."

"How?"

"Oh, I don't know. Imagine."

"I know what you mean. You think I can't be sincere with anybody."

"Oh, no I don't."

"What do you think?"

"That you can't—try." Alma gave another victorious laugh.

Miss Woodburn and Fulkerson would once have both feigned a great interest in Alma's sketching Beaton, and made it the subject of talk, in which they approached as nearly as possible the real interest of their lives. Now they frankly remained away, in the dining-room, which was very cozy after the dinner had disappeared; the colonel sat with his lamp and paper in the gallery beyond; Mrs. Leighton was about her housekeeping affairs, in the content she always felt when Alma was with Beaton.

"They seem to be having a pretty good time in there,"

said Fulkerson, detaching himself from his own absolute good time as well as he could.

"At least Alma does," said Miss Woodburn.

"Do you think she cares for him?"

"Quahte as moch as he desoves."

"What makes you all down on Beaton around here? He's not such a bad fellow."

"We awe not all doan on him. Mrs. Leighton isn't doan on him."

"Oh, I guess if it was the old lady, there wouldn't be much question about it."

They both laughed, and Alma said, "They seem to be greatly amused with something in there."

"Me, probably," said Beaton. "I seem to amuse everybody to-night."

"Don't you always?"

"I always amuse you, I'm afraid, Alma."

She looked at him as if she were going to snub him openly for using her name; but apparently she decided to do it covertly. "You didn't at first. I really used to believe you could be serious once."

"Couldn't you believe it again? Now?"

"Not when you put on that wind-harp stop."

"Wetmore has been talking to you about me. He would sacrifice his best friend to a phrase. He spends his time making them."

"He's made some very pretty ones about you."

"Like the one you just quoted?"

"No, not exactly. He admires you ever so much. He says———." She stopped, teasingly.

"What?"

"He says you could be almost anything you wished, if you didn't wish to be everything."

"That sounds more like the *school* of Wetmore. That's what *you* say, Alma. Well, if there were something you wished me to be, I could be it."

"We might adapt Kingsley:*'Be good, sweet maid, and let who will be clever.'" He could not help laughing. She

348

went on: "I always thought that was the most patronising and exasperating thing ever addressed to a human girl; and we've had to stand a good deal in our time. I should like to have it applied to the other 'sect' a while. As if any girl that *was* a girl would be good if she had the remotest chance of being clever."

"Then you wouldn't wish me to be good?" Beaton asked.

"Not if you were a girl."

"You want to shock me. Well, I suppose I deserve it. But if I were one-tenth part as good as you are, Alma, I should have a lighter heart than I have now. I know that I'm fickle, but I'm not false, as you think I am."

"Who said I thought you were false?"

"No one," said Beaton. "It isn't necessary, when you look it—live it."

"Oh, dear! I didn't know I devoted my whole time to the subject."

"I know I'm despicable. I could tell you something—the history of this day, even—that would make you despise me." Beaton had in mind his purchase of the overcoat, which Alma was getting in so effectively, with the money he ought to have sent his father. "But," he went on darkly, with a sense that what he was that moment suffering for his selfishness must somehow be a kind of atonement, which would finally leave him to the guiltless enjoyment of the overcoat, "you wouldn't believe the depths of baseness I could descend to."

"I would try," said Alma, rapidly shading the collar, "if you'd give me some hint."

Beaton had a sudden wish to pour out his remorse to her, but he was afraid of her laughing at him. He said to himself that this was a very wholesome fear, and that if he could always have her at hand he should not make a fool of himself so often. A man conceives of such an office as the very noblest for a woman; he worships her for it if he is magnanimous. But Beaton was silent, and Alma put back her head for the right distance on her sketch. "Mr. Fulkerson thinks you are the sublimest of human beings for advising him to

349

get Colonel Woodburn to interview Mr. Dryfoos about Lindau. What have you ever done with your Judas?"

"I haven't done anything with it. Nadel thought he would take hold of it at one time, but he dropped it again. After all, I don't suppose it could be popularised. Fulkerson wanted to offer it as a premium to subscribers for *Every Other Week*, but I sat down on that."

Alma could not feel the absurdity of this, and she merely said, "*Every Other Week* seems to be going on just the same as ever."

"Yes, the trouble has all blown over, I believe. Fulkerson," said Beaton, with a return to what they were saying, "has managed the whole business very well. But he exaggerates the value of my advice."

"Very likely," Alma suggested vaguely. "Or no! Excuse me! He couldn't, he couldn't!" She laughed delightedly at Beaton's foolish look of embarrassment.

He tried to recover his dignity in saying, "He's a very good fellow, and he deserves his happiness."

"Oh, indeed!" said Alma perversely. "Does any one deserve happiness?"

"I know I don't," sighed Beaton.

"You mean you don't get it."

"I certainly don't get it."

"Ah, but that isn't the reason."

"What is?"

"That's the secret of the universe." She bit in her lower lip, and looked at him with eyes of gleaming fun.

"Are you *never* serious?" he asked.

"With serious people—always."

"*I* am serious; and you have the secret of my happiness——." He threw himself impulsively forward in his chair.

"Oh, pose, pose!" she cried.

"I *won't* pose," he answered, "and you have got to listen to me. You know I'm in love with you; and I know that once you cared for me. Can't that time—won't it—come back again? Try to think so, Alma!"

"No," she said, briefly and seriously enough.

"But that seems impossible. What is it I've done—what have you against me?"

"Nothing. But that time is *past*. I couldn't recall it if I wished. Why did you bring it up? You've broken your word. You know I wouldn't have let you keep coming here if you hadn't promised never to refer to it."

"How could I help it? With that happiness near us—Fulkerson——"

"Oh, it's *that*? I might have known it!"

"No, it isn't that—it's something far deeper. But if it's nothing you have against me, what is it, Alma, that keeps you from caring for me now as you did then? I haven't changed."

"But *I* have. I shall never care for you again, Mr. Beaton; you might as well understand it once for all. Don't think it's anything in yourself, or that I think you unworthy of me. I'm not so self-satisfied as that; I know very well that I'm not a perfect character, and that I've no claim on perfection in anybody else. I think women who want that are fools; they won't get it, and they don't deserve it. But I've learned a good deal more about myself than I knew in St. Barnaby, and a life of work, of art, and of art alone—that's what I've made up my mind to."

"A woman that's made up her mind to that has no heart to hinder her!"

"Would a man have that had done so?"

"But I don't believe you, Alma. You're merely laughing at me. And besides, with me you needn't give up art. We could work together. You know how much I admire your talent. I believe I could help it—serve it; I would be its willing slave, and yours, Heaven knows!"

"I don't want any slave—nor any slavery. I want to be free—always. Now do you see? I *don't* care for you, and I never could in the old way; but I should have to care for some one more than I believe I ever shall to give up my work. Shall we go on?" She looked at her sketch.

"No, we shall not go on," he said, gloomily as he rose.

"I suppose you blame me," she said, rising too.

"Oh no! I blame no one—or only myself. I threw my chance away."

"I'm glad you see that; and I'm glad you did it. You don't believe me, of course. Why do men think life can be only the one thing to women? And if you come to the selfish view, who are the happy women? I'm sure that if work doesn't fail me, health won't, and happiness won't."

"But you could work on with me——"

"Second fiddle. Do you suppose I shouldn't be woman enough to wish my work always less and lower than yours? At least I've heart enough for that!"

"You've heart enough for anything, Alma. I was a fool to say you hadn't."

"I think the women who keep their hearts have an even chance, at least, of having heart——"

"Ah, there's where you're wrong!"

"But mine isn't mine to give *you*, anyhow. And now I don't want you ever to speak to me about this again."

"Oh, there's no danger!" he cried bitterly. "I shall never willingly see you again."

"That's as you like, Mr. Beaton. We've had to be very frank, but I don't see why we shouldn't be friends. Still, we needn't, if you don't like."

"And I may come—I may come here—as—as usual?"

"Why, if you can consistently," she said, with a smile, and she held out her hand to him.

He went home dazed, and feeling as if it were a bad joke that had been put upon him. At least the affair went so deep that it estranged the aspect of his familiar studio. Some of the things in it were not very familiar; he had spent lately a great deal on rugs, on stuffs, on Japanese bric-à-brac. When he saw these things in the shops he had felt that he must have them; that they were necessary to him; and he was partly in debt for them, still without having sent any of his earnings to pay his father. As he looked at them now he liked to fancy something weird and conscious in them as the silent witnesses of a broken life. He felt about among some of the smaller objects on the mantel for his pipe. Before he slept he was aware, in the luxury of his despair, of a remote relief, an escape; and after all, the understanding he had come to with Alma was only the explicit formulation of terms long tacit between them. Beaton would have been puzzled more than he knew if she had taken him seriously. It was inevitable that he should declare himself in love with her; but he was not disappointed at her rejection of his love; perhaps not so much as he would have been at its acceptance, though he tried to think otherwise, and to give himself airs of tragedy. He did not really feel that the result was worse than what had gone before, and it left him free.

But he did not go to the Leightons again for so long a time that Mrs. Leighton asked Alma what had happened. Alma told her.

"And he won't come any more?" her mother sighed, with reserved censure.

"Oh, I think he will. He couldn't very well come the next night. But he has the habit of coming, and with Mr. Beaton habit is everything—even the habit of thinking he's in love with some one."

"Alma," said her mother, "I don't think it's very nice for a girl to let a young man keep coming to see her after she's refused him."

"Why not, if it amuses him and doesn't hurt the girl?"

"But it does hurt her, Alma. It—it's indelicate. It isn't fair to him; it gives him hopes."

"Well, mamma, it hasn't happened in the given case yet. If Mr. Beaton comes again I won't see him, and you can forbid him the house."

"If I could only feel sure, Alma," said her mother, taking up another branch of the inquiry, "that you really knew your own mind, I should be easier about it."

"Then you can rest perfectly quiet, mamma. I do know my own mind; and what's worse, I know Mr. Beaton's mind."

"What do you mean?"

"I mean that he spoke to me the other night simply

because Mr. Fulkerson's engagement had broken him all up."

"What expressions!" Mrs. Leighton lamented.

"He let it out himself," Alma went on. "And you wouldn't have thought it was very flattering yourself. When I'm made love to, after this, I prefer to be made love to in an off-year, when there isn't another engaged couple anywhere about."

"Did you tell him that, Alma?"

"Tell him that! What do you mean, mamma? I may be indelicate, but I'm not quite so indelicate as that."

"I didn't mean you were indelicate, really, Alma, but I wanted to warn you. I think Mr. Beaton was very much in earnest."

"Oh, so did he!"

"And you didn't?"

"Oh yes, for the time being. I suppose he's very much in earnest with Miss Vance at times, and with Miss Dryfoos at others. Sometimes, he's a painter, and sometimes he's an architect, and sometimes he's a sculptor. He has too many gifts—too many tastes."

"And if Miss Vance, and Miss Dryfoos——"

"Oh, do say Sculpture and Architecture, mamma! It's getting so dreadfully personal!"

"Alma, you know that I only wish to get at your real feeling in the matter."

"And you know that I don't want to let you—especially when I haven't got any real feeling in the matter. But I should think—speaking in the abstract entirely—that if either of those arts was ever going to be in earnest about him, it would want his exclusive devotion for a week at least."

"I didn't know," said Mrs. Leighton, "that he was doing anything now at the others. I thought he was entirely taken up with his work on *Every Other Week*."

"Oh, he is! he is!"

"And you certainly can't say, my dear, that he hasn't been very kind—very useful to you, in that matter."

"And so I ought to have said yes out of gratitude? Thank you, mamma! I didn't know you held me so cheap."

"You know whether I hold you cheap or not, Alma. I don't want you to cheapen yourself. I don't want you to trifle with any one. I want you to be honest with yourself."

"Well, come now, mamma! Suppose you begin. I've been perfectly honest with myself, and I've been honest with Mr. Beaton. I don't care for him, and I've told him I didn't; so he may be supposed to know it. If he comes here after this, he'll come as a plain, unostentatious friend of the family, and it's for you to say whether he shall come in that capacity or not. I hope you won't trifle with him, and let him get the notion that he's coming on any other basis."

Mrs. Leighton felt the comfort of the critical attitude far too keenly to abandon it for anything constructive. She only said, "You know very well, Alma, that's a matter I can have nothing to do with."

"Then you leave him entirely to me?"

"I hope you will regard his right to candid and open treatment."

"He's had nothing but the most open and candid treatment from me, mamma. It's you that want to play fast and loose with him. And to tell you the truth, I believe he would like that a good deal better; I believe that if there's anything he hates, it's openness and candour."

Alma laughed, and put her arms round her mother, who could not help laughing a little too.

II

THE winter did not renew for Christine and Mela the social opportunity which the spring had offered. After the *musicale* at Mrs. Horn's, they both made their party-call, as Mela said, in due season; but they did not find Mrs. Horn at home, and neither she nor Miss Vance came to see them after people returned to town in the fall. They tried to believe for a time that Mrs. Horn had not got their cards; this pretence failed them, and they fell back upon their pride, or rather Christine's pride. Mela had little but her good-nature to avail her in any exigency, and if Mrs. Horn or Miss Vance had come to call after a year of neglect, she would have received them as amiably as if they had not lost a day in coming. But Christine had drawn a line, beyond which they would not have been forgiven; and she had planned the words and the behaviour with which she would have punished them if they had appeared then. Neither sister imagined herself in anywise inferior to them; but Christine was suspicious, at least, and it was Mela who invented the hypothesis of the lost cards. As nothing happened to prove or to disprove the fact, she said, "I move we put Coonrod up to gittun' it out of Miss Vance, at some of their meetings."

"If you do," said Christine, "I'll kill you."

Christine, however, had the visits of Beaton to console her, and if these seemed to have no definite aim, she was willing to rest in the pleasure they gave her vanity; but Mela had nothing. Sometimes she even wished they were all back on the farm.

"It would be the best thing for both of you," said Mrs. Dryfoos, in answer to such a burst of desperation. "I don't think New York is any place for girls."

"Well, what I hate, mother," said Mela, "is, it don't seem to be any place for young men, either." She found this so good when she had said it that she laughed over it till Christine was angry.

"A body would think there had never been any joke before."

"I don't see as it's a joke," said Mrs. Dryfoos. "It's the plain truth."

"Oh, don't mind her, mother," said Mela. "She's put out because her old Mr. Beaton ha'n't been round for a couple o' weeks. If you don't watch out, that fellow'll give you the slip, yit, Christine, after all your pains."

"Well, there ain't anybody to give *you* the slip, Mela," Christine clawed back.

"No; I ha'n't ever set my traps for anybody." This was what Mela said for want of a better retort; but it was not quite true. When Kendricks came with Beaton to call after her father's dinner, she used all her cunning to ensnare him, and she had him to herself as long as Beaton stayed; Dryfoos sent down word that he was not very well, and had gone to bed. The novelty of Mela had worn off for Kendricks, and she found him, as she frankly told him, not half as entertaining as he was at Mrs. Horn's; but she did her best with him as the only flirtable material which had yet come to her hand. It would have been her ideal to have the young men stay till past midnight, and her father come downstairs in his stocking-feet, and tell them it was time to go. But they made a visit of decorous brevity, and Kendricks did not come again. She met him afterward, once, as she was crossing the pavement in Union Square, to get into her coupé, and made the most of him; but it was necessarily very little, and so he passed out of her life without having left any trace in her heart, though Mela had a heart that she would have put at the disposition of almost any young man that wanted it. Kendricks himself, Manhattan cockney as he was, with scarcely more outlook into the average American nature than if he had been kept a prisoner in New York society all his days, perceived a property in her which forbade him as a man of conscience to trifle with her; something earthly good and kind, if it was simple and vulgar. In revising his impressions of her, it seemed to him that she would come even to better literary effect if this were recognized in her; and it made her sacred, in spite of her willingness to fool and to be fooled, in her merely human quality. After all, he saw that she wished honestly to love and to be loved, and the lures she threw out to that end seemed to him pathetic rather than ridiculous; he could not join Beaton in laughing at her; and he did not like Beaton's laughing at the other girl, either. It seemed to Kendricks, with the code of honour which he mostly kept to himself because he was a little ashamed to find there were so few others like it, that if Beaton cared nothing for the other girl—and Christine appeared simply detestable to Kendricks—he had better keep away from her, and not give her the impression he was in love with her. He rather fancied that this was the part of a gentleman, and he

could not have penetrated to that æsthetic and moral complexity which formed the consciousness of a nature like
Beaton, and was chiefly a torment to itself; he could not have
conceived of the wayward impulses indulged at every
moment in little things, till the straight highway was
traversed and wellnigh lost under their tangle. To do whatever one likes is finally to do nothing that one likes, even
though one continues to do what one will; but Kendricks,
though a sage of twenty-seven, was still too young to understand this.

Beaton scarcely understood it himself, perhaps because
he was not yet twenty-seven. He only knew that his will was
somehow sick; that it spent itself in caprices, and brought
him no happiness from the fulfilment of the most vehement
wish. But he was aware that his wishes grew less and less
vehement; he began to have a fear that some time he might
have none at all. It seemed to him that if he could once do
something that was thoroughly distasteful to himself, he
might make a beginning in the right direction; but when he
tried this on a small scale it failed, and it seemed stupid.
Some sort of expiation was the thing he needed, he was sure;
but he could not think of anything in particular to expiate;
a man could not expiate his temperament, and his temperament was what Beaton decided to be at fault. He perceived
that it went deeper than even fate would have gone; he
could have fulfilled an evil destiny and had done with it,
however terrible. His trouble was that he could not escape
from himself; and for the most part, he justified himself in
refusing to try. After he had come to that distinct understanding with Alma Leighton, and experienced the relief it
really gave him, he thought for a while that if it had fallen
out otherwise, and she had put him in charge of her destiny,
he might have been better able to manage his own. But as it
was, he could only drift, and let all other things take their
course. It was necessary that he should go to see her afterward, to show her that he was equal to the event; but he did
not go so often, and he went rather oftener to the Dryfooses;
it was not easy to see Margaret Vance, except on the society

terms. With much sneering and scorning, he fulfilled the duties to Mrs. Horn without which he knew he should be dropped from her list; but one might go to many of her Thursdays without getting many words with her niece. Beaton hardly knew whether he wanted many; the girl kept the charm of her innocent stylishness; but latterly she wanted to talk more about social questions than about the psychical problems that young people usually debate so personally. Son of the working-people as he was, Beaton had never cared anything about such matters; he did not know about them or wish to know; he was perhaps too near them. Besides, there was an embarrassment, at least on her part, concerning the Dryfooses. She was too high-minded to blame him for having tempted her to her failure with them by his talk about them; but she was conscious of avoiding them in her talk. She had decided not to renew the effort she had made in the spring; because she could not do them good as fellow-creatures needing food and warmth and work, and she would not try to befriend them socially; she had a horror of any such futile sentimentality. She would have liked to account to Beaton in this way for a course which she sus-pected he must have heard their comments upon, but she did not quite know how to do it; she could not be sure how much or how little he cared for them. Some tentative ap-proaches which she made toward explanation were met with such eager disclaim of personal interest that she knew less than before what to think; and she turned the talk from the sisters to the brother, whom it seemed she still continued to meet in their common work among the poor.

"He seems very different," she ventured.

"Oh, quite," said Beaton. "He's the kind of person that you might suppose gave the Catholics a hint for the cloistral life; he's a cloistered nature—the nature that atones and suffers for. But he's awfully dull company, don't you think? I never can get anything out of him."

"He's very much in earnest."

"Remorselessly. We've got a profane and mundane crea-ture there at the office who runs us all, and it's shocking merely to see the contact of the two natures. When Fulkerson gets to joking Dryfoos—he likes to put his joke in the form of a pretence that Dryfoos is actuated by a selfish motive, that he has an eye to office, and is working up a political interest for himself on the East side—it's something inexpressible."

"I should think so," said Miss Vance, with such lofty disapproval that Beaton felt himself included in it for having merely told what caused it.

He could not help saying, in natural rebellion, "Well, the man of one idea is always a little ridiculous."

"When his idea is right?" she demanded. "A right idea can't be ridiculous."

"Oh, I only said the man that held it alone. He's flat; he has no relief, no projection."

She seemed unable to answer, and he perceived that he had silenced her to his own disadvantage. It appeared to Beaton that she was becoming a little too exacting for comfort in her idealism. He put down the cup of tea he had been tasting, and said, in his solemn staccato, "I must go. Good-bye!" and got instantly away from her, with an effect he had of having suddenly thought of something imperative.

He went up to Mrs. Horn for a moment's hail and farewell, and felt himself subtly detained by her through fugitive passages of conversation with half a dozen other people. He fancied that at crises of this strange interview Mrs. Horn was about to become confidential with him, and confidential, of all things, about her niece. She ended by not having palpably been so. In fact, the concern in her mind would have been difficult to impart to a young man, and after several experiments Mrs. Horn found it impossible to say that she wished Margaret could somehow be interested in lower things than those which occupied her. She had watched with growing anxiety the girl's tendency to various kinds of self-devotion. She had dark hours in which she even feared her entire withdrawal from the world in a life of good works. Before now, girls had entered the Protestant sisterhoods, which appeal so potently to the young and generous imagination, and Margaret was of just the temperament to be influenced by them. During the past summer she had been unhappy at her separation from the cares that had engrossed her more and more as their stay in the city drew to an end in the spring, and she had hurried her aunt back to town earlier in the fall than she would have chosen to come. Margaret had her correspondents among the working-women whom she befriended. Mrs. Horn was at one time alarmed to find that Margaret was actually promoting a strike of the button-hole workers. This, of course, had its ludicrous side, in connection with a young lady in good society, and a person of even so little humour as Mrs. Horn could not help seeing it. At the same time she could not help foreboding the worst from it; she was afraid that Margaret's health would give way under the strain, and that if she did not go into a sisterhood she would at least go into a decline. She began the winter with all such counteractive measures as she could employ. At an age when such things weary, she threw herself into the pleasures of society with the hope of dragging Margaret after her; and a sympathetic witness must have followed with compassion her course from ball to ball, from reception to reception, from parlour-reading to parlour-reading, from *musicale* to *musicale*, from play to play, from opera to opera. She tasted, after she had practically renounced them, the bitter and the insipid flavours of fashionable amusement, in the hope that Margaret might find them sweet, and now at the end she had to own to herself that she had failed. It was coming Lent again, and the girl had only grown thinner and more serious with the diversions that did not divert her from the baleful works of beneficence on which Mrs. Horn felt that she was throwing her youth away. Margaret could have borne either alone, but together they were wearing her out. She felt it a duty to undergo the pleasures her aunt appointed for her, but she could not forego the other duties in which she found her only pleasure.

She kept up her music still because she could employ it at the meetings for the entertainment, and, as she hoped, the elevation of her working-women; but she neglected the other

æsthetic interests which once occupied her; and at sight of
Beaton talking with her, Mrs. Horn caught at the hope that
he might somehow be turned to account in reviving Margaret's former interest in art. She asked him if Mr. Wetmore
had his classes that winter as usual; and she said she wished
Margaret could be induced to go again: Mr. Wetmore
always said that she did not draw very well, but that she had
a great deal of feeling for it, and her work was interesting.
She asked, were the Leightons in town again; and she murmured a regret that she had not been able to see anything of
them, without explaining why; she said she had a fancy that
if Margaret knew Miss Leighton, and what she was doing,
it might stimulate her, perhaps. She supposed Miss Leighton was still going on with her art?

Beaton said, Oh yes, he believed so.

But his manner did not encourage Mrs. Horn to pursue her
aims in that direction, and she said, with a sigh, she wished
he still had a class; she always fancied that Margaret got more
good from his instruction than from any one else's.

He said that she was very good; but there was really nobody who knew half as much as Wetmore, or could make any
one understand half as much.

Mrs. Horn was afraid, she said, that Mr. Wetmore's
terrible sincerity discouraged Margaret; he would not let
her have any illusions about the outcome of what she was
doing; and did not Mr. Beaton think that some illusion was
necessary with young people? Of course it was very nice of
Mr. Wetmore to be so honest, but it did not always seem to
be the wisest thing. She begged Mr. Beaton to try to think
of some one who would be a little less severe. Her tone
assumed a deeper interest in the people who were coming up
and going away, and Beaton perceived that he was dismissed.

He went away with vanity flattered by the sense of having
been appealed to concerning Margaret, and then he began
to chafe at what she had said of Wetmore's honesty, apropos
of her wish that he still had a class himself. Did she mean,
confound her! that *he* was insincere, and would let Miss
Vance suppose she had more talent than she really had?

The more Beaton thought of this, the more furious he became; and the more he was convinced that something like it had been unconsciously if not consciously in her mind. He framed some keen retorts, to the general effect that with the atmosphere of illusion preserved so completely at home, Miss Vance hardly needed it in her art studies. Having just determined never to go near Mrs. Horn's Thursdays again, he decided to go once more, in order to plant this sting in her capacious but somewhat callous bosom; and he planned how he would lead the talk up to the point from which he should launch it.

In the meantime he felt the need of some present solace, such as only unqualified worship could give him; a cruel wish to feel his power in some direction where, even if it were resisted, it could not be overcome, drove him on. That a woman who was to Beaton the embodiment of artificiality should intimate, however innocently—the innocence made it all the worse—that he was less honest than Wetmore, whom he knew to be so much more honest, was something that must be retaliated somewhere before his self-respect could be restored. It was only five o'clock, and he went on uptown to the Dryfooses', though he had been there only the night before last. He asked for the ladies, and Mrs. Mandel received him.

"The young ladies are down-town shopping," she said, "but I am very glad of the opportunity of seeing you alone, Mr. Beaton. You know I lived several years in Europe."

"Yes," said Beaton, wondering what that could have to do with her pleasure in seeing him alone. "I believe so?" He involuntarily gave his words the questioning inflection.

"You have lived abroad, too, and so you won't find what I am going to ask so strange. Mr. Beaton, why do you come so much to this house?" Mrs. Mandel bent forward with an aspect of lady-like interest, and smiled.

Beaton frowned. "Why do I come so much?"

"Yes."

"Why do I——. Excuse me, Mrs. Mandel, but will you allow me to ask why you ask?"

"Oh, certainly. There's no reason why I shouldn't say, for I wish you to be very frank with me. I ask because there are two young ladies in this house; and, in a certain way, I have to take the place of a mother to them. I needn't explain why; you know all the people here, and you understand. I have nothing to say about them, but I should not be speaking to you now if they were not all rather helpless people. They do not know the world they have come to live in here, and they cannot help themselves nor one another. But you do know it, Mr. Beaton, and I am sure you know just how much or how little you mean by coming here. You are either interested in one of these young girls or you are not. If you are, I have nothing more to say. If you are not——." Mrs. Mandel continued to smile, but the smile had grown more perfunctory, and it had an icy gleam.

Beaton looked at her with surprise that he gravely kept to himself. He had always regarded her as a social nullity, with a kind of pity, to be sure, as a civilised person living among such people as the Dryfooses, but not without a humorous contempt; he had thought of her as Mandel, and sometimes as old Mandel, though she was not half a score of years his senior, and was still well on the sunny side of forty. He reddened, and then turned an angry pallor. "Excuse me again, Mrs. Mandel. Do you ask this from the young ladies?"

"Certainly not," she said, with the best temper, and with something in her tone that convicted Beaton of vulgarity in putting his question of her authority in the form of a sneer. "As I have suggested, they would hardly know how to help themselves at all in such a matter. I have no objection to saying that I ask it from the father of the young ladies. Of course, in and for myself I should have no right to know anything about your affairs. I assure you the duty of knowing isn't very pleasant." The little tremor in her clear voice struck Beaton as something rather nice.

"I can very well believe that, Mrs. Mandel," he said, with a dreamy sadness in his own. He lifted his eyes, and looked into hers. "If I told you that I cared nothing about them in the way you intimate?"

"Then I should prefer to let you characterise your own conduct in continuing to come here for the year past, as you have done, and tacitly leading them on to infer differently." They both mechanically kept up the fiction of plurality in speaking of Christine, but there was no doubt in the mind of either which of the young ladies the other meant.

A good many thoughts went through Beaton's mind, and none of them were flattering. He had not been unconscious that the part he had played toward this girl was ignoble, and that it had grown meaner as the fancy which her beauty had at first kindled in him had grown cooler. He was aware that of late he had been amusing himself with her passion in a way that was not less than cruel, not because he wished to do so, but because he was listless and wished nothing. He rose in saying, "I might be a little more lenient than you think, Mrs. Mandel; but I won't trouble you with any palliating theory. I will not come any more."

He bowed, and Mrs. Mandel said, "Of course, it's only your action that I am concerned with."

She seemed to him merely triumphant, and he could not conceive what it had cost her to nerve herself up to her too easy victory. He left Mrs. Mandel to a far harder lot than had fallen to him, and he went away hating her as an enemy who had humiliated him at a moment when he particularly needed exalting. It was really very simple for him to stop going to see Christine Dryfoos, but it was not at all simple for Mrs. Mandel to deal with the consequences of his not coming. He only thought how lightly she had stopped him, and the poor woman whom he had left trembling for what she had been obliged to do embodied for him the conscience that accused him of unpleasant things.

"By heavens! this is piling it up," he said to himself through his set teeth, realising how it had happened right on top of that stupid insult from Mrs. Horn. Now he should have to give up his place on *Every Other Week*; he could not keep that, under the circumstances, even if some pretence were not made to get rid of him; he must hurry and anticipate any such pretence; he must see Fulkerson at once; he wondered where he should find him at that hour. He thought, with bitterness so real that it gave him a kind of tragical satisfaction, how certainly he could find him a little later at Mrs. Leighton's; and Fulkerson's happiness became an added injury.

The thing had of course come about just at the wrong time. There never had been a time when Beaton needed money more; when he had spent what he had and what he expected to have so recklessly. He was in debt to Fulkerson personally and officially for advance payments of salary. The thought of sending money home made him break into a scoffing laugh, which he turned into a cough in order to deceive the passers. What sort of face should he go to Fulkerson with and tell him that he renounced his employment on *Every Other Week*; and what should he do when he had renounced it? Take pupils, perhaps; open a class? A lurid conception of a class conducted on those principles of shameless flattery at which Mrs. Horn had hinted—he believed now she had meant to insult him—presented itself. Why should not he act upon the suggestion? He thought—with loathing for the whole race of women-dabblers in art—how easy the thing would be: as easy as to turn back now and tell that old fool's girl that he loved her, and rake in half his millions. Why should not he do that? No one else cared for him; and at a year's end, probably, one woman would be like another as far as the love was concerned, and probably he should not be more tired if the woman were Christine Dryfoos than if she were Margaret Vance. He kept Alma Leighton out of the question, because at the bottom of his heart he believed that she must be for ever unlike every other woman to him.

The tide of his confused and aimless reverie had carried him far down-town, he thought; but when he looked up from it to see where he was, he found himself on Sixth Avenue, only a little below Thirty-ninth Street, very hot and blown; that idiotic fur overcoat was stifling. He could not possibly walk down to Eleventh; he did not want to walk even to the Elevated station at Thirty-fourth; he stopped at the corner to wait for a surface-car, and fell again into his bitter fancies. After a while he roused himself and looked up the track, but there was no car coming. He found himself beside a policeman, who was lazily swinging his club by its thong from his wrist.

"When do you suppose a car will be along?" he asked, rather in a general sarcasm of the absence of the cars than in any special belief that the policeman could tell him.

The policeman waited to discharge his tobacco juice into the gutter. "In about a week," he said nonchalantly.

"What's the matter?" asked Beaton, wondering what the joke could be.

"Strike,"* said the policeman. His interest in Beaton's ignorance seemed to overcome his contempt of it. "Knocked off everywhere this morning except Third Avenue and one or two cross-town lines." He spat again and kept his bulk at its incline over the gutter to glance at a group of men on the corner below. They were neatly dressed, and looked like something better than working men, and they had a holiday air of being in their best clothes.

"Some of the strikers?" asked Beaton.

The policeman nodded.

"Any trouble yet?"

"There won't be any trouble till we begin to move the cars," said the policeman.

Beaton felt a sudden turn of his rage toward the men whose action would now force him to walk five blocks and mount the stairs of the Elevated station. "If you'd take out eight or ten of those fellows," he said ferociously, "and set them up against a wall and shoot them, you'd save a great deal of bother."

"I guess we sha'n't have to shoot much," said the policeman, still swinging his locust. "Anyway, we sha'n't begin it. If it comes to a fight, though," he said, with a look at the men under the scooping rim of his helmet, "we can drive the whole six thousand of 'em into the East River without pullin' a trigger."

367

"Are there six thousand in it?"

"About."

"What do the infernal fools expect to live on?"

"The interest of their money, I suppose," said the officer, with a grin of satisfaction in his irony. "It's got to run its course. Then they'll come back with their heads tied up and their tails between their legs, and plead to be taken on again."

"If I was a manager of the roads," said Beaton, thinking of how much he was already inconvenienced by the strike, and obscurely connecting it as one of the series with the wrongs he had suffered at the hands of Mrs. Horn and Mrs. Mandel, "I would see them starve before I'd take them back—every one of them."

"Well," said the policeman impartially, as a man might whom the companies allowed to ride free, but who had made friends with a good many drivers and conductors in the course of his free riding, "I guess that's what the roads would like to do if they could; but the men are too many for them, and there ain't enough other men to take their places."

"No matter," said Beaton severely. "They can bring in men from other places."

"Oh, they'll do that fast enough," said the policeman.

A man came out of the saloon on the corner where the strikers were standing, noisy drunk, and they began, as they would have said, to have some fun with him. The policeman left Beaton, and sauntered slowly down toward the group as if in the natural course of an afternoon ramble. On the other side of the street Beaton could see another officer sauntering up from the block below. Looking up and down the avenue, so silent of its horse-car bells, he saw a policeman at every corner. It was rather impressive.

III

THE strike made a good deal of talk in the office of *Every Other Week*—that is, it made Fulkerson talk a good deal. He congratulated himself that he was not personally incommoded by it, like some of the fellows who lived up-town, and had not everything under one roof, as it were. He enjoyed the excitement of it, and he kept the office-boy running out to buy the extras which the newsmen came crying through the street almost every hour with a lamentable, unintelligible noise. He read not only the latest intelligence of the strike, but the editorial comments on it, which praised the firm attitude of both parties, and the admirable measures taken by the police to preserve order. Fulkerson enjoyed the interviews with the police captains and the leaders of the strike; he equally enjoyed the attempts of the reporters to interview the road managers, which were so graphically detailed, and with such a fine feeling for the right use of scare-heads as to have almost the value of direct expressions from them, though it seemed that they had resolutely refused to speak. He said, at second-hand from the papers, that if the men behaved themselves and respected the rights of property, they would have public sympathy with them every time; but just as soon as they began to interfere with the roads' right to manage their own affairs in their own way, they must be put down with an iron hand; the phrase "iron hand" did Fulkerson almost as much good as if it had never been used before. News began to come of fighting between the police and the strikers when the roads tried to move their cars with men imported from Philadelphia, and then Fulkerson rejoiced at the splendid courage of the police. At the same time he believed what the strikers said, and that the trouble was not made by them, but by gangs of roughs acting without their approval. In this juncture he was relieved by the arrival of the State Board of Arbitration, which took up its quarters, with a great many scare-heads,* at one of the principal hotels, and invited the roads and the strikers to lay the matter in dispute before them; he said that now we should see the working of the greatest piece of social machinery in modern times. But it appeared to work only in the alacrity of the strikers to submit their grievance. The roads were as one road in declaring that there was nothing to arbitrate, and that they were merely asserting their right to manage their own affairs in their own way. One of the presidents was reported to have told a member of the Board, who personally summoned him, to get out and to go about his business. Then, to Fulkerson's extreme disappointment, the august tribunal, acting on behalf of the sovereign people in the interest of peace, declared itself powerless and got out, and would, no doubt, have gone about its business if it had had any. Fulkerson did not know what to say, perhaps because the extras did not; but March laughed at this result.

"It's a good deal like the military manœuvre of the King of France and his forty thousand men. I suppose somebody told him at the top of the hill that there was nothing to arbitrate, and to get out and go about his business, and that was the reason he marched down after he had marched up with all that ceremony. What amuses me is to find that in an affair of this kind the roads have rights and the strikers have rights, but the public has no rights at all. The roads and the strikers are allowed to fight out a private war in our midst—as thoroughly and precisely a private war as any we despise the Middle Ages for having tolerated—as any street war in Florence or Verona—and to fight it out at our pains and expense, and we stand by like sheep, and wait till we get tired. It's a funny attitude for a city of fifteen hundred thousand inhabitants."

"What would you do?" asked Fulkerson, a good deal daunted by this view of the case.

"Do? Nothing. Hasn't the State Board of Arbitration declared itself powerless? We have no hold upon the strikers; and we're so used to being snubbed and disobliged by common carriers that we have forgotten our hold on the roads, and always allow them to manage their own affairs in their own way, quite as if we had nothing to do with them, and they owed us no services in return for their privileges."

"That's a good deal so," said Fulkerson, disordering his hair. "Well, it's nuts for the colonel nowadays. He says if he was boss of this town he would seize the roads on behalf of the people, and man 'em with policemen, and run 'em till the managers had come to terms with the strikers; and he'd do that every time there was a strike."

"Doesn't that rather savour of the paternalism he condemned in Lindau?" asked March.

"I don't know. It savours of horse-sense."

"You are pretty far gone, Fulkerson. I thought you were the most engaged man I ever saw; but I guess you're more father-in-lawed. And before you're married too."

"Well, the colonel's a glorious old fellow, March. I wish he had the power to do that thing, just for the fun of looking on while he waltzed in. He's on the keen jump from morning till night, and he's up late and early to see the row. I'm afraid he'll get shot at some of the fights; he sees them all; *I* can't get any show at them: haven't seen a brickbat shied or a club swung yet. Have you?"

"No, I find I can philosophise the situation about as well from the papers, and that's what I really want to do, I suppose. Besides I'm solemnly pledged by Mrs. March not to go near any sort of crowd, under penalty of having her bring the children and go with me. Her theory is that we must all die together; the children haven't been at school since the strike began. There's no precaution that Mrs. March hasn't used. She watches me whenever I go out, and sees that I start straight for this office."

Fulkerson laughed and said: "Well, it's probably the only thing that's saved your life. Have you seen anything of Beaton lately?"

"No. You don't mean to say *he's* killed!"

"Not if he knows it. But I don't know——. What do you say, March? What's the reason you couldn't get us up a paper on the strike?"

"I knew it would fetch round to *Every Other Week*, somehow."

"No, but seriously. There'll be plenty of newspaper accounts. But you could treat it in the historical spirit—like something that happened several centuries ago; De Foe's Plague of London style. Heigh? What made me think of it was Beaton. If I could get hold of him, you two could go round together and take down its æsthetic aspects. It's a big thing, March, this strike is. I tell you it's imposing to have a private war, as you say, fought out this way, in the heart of New York, and New York not minding it a bit. See? Might take that view of it. With your descriptions and Beaton's sketches—well, it would just be the greatest card! Come! What do you say?"

"Will you undertake to make it right with Mrs. March if I'm killed and she and the children are not killed with me?"

"Well, it would be difficult. I wonder how it would do to get Kendricks to do the literary part?"

"I've no doubt he'd jump at the chance. I've yet to see the form of literature that Kendricks wouldn't lay down his life for."

"Say!" March perceived that Fulkerson was about to vent another inspiration, and smiled patiently. "Look here! What's the reason we couldn't get one of the strikers to write it up for us?"

"Might have a symposium of strikers and presidents," March suggested.

"No; I'm in earnest. They say some of those fellows—especially the foreigners—are educated men. I know one fellow—a Bohemian—that used to edit a Bohemian newspaper here. He could write it out in his kind of Dutch, and we could get Lindau to translate it."

"I guess not," said March dryly.

"Why not? He'd do it for the cause, wouldn't he? Suppose you put it up on him, the next time you see him."

"I don't see Lindau any more," said March. He added, "I guess he's renounced me along with Mr. Dryfoos's money."

"Pshaw! You don't mean he hasn't been round since?"

"He came for a while, but he's left off coming now. I don't

feel particularly gay about it," March said, with some resentment of Fulkerson's grin. "He's left me in debt to him for lessons to the children."

Fulkerson laughed out. "Well, he *is* the greatest old fool! Who'd 'a' thought he'd 'a' been in earnest with those 'brincibles' of his? But I suppose there have to be just such cranks; it takes all kinds to make a world."

"There has to be *one* such crank, it seems," March partially assented. "One's enough for me."

"I reckon this thing is nuts for Lindau, too," said Fulkerson. "Why, it must act like a schooner of beer on him all the while, to see 'gabidal' embarrassed like it is by this strike. It must make old Lindau feel like he was back behind those barricades at Berlin. Well, he's a splendid old fellow; pity he drinks, as I remarked once before."

When March left the office he did not go home so directly as he came, perhaps because Mrs. March's eye was not on him. He was very curious about some aspects of the strike, whose importance, as a great social convulsion, he felt people did not recognise; and with his temperance in everything, he found its negative expressions as significant as its more violent phases. He had promised his wife solemnly that he would keep away from these, and he had a natural inclination to keep his promise; he had no wish to be that peaceful spectator who always gets shot when there is any firing on a mob. He interested himself in the apparent indifference of the mighty city, which kept on about its business as tranquilly as if the private war being fought out in its midst were a vague rumour of Indian troubles on the frontier; and he realised how there might once have been a street feud of forty years in Florence without interfering materially with the industry and prosperity of the city. On Broadway there was a silence where a jangle and clatter of horse-car bells and hoofs had been, but it was not very noticeable; and on the avenues, roofed by the elevated roads, this silence of the surface tracks was not noticeable at all in the roar of the trains overhead. Some of the cross-town cars were beginning to run again; with a policeman on the rear of each; on the Third Avenue line, operated by non-union men, who had not struck, there were two policemen beside the driver of every car, and two beside the conductor, to protect them from the strikers. But there were no strikers in sight, and on Second Avenue they stood quietly about in groups on the corners. While March watched them at a safe distance, a car laden with policemen came down the track, but none of the strikers offered to molest it. In their simple Sunday best, March thought them very quiet, decent-looking people, and he could well believe that they had nothing to do with the riotous outbreaks in other parts of the city. He could hardly believe that there were any such out-breaks; he began more and more to think them mere news-paper exaggerations in the absence of any disturbance, or the disposition to it, that he could see. He walked on to the East River: Avenues A, B, and C presented the same quiet aspect as Second Avenue; groups of men stood on the corners and now and then a police-laden car was brought un-molested down the tracks before them; they looked at it and talked together, and some laughed, but there was no trouble.

March got a cross-town car, and came back to the West side. A policeman, looking very sleepy and tired, lounged on the platform.

"I suppose you'll be glad when this cruel war is over," March suggested, as he got in.

The officer gave him a surly glance and made him no answer.

His behaviour, from a man born to the joking give and take of our life, impressed March. It gave him a fine sense of the ferocity which he had read of the French troops putting on toward the populace just before the *coup d'état*; he began to feel like populace; but he struggled with himself and regained his character of philosophical observer. In this character he remained in the car and let it carry him by the corner where he ought to have got out and gone home, and let it keep on with him to one of the furthermost tracks west-ward, where so much of the fighting was reported to have taken place. But everything on the way was as quiet as on the East side.

Suddenly the car stopped with so quick a turn of the brake that he was half thrown from his seat, and the policeman jumped down from the platform and ran forward.

IV

DRYFOOS sat at breakfast that morning with Mrs. Mandel as usual to pour out his coffee. Conrad had already gone down-town; the two girls lay abed much later than their father breakfasted, and their mother had gradually grown too feeble to come down till lunch. Suddenly Christine appeared at the door. Her face was white to the edges of her lips, and her eyes were blazing.

"Look here, father! Have you been saying anything to Mr. Beaton?"

The old man looked up at her across his coffee-cup through his frowning brows. "No."

Mrs. Mandel dropped her eyes, and the spoon shook in her hand.

"Then what's the reason he don't come here any more?" demanded the girl; and her glance darted from her father to Mrs. Mandel. "Oh, it's *you*, is it? I'd like to know who told *you* to meddle in other people's business?"

"*I* did," said Dryfoos savagely. "*I* told her to ask him what he wanted here, and he said he didn't want anything, and he stopped coming. That's all. I did it myself."

"Oh, you *did*, did you?" said the girl, scarcely less insolently than she had spoken to Mrs. Mandel. "I should like to know what you did it for? I'd like to know what made you think I wasn't able to take care of myself. I just knew somebody had been meddling, but I didn't suppose it was *you*. I can manage my own affairs in my own way, if you please, and I'll thank you after this to leave me to myself in what don't concern you."

"Don't concern me? You impudent jade!" her father began.

Christine advanced from the doorway toward the table; she had her hands closed upon what seemed trinkets, some of which glittered and dangled from them. She said, "Will you go to him and tell him that this meddlesome minx here had no business to say anything about me to him, and you take it all back?"

"No!" shouted the old man. "And if——"

"That's all I want of *you*!" the girl shouted in her turn. "Here are your presents." With both hands she flung the jewels—pins and rings and ear-rings and bracelets—among the breakfast dishes, from which some of them sprang to the floor. She stood a moment to pull the intaglio ring from the finger where Beaton put it a year ago, and dashed that at her father's plate. Then she whirled out of the room, and they heard her running upstairs.

The old man made a start toward her, but he fell back in his chair before she was gone, and with a fierce, grinding movement of his jaws, controlled himself. "Take—take those things up," he gasped to Mrs. Mandel. He seemed unable to rise again from his chair, but when she asked him if he were unwell, he said no, with an air of offence, and got quickly to his feet. He mechanically picked up the intaglio ring from the table while he stood there, and put it on his little finger; his hand was not much bigger than Christine's. "How do you suppose she found it out?" he asked, after a moment.

"She seems to have merely suspected it," said Mrs. Mandel, in a tremor, and with the fright in her eyes which Christine's violence had brought there.

"Well, it don't make any difference. She had to know, somehow, and now she knows." He started toward the door of the library, as if to go into the hall, where his hat and coat always hung.

"Mr. Dryfoos," palpitated Mrs. Mandel, "I can't remain here, after the language your daughter has used to me—I can't let you leave me—I—I'm afraid of her——"

"Lock yourself up, then," said the old man rudely. He added, from the hall before he went out, "I reckon she'll quiet down now."

He took the elevated road. The strike seemed a very far-off thing, though the paper he bought to look up the stock market was full of noisy typography about yesterday's troubles on the surface lines. Among the millions in Wall Street there was some joking and some swearing, but not much thinking about the six thousand men who had taken such chances in their attempt to better their condition. Dryfoos heard nothing of the strike in the lobby of the Stock Exchange, where he spent two or three hours watching a favourite stock of his go up and go down under the betting. By the time the Exchange closed it had risen eight points, and on this and some other investments he was five thousand dollars richer than he had been in the morning. But he had expected to be richer still, and he was by no means satisfied with his luck. All through the excitement of his winning and losing had played the dull, murderous rage he felt toward the child who had defied him, and when the game was over and he started home, his rage mounted into a sort of frenzy; he would teach her, he would break her. He walked a long way without thinking, and then waited for a car. None came, and he hailed a passing coupé.

"What has got all the cars?" he demanded of the driver, who jumped down from his box to open the door for him and get his direction.

"Been away?" asked the driver. "Hasn't been any car along for a week. Strike."

"Oh yes," said Dryfoos. He felt suddenly giddy, and he remained staring at the driver after he had taken his seat.

The man asked, "Where to?"

Dryfoos could not think of his street or number, and he said with uncontrollable fury, "I told you once! Go up to West Eleventh, and drive along slow on the south side; I'll show you the place."

He could not remember the number of *Every Other Week* office, where he suddenly decided to stop before he went home. He wished to see Fulkerson, and ask him something about Beaton: whether he had been about lately, and whether he had dropped any hint of what had happened concerning Christine; Dryfoos believed that Fulkerson was in the fellow's confidence.

There was nobody but Conrad in the counting-room, whither Dryfoos returned after glancing into Fulkerson's empty office. "Where's Fulkerson?" he asked, sitting down with his hat on.

"He went out a few moments ago," said Conrad, glancing at the clock. "I'm afraid he isn't coming back again to-day, if you wanted to see him."

Dryfoos twisted his head sidewise and upward to indicate March's room. "That other fellow out, too?"

"He went just before Mr. Fulkerson," answered Conrad.

"Do you generally knock off here in the middle of the afternoon?" asked the old man.

"No," said Conrad, as patiently as if his father had not been there a score of times, and found the whole staff of *Every Other Week* at work between four and five. "Mr. March, you know, always takes a good deal of his work home with him, and I suppose Mr. Fulkerson went out so early because there isn't much doing to-day. Perhaps it's the strike that makes it dull."

"The strike—yes! It's a pretty piece of business to have everything thrown out because a parcel of lazy hounds want a chance to lay off and get drunk." Dryfoos seemed to think Conrad would make some answer to this, but the young man's mild face merely saddened, and he said nothing. "I've got a coupé out there now that I had to take because I couldn't get a car. If I had my way I'd have a lot of those vagabonds hung. They're waiting to get the city into a snarl, and then rob the houses—pack of dirty, worthless whelps. They ought to call out the militia, and fire into 'em. Clubbing is too good for them." Conrad was still silent, and his father sneered, "But I reckon *you* don't think so."

"I think the strike is useless," said Conrad.

"Oh, you *do*, do you? Comin' to your senses a little. Gettin' tired walkin' so much. I should like to know what your gentlemen over there on the East side think about the strike, anyway."

The young fellow dropped his eyes. "I am not authorised to speak for them."

"Oh, indeed! And perhaps you're not authorised to speak for yourself?"

"Father, you know we don't agree about these things. I'd rather not talk——"

"But I'm goin' to *make* you talk this time!" cried Dryfoos, striking the arm of the chair he sat in with the side of his fist. A maddening thought of Christine came over him. "As long as you eat my bread, you have got to do as I say. I won't have my children telling me what I shall do and sha'n't do, or take on airs of being holier than me. Now, you just speak up! Do you think those loafers are right, or don't you? Come!"

Conrad apparently judged it best to speak. "I think they were very foolish to strike—at this time, when the elevated roads can do the work."

"Oh, at this time, heigh! And I suppose they think over there on the East side that it'd been wise to strike before we got the elevated." Conrad again refused to answer, and his father roared, "What do you think?"

"I think a strike is always bad business. It's war; but sometimes there don't seem any other way for the working men to get justice. They say that sometimes strikes do raise the wages, after a while."

"Those lazy devils were paid enough already," shrieked the old man. "They got two dollars a day. How much do you think they ought to 'a' got? Twenty?"

Conrad hesitated, with a beseeching look at his father. But he decided to answer. "The men say that with partial work, and fines, and other things, they get sometimes a dollar, and sometimes ninety cents a day."

"They lie, and you *know* they lie," said his father, rising and coming toward him. "And what do you think the upshot of it all will be, after they've ruined business for another week, and made people hire hacks, and stolen the money of honest men? How is it going to end?"

"They will have to give in."

"Oh, give in, heigh! And what will you say *then*, I

should like to know? How will you feel about it then? Speak!"

"I shall feel as I do now. I know you don't think that way, and I don't blame you—or anybody. But if I have got to say how I shall feel, why, I shall feel sorry they didn't succeed, for I believe they have a righteous cause, though they go the wrong way to help themselves."

His father came close to him, his eyes blazing, his teeth set. "Do you *dare* to say that to me?"

"Yes. I can't help it. I pity them; my whole heart is with those poor men."

"You impudent puppy!" shouted the old man. He lifted his hand and struck his son in the face. Conrad caught his hand with his own left, and while the blood began to trickle from a wound that Christine's intaglio ring had made in his temple, he looked at him with a kind of grieving wonder, and said, "Father!"

The old man wrenched his fist away, and ran out of the house. He remembered his address now, and he gave it as he plunged into the coupé. He trembled with his evil passion, and glared out of the windows at the passers as he drove home; he only saw Conrad's mild grieving, wondering eyes, and the blood slowly trickling from the wound in his temple.

Conrad went to the neat set-bowl* in Fulkerson's comfortable room, and washed the blood away, and kept bathing the wound with the cold water till it stopped bleeding. The cut was not deep, and he thought he would not put anything on it. After a while he locked up the office, and started out, he hardly knew where. But he walked on, in the direction he had taken, till he found himself in Union Square, on the pavement in front of Brentano's. It seemed to him that he heard some one calling gently to him, "Mr. Dryfoos!"

V

CONRAD looked confusedly around, and the same voice said again, "Mr. Dryfoos!" and he saw that it was a lady speaking to him from a coupé beside the curbing, and then he saw that it was Miss Vance.

She smiled when he gave signs of having discovered her, and came up to the door of her carriage. "I am so glad to meet you. I have been longing to talk to somebody; nobody seems to feel about it as I do. Oh, isn't it horrible? *Must* they fail? I saw cars running on all the lines as I came across; it made me sick at heart. *Must* those brave fellows give in? And everybody seems to hate them so—I can't bear it." Her face was estranged with excitement, and there were traces of tears on it. "You must think me almost crazy to stop you in the street this way; but when I caught sight of you I had to speak. I knew you would sympathise—I knew you would feel as I do. Oh, how can anybody help honouring those poor men for standing by one another as they do? They are risking all they have in the world for the sake of justice! Oh, they are true heroes! They are staking the bread of their wives and children on the dreadful chance they've taken! But no one seems to understand it. No one seems to see that they are willing to suffer more now that other poor men may suffer less hereafter. And those wretched creatures that are coming in to take their places—those traitors."

"We can't blame them for wanting to earn a living, Miss Vance," said Conrad.

"No, no! I don't blame them. Who am I, to do such a thing? It's *we*—people like me, of my class—who make the poor betray one another. But this dreadful fighting—this hideous paper is full of it!" She held up an extra, crumpled with her nervous reading. "Can't something be done to stop it? Don't you think that if some one went among them, and tried to make them see how perfectly hopeless it was to resist the companies, and drive off the new men, he might do some good? I have wanted to go and try it; but I am a woman, and I mustn't! I shouldn't be afraid of the strikers, but I'm afraid of what people would say!" Conrad kept pressing his handkerchief to the cut in his temple, which he thought might be bleeding, and now she noticed this. "Are you hurt, Mr. Dryfoos? You look so pale."

"No, it's nothing—a little scratch I've got."

"Indeed you look pale. Have you a carriage? How will you get home? Will you get in here with me, and let me drive you?"

"No, no," said Conrad, smiling at her excitement. "I'm perfectly well——"

"And you don't think I'm foolish and wicked for stopping you here, and talking in this way? But I know you feel as I do!"

"Yes, I feel as you do. You are right—right in every way— I mustn't keep you—Good-bye." He stepped back to bow, but she put her beautiful hand out of the window, and when he took it she wrung his hand hard.

"Thank you, thank you! You are good and you are just! But no one can do anything. It's useless!"

The type of irreproachable coachman on the box whose respectability had suffered through the strange behaviour of his mistress in this interview, drove quickly off at her signal, and Conrad stood a moment looking after the carriage. His heart was full of joy; it leaped; he thought it would burst. As he turned to walk away it seemed to him as if he mounted upon the air. The trust she had shown him, the praise she had given him; that crush of the hand: he hoped nothing, he formed no idea from it, but it all filled him with love that cast out the pain and shame he had been suffering. He believed that he could never be unhappy any more; the hardness that was in his mind toward his father went out of it; he saw how sorely he had tried him; he grieved that he had done it, but the means, the difference of his feeling about the cause of their quarrel, he was solemnly glad of that since she shared it. He was only sorry for his father. "Poor father!" he said under his breath as he went along. He explained to her about his father in his reverie, and she pitied his father too.

He was walking over toward the West side, aimlessly at first, and then at times with the longing to do something to save those mistaken men from themselves forming itself into a purpose. Was not that what she meant, when she bewailed her woman's helplessness? She must have wished him to try, if he, being a man, could not do something; or if she did not, still he would try, and if she heard of it, she would recall what she had said, and would be glad he had understood her so. Thinking of her pleasure in what he was going to do, he forgot almost what it was; but when he came to a street-car track he remembered it, and looked up and down to see if there were any turbulent gathering of men, whom he might mingle with and help to keep from violence. He saw none anywhere; and then suddenly, as if at the same moment, for in his exalted mood all events had a dream-like simultaneity, he stood at the corner of an avenue, and in the middle of it, a little way off, was a street-car, and around the car a tumult of shouting, cursing, struggling men. The driver was lashing his horses forward, and a policeman was at their heads, with the conductor, pulling them; stones, clubs, brick-bats hailed upon the car, the horses, the men trying to move them. The mob closed upon them in a body, and then a patrol-wagon whirled up from the other side, and a squad of policemen leaped out, and began to club the rioters. Conrad could see how they struck them under the rims of their hats; the blows on their skulls sounded as if they had fallen on stone; the rioters ran in all directions.

One of the officers rushed up toward the corner where Conrad stood, and then he saw at his side a tall old man with a long white beard. He was calling out at the policeman: "Ah, yes! Glup the strikerss—gif it to them! Why don't you co and glup the bresidents that insoalt your lawss, and gick your Boart of Arpidration out-of-toors? Glup the strikerss—they cot no friendts! They cot no money to pribe you, to dreat you!"

The officer whirled his club, and the old man threw his

left arm up to shield his head. Conrad recognised Lindau, and now he saw the empty sleeve dangle in the air, over the stump of his wrist. He heard a shot in that turmoil beside the car, and something seemed to strike him in the breast. He was going to say to the policeman, "Don't strike him! He's an old soldier! You see he has no hand!" but he could not speak, he could not move his tongue. The policeman stood there; he saw his face: it was not bad, nor cruel; it was like the face of a statue, fixed, perdurable; a mere image of irresponsible and involuntary authority. Then Conrad fell forward, pierced through the heart by that shot fired from the car.

March heard the shot as he scrambled out of his car, and at the same moment he saw Lindau drop under the club of the policeman, who left him where he fell, and joined the rest of the squad in pursuing the rioters. The fighting round the car in the avenue ceased; the driver whipped his horses into a gallop, and the place was left empty.

March would have liked to run; he thought how his wife had implored him to keep away from the rioting; but he could not have left Lindau lying there if he would. Something stronger than his will drew him to the spot, and there he saw Conrad dead beside the old man.

VI

In the cares which Mrs. March shared with her husband that night she was supported partly by principle, but mainly by the potent excitement which bewildered Conrad's family and took all reality from what had happened. It was nearly midnight when the Marches left them and walked away toward the elevated station with Fulkerson. Everything had been done, by that time, that could be done; and Fulkerson was not without that satisfaction in the business-like despatch of all the details which attends each step in such an affair, and helps to make death tolerable even to the most sorely stricken. We are creatures of the moment; we live from one little space to another; and only one interest at a time fills these. Fulkerson was cheerful when they got into the street, almost gay; and Mrs. March experienced a rebound from her depression which she felt that she ought not to have experienced. But she condoned the offence a little in herself, because her husband remained so constant in his gravity; and pending the final accounting he must make her for having been where he could be of so much use from the first instant of the calamity, she was tenderly, gratefully proud of all the use he had been to Conrad's family, and especially his miserable old father. To her mind March was the principal actor in the whole affair, and much more important in having seen it than those who had suffered in it. In fact, he had suffered incomparably.

"Well, well," said Fulkerson. "They'll get along now. We've done all *we* could, and there's nothing left but for them to bear it. Of course it's awful, but I guess it'll come out all right. I mean," he added, "they'll pull through now."

"I suppose," said March, "that nothing is put on us that we can't bear. But I should think," he went on musingly, "that when God sees what we poor finite creatures *can* bear, hemmed round with this eternal darkness of death, He must respect us."

"Basil!" said his wife. But in her heart she drew nearer to him for the words she thought she ought to rebuke him for.

"Oh, I know," he said, "we school ourselves to despise human nature. But God did not make us despicable, and I say whatever end He meant us for, He must have some such thrill of joy in our adequacy to fate as a father feels when his son shows himself a man. When I think what we can be if we must, I can't believe the least of us shall finally perish."

"Oh, I reckon the Almighty won't scoop any of us," said Fulkerson, with a piety of his own.

"That poor boy's father!" sighed Mrs. March. "I can't get his face out of my sight. He looked so much worse than death."

"Oh, death doesn't look bad," said March. "It's life that looks so in its presence. Death is peace and pardon. I only wish poor old Lindau was as well out of it as Conrad there."

"Ah, Lindau! He has done harm enough," said Mrs. March. "I hope he will be careful after this."

March did not try to defend Lindau against her theory of the case, which inexorably held him responsible for Conrad's death.

"Lindau's going to come out all right, I guess," said Fulkerson. "He was first-rate when I saw him at the hospital to-night." He whispered in March's ear, at a chance he got in mounting the station stairs: "I didn't like to tell you there at the house, but I guess you'd better know. They had to take Lindau's arm off near the shoulder. Smashed all to pieces by the clubbing."

In the house, vainly rich and foolishly unfit for them, the bereaved family whom the Marches had just left lingered together, and tried to get strength to part for the night. They were all spent with the fatigue that comes from heaven to such misery as theirs, and they sat in a torpor in which each waited for the other to move, to speak.

Christine moved, and Mela spoke. Christine rose and went out of the room without saying a word, and they heard her going upstairs. Then Mela said, "I reckon the rest of us better be goin' too, father. Here, let's git mother started."

She put her arm round her mother, to lift her from her chair, but the old man did not stir, and Mela called Mrs. Mandel from the next room. Between them they raised her to her feet.

"Ain't there anybody a-goin' to set up with it?" she asked, in her hoarse pipe. "It appears like folks hain't got any feelin's in New York. Woon't some o' the neighbours come and offer to set up, without waitin' to be asked?"

"Oh, that's all right, mother. The men'll attend to that. Don't you bother any," Mela coaxed, and she kept her arm round her mother, with tender patience.

"Why, Mely, child! I can't feel right to have it left to hirelun's, so. But there ain't anybody any more to see things done as they ought. If Coonrod was on'y here——"

"Well, mother, you *are* pretty mixed!" said Mela, with a strong tendency to break into her large guffaw. But she checked herself and said, "I know just how you feel, though. It keeps a-comun' and a-goun'; and it's so and it ain't so, all at once; that's the plague of it. Well, father! Ain't you goun' to come?"

"I'm goin' to stay, Mela," said the old man gently, without moving. "Get your mother to bed, that's a good girl."

"You goin' to set up with him, Jacob?" asked the old woman.

"Yes, 'Liz'beth, I'll set up. You go to bed."

"Well, I will, Jacob. And I believe it'll do you good to set up. I wished I could set up with you; but I don't seem to have the stren'th I did when the twins died. I must git my sleep, so's to——I don't like very well to have you broke of your rest, Jacob, but there don't appear to be anybody else. You wouldn't have to do it if Coonrod was here. There I go ag'in! Mercy! mercy!"

"Well, do come along, then, mother," said Mela; and she got her out of the room, with Mrs. Mandel's help, and up the stairs.

From the top the old woman called down: "You tell Coonrod——" She stopped, and he heard her groan out, "My Lord! my Lord!"

He sat, one silence in the dining-room, where they had all lingered together, and in the library beyond the hireling watcher sat, another silence. The time passed, but neither moved, and the last noise in the house ceased, so that they heard each other breathe, and the vague, remote rumour of the city invaded the inner stillness. It grew louder toward morning, and then Dryfoos knew from the watcher's deeper breathing that he had fallen into a doze.

He crept by him to the drawing-room, where his son was; the place was full of the awful sweetness of the flowers that Fulkerson had brought, and that lay above the pulseless breast. The old man turned up a burner in the chandelier, and stood looking on the majestic serenity of the dead face.

He could not move when he saw his wife coming down the

stairway in the hall. She was in her long white flannel bed-gown, and the candle she carried shook with her nervous tremor. He thought she might be walking in her sleep, but she said, quite simply, "I woke up, and I couldn't git to sleep ag'in without comin' to have a look." She stood beside their dead son with him. "Well, he's beautiful, Jacob. He was the prettiest baby! And he was always good, Coonrod was; I'll say that for him. I don't believe he ever give me a minute's care in his whole life. I reckon I liked him about the best of all the childern; but I don't know as I ever done much to show it. But you was always good to him, Jacob; you always done the best for him, ever since he was a little feller. I used to be afraid you'd spoil him sometimes in them days; but I guess you're glad now for every time you didn't cross him. I don't suppose since the twins died you ever hit him a lick." She stooped and peered closer at the face. "Why, Jacob, what's that there by his pore eye?"

Dryfoos saw it too, the wound that he had feared to look for, and that now seemed to redden on his sight. He broke into a low, wavering cry, like a child's in despair, like an animal's in terror, like a soul's in the anguish of remorse.

VII

THE evening after the funeral, while the Marches sat together talking it over, and making approaches, through its shadow, to the question of their own future, which it involved, they were startled by the twitter of the electric bell at their apartment door. It was really not so late as the children's having gone to bed made it seem; but at nine o'clock it was too late for any probable visitor except Fulkerson. It might be he, and March was glad to postpone the impending question to his curiosity concerning the immediate business Fulkerson might have with him. He went himself to the door, and confronted there a lady deeply veiled in black, and attended by a very decorous serving-woman.

"Are you alone, Mr. March—you and Mrs. March?" asked the lady, behind her veil; and as he hesitated, she said, "You don't know me! Miss Vance;" and she threw back her veil, showing her face wan and agitated in the dark folds. "I am very anxious to see you—to speak with you both. May I come in?"

"Why, certainly, Miss Vance," he answered, still too much stupefied by her presence to realise it.

She promptly entered, and saying, with a glance at the hall chair by the door, "My maid can sit here?" followed him to the room where he had left his wife.

Mrs. March showed herself more capable of coping with the fact. She welcomed Miss Vance with the liking they both felt for the girl, and with the sympathy which her troubled face inspired.

"I won't tire you with excuses for coming, Mrs. March," she said, "for it was the only thing left for me to do; and I come at my aunt's suggestion." She added this as if it would help to account for her more on the conventional plane, and she had the instinctive good taste to address herself throughout to Mrs. March as much as possible, though what she had to say was mainly for March. "I don't know how to begin—I don't know how to speak of this terrible affair. But you know what I mean. I feel as if I had lived a whole lifetime since it—happened. I don't want you to pity me for it," she said, forestalling a politeness from Mrs. March. "I'm the last one to be thought of, and you mustn't mind me if I try to make you. I came to find out all of the truth that I can, and when I know just what that is I shall know what to do. I have read the inquest; it's all burnt into my brain. But I don't care for that—for myself: you must let me say such things without minding me. I know that your husband— that Mr. March was there; I read his testimony; and I wished to ask him—to ask him——" She stopped and looked distractedly about. "But what folly! He must have said everything he knew—he had to." Her eyes wandered to him from his wife, on whom she had kept them with instinctive tact.

"I said everything—yes," he replied. "But if you would like to know——"

"Perhaps I had better tell you something first. I had just parted with him—it couldn't have been more than half an hour—in front of Brentano's; he must have gone straight to his death. We were talking, and I—I said, Why didn't some one go among the strikers and plead with them to be peaceable, and keep them from attacking the new men. I knew that he felt as I did about the strikers; that he was their friend. Did you see—do you know anything that makes you think he had been trying to do that?"

"I am sorry," March began, "I didn't see him at all till— till I saw him lying dead."

"My husband was there purely by accident," Mrs. March put in. "I had begged and entreated him not to go near the striking anywhere. And he had just got out of the car, and saw the policeman strike that wretched Lindau—he's been such an anxiety to me ever since we have had anything to do with him here; my husband knew him when he was a boy in the West. Mr. March came home from it all perfectly prostrated; it made us all sick! Nothing so horrible ever came into our lives before. I assure you it was the most shocking experience."

Miss Vance listened to her with that look of patience which those who have seen much of the real suffering of the world— the daily portion of the poor—have for the nervous woes of comfortable people. March hung his head; he knew it would be useless to protest that his share of the calamity was, by comparison, infinitesimally small.

After she had heard Mrs. March to the end even of her repetitions, Miss Vance said, as if it were a mere matter of course that she should have looked the affair up, "Yes, I have seen Mr. Lindau at the hospital——"

"My husband goes every day to see him," Mrs. March interrupted, to give a final touch to the conception of March's magnanimity throughout.

"The poor man seems to have been in the wrong at the time," said Miss Vance.

"I could almost say he had earned the right to be wrong. He's a man of the most generous instincts, and a high ideal of justice, of equity—too high to be considered by a policeman with a club in his hand," said March, with a bold defiance of his wife's different opinion of Lindau. "It's the policeman's business, I suppose, to club the ideal when he finds it inciting a riot."

"Oh, I don't blame Mr. Lindau; I don't blame the policeman; he was as much a mere instrument as his club was. I am only trying to find out how much I am to blame myself. I had no thought of Mr. Dryfoos's going there—of his attempting to talk with the strikers and keep them quiet; I was only thinking, as women do, of what I should try to do if I were a man. But perhaps he understood me to ask him to go—perhaps my words sent him to his death."

She had a sort of calm in her courage to know the worst truth as to her responsibility that forbade any wish to flatter her out of it. "I'm afraid," said March, "that is what can never be known now." After a moment he added, "But why should you wish to know? If he went there as a peacemaker, he died in a good cause, in such a way as he would wish to die, I believe."

"Yes," said the girl; "I have thought of that. But death is awful; we must not think patiently, forgivingly of sending any one to their death in the best cause."

"I fancy life was an awful thing to Conrad Dryfoos," March replied. "He was thwarted and disappointed, without even pleasing the ambition that thwarted and disappointed him. That poor old man, his father, warped him from his simple, lifelong wish to be a minister, and was trying to make a business-man of him. If it will be any consolation to you to know it, Miss Vance, I can assure you that he was very unhappy, and I don't see how he could ever have been happy here."

"It won't," said the girl steadily. "If people are born into this world, it's because they were meant to live in it. It isn't a question of being happy here; no one is happy, in that old selfish way, or can be; but he could have been of great use."

"Perhaps he was of use in dying. Who knows? He may have been trying to silence Lindau."

"Oh, Lindau wasn't worth it!" cried Mrs. March.

Miss Vance looked at her as if she did not quite understand. Then she turned to March. "He might have been unhappy, as we all are; but I know that his life here would have had a higher happiness than we wish for or aim for." The tears began to run silently down her cheeks.

"He looked strangely happy that day when he left me. He had hurt himself somehow, and his face was bleeding from a scratch; he kept his handkerchief up; he was pale, but such a *light* came into his face when he shook hands— ah, I know he went to try and do what I said!" They were all silent, while she dried her eyes and then put her handkerchief back into the pocket from which she had suddenly pulled it, with a series of vivid, young-ladyish gestures, which struck March by their incongruity with the occasion of their talk, and yet by their harmony with the rest of her elegance. "I am sorry, Miss Vance," he began, "that I can't really tell you anything more——"

"You are very kind," she said, controlling herself and rising quickly. "I thank you—thank you both very much." She turned to Mrs. March and shook hands with her and then with him. "I might have known—I did know that there wasn't anything more for you to tell. But at least I've found out from you that there *was* nothing, and now I can begin to bear what I must. How are those poor creatures—his mother and father, his sisters? Some day, I hope, I shall be ashamed to have postponed them to the thought of myself; but I can't pretend to be yet. I could not come to the funeral; I wanted to."

She addressed her question to Mrs. March, who answered: "I can understand. But they were pleased with the flowers you sent; people are, at such times, and they haven't many friends."

"Would you go to see them?" asked the girl. "Would you tell them what I've told you?"

Mrs. March looked at her husband.

"I don't see what good it would do. They wouldn't understand. But if it would relieve you——"

"I'll wait till it isn't a question of self-relief," said the girl. "Good-bye!"

She left them to long debate of the event. At the end Mrs. March said, "She is a strange being; such a mixture of the society girl and the saint."

Her husband answered: "She's the potentiality of several kinds of fanatic. She's very unhappy, and I don't see how she's to be happier about that poor fellow. I shouldn't be surprised if she *did* inspire him to attempt something of that kind."

"Well, you got out of it very well, Basil. I admired the way you managed. I was afraid you'd say something awkward."

"Oh, with a plain line of truth before me, as the only possible thing, I can get on pretty well. When it comes to anything decorative, I'd rather leave it to you, Isabel."

She seemed insensible of his jest. "Of course he was in love with her. *That* was the light that came into his face when he was going to do what he thought she wanted him to do."

"And she—do you think that she was——"

"What an idea! It would have been perfectly grotesque!"

VIII

THEIR affliction brought the Dryfooses into humaner relations with the Marches, who had hitherto regarded them as a necessary evil, as the odious means of their own prosperity. Mrs. March found that the women of the family seemed glad of her coming, and in the sense of her usefulness to them all she began to feel a kindness even for Christine. But she could not help seeing that between the girl and her father there was an unsettled account, somehow, and that it was Christine and not the old man who was holding out. She thought that their sorrow had tended to refine the others. Mela was much more subdued, and except when she abandoned herself to a childish interest in her mourning, she did nothing to shock Mrs. March's taste, or to seem unworthy of her grief. She was very good to her mother, whom the blow had left unchanged, and to her father, whom it had apparently fallen upon with crushing weight. Once, after visiting their house, she described to her husband a little scene between Dryfoos and Mela, when he came home from Wall Street, and the girl met him at the door with a kind of country simpleness, and took his hat and stick, and brought him into the room where Mrs. March sat, looking tired and broken.

She found this look of Dryfoos's pathetic, and dwelt on the sort of stupefaction there was in it; he must have loved his son more than they ever realised. "Yes," said March, "I suspect he did. He's never been about the place since that day; he was always dropping in before, on his way uptown. He seems to go down to Wall Street every day, just as before, but I suppose that's mechanical; he wouldn't know what else to do; I dare say it's best for him. The sanguine Fulkerson is getting a little anxious about the future of *Every Other Week*. Now Conrad's gone, he isn't sure the old man will want to keep on with it, or whether he'll have to look up another Angel. He wants to get married, I imagine, and he can't venture till this point is settled."

"It's a very material point to *us*, too, Basil," said Mrs. March.

"Well, of course. I hadn't overlooked that, you may be sure. One of the things that Fulkerson and I have discussed is a scheme for buying the magazine. Its success is pretty well assured now, and I shouldn't be afraid to put money into it—if I had the money."

"I couldn't let you sell the house in Boston, Basil!"

"And I don't want to. I wish we could go back and live in it, and get the rent too! It would be quite a support. But I suppose if Dryfoos won't keep on, it must come to another Angel. I hope it won't be a literary one, with a fancy for running my department."

"Oh, I guess whoever takes the magazine will be glad enough to keep you!"

"Do you think so? Well, perhaps. But I don't believe Fulkerson would let me stand long between him and an Angel of the right description."

"Well, then, I believe he *would*. And you've never seen anything, Basil, to make you really think that Mr. Fulkerson didn't appreciate you to the utmost."

"I think I came pretty near an undervaluation in that Lindau trouble. I shall always wonder what put a backbone into Fulkerson, just at that crisis. Fulkerson doesn't strike me as the stuff of a moral hero."

"At any rate, he *was* one," said Mrs. March, "and that's quite enough for me."

March did not answer. "What a noble thing life is, anyway! Here I am, well on the way to fifty, after twenty-five years of hard work, looking forward to the potential poorhouse as confidently as I did in youth. We might have saved a little more than we have saved; but the little more wouldn't avail if I were turned out of my place now; and we should have lived sordidly to no purpose. Some one always has you by the throat, unless you have some one else in *your* grip. I wonder if that's the attitude the Almighty intended his respectable creatures to take toward one another! I wonder if he meant our civilisation, the battle we fight in, the game we trick in! I wonder if he considers it final, and if the kingdom of heaven on earth, which we pray for——"

"Have you seen Lindau to-day?" Mrs. March asked.

"You inferred it from the quality of my piety?" March laughed, and then suddenly sobered. "Yes, I saw him. It's going rather hard with him, I'm afraid. The amputation doesn't heal very well; the shock was very great, and he's old. It'll take time. There's so much pain that they have to keep him under opiates, and I don't think he fully knew me. At any rate, I didn't get my piety from him to-day."

"It's horrible! Horrible!" said Mrs. March. "I can't get over it! After losing his hand in the war, to lose his whole arm now in *this* way! It does seem too cruel! Of course he oughtn't to have been there; we can say that. But *you* oughtn't to have been there either, Basil."

"Well, I wasn't exactly advising the police to go and club the railroad presidents."

"Neither was poor Conrad Dryfoos."

"I don't deny it. All that was distinctly the chance of life and death. That belonged to God; and no doubt it was law, though it seems chance. But what I object to is this economic chance-world in which we live, and which we men seem to have created. It ought to be law as inflexible in human affairs as the order of day and night in the physical world, that if a man will work he shall both rest and eat, and shall not be harassed with any question as to how his repose and his provision shall come. Nothing less ideal than this satisfies the reason. But in our state of things no one is secure of this. No one is sure of finding work; no one is sure of not losing it. I may have my work taken away from me at any moment by the caprice, the mood, the indigestion of a man who has not the qualification for knowing whether I do it well or ill. At my time of life—at every time of life—a man ought to feel that if he will keep on doing his duty he shall not suffer in himself or in those who are dear to him, except through natural causes. But no man can feel this as things are now; and so we go on, pushing and pulling, climbing and crawling, thrusting aside and trampling underfoot; lying, cheating, stealing; and when we get to the end, covered with blood and dirt and sin and shame, and look back over the way we've come to a palace of our own, or the poor-house, which is about the only possession we can claim in common with our brother-men, I don't think the retrospect can be pleasing."

"I know, I know!" said his wife. "I think of those things too, Basil. Life isn't what it seems when you look forward to it. But I think people would suffer less, and wouldn't have to work so hard, and could make all reasonable provision for the future, if they were not so greedy and so foolish."

"Oh, without doubt! We can't put it all on the conditions; we must put some of the blame on character. But conditions *make* character; and people are greedy and foolish, and wish to have and to shine, because having and shining are held up to them by civilisation as the chief good of life. We all know they are not the chief good, perhaps not good at all; but if some one ventures to say so, all the rest of us call him a fraud and a crank, and go moiling and toiling on to the palace or the poor-house. We can't help it. If one were less greedy, or less foolish, some one else would have, and would shine at his expense. We don't moil and toil to ourselves alone; the palace or the poor-house is not merely for ourselves, but for our children, whom we've brought up in the superstition that having and shining is the chief good. We dare not teach them otherwise, for fear they may falter in the fight, when it comes their turn; and the children of others will crowd them out of the palace into the poor-house. If we felt sure that honest work shared by all would bring them honest food shared by all, some heroic few of us, who did not wish our children to rise above their fellows—though we could not bear to have them fall below—might trust them with the truth. But we have no such assurance; and so we go on trembling before Dryfooses, and living in gimcrackeries."

"Basil, Basil! I was always willing to live more simply than you. You know I was!"

"I know you always said so, my dear. But how many bell-ratchets and speaking-tubes would you be willing to have at the street door below? I remember that when we were looking for a flat you rejected every building that had a bell-ratchet or a speaking-tube, and would have nothing to do with any that had more than an electric button; you wanted a hall-boy, with electric buttons all over him. I don't blame you. I find such things quite as necessary as you do."

"And do you mean to say, Basil," she asked, abandoning this unprofitable branch of the inquiry, "that you are really uneasy about your place? that you are afraid Mr. Dryfoos may give up being an Angel, and Mr. Fulkerson may play you false?"

"Play me false? Oh, it wouldn't be playing me false. It would be merely looking out for himself, if the new Angel had editorial tastes, and wanted my place. It's what any one would do."

"*You* wouldn't do it, Basil!"

"Wouldn't I? Well, if any one offered me more salary than *Every Other Week* pays—say twice as much—what do you think my duty to my suffering family would be? It's give and take in the business world, Isabel; especially take. But as to being uneasy, I'm not, in the least. I've the spirit of a lion, when it comes to such a chance as that. When I see how readily the sensibilities of the passing stranger can be worked in New York, I think of taking up the *rôle* of that desperate man on Third Avenue, who went along looking for garbage in the gutter to eat. I think I could pick up at least twenty or thirty cents a day by that little game, and maintain my family in the affluence it's been accustomed to."

"*Basil!*" cried his wife. "You don't mean to say that man was an impostor! And I've gone about, ever since, feeling that one such case in a million, the bare possibility of it, was enough to justify all that Lindau said about the rich and the poor!"

March laughed teasingly. "Oh, I don't say he was an impostor. Perhaps he really was hungry; but if he wasn't, what do you think of a civilisation that makes the opportunity of such a fraud? that gives us all such a bad conscience for the need which is, that we weaken to the need that isn't? Suppose that poor fellow wasn't personally founded on fact: nevertheless, he represented the truth; he was the ideal of the suffering which would be less effective if realistically treated. That man is a great comfort to me. He probably rioted for days on that quarter I gave him; made a dinner very likely, or a champagne supper; and if *Every Other Week* wants to get rid of me, I intend to work that racket. You can hang round the corner with Bella, and Tom can come up to me in tears, at stated intervals, and ask me if I've found anything yet. To be sure, we might be arrested and sent up somewhere. But even in that extreme case we should be provided for. Oh no, I'm not afraid of losing my place! I've merely a sort of psychological curiosity to know how men like Dryfoos and Fulkerson will work out the problem before them."

IX

It was a curiosity which Fulkerson himself shared, at least concerning Dryfoos. "I don't know what the old man's going to do," he said to March, the day after the Marches had talked their future over. "Said anything to you yet?"

"No, not a word."

"You're anxious, I suppose, same as I am. Fact is," said Fulkerson, blushing a little, "I can't ask to have a day named till I know where I am in connection with the old man. I can't tell whether I've got to look out for something else, or somebody else. Of course, it's full soon yet."

"Yes," March said, "much sooner than it seems to us. We're so anxious about the future that we don't remember how very recent the past is."

"That's something so. The old man's hardly had time yet to pull himself together. Well, I'm glad you feel that way about it, March. I guess it's more of a blow to him than we realise. He was a good deal bound up in Coonrod, though he didn't always use him very well. Well, I reckon it's apt to happen so oftentimes; curious how cruel love can be. Heigh? We're an awful mixture, March!"

"Yes, that's the marvel and the curse, as Browning says."

"Why, that poor boy himself," pursued Fulkerson, "had streaks of the mule in him that could give odds to Beaton, and he must have tried the old man by the way he would give in to his will, and hold out against his judgment. I don't believe he ever budged a hair's-breadth from his original position about wanting to be a preacher and not wanting to be a business man. Well, of course! *I* don't think business is all in all; but it must have made the old man mad to find that without saying anything, or doing anything to show it, and after seeming to come over to his ground, and really coming, practically, Coonrod was just exactly where he first planted himself, every time."

"Yes, people that have convictions are difficult. Fortunately, they're rare."

"Do you think so? It seems to me that everybody's got convictions. Beaton himself, who hasn't a principle to throw at a dog, has got convictions the size of a barn. They ain't always the same ones, I know, but they're always to the same effect, as far as Beaton's being Number One is concerned. The old man's got convictions—or did have, unless this thing lately has shaken him all up—and he believes that money will do everything. Colonel Woodburn's got convictions that he wouldn't part with for untold millions. Why, March, you got convictions yourself!"

"Have I?" said March. "I don't know what they are."

"Well, neither do I; but I know you were ready to kick the trough over for them when the old man wanted us to bounce Lindau that time."

"Oh yes," said March; he remembered the fact; but he was still uncertain just what the convictions were that he had been so staunch for.

"I suppose we could have got along without you," Fulkerson mused aloud. "It's astonishing how you always *can* get along in this world without the man that is simply indispensable. Makes a fellow realise that he could take a day off now and then without deranging the solar system a great deal. Now here's Coonrod—or rather, he isn't. But that boy managed his part of the schooner so well that I used to tremble when I thought of his getting the better of the old man, and going into a convent or something of that kind; and now here he is, snuffed out in half a second, and I don't believe but what we shall be sailing along just as chipper as usual inside of thirty days. I reckon it will bring the old man to the point when I come to talk with him about who's to be put in Coonrod's place. I don't like very well to start the subject with him; but it's got to be done some time."

"Yes," March admitted. "It's terrible to think how unnecessary even the best and wisest of us is to the purposes of Providence. When I looked at that poor young fellow's face sometimes—so gentle and true and pure—I used to

think the world was appreciably richer for his being in it.
But are we appreciably poorer for his being out of it now?"

"No, I don't reckon we are," said Fulkerson. "And what
a lot of the raw material of all kinds the Almighty must have,
to *waste* us the way he seems to do. Think of throwing away
a precious creature like Coonrod Dryfoos on one chance in
a thousand of getting that old fool of a Lindau out of the way
of being clubbed! For I suppose that was what Coonrod was
up to. Say! Have you been round to see Lindau to-day?"

Something in the tone or the manner of Fulkerson startled
March. "No! I haven't seen him since yesterday."

"Well, I don't know," said Fulkerson. "I guess I saw him
a little while after you did, and that young doctor there
seemed to feel kind of worried about him. Or not worried,
exactly; they can't afford to let such things worry them, I
suppose; but——"

"He's worse?" asked March.

"Oh, he didn't say so. But I just wondered if you'd seen
him to-day."

"I think I'll go now," said March, with a pang at heart.
He had gone every day to see Lindau, but this day he had
thought he would not go, and that was why his heart smote
him. He knew that if he were in Lindau's place Lindau would
never have left his side if he could have helped it. March
tried to believe that the case was the same, as it stood now;
it seemed to him that he was always going to or from the
hospital; he said to himself that it must do Lindau harm to
be visited so much. But he knew that this was not true when
he was met at the door of the ward where Lindau lay by the
young doctor, who had come to feel a personal interest in
March's interest in Lindau.

He smiled without gaiety, and said, "He's just going."

"What! Discharged?"

"Oh no. He has been failing very fast since you saw him
yesterday, and now——" They had been walking softly and
talking softly down the aisle between the long rows of beds.
"Would you care to see him?"

The doctor made a slight gesture toward the white canvas

screen which in such places forms the death-chamber of the poor and friendless. "Come round this way—he won't know you! I've got rather fond of the poor old fellow. He wouldn't have a clergyman—sort of agnostic, isn't he? A good many of these Germans are—but the young lady who's been coming to see him——"

They both stopped. Lindau's grand, patriarchal head, foreshortened to their view, lay white upon the pillow, and his broad white beard flowed out over the sheet, which heaved with those long last breaths. Beside his bed Margaret Vance was kneeling; her veil was thrown back, and her face was lifted; she held clasped between her hands the hand of the dying man; she moved her lips inaudibly.

X

IN spite of the experience of the whole race from time immemorial, when death comes to any one we know we helplessly regard it as an incident of life, which will presently go on as before. Perhaps this is an instinctive perception of the truth that it does go on somewhere; but we have a sense of death as absolutely the end even for earth, only if it relates to some one remote or indifferent to us. March tried to project Lindau to the necessary distance from himself in order to realise the fact in his case, but he could not, though the man with whom his youth had been associated in a poetic friendship had not actually re-entered the region of his affection to the same degree, or in any like degree. The changed conditions forbade that. He had a soreness of heart concerning him; but he could not make sure whether this soreness was grief for his death, or remorse for his own uncandour with him about Dryfoos, or a foreboding of that accounting with his conscience which he knew his wife would now exact of him down to the last minutest particular of their joint and several behaviour toward Lindau ever since they had met him in New York.

He felt something knock against his shoulder, and he

looked up to have his hat struck from his head by a horse's nose. He saw the horse put his foot on the hat, and he reflected, "Now it will always look like an accordion," and he heard the horse's driver address him some sarcasms before he could fully awaken to the situation. He was standing bare-headed in the middle of Fifth Avenue, and blocking the tide of carriages flowing in either direction. Among the faces put out of the carriage windows he saw that of Dryfoos looking from a coupé. The old man knew him, and said, "Jump in here, Mr. March"; and March, who had mechanically picked up his hat, and was thinking, "Now I shall have to tell Isabel about this at once, and she will never trust me on the street again without her," mechanically obeyed. Her confidence in him had been undermined by his being so near Conrad when he was shot; and it went through his mind that he would get Dryfoos to drive him to a hatter's, where he could buy a new hat, and not be obliged to confess his narrow escape to his wife till the incident was some days old and she could bear it better. It quite drove Lindau's death out of his mind for the moment; and when Dryfoos said if he was going home he would drive up to the first cross-street and turn back with him, March said he would be glad if he would take him to a hat-store. The old man put his head out again and told the driver to take them to the Fifth Avenue Hotel. "There's a hat-store around there somewhere, seems to me," he said; and they talked of March's accident as well as they could in the rattle and clatter of the street till they reached the place. March got his hat, passing a joke with the hatter about the impossibility of pressing his old hat over again, and came out to thank Dryfoos and take leave of him.

"If you ain't in any great hurry," the old man said, "I wish you'd get in here a minute. I'd like to have a little talk with you."

"Oh, certainly," said March, and he thought: "It's coming now about what he intends to do with *Every Other Week*. Well, I might as well have all the misery at once and have it over."

Dryfoos called up to his driver, who bent his head down sidewise to listen: "Go over there on Madison Avenue, onto that asphalte, and keep drivin' up and down till I stop you. I can't hear myself think on these pavements," he said to March. But after they got upon the asphalte, and began smoothly rolling over it, he seemed in no haste to begin. At last he said, "I wanted to talk with you about that—that Dutchman that was at my dinner—Lindau," and March's heart gave a jump with wonder whether he could have already heard of Lindau's death; but in an instant he perceived that this was impossible. "I been talkin' with Fulkerson about him, and he says they had to take the balance of his arm off."

March nodded; it seemed to him he could not speak. He could not make out from the close face of the old man anything of his motive. It was set, but set as a piece of broken mechanism is when it has lost the power to relax itself. There was no other history in it of what the man had passed through in his son's death.

"I don't know," Dryfoos resumed, looking aside at the cloth window-strap, which he kept fingering, "as you quite understood what made me the maddest. I didn't tell him I could talk Dutch, because I can't keep it up with a regular German; but my father was Pennsylvany Dutch, and I could understand what he was saying to you about me. I know I had no business to understood it, after I let him think I couldn't; but I did, and I didn't like very well to have a man callin' me a traitor and a tyrant at my own table. Well, I look at it differently now, and I reckon I had better have tried to put up with it; and I would, if I could have known——" He stopped with a quivering lip, and then went on. "Then, again, I didn't like his talkin' that paternalism of his. I always heard it was the worst kind of thing for the country; I was brought up to think the best government was the one that governs the least; and I didn't want to hear that kind of talk from a man that was livin' on my money. I couldn't bear it from him. Or I thought I couldn't before—before——" He stopped again, and gulped. "I reckon now there ain't anything I couldn't bear."

March was moved by the blunt words and the mute stare forward with which they ended. "Mr. Dryfoos, I didn't know that you understood Lindau's German, or I shouldn't have allowed him—he wouldn't have allowed himself—to go on. He wouldn't have knowingly abused his position of guest to censure you, no matter how much he condemned you."

"I don't care for it now," said Dryfoos. "It's all past and gone, as far as I'm concerned; but I wanted you to see that I wasn't tryin' to punish him for his opinions, as you said."

"No; I see now," March assented, though he thought his position still justified. "I wish——"

"I don't know as I understand much about his opinions, anyway; but I ain't ready to say I want the men dependent on me to manage my business for me. I always tried to do the square thing by my hands; and in that particular case out there, I took on all the old hands just as fast as they left their Union. As for the game I came on them, it was dog eat dog, anyway."

March could have laughed to think how far this old man was from even conceiving of Lindau's point of view, and how he was saying the worst of himself that Lindau could have said of him. No one could have characterised the kind of thing he had done more severely than he when he called it dog eat dog.

"There's a great deal to be said on both sides," March began, hoping to lead up through this generality to the fact of Lindau's death; but the old man went on—

"Well, all I wanted him to know is that I wasn't trying to punish him for what he said about things in general. You naturally got that idea, I reckon; but I always went in for lettin' people say what they please and think what they please; it's the only way in a free country."

"I'm afraid, Mr. Dryfoos, that it would make little difference to Lindau now——"

"I don't suppose he bears malice for it," said Dryfoos, "but what I want to do is to have him told so. He could understand just why I didn't want to be called hard names,

and yet I didn't object to his thinkin' whatever he pleased.
I'd like him to know——"

"No one can speak to him, no one can tell him," March
began again, but again Dryfoos prevented him from going on.

"I understand it's a delicate thing; and I'm not askin'
you to do it. What I would really like to do—if you think he
could be prepared for it, some way, and could stand it—
would be to go to him myself, and tell him just what the
trouble was. I'm in hopes, if I done that, he could see how
I felt about it."

A picture of Dryfoos going to the dead Lindau with his
vain regrets presented itself to March, and he tried once
more to make the old man understand. "Mr. Dryfoos," he
said, "Lindau is past all that for ever," and he felt the ghastly
comedy of it when Dryfoos continued, without heeding
him—

"I got a particular reason why I want him to believe it
wasn't his ideas I objected to—them ideas of his about the
government carryin' everything on and givin' work. I don't
understand 'em exactly, but I found a writin'—among—my
son's—things" (he seemed to force the words through his
teeth), "and I reckon he—thought—that way. Kind of a
diary—where he—put down—his thoughts. My son and
me—we differed about a good—many things." His chin
shook, and from time to time he stopped. "I wasn't very
good to him, I reckon; I crossed him where I guess I got no
business to crossed him; but I thought everything of—
Coonrod. He was the best boy, from a baby, that ever was;
just so patient and mild, and done whatever he was told.
I ought to 'a' let him been a preacher! O my son, my son!"

The sobs could not be kept back any longer; they shook
the old man with a violence that made March afraid for him;
but he controlled himself at last with a series of hoarse
sounds like barks. "Well, it's all past and gone! But as I
understand you from what you saw, when—Coonrod—was
—killed, he was tryin' to save that old man from trouble?"

"Yes, yes! It seemed so to me."

"That'll do, then! I want you to have him come back and write for the book when he gets well. I want you to find out and let me know if there's anything I can do for him. I'll feel as if I done it—for my—son. I'll take him into my own house, and do for him there, if you say so, when he gets so he can be moved. I'll wait on him myself. It's what Coonrod 'd do, if he was here. I don't feel any hardness to him because it was him that got Coonrod killed, as you might say, in one sense of the term; but I've tried to think it out, and I feel like I was all the more beholden to him because my son died tryin' to save him. Whatever I do, I'll be doin' it for Coonrod, and that's enough for me." He seemed to have finished, and he turned to March as if to hear what he had to say.

March hesitated. "I'm afraid, Mr. Dryfoos—— Didn't Fulkerson tell you that Lindau was very sick!"

"Yes, of course. But he's all right, he said."

Now it had to come, though the fact had been latterly playing fast and loose with March's consciousness. Something almost made him smile; the willingness he had once felt to give this old man pain; then he consoled himself by thinking that at least he was not obliged to meet Dryfoos's wish to make atonement with the fact that Lindau had renounced him, and would on no terms work for such a man as he, or suffer any kindness from him. In this light Lindau seemed the harder of the two, and March had the momentary force to say: "Mr. Dryfoos—it can't be. Lindau—I have just come from him—is dead."

XI

"How did he take it? How could he bear it? O Basil! I wonder you could have the heart to say it to him. It was cruel!"

"Yes, cruel enough, my dear," March owned to his wife, when they talked the matter over on his return home. He could not wait till the children were out of the way, and afterward neither he nor his wife was sorry that he had

spoken of it before them. The girl cried plentifully for her
old friend who was dead, and said she hated Mr. Dryfoos,
and then was sorry for him, too; and the boy listened to all,
and spoke with a serious sense that pleased his father. "But
as to how he took it," March went on to answer his wife's
question about Dryfoos, "how do any of us take a thing that
hurts? Some of us cry out, and some of us—don't. Dryfoos
drew a kind of long, quivering breath, as a child does when
it grieves—there's something curiously simple and primitive about him—and didn't say anything. After a while he
asked me how he could see the people at the hospital about
the remains; I gave him my card to the young doctor there
that had charge of Lindau. I suppose he was still carrying
forward his plan of reparation in his mind—to the dead for
the dead. But how useless! If he could have taken the living
Lindau home with him, and cared for him all his days, what
would it have profited the gentle creature whose life his
wordly ambition vexed and thwarted here? He might as
well offer a sacrifice at Conrad's grave. Children," said
March, turning to them, "death is an exile that no remorse
and no love can reach. Remember that, and be good to
every one here on earth, for your longing to retrieve any
harshness or unkindness to the dead will be the very ecstasy
of anguish to you. I wonder," he mused, "if one of the
reasons why we're shut up to our ignorance of what is to
be hereafter isn't that we should be still more brutal to
one another here, in the hope of making reparation
somewhere else. Perhaps, if we ever come to obey the
law of love on earth, the mystery of death will be taken
away."

"Well"—the ancestral Puritanism spoke in Mrs. March—
"these two old men have been terribly punished. They have
both been violent and wilful, and they have both been
punished. No one need ever tell *me* there is not a moral
government of the universe!"

March always disliked to hear her talk in this way, which
did both her head and heart injustice. "And Conrad," he
said, "what was *he* punished for?"

"He?" she answered, in an exultation; "he suffered for the sins of others."

"Ah, well, if you put it in that way, yes. That goes on continually. That's another mystery."

He fell to brooding on it, and presently he heard his son saying, "I suppose, papa, that Mr. Lindau died in a bad cause?"

March was startled. He had always been so sorry for Lindau, and admired his courage and generosity so much, that he had never fairly considered this question. "Why, yes," he answered; "he died in the cause of disorder; he was trying to obstruct the law. No doubt there was a wrong there, an inconsistency and an injustice that he felt keenly; but it could not be reached in his way without greater wrong."

"Yes; that's what I thought," said the boy. "And what's the use of our ever fighting about anything in America? I always thought we could vote anything we wanted."

"We can, if we're honest, and don't buy and sell one another's votes," said his father. "And men like Lindau, who renounce the American means as hopeless, and let their love of justice hurry them into sympathy with violence, yes, they are wrong; and poor Lindau did die in a bad cause, as you say, Tom."

"I think Conrad had no business there, or you either, Basil," said his wife.

"Oh, I don't defend myself," said March. "I was there in the cause of literary curiosity and of conjugal disobedience. But Conrad—yes, he had some business there: it was his business to suffer there for the sins of others. Isabel, we can't throw aside that old doctrine of the Atonement yet. The life of Christ, it wasn't only in healing the sick and going about to do good; it was suffering for the sins of others! That's as great a mystery as the mystery of death. Why should there be such a principle in the world? But it's been felt, and more or less dumbly, blindly recognised ever since Calvary. If we love mankind, pity them, we even *wish* to suffer for them. That's what has created the religious orders in all times—the brotherhoods and sisterhoods that belong to our day—as much as to the mediæval past. That's what is driving a girl like Margaret Vance, who has everything that the world can offer her young beauty, on to the work of a Sister of Charity among the poor and the dying."

"Yes, yes!" cried Mrs. March. "How—how did she look there, Basil?" She had her feminine misgivings; she was not sure but the girl was something of a *poseuse*, and enjoyed the picturesqueness, as well as the pain; and she wished to be convinced that it was not so.

"Well," she said, when March had told again the little there was to tell, "I suppose it must be a great trial to a woman like Mrs. Horn to have her niece going that way."

"The way of Christ?" asked March, with a smile.

"Oh, Christ came into the world to teach us how to live rightly in it, too. If we were all to spend our time in hospitals, it would be rather dismal for the homes. But perhaps you don't think the homes are worth minding?" she suggested, with a certain note in her voice that he knew.

He got up and kissed her. "I think the gimcrackeries are." He took the hat he had set down on the parlour table on coming in, and started to put it in the hall, and that made her notice it.

"You've been getting a new hat!"

"Yes," he hesitated; "the old one had got—was decidedly shabby."

"Well, that's right. I don't like you to wear them too long. Did you leave the old one to be pressed?"

"Well, the hatter seemed to think it was hardly worth pressing," said March. He decided that for the present his wife's nerves had quite all they could bear.

XII

It was in a manner grotesque, but to March it was all the more natural for that reason, that Dryfoos should have Lindau's funeral from his house. He knew the old man to be darkly groping, through the payment of these vain honours to the dead, for some atonement to his son, and he imagined him finding in them such comfort as comes from doing all one can, even when all is useless.

No one knew what Lindau's religion was, and in default they had had the Anglican burial service read over him; it seems the refuge of all the homeless dead. Mrs. Dryfoos came down for the ceremony. She understood that it was for Coonrod's sake that his father wished the funeral to be there; and she confided to Mrs. March that she believed Coonrod would have been pleased. "Coonrod was a member of the 'Piscopal Church; and fawther's doin' the whole thing for Coonrod as much as for anybody. He thought the world of Coonrod, fawther did. Mela, she kind of thought it would look queer to have two funerals from the same house, hand-runnin', as you might call it, and one of 'em no relation, either; but when she saw how fawther was bent on it, she give in. Seems as if she was tryin' to make up to fawther for Coonrod as much as she could. Mela always was a good child, but nobody can ever come up to Coonrod."

March felt all the grotesqueness, the hopeless absurdity of Dryfoos's endeavour at atonement in these vain obsequies to the man for whom he believed his son to have died; but the effort had its magnanimity, its pathos, and there was a poetry that appealed to him in this reconciliation through death of men, of ideas, of conditions, that could only have gone warring on in life. He thought, as the priest went on with the solemn liturgy, how all the world must come together in that peace which, struggle and strive as we may, shall claim us at last. He looked at Dryfoos, and wondered whether he would consider these rites a sufficient tribute, or

411

whether there was enough in him to make him realise their futility, except as a mere sign of his wish to retrieve the past. He thought how we never can atone for the wrong we do; the heart we have grieved and wounded cannot kindle with pity for us when once it is stilled; and yet we can put our evil from us with penitence; and somehow, somewhere, the order of loving-kindness, which our passion or our wilfulness has disturbed, will be restored.

Dryfoos, through Fulkerson, had asked all the more intimate contributors of *Every Other Week* to come. Beaton was absent, but Fulkerson had brought Miss Woodburn, with her father, and Mrs. Leighton and Alma, to fill up, as he said. Mela was much present, and was official with the arrangement of the flowers and the welcome of the guests. She imparted this impersonality to her reception of Kendricks, whom Fulkerson met in the outer hall with his party, and whom he presented in whisper to them all. Kendricks smiled under his breath, as it were, and was then mutely and seriously polite to the Leightons. Alma brought a little bunch of flowers, which were lost in the presence of those which Dryfoos had ordered to be unsparingly provided.

It was a kind of satisfaction to Mela to have Miss Vance come, and reassuring as to how it would look to have the funeral there; Miss Vance would certainly not have come unless it had been all right; she had come, and had sent some Easter lilies.

"Ain't Christine coming down?" Fulkerson asked Mela.

"No, she ain't a bit well, and she ain't been, ever since Coonrod died. I don't know what's got over her," said Mela. She added, "Well, I should 'a' thought Mr. Beaton would 'a' made out to 'a' come!"

"Beaton's peculiar," said Fulkerson. "If he thinks you want him he takes a pleasure in not letting you have him."

"Well, goodness knows, *I* don't want him," said the girl.

Christine kept her room, and for the most part kept her bed; but there seemed nothing definitely the matter with her, and she would not let them call a doctor. Her mother said she reckoned she was beginning to feel the spring weather, that always perfectly pulled a body down in New York; and Mela said if being as cross as two sticks was any sign of spring-fever, Christine had it bad. She was faithfully kind to her, and submitted to all her humours, but she recompensed herself by the freest criticism of Christine when not in actual attendance on her. Christine would not suffer Mrs. Mandel to approach her, and she had with her father a sullen submission which was not resignation. For her, apparently, Conrad had not died, or had died in vain.

"Pshaw!" said Mela, one morning when she came to breakfast, "I reckon if we was to send up an old card of Mr. Beaton's she'd rattle downstairs fast enough. If she's sick, she's love-sick. It makes *me* sick to *see* her."

Mela was talking to Mrs. Mandel, but her father looked up from his plate, and listened. Mela went on: "*I* don't know what's made the fellow quit comun'. But he *was* an aggravatun' thing, and no more dependable than water. It's just like Mr. Fulkerson said, if he thinks you want him he'll take a pleasure in not lettun' you have him. I reckon that's what's the matter with Christine. I believe in my heart the girl'll die if she don't git him."

Mela went on to eat her breakfast with her own good appetite. She now always came down to keep her father company, as she said, and she did her best to cheer and comfort him. At least she kept the talk going, and she had it nearly all to herself, for Mrs. Mandel was now merely staying on provisionally, and in the absence of any regrets or excuses from Christine, was looking ruefully forward to the moment when she must leave even this ungentle home for the chances of the ruder world outside.

The old man said nothing at table, but when Mela went up to see if she could do anything for Christine, he asked Mrs. Mandel again about all the facts of her last interview with Beaton.

She gave them as fully as she could remember them, and the old man made no comment on them. But he went out directly after, and at *Every Other Week* office he climbed the stairs to Fulkerson's room, and asked for Beaton's address. No one yet had taken charge of Conrad's work, and Fulkerson was running the thing himself, as he said, till he could talk with Dryfoos about it. The old man would not look into the empty room where he had last seen his son alive; he turned his face away, and hurried by the door.

XIII

THE course of public events carried Beaton's private affairs beyond the reach of his simple first intention to renounce his connection with *Every Other Week*. In fact this was not perhaps so simple as it seemed, and long before it could be put in effect it appeared still simpler to do nothing about the matter: to remain passive and leave the initiative to Dryfoos, to maintain the dignity of unconsciousness and let recognition of any change in the situation come from those who had caused the change. After all, it was rather absurd to propose making a purely personal question the pivot on which his relations with *Every Other Week* turned. He took a hint from March's position and decided that he did not know Dryfoos in these relations; he only knew Fulkerson, who had certainly had nothing to do with Mrs. Mandel's asking his intentions. As he reflected upon this he became less eager to look Fulkerson up and make the magazine a partner of his own sufferings. This was the soberer mood to which Beaton trusted that night even before he slept, and he awoke fully confirmed in it. As he examined the offence done him in the cold light of day, he perceived that it had not come either from Mrs. Mandel, who was visibly the faltering and unwilling instrument of it, or from Christine, who was altogether ignorant of it, but from Dryfoos, whom he could not hurt by giving up his place. He could only punish Fulkerson by that, and Fulkerson was innocent. Justice and interest alike dictated the passive course to which Beaton inclined; and he reflected that he might safely leave the punishment of Dryfoos to Christine, who would find out what had happened, and would be able to take care of herself in any encounter of tempers with her father.

Beaton did not go to the office during the week that followed upon this conclusion; but they were used there to these sudden absences of his, and as his work for the time was in train, nothing was made of his staying away, except the sarcastic comment which the thought of him was apt to excite in the literary department. He no longer came so much to the Leightons, and Fulkerson was in no state of mind to miss any one there except Miss Woodburn, whom he never missed. Beaton was left, then, unmolestedly awaiting the return of destiny, when he read in the morning paper, over his coffee at Maroni's, the deeply scare-headed story of Conrad's death and the clubbing of Lindau. He probably cared as little for either of them as any man that ever saw them; but he felt a shock if not a pang at Conrad's fate, so out of keeping with his life and character. He did not know what to do; and he did nothing. He was not asked to the funeral, but he had not expected that, and when Fulkerson brought him notice that Lindau was also to be buried from Dryfoos's house, it was without his usual sullen vindictiveness that he kept away. In his sort, and as much as a man could who was necessarily so much taken up with himself, he was sorry for Conrad's father; Beaton had a peculiar tenderness for his own father, and he imagined how his father would feel if it were he who had been killed in Conrad's place, as it might very well have been; he sympathised with himself in view of the possibility; and for once they were mistaken who thought him indifferent and merely brutal in his failure to appear at Lindau's obsequies.

He would really have gone if he had known how to reconcile his presence in that house with the terms of his effective banishment from it; and he was rather forgivingly finding himself wronged in the situation, when Dryfoos knocked at the studio door the morning after Lindau's funeral. Beaton roared out "Come in!" as he always did to a knock if he had not a model: if he had a model he set the door slightly ajar, and with his palette on his thumb frowned at his visitor, and told him he could not come in. Dryfoos fumbled about for the knob in the dim passageway outside, and Beaton, who had experience of people's difficulties with it, suddenly jerked the door open. The two men stood confronted, and at first sight of each other their quiescent dislike revived. Each would have been willing to turn away from the other, but that was not possible. Beaton snorted some sort of inarticulate salutation, which Dryfoos did not try to return; he asked if he could see him alone for a minute or two, and Beaton bade him come in, and swept some paint-blotched rags from the chair which he told him to take. He noticed, as the old man sank tremulously into it, that his movement was like that of his own father, and also that he looked very much like Christine. Dryfoos folded his hands tremulously on the top of his horn-handled stick, and he was rather finely haggard, with the dark hollows round his black eyes, and the fall of the muscles on either side of his chin. He had forgotten to take his soft, wide-brimmed hat off; and Beaton felt a desire to sketch him just as he sat.

Dryfoos suddenly pulled himself together from the dreary absence into which he fell at first. "Young man," he began, "may be I've come here on a fool's errand," and Beaton rather fancied that beginning.

But it embarrassed him a little, and he said, with a shy glance aside, "I don't know what you mean."

"I reckon," Dryfoos answered quietly, "you got your notion, though. I set that woman on to speak to you the way she done. But if there was anything wrong in the way she spoke; or if you didn't feel like she had any right to question you up as if we suspected you of anything mean, I want you to say so."

Beaton said nothing and the old man went on.

"I ain't very well up in the ways of the world, and I don't pretend to be. All I want is to be fair and square with everybody. I've made mistakes, though, in my time——" He stopped, and Beaton was not proof against the misery of his face, which was twisted as with some strong physical ache. "I don't know as I want to make any more, if I can help it.

I don't know but what you had a right to keep on comin',
and if you had I want you to say so. Don't you be afraid but
what I'll take it in the right way. I don't want to take advantage of anybody; and I don't ask you to say any more than
that."

Beaton did not find the humiliation of the man who had
humiliated him so sweet as he could have fancied it might be.
He knew how it had come about, and that it was an effect of
love for his child; it did not matter by what ungracious means
she had brought him to know that he loved her better than
his own will, that his wish for her happiness was stronger
than his pride; it was enough that he was now somehow
brought to give proof of it. Beaton could not be aware of all
that dark coil of circumstance through which Dryfoos's
present action evolved itself; the worst of this was buried in
the secret of the old man's heart, a worm of perpetual torment. What was apparent to another was that he was broken
by the sorrow that had fallen upon him, and it was this that
Beaton respected and pitied in his impulse to be frank and
kind in his answer.

"No, I had no right to keep coming to your house in the
way I did, unless—unless I meant more than I ever said."
Beaton added, "I don't say that what you did was usual—in
this country, at any rate; but I can't say you were wrong.
Since you speak to me about the matter, it's only fair to myself to say that a good deal goes on in life without much
thinking of consequences. That's the way I excuse myself."

"And you say Mrs. Mandel done right?" asked Dryfoos,
as if he wished simply to be assured of a point of etiquette.

"Yes, she did right. I've nothing to complain of."

"That's all I wanted to know," said Dryfoos; but apparently he had not finished, and he did not go, though the
silence that Beaton now kept gave him a chance to do so.
He began a series of questions which had no relation to the
matter in hand, though they were strictly personal to
Beaton. "What countryman are you?" he asked, after a
moment.

"What countryman?" Beaton frowned back at him.

"Yes, are you an American by birth?"

"Yes; I was born in Syracuse."

"Protestant?"

"My father is a Scotch Seceder."*

"What business is your father in?"

Beaton faltered and blushed; then he answered, "He's in the monument business, as he calls it. He's a tombstone cutter." Now that he was launched, Beaton saw no reason for not declaring, "My father's always been a poor man, and worked with his own hands for his living." He had too slight esteem socially for Dryfoos to conceal a fact from him that he might have wished to blink with others.

"Well, that's right," said Dryfoos. "I used to farm it myself. I've got a good pile of money together, now. At first it didn't come easy; but now it's got started it pours in and *pours* in; it seems like there was no end to it. I've got well on to three million; but it couldn't keep me from losin' my son. It can't buy me back a minute of his life; not all the money in the world can do it!"

He grieved this out as if to himself rather than to Beaton, who scarcely ventured to say, "I know—I am very sorry——"

"How did you come," Dryfoos interrupted, "to take up paintin'?"

"Well, I don't know," said Beaton, a little scornfully. "You don't take a thing of that kind up, I fancy. I always wanted to paint."

"Father try to stop you?"

"No. It wouldn't have been of any use. Why——"

"My son, he wanted to be a preacher, and I did stop *him*— or I thought I did. But I reckon he was a preacher, all the same, every minute of his life. As you say, it ain't any use to try to stop a thing like that. I reckon if a child has got any particular bent, it was given to it; and it's goin' against the grain, it's goin' against the law, to try to bend it some other way. There's lots of good business men Mr. Beaton, twenty of 'em to every good preacher."

"I imagine more than twenty," said Beaton, amused and

touched through his curiosity as to what the old man was driving at by the quaint simplicity of his speculations.

"Father ever come to the city?"

"No; he never has the time; and my mother's an invalid."

"Oh! Brothers and sisters?"

"Yes; we're a large family."

"I lost two little fellers—twins," said Dryfoos sadly. "But we hain't ever had but just the five. Ever take portraits?"

"Yes," said Beaton, meeting this zigzag in the queries as seriously as the rest. "I don't think I am good at it."

Dryfoos got to his feet. "I wished you'd paint a likeness of my son. You've seen him plenty of times. We won't fight about the price, don't you be afraid of that."

Beaton was astonished, and in a mistaken way he was disgusted. He saw that Dryfoos was trying to undo Mrs. Mandel's work practically, and get him to come again to his house; that he now conceived of the offence given him as condoned, and wished to restore the former situation. He knew that he was attempting this for Christine's sake, but he was not the man to imagine that Dryfoos was trying not only to tolerate him but to like him; and in fact Dryfoos was not wholly conscious himself of this end. What they both understood was that Dryfoos was endeavouring to get at Beaton through Conrad's memory; but with one this was its dedication to a purpose of self-sacrifice and with the other a vulgar and shameless use of it.

"I couldn't do it," said Beaton. "I couldn't think of attempting it."

"Why not?" Dryfoos persisted. "We got some photographs of him; he didn't like to sit very well; but his mother got him to; and you know how he looked."

"I couldn't do it—I couldn't. I can't even consider it. I'm very sorry. I would, if it were possible. But it isn't possible."

"I reckon if you see the photographs once——"

"It isn't that, Mr. Dryfoos. But I'm not in the way of that kind of thing any more."

"I'd give any price you've a mind to name——"

"Oh, it isn't the money!" cried Beaton, beginning to lose control of himself.

The old man did not notice him. He sat with his head fallen forward, and his chin resting on his folded hands. Thinking of the portrait, he saw Conrad's face before him, reproachful, astonished, but all gentle as it looked when Conrad caught his hand that day after he struck him; he heard him say, "Father!" and the sweat gathered on his forehead. "O my God!" he groaned. "No; there ain't anything I can do now."

Beaton did not know whether Dryfoos was speaking to him or not. He started toward him: "Are you ill?"

"No, there ain't anything the matter," said the old man. "But I guess I'll lay down on your settee a minute." He tottered with Beaton's help to the æsthetic couch covered with a tiger-skin, on which Beaton had once thought of painting a Cleopatra; but he could never get the right model. As the old man stretched himself out on it, pale and suffering, he did not look much like a Cleopatra, but Beaton was struck with his effectiveness, and the likeness between him and his daughter; she would make a very good Cleopatra in some ways. All the time, while these thoughts passed through his mind, he was afraid Dryfoos would die. The old man fetched his breath in gasps, which presently smoothed and lengthened into his normal breathing. Beaton got him a glass of wine, and after tasting it he sat up.

"You've got to excuse me," he said, getting back to his characteristic grimness with surprising suddenness, when once he began to recover himself. "I've been through a good deal lately; and sometimes it ketches me round the heart like a pain."

In his life of selfish immunity from grief Beaton could not understand this experience that poignant sorrow brings; he said to himself that Dryfoos was going the way of *angina pectoris*; as he began shuffling off the tiger-skin he said, "Had you better get up? Wouldn't you like me to call a doctor?"

"I'm all right, young man." Dryfoos took his hat and

stick from him, but he made for the door so uncertainly that
Beaton put his hand under his elbow and helped him out,
and down the stairs, to his coupé.

"Hadn't you better let me drive home with you?" he
asked.

"What?" said Dryfoos suspiciously.

Beaton repeated his question.

"I guess I'm able to go home alone," said Dryfoos, in a
surly tone, and he put his head out of the window and called
up "Home!" to the driver, who immediately started off, and
left Beaton standing beside the curb-stone.

XIV

BEATON wasted the rest of the day in the emotions and
speculations which Dryfoos's call inspired. It was not that
they continuously occupied him, but they broke up the
train of other thoughts, and spoiled him for work; a very
little spoiled Beaton for work; he required just the right
mood for work. He comprehended perfectly well that
Dryfoos had made him that extraordinary embassy because
he wished him to renew his visits, and he easily imagined
the means that had brought him to this pass. From what he
knew of that girl he did not envy her father his meeting with
her when he must tell her his mission had failed. But had it
failed? When Beaton came to ask himself this question, he
could only perceive that he and Dryfoos had failed to find any
ground of sympathy, and had parted in the same dislike with
which they had met. But as to any other failure, it was
certainly tacit, and it still rested with him to give it effect.
He could go back to Dryfoos's house, as freely as before,
and it was clear that he was very much desired to come back.
But if he went back it was also clear that he must go back
with intentions more explicit than before, and now he had
to ask himself just how much or how little he had meant by
going there. His liking for Christine had certainly not
increased, but the charm, on the other hand, of holding a

leopardess in leash had not yet palled upon him. In his life
of inconstancies, it was a pleasure to rest upon something
fixed, and the man who had no control over himself liked
logically enough to feel his control of some one else. The
fact cannot otherwise be put in terms, and the attraction
which Christine Dryfoos had for him, apart from this,
escapes from all terms, as anything purely and merely
passional must. He had seen from the first that she was a cat,
and so far as youth forecasts such things, he felt that she
would be a shrew. But he had a perverse sense of her beauty,
and he knew a sort of life in which her power to molest him
with her temper could be reduced to the smallest proportions, and even broken to pieces. Then the consciousness
of her money entered. It was evident that the old man had
mentioned his millions in the way of a hint to him of what he
might reasonably expect if he would turn and be his son-in-
law. Beaton did not put it to himself in those words; and in
fact his cogitations were not in words at all. It was the play
of cognitions, of sensations, formlessly tending to the effect
which can only be very clumsily interpreted in language.
But when he got to this point in them, Beaton rose to
magnanimity and in a flash of dramatic reverie disposed of
a part of Dryfoos's riches in placing his father and mother,
and his brothers and sisters, beyond all pecuniary anxiety
for ever. He had no shame, no scruple in this, for he had
been a pensioner upon others ever since a Syracusan
amateur of the arts had detected his talent, and given him
the money to go and study abroad. Beaton had always considered the money a loan, to be repaid out of his future
success; but he now never dreamt of repaying it; as the man
was rich, he had even a contempt for the notion of repaying
him; but this did not prevent him from feeling very keenly
the hardships he put his father to in borrowing money from
him, though he never repaid his father, either. In this reverie
he saw himself sacrificed in marriage with Christine Dryfoos,
in a kind of admiring self-pity, and he was melted by the
spectacle of the dignity with which he suffered all the lifelong trials ensuing from his unselfishness. The fancy that

422

Alma Leighton came bitterly to regret him, contributed to soothe and flatter him, and he was not sure that Margaret Vance did not suffer a like loss in him.

There had been times when, as he believed, that beautiful girl's high thoughts had tended toward him; there had been looks, gestures, even words, that had this effect to him, or even seemed to have had it; and Beaton saw that he might easily construe Mrs. Horn's confidential appeal to him to get Margaret interested in art again as something by no means necessarily offensive, even though it had been made to him as to a master of illusion. If Mrs. Horn had to choose between him and the life of good works to which her niece was visibly abandoning herself, Beaton could not doubt which she would choose; the only question was how real the danger of a life of good works was.

As he thought of these two girls, one so charming and the other so divine, it became indefinitely difficult to renounce them for Christine Dryfoos, with her sultry temper, and her earthbound ideals. Life had been so flattering to Beaton hitherto that he could not believe them both finally indifferent; and if they were not indifferent, perhaps he did not wish either of them to be very definite. What he really longed for was their sympathy; for a man who is able to walk round quite ruthlessly on the feelings of others often has very tender feelings of his own, easily lacerated, and eagerly responsive to the caresses of compassion. In this frame Beaton determined to go that afternoon, though it was not Mrs. Horn's day, and call upon her in the hope of possibly seeing Miss Vance alone. As he continued in it, he took this for a sign, and actually went. It did not fall out at once as he wished, but he got Mrs. Horn to talking again about her niece, and Mrs. Horn again regretted that nothing could be done by the fine arts to reclaim Margaret from good works.

"Is she at home? Will you let me see her?" asked Beaton with something of the scientific interest of a physician inquiring for a patient whose symptoms have been rehearsed to him. He had not asked for her before.

"Yes, certainly," said Mrs. Horn, and she went herself to

call Margaret, and she did not return with her. The girl
entered with the gentle grace peculiar to her; and Beaton,
bent as he was on his own consolation, could not help being
struck with the spiritual exaltation of her look. At sight of her,
the vague hope he had never quite relinquished, that they
might be something more than æsthetic friends, died in his
heart. She wore black, as she often did; but in spite of its
fashion her dress received a nun-like effect from the pensive
absence of her face. "Decidedly," thought Beaton, "she is
far gone in good works."

But he rose, all the same, to meet her on the old level, and
he began at once to talk to her of the subject he had been discussing with her aunt. He said frankly that they both felt
she had unjustifiably turned her back upon possibilities
which she ought not to neglect.

"You know very well," she answered, "that I couldn't do
anything in that way worth the time I should waste on it.
Don't talk of it, please. I suppose my aunt has been asking
you to say this, but it's no use. I'm sorry it's no use, she
wishes it so much; but I'm not sorry otherwise. You can find
the pleasure at least of doing good work in it; but I couldn't
find anything in it but a barren amusement. Mr. Wetmore
is right; for me, it's like enjoying an opera, or a ball."

"That's one of Wetmore's phrases. He'd sacrifice anything to them."

She put aside the whole subject with a look. "You were
not at Mr. Dryfoos's the other day. Have you seen them, any
of them, lately?"

"I haven't been there for some time, no," said Beaton
evasively. But he thought if he was to get on to anything, he
had better be candid. "Mr. Dryfoos was at my studio this
morning. He's got a queer notion. He wants me to paint his
son's portrait."

She started. "And will you——"

"No, I couldn't do such a thing. It isn't in my way. I told
him so. His son had a beautiful face—an antique profile; a
sort of early Christian type; but I'm too much of a pagan for
that sort of thing."

"Yes."

"Yes," Beaton continued, not quite liking her assent, after he had invited it. He had his pride in being a pagan, a Greek, but it failed him in her presence, now; and he wished that she had protested he was none. "He was a singular creature; a kind of survival; an exile in our time and place. I don't know: we don't quite expect a saint to be rustic; but with all his goodness Conrad Dryfoos was a country person. If he were not dying for a cause you could imagine him milking." Beaton intended a contempt that came from the bitterness of having himself once milked the family cow.

His contempt did not reach Miss Vance. "He died for a cause," she said. "The holiest."

"Of labour?"

"Of peace. He was there to persuade the strikers to be quiet and go home."

"I haven't been quite sure," said Beaton. "But in any case he had no business there. The police were on hand to do the persuading."

"I can't let you talk so!" cried the girl. "It's shocking! Oh, I know it's the way people talk, and the worst is that in the sight of the world it's the right way. But the blessing on the peace-makers is not for the policemen with their clubs."

Beaton saw that she was nervous; he made his reflection that she was altogether too far gone in good works for the fine arts to reach her; he began to think how he could turn her primitive Christianity to the account of his modern heathenism. He had no deeper design than to get flattered back into his own favour far enough to find courage for some sort of decisive step. In his heart he was trying to will whether he should or should not go back to Dryfoos's house. It could not be from the caprice that had formerly taken him; it must be from a definite purpose; again he realised this. "Of course; you are right," he said. "I wish I could have answered that old man differently. I fancy he was bound up in his son, though he quarrelled with him, and crossed him. But I couldn't do it; it wasn't possible." He said to himself that if she said, "No," now, he would be ruled by her

425

agreement with him; and if she disagreed with him, he would be ruled still by the chance, and would go no more to the Dryfoos's. He found himself embarrassed to the point of blushing when she said nothing, and left him, as it were, on his own hands. "I should like to have given him that comfort; I fancy he hasn't much comfort in life; but there seems no comfort in me." He dropped his head in a fit attitude for compassion; but she poured no pity upon it.

"There is no comfort for us in ourselves," she said. "It's hard to get outside; but there's only despair within. When we think we have done something for others, by some great effort, we find it's all for our own vanity."

"Yes," said Beaton. "If I could paint pictures for righteousness' sake, I should have been glad to do Conrad Dryfoos for his father. I felt sorry for him. Did the rest seem very much broken up? You saw them all?"

"Not all. Miss Dryfoos was ill, her sister said. It's hard to tell how much people suffer. His mother seemed bewildered. The younger sister is a simple creature; she looks like him; I think she must have something of his spirit."

"Not much spirit of any kind, I imagine," said Beaton. "But she's amiably material. Did they say Miss Dryfoos was seriously ill?"

"No. I supposed she might be prostrated by her brother's death."

"Does she seem that kind of person to you, Miss Vance?" asked Beaton.

"I don't know. I haven't tried to see so much of them as I might, the past winter. I was not sure about her when I met her; I've never seen much of people, except in my own set, and the—very poor. I have been afraid I didn't understand her. She may have a kind of pride that would not let her do herself justice."

Beaton felt the unconscious dislike in the endeavour of praise. "Then she seems to you like a person whose life— its trials, its chances—would make more of than she is now?"

"I didn't say that. I can't judge of her at all; but where we don't know, don't you think we ought to imagine the best?"

"Oh yes," said Beaton. "I didn't know but what I once said of them might have prejudiced you against them. I have accused myself of it." He always took a tone of conscientiousness, of self-censure, in talking with Miss Vance; he could not help it.

"Oh no. And I never allowed myself to form any judgment of her. She is very pretty, don't you think, in a kind of way?"

"Very."

"She has a beautiful brunette colouring: that floury white and the delicate pink in it. Her eyes are beautiful."

"She's graceful, too," said Beaton. "I've tried her in colour; but I didn't make it out."

"I've wondered sometimes," said Miss Vance, "whether that elusive quality you find in some people you try to paint doesn't characterise them all through. Miss Dryfoos might be ever so much finer and better than we would find out in the society way that seems the only way."

"Perhaps," said Beaton gloomily; and he went away profoundly discouraged by this last analysis of Christine's character. The angelic imperviousness of Miss Vance to properties of which his own wickedness was so keenly aware in Christine might have made him laugh, if it had not been such a serious affair with him. As it was, he smiled to think how very differently Alma Leighton would have judged her from Miss Vance's premises. He liked that clear vision of Alma's even when it pierced his own disguises. Yes, that was the light he had let die out, and it might have shone upon his path through life. Beaton never felt so poignantly the disadvantage of having on any given occasion been wanting to his own interests through his self-love as in this. He had no one to blame but himself for what had happened, but he blamed Alma for what might happen in the future because she shut out the way of retrieval and return. When he thought of the attitude she had taken toward him, it seemed incredible, and he was always longing to give her a final chance to reverse her final judgment. It appeared to him that the time had come for this now, if ever.

XV

WHILE we are still young we feel a kind of pride, a sort of
fierce pleasure, in any important experience, such as we have
read of or heard of in the lives of others, no matter how painful. It was this pride, this pleasure, which Beaton now felt
in realising that the toils of fate were about him, that between him and a future of which Christine Dryfoos must be
the genius, there was nothing but the will, the mood, the
fancy of a girl who had not given him the hope that either
could ever again be in his favour. He had nothing to trust to,
in fact, but his knowledge that he had once had them all;
she did not deny that; but neither did she conceal that he
had flung away his power over them, and she had told him
that they never could be his again. A man knows that he can
love and wholly cease to love, not once merely, but several
times; he recognises the fact in regard to himself, both
theoretically and practically; but in regard to women he
cherishes the superstition of the romances that love is once
for all, and for ever. It was because Beaton would not believe
that Alma Leighton, being a woman, could put him out of
her heart after suffering him to steal into it, that he now
hoped anything from her, and she had been so explicit when
they last spoke of that affair that he did not hope much. He
said to himself that he was going to cast himself on her
mercy, to take whatever chance of life, love, and work there
was in her having the smallest pity on him. If she would have
none, then there was but one thing he could do: marry
Christine and go abroad. He did not see how he could bring
this alternative to bear upon Alma; even if she knew what
he would do in case of a final rejection, he had grounds for
fearing she would not care; but he brought it to bear upon
himself, and it nerved him to a desperate courage. He could
hardly wait for evening to come, before he went to see her;
when it came, it seemed to have come too soon. He had
wrought himself thoroughly into the conviction that he was

in earnest, and that everything depended upon her answer to him, but it was not till he found himself in her presence, and alone with her, that he realised the truth of his conviction. Then the influences of her grace, her gaiety, her arch beauty, above all, her good sense, penetrated his soul like a subtle intoxication, and he said to himself that he was right; he could not live without her; these attributes of hers were what he needed to win him, to cheer him, to charm him, to guide him. He longed so to please her, to ingratiate himself with her, that he attempted to be light like her in his talk, but lapsed into abysmal absences, and gloomy recesses of introspection.

"What are you laughing at?" he asked, suddenly starting from one of these.

"What you are thinking of."

"It's nothing to laugh at. Do you know what it is I'm thinking of?"

"Don't tell, if it's dreadful."

"Oh, I dare say you wouldn't think it's dreadful," he said, with bitterness. "It's simply the case of a man who has made a fool of himself, and sees no help of retrieval in himself."

"Can any one else help a man unmake a fool of himself?" she asked, with a smile.

"Yes. In a case like this."

"Dear me! This is very interesting."

She did not ask him what the case was, but he was launched now, and he pressed on. "I am the man who has made a fool of himself——"

"Oh!"

"And you can help me out if you will. Alma, I wish you could see me as I really am."

"Do you, Mr. Beaton? Perhaps I do."

"No; you don't. You formulated me in a certain way, and you won't allow for the change that takes place in every one. *You* have changed; why shouldn't I?"

"Has this to do with your having made a fool of yourself?"

"Yes."

"Oh! Then I don't see how you have changed."

429

She laughed, and he too, ruefully. "You're cruel. Not but what I deserve your mockery. But the change was not from the capacity of making a fool of myself. I suppose I shall always do that more or less—unless you help me. Alma! Why can't you have a little compassion? You know that I must always love you."

"Nothing makes me doubt that like your saying it, Mr. Beaton. But now you've broken your word——"

"You are to blame for that. You knew I couldn't keep it!"

"Yes, I'm to blame. I was wrong to let you come—after that. And so I forgive you for speaking to me in that way again. But it's perfectly impossible and perfectly useless for *me* to hear you any more on that subject; and so—good-bye!"

She rose, and he perforce with her. "And do you mean it?" he asked. "For ever?"

"For ever. This is truly the last time I will ever see you if I can help it. Oh, I feel sorry enough for you!" she said, with a glance at his face. "I do believe you are in earnest. But it's too late now. Don't let us talk about it any more! But we shall, if we meet, and so——"

"And so good-bye! Well I've nothing more to say, and I might as well say that. I think you've been very good to me. It seems to me as if you had been—shall I say it?—trying to give me a chance. Is that so?"

She dropped her eyes and did not answer.

"You found it was no use! Well, I thank you for trying. It's curious to think that I once had your trust, your regard, and now I haven't it. You don't mind my remembering that I had? It'll be some little consolation, and I believe it will be some help. I know I can't retrieve the past now. It *is* too late. It seems too preposterous--perfectly lurid—that I could have been going to tell you what a tangle I'd got myself in, and to ask you to help untangle me. I must choke in the infernal coil, but I'd like to have the sweetness of your pity in it—whatever it is.'

She put out her hand. "Whatever it is, I do pity you; I said that."

"Thank you." He kissed the hand she gave him and went. He had gone on some such terms before; was it now for the last time? She believed it was. She felt in herself a satiety, a fatigue, in which his good looks, his invented airs and poses, his real trouble, were all alike repulsive. She did not acquit herself of the wrong of having let him think she might yet have liked him as she once did; but she had been honestly willing to see whether she could. It had mystified her to find that when they first met in New York, after their summer in St. Barnaby, she cared nothing for him; she had expected to punish him for his neglect, and then fancy him as before, but she did not. More and more she saw him selfish and mean, weak-willed, narrow-minded and hard-hearted; and aimless, with all his talent. She admired his talent in proportion as she learned more of artists, and perceived how uncommon it was; but she said to herself that if she were going to devote herself to art, she would do it at first hand. She was perfectly serene and happy in her final rejection of Beaton; he had worn out not only her fancy, but her sympathy too.

This was what her mother would not believe when Alma reported the interview to her; she would not believe it was the last time they should meet; death itself can hardly convince us that it is the last time of anything, of everything between ourselves and the dead. "Well, Alma," she said, "I hope you'll never regret what you've done."

"You may be sure I shall not regret it. If ever I'm low-spirited about anything, I'll think of giving Mr. Beaton his freedom, and that will cheer me up."

"And don't you expect to get married? Do you intend to be an old maid?" demanded her mother, in the bonds of the superstition women have so long been under to the effect that every woman must wish to get married, if for no other purpose than to avoid being an old maid.

"Well, mamma," said Alma, "I intend being a young one for a few years yet; and then I'll see. If I meet the right person, all well and good; if not, not. But I shall pick and chose, as a man does; I won't merely be picked and chosen."

"You can't help yourself; you may be very glad if you *are* picked and chosen."

"What nonsense, mamma! A girl can get any man she wants, if she goes about it the right way. And when *my* 'fated fairy prince'* comes along, I shall just simply make furious love to him, and grab him. Of course, I shall make a decent pretence of talking in my sleep. I believe it's done that way, more than half the time. The fated fairy prince wouldn't *see* the princess in nine cases out of ten if she didn't say something; he would go mooning along after the maids of honour."

Mrs. Leighton tried to look unspeakable horror; but she broke down and laughed. "Well, you are a strange girl, Alma."

"I don't know about that. But one thing I *do* know, mamma, and that is that Prince Beaton isn't the F. F. P. for *me*. How strange *you* are, mamma! Don't you think it would be perfectly *disgusting* to accept a person you didn't care for, and let him go on and love you and marry you? It's sickening."

"Why, certainly, Alma. It's only because I know you *did* care for him once——"

"And now I don't. And he *didn't* care for me once, and now he does. And so we're quits."

"If I could believe——"

"You had better brace up and try, mamma; for as Mr. Fulkerson says, it's as sure as guns. From the crown of his head to the sole of his foot, he's loathsome to me; and he keeps getting loathsomer. Ugh! Good night!"

XVI

"WELL, I guess she's given him the grand bounce, at last," said Fulkerson to March in one of their moments of confidence at the office. "That's Mad's inference from appearances—and disappearances; and some little hints from Ma Leighton."

"Well, I don't know that I have any criticisms to offer," said March. "It may be bad for Beaton, but it's a very good thing for Miss Leighton. Upon the whole, I believe I congratulate her."

"Well, I don't know. I always kind of hoped it would turn out the other way. You know I always had a sneaking fondness for the fellow."

"Miss Leighton seems not to have had."

"It's a pity she hadn't. I tell you, March, it ain't so easy for a girl to get married, here in the East, that she can afford to despise any chance."

"Isn't that rather a low view of it?"

"It's a common-sense view. Beaton has the making of a first-rate fellow in him. He's the raw material of a great artist and a good citizen. All he wants is somebody to take him in hand and keep him from makin' an ass of himself and kickin' over the traces generally, and ridin' two or three horses bareback at once."

"It seems a simple problem, though the metaphor is rather complicated," said March. "But talk to Miss Leighton about it. *I* haven't given Beaton the grand bounce."

He began to turn over the manuscripts on his table, and Fulkerson went away. But March found himself thinking of the matter from time to time during the day, and he spoke to his wife about it when he went home. She surprised him by taking Fulkerson's view of it.

"Yes, it's a pity she couldn't have made up her mind to have him. It's better for a woman to be married."

"I thought Paul only went so far*as to say it was well. But what would become of Miss Leighton's artistic career if she married?"

"Oh, her artistic career!" said Mrs. March, with matronly contempt of it.

"But look here!" cried her husband. "Suppose she doesn't like him?"

"How can a girl of that age tell whether she likes any one or not?"

"It seems to me *you* were able to tell at that age, Isabel.

433

But let's examine this thing. (This thing! I believe Fulkerson is characterising my whole parlance, as well as your morals.) Why shouldn't we rejoice as much at a non-marriage as a marriage? When we consider the enormous risks people take in linking their lives together, after not half so much thought as goes to an ordinary horse trade, I think we ought to be glad whenever they don't do it. I believe that this popular demand for the matrimony of others comes from our novel-reading. We get to thinking that there is no other happiness or good fortune in life except marriage; and it's offered in fiction as the highest premium for virtue, courage, beauty, learning, and saving human life. We all know it isn't. We know that in reality marriage is dog cheap, and anybody can have it for the asking—if he keeps asking enough people. By-and-by some fellow will wake up and see that a first-class story can be written from the anti-marriage point of view; and he'll begin with an engaged couple, and devote his novel to *dis*engaging them, and rendering them separately happy ever after in the *dénoûment*. It will make his everlasting fortune."

"Why don't *you* write it, Basil?" she asked. "It's a delightful idea. You could do it splendidly."

He became fascinated with the notion. He developed it in detail; but at the end he sighed and said, "With this *Every Other Week* work on my hands, of course I can't attempt a novel. But perhaps I sha'n't have it long."

She was instantly anxious to know what he meant, and the novel and Miss Leighton's affair were both dropped out of their thoughts. "What do you mean? Has Mr. Fulkerson said anything yet?"

"Not a word. He knows no more about it than I do. Dryfoos hasn't spoken, and we're both afraid to ask him. Of course, I *couldn't* ask him."

"No."

"But it's pretty uncomfortable, to be kept hanging by the gills, so, as Fulkerson says."

"Yes, we don't know what to do."

March and Fulkerson said the same to each other; and

Fulkerson said that if the old man pulled out, he did not know what would happen. He had no capital to carry the thing on, and the very fact that the old man had pulled out would damage it so that it would be hard to get anybody else to put it. In the meantime Fulkerson was running Conrad's office-work, when he ought to be looking after the outside interests of the thing; and he could not see the day when he could get married.

"I don't know which it's worse for, March: you or me. I don't know, under the circumstances, whether it's worse to have a family or to want to have one. Of course—of course! We can't hurry the old man up. It wouldn't be decent, and it would be dangerous. We got to wait."

He almost decided to draw upon Dryfoos for some money; he did not need any, but he said may be the demand would act as a hint upon him. One day, about a week after Alma's final rejection of Beaton, Dryfoos came into March's office. Fulkerson was out, but the old man seemed not to have tried to see him.

He put his hat on the floor by his chair, after he sat down, and looked at March a while with his old eyes, which had the vitreous glitter of old eyes stimulated to sleeplessness. Then he said, abruptly, "Mr. March, how would you like to take this thing off my hands?"

"I don't understand, exactly," March began; but of course he understood that Dryfoos was offeiing to let him have *Every Other Week*, on some terms or other, and his heart leaped with hope.

The old man knew he understood, and so he did not explain. He said, "I am going to Europe, to take my family there. The doctor thinks it might do my wife some good; and I ain't very well myself, and my girls both want to go; and so we're goin'. If you want to take this thing off my hands, I reckon I can let you have it in 'most any shape you say. You're all settled here in New York, and I don't suppose you want to break up, much, at your time of life, and I've been thinkin' whether you wouldn't like to take the thing."

The word, which Dryfoos had now used three times, made March at last think of Fulkerson; he had been filled too full of himself to think of any one else till he had mastered the notion of such wonderful good fortune as seemed about falling to him. But now, he did think of Fulkerson, and with some shame and confusion; for he remembered how when Dryfoos had last approached him there on the business of his connection with *Every Other Week*, he had been very haughty with him, and told him that he did not know him in this connection. He blushed to find how far his thoughts had now run without encountering this obstacle of etiquette.

"Have you spoken to Mr. Fulkerson?" he asked.

"No, I hain't. It ain't a question of management. It's a question of buying and selling. I offer the thing to you first. I reckon Fulkerson couldn't get on very well without you."

March saw the real difference in the two cases, and he was glad to see it, because he could act more decisively if not hampered by an obligation to consistency. "I am gratified, of course, Mr. Dryfoos; extremely gratified; and it's no use pretending that I shouldn't be happy beyond bounds to get possession of *Every Other Week*. But I don't feel quite free to talk about it apart from Mr. Fulkerson."

"Oh, all right!" said the old man, with quick offence.

March hastened to say, "I feel bound to Mr. Fulkerson in every way. He got me to come here, and I couldn't even *seem* to act without him."

He put it questioningly, and the old man answered, "Yes, I can see that. When'll he be in? I can wait." But he looked impatient.

"Very soon, now," said March, looking at his watch. "He was only to be gone a moment," and while he went on to talk with Dryfoos, he wondered why the old man should have come first to speak with him, and whether it was from some obscure wish to make him reparation for displeasures in the past, or from a distrust or dislike of Fulkerson. Whichever light he looked at it in, it was flattering.

"Do you think of going abroad soon?" he asked.

"What? Yes—I don't know—I reckon. We got our

passage engaged. It's on one of them French boats. We're goin' to Paris."

"Oh! That will be interesting to the young ladies."

"Yes. I reckon we're goin' for them. 'Tain't likely my wife and me would want to pull up stakes at our age," said the old man sorrowfully.

"But you may find it do you good, Mr. Dryfoos," said March, with a kindness that was real, mixed as it was with the selfish interest he now had in the intended voyage.

"Well, may be, may be," sighed the old man; and he dropped his head forward. "It don't make a great deal of difference what we do or we don't do, for the few years left."

"I hope Mrs. Dryfoos is as well as usual," said March, finding the ground delicate and difficult.

"Middlin', middlin'," said the old man. "My daughter Christine, she ain't very well."

"Oh," said March. It was quite impossible for him to affect a more explicit interest in the fact. He and Dryfoos sat silent for a few moments, and he was vainly casting about in his thought for something else which would tide them over the interval till Fulkerson came, when he heard his step on the stairs.

"Hello, hello!" he said. "Meeting of the clans!" It was always a meeting of the clans, with Fulkerson, or a field day, or an extra session, or a regular conclave, whenever he saw people of any common interest together. "Hain't seen you here for a good while, Mr. Dryfoos. *Did* think some of running away with *Every Other Week* one while, but couldn't seem to work March up to the point."

He gave Dryfoos his hand, and pushed aside the papers on the corner of March's desk, and sat down there, and went on briskly with the nonsense he could always talk, while he was waiting for another to develop any matter of business; he told March afterward that he scented business in the air as soon as he came into the room where he and Dryfoos were sitting.

Dryfoos seemed determined to leave the word to March, who said, after an inquiring look at him, "Mr. Dryfoos

437

has been proposing to let us have *Every Other Week*, Fulkerson."

"Well, that's good; that suits yours truly; March & Fulkerson, publishers and proprietors, won't pretend it don't, *if* the terms are all right."

"The terms," said the old man, "are whatever you want 'em. I haven't got any more use for the concern——" He gulped, and stopped; they knew what he was thinking of, and they looked down in pity. He went on. "I woon't put any more money in it; but what I've put in a'ready, can stay; and you can pay me four per cent."

He got upon his feet; and March and Fulkerson stood, too.

"Well, I call that pretty white," said Fulkerson. "It's a bargain as far as I'm concerned. I suppose you'll want to talk it over with your wife, March?"

"Yes; I shall," said March. "I can see that it's a great chance; but I want to talk it over with my wife."

"Well, that's right," said the old man. "Let me hear from you to-morrow."

He went out, and Fulkerson began to dance round the room. He caught March about his stalwart girth and tried to make him waltz; the office-boy came to the door, and looked on with approval.

"Come, come, you idiot!" said March, rooting himself to the carpet.

"It's just throwing the thing into our mouths," said Fulkerson. "The wedding will be this day week. No cards! Teedle-lumpty diddle! Teedle-lumpty-dee! What do you suppose he *means* by it, March?" he asked, bringing himself soberly up, of a sudden. "What is his little game? Or is he crazy? It don't seem like the Dryfoos or *my* previous acquaintance."

—"I suppose," March suggested, "that he's got money enough, so that he don't care for this——"

"Pshaw! You're a poet! Don't you know that the more money that kind of man has got, the more he cares for money? It's some fancy of his—like having Lindau's funeral at his house——— By jings, March, I believe *you're* his fancy!"

"Oh, now! Don't *you* be a poet, Fulkerson!"

"I do! He seemed to take a kind of shine to you from the day you wouldn't turn off old Lindau; he did indeed. It kind of shook him up. It made him think you had something *in* you. He was deceived by appearances. Look here! I'm going round to see Mrs. March with you, and explain the thing to her. I *know* Mrs. March! She wouldn't believe you knew what you were going in for. She has a great respect for your mind, but she don't think you've got any sense. Heigh?"

"All right," said March, glad of the notion; and it was really a comfort to have Fulkerson with him to develop all the points; and it was delightful to see how clearly and quickly she seized them; it made March proud of her. She was only angry that they had lost any time in coming to submit so plain a case to her. Mr. Dryfoos might change his mind in the night, and then everything would be lost. They must go to him instantly, and tell him that they accepted; they must telegraph him.

"Might as well send a district messenger; he'd get there next week," said Fulkerson. "No, no! It'll all keep till to-morrow, and be the better for it. If he's got this fancy for March, as I say, he ain't agoing to change it in a single night. People don't change their fancies for March in a lifetime. Heigh?"

When Fulkerson turned up very early at the office next morning, as March did, he was less strenuous about Dryfoos's fancy for March. It was as if Miss Woodburn might have blown cold upon that theory, as something unjust to his own merit, for which she would naturally be more jealous than he.

March told him, what he had forgotten to tell him the day before, though he had been trying, all through their excited talk, to get it in, that the Dryfooses were going abroad.

"Oh, ho!" cried Fulkerson. "*That's* the milk in the cocoa-nut, is it? Well, I *thought* there must be something."

But this fact had not changed Mrs. March at all in her

conviction that it was Mr. Dryfoos's fancy for her husband which had moved him to make him this extraordinary offer, and she reminded him that it had first been made to him, without regard to Fulkerson. "And perhaps," she went on, "Mr. Dryfoos has been changed—softened; and doesn't find money all in all any more. He's had enough to change him, poor old man!"

"Does anything from without change us?" her husband mused aloud. "We're brought up to think so by the novelists, who really have the charge of people's thinking, nowadays. But I doubt it, especially if the thing outside is some great event, something cataclysmal, like this tremendous sorrow of Dryfoos's."

"Then what *is* it that changes us?" demanded his wife, almost angry with him for his heresy.

"Well, it won't do to say, the Holy Spirit indwelling. That would sound like cant at this day. But the old fellows that used to say that had some glimpses of the truth. They knew that it is the still, small voice that the soul heeds, not the deafening blasts of doom. I suppose I should have to say that we didn't change at all. We develop. There's the making of several characters in each of us; we *are* each several characters, and sometimes this character has the lead in us, and sometimes that. From what Fulkerson has told me of Dryfoos I should say he had always had the potentiality of better things in him than he has ever been yet; and perhaps the time has come for the good to have its chance. The growth in one direction has stopped; it's begun in another; that's all. The man hasn't been changed by his son's death; it stunned, it benumbed him; but it couldn't change him. It was an event, like any other, and it had to happen as much as his being born. It was forecast from the beginning of time, and was as entirely an effect of his coming into the world——"

"Basil! Basil!" cried his wife. "This is fatalism!"

"Then you think," he said, "that a sparrow falls to the ground* *without* the will of God?" and he laughed provokingly. But he went on more soberly. "*I* don't know what it all means, Isabel, though I believe it means good. What did Christ himself say? That if one rose from the dead it would not avail.* And yet we are always looking for the miraculous! I believe that unhappy old man truly grieves for his son, whom he treated cruelly without the final intention of cruelty, for he loved him and wished to be proud of him; but I don't think his death has changed him, any more than the smallest event in the chain of events remotely working through his nature from the beginning. But why do you think he's changed at all? Because he offers to sell me *Every Other Week* on easy terms? He says himself that he has no further use for the thing; and he knows perfectly well that he couldn't get his money out of it now, without an enormous shrinkage. He couldn't appear at this late day as the owner, and sell it to anybody but Fulkerson and me for a fifth of what it's cost him. He *can* sell it to us for *all* it's cost him; and four per cent. is no bad interest on his money till we can pay it back. It's a good thing for us; but we have to ask whether Dryfoos has done us the good, or whether it's the blessing of Heaven. If it's merely the blessing of Heaven, I don't propose being grateful for it."

March laughed again, and his wife said, "It's disgusting."

"It's business," he assented. "Business is business; but I don't say it isn't disgusting. Lindau had a low opinion of it."

"I think that with all his faults Mr. Dryfoos is a better man than Lindau," she proclaimed.

"Well, he's certainly able to offer us a better thing in *Every Other Week*," said March.

She knew he was enamoured of the literary finish of his cynicism, and that at heart he was as humbly and truly grateful as she was for the good fortune opening to them.

XVII

BEATON was at his best when he parted for the last time with Alma Leighton, for he saw then that what had happened to him was the necessary consequence of what he had been, if not what he had done. Afterward he lost this clear vision; he began to deny the fact; he drew upon his knowledge of life, and in arguing himself into a different frame of mind he alleged the case of different people who had done and been much worse things than he, and yet no such disagreeable consequence had befallen them. Then he saw that it was all the work of blind chance, and he said to himself that it was this that made him desperate, and willing to call evil his good, and to take his own wherever he could find it. There was a great deal that was literary and factitious and tawdry in the mood in which he went to see Christine Dryfoos, the night when the Marches sat talking their prospects over; and nothing that was decided in his purpose. He knew what the drift of his mind was, but he had always preferred to let chance determine his events, and now since chance had played him such an ill turn with Alma, he left it the whole responsibility. Not in terms, but in effect, this was his thought as he walked on uptown to pay the first of the visits which Dryfoos had practically invited him to resume. He had an insolent satisfaction in having delayed it so long; if he was going back he was going back on his own conditions, and these were to be as hard and humiliating as he could make them. But this intention again was inchoate, floating, the stuff of an intention, rather than intention; an expression of temperament chiefly.

He had been expected before that. Christine had got out of Mela that her father had been at Beaton's studio, and then she had gone at the old man and got from him every smallest fact of the interview there. She had flung back in his teeth the good-will toward herself with which he had gone to Beaton. She was furious with shame and resentment; she told him he had made bad worse, that he had made a fool of himself to no end; she spared neither his age, nor his grief-broken spirit, in which his will could not rise against hers. She filled the house with her rage, screaming it out upon him; but when her fury was once spent, she began to have some hopes from what her father had done. She no longer kept her bed; every evening she dressed herself in the dress Beaton admired the most, and sat up till a certain hour to receive him. She had fixed a day in her own mind before which, if he came, she would forgive him all he had made her suffer: the mortification, the suspense, the despair. Beyond this, she had the purpose of making her father go to Europe; she felt that she could no longer live in America, with the double disgrace that had been put upon her.

Beaton rang, and while the servant was coming the insolent caprice seized him to ask for the young ladies instead of the old man, as he had supposed of course he should do. The maid who answered the bell, in the place of the reluctant Irishman of other days, had all his hesitation in admitting that the young ladies were at home.

He found Mela in the drawing-room. At sight of him she looked scared; but she seemed to be reassured by his calm. He asked if he was not to have the pleasure of seeing Miss Dryfoos too; and Mela said she reckoned the girl had gone upstairs to tell her. Mela was in black, and Beaton noted how well the solid sable became her rich, red blond beauty; he wondered what the effect would be with Christine.

But she, when she appeared, was not in mourning. He fancied that she wore the lustrous black silk, with the breadths of white Venetian lace about the neck which he had praised, because he praised it. Her cheeks burned with a Jacqueminot*crimson, what should be white in her face was chalky white. She carried a plumed ostrich fan, black and soft, and after giving him her hand, sat down and waved it to and fro slowly, as he remembered her doing the night they first met. She had no ideas, except such as related intimately to herself, and she had no gabble, like Mela; and she let him talk. It was past the day when she had promised

443

herself she would forgive him; but as he talked on she felt all her passion for him revived, and the conflict of desires, the desire to hate, the desire to love, made a dizzying whirl in her brain. She looked at him, half doubting whether he was really there or not. He had never looked so handsome, with his dreamy eyes floating under his heavy overhanging hair, and his pointed brown beard defined against his lustrous shirt-front. His mellowly modulated, mysterious voice lulled her; when Mela made an errand out of the room, and Beaton crossed to her and sat down by her she shivered.

"Are you cold?" he asked, and she felt the cruel mockery and exultant consciousness of power in his tone, as perhaps a wild thing feels captivity in the voice of its keeper. But now, she said she would still forgive him if he asked her.

Mela came back, and the talk fell again to the former level; but Beaton had not said anything that really meant what she wished, and she saw that he intended to say nothing. Her heart began to burn like a fire in her breast.

"You been tellun' him about our goun' to Europe?" Mela asked.

"No," said Christine briefly, and looking at the fan spread out on her lap.

Beaton asked when; and then he rose, and said if it was so soon, he supposed he should not see them again, unless he saw them in Paris; he might very likely run over, during the summer. He said to himself that he had given it a fair trial with Christine, and he could not make it go.

Christine rose, with a kind of gasp, and mechanically followed him to the door of the drawing-room; Mela came too; and while he was putting on his overcoat, she gurgled and bubbed in good-humour with all the world. Christine stood looking at him, and thinking how handsomer still he was in his overcoat; and that fire burned fiercer in her. She felt him more than life to her and knew him lost, and the frenzy that makes a woman kill the man she loves, or fling vitriol to destroy the beauty she cannot have for all hers, possessed her lawless soul. He gave his hand to Mela, and said, in his wind-harp stop, "Good-bye."

As he put out his hand to Christine, she pushed it aside with a scream of rage; she flashed at him, and with both hands made a feline pass at the face he bent toward her. He sprang back, and after an instant of stupefaction he pulled open the door behind him, and ran out into the street.

"Well, Christine Dryfoos!" said Mela. "Spag at him like a wild-cat!"*

"I don't care," Christine shrieked. "I'll tear his eyes out!" She flew upstairs to her own room, and left the burden of the explanation to Mela, who did it justice.

Beaton found himself, he did not know how, in his studio, reeking with perspiration and breathless. He must almost have run. He struck a match with a shaking hand, and looked at his face in the glass. He expected to see the bleeding marks of her nails on his cheeks, but he could see nothing. He grovelled inwardly; it was all so low and coarse and vulgar; it was all so just and apt to his deserts.

There was a pistol among the dusty bric-à-brac on the mantel which he had kept loaded to fire at a cat in the area. He took it and sat looking into the muzzle, wishing it might go off by accident and kill him. It slipped through his hand and struck the floor, and there was a report; he sprang into the air, feeling that he had been shot. But he found himself still alive, with only a burning line along his cheek, such as one of Christine's finger-nails might have left.

He laughed with cynical recognition of the fact that he had got his punishment in the right way, and that his case was not to be dignified into tragedy.

XVIII

THE Marches, with Fulkerson, went to see the Dryfooses off on the French steamer. There was no longer any business obligation on them to be civil, and there was greater kindness for that reason in the attention they offered. *Every Other Week* had been made over to the joint ownership of March and Fulkerson, and the details arranged with a hardness on

Dryfoos's side which certainly left Mrs. March with a sense of his incomplete regeneration. Yet when she saw him there on the steamer, she pitied him; he looked wearied and bewildered; even his wife, with her twitching head, and her prophecies of evil, croaked hoarsely out, while she clung to Mrs. March's hand where they sat together till the leave-takers were ordered ashore, was less pathetic. Mela was looking after both of them, and trying to cheer them, in a joyful excitement. "I tell 'em it's goun' to add ten years to both their lives," she said. "The voyage'll do their healths good; and then, we're gittun' away from that miser'ble pack o' servants that was eatun' us up, there in New York. I *hate* the place!" she said, as if they had already left it. "Yes, Mrs. Mandel's goun', too,' she added, following the direction of Mrs. March's eyes where they noted Mrs. Mandel speaking to Christine on the other side of the cabin. "Her and Christine had a kind of a spat, and she was goun' to leave, but here only the other day, Christine offered to make it up with her, and now they're as thick as thieves. Well, I reckon we couldn't very well 'a' got along without her. She's about the only one that speaks French in *this* family."

Mrs. March's eyes still dwelt upon Christine's face; it was full of a furtive wildness. She seemed to be keeping a watch to prevent herself from looking as if she were looking for some one. "Do you know," Mrs. March said to her husband as they jingled along homeward in the Christopher Street bob-tail car, "I thought she was in love with that detestable Mr. Beaton of yours, at one time, and that he was amusing himself with her."

"I can bear a good deal, Isabel," said March, "but I *wish* you wouldn't attribute Beaton to me. He's the invention of that Mr. Fulkerson of yours."

"Well, at any rate, I hope, now, you'll both get rid of him, in the reforms you're going to carry out."

These reforms were for a greater economy in the management of *Every Other Week*; but in their very nature they could not include the suppression of Beaton. He had always shown himself capable and loyal to the interests of the magazine, and both the new owners were glad to keep him. He was glad to stay, though he made a gruff pretence of indifference, when they came to look over the new arrangement with him. In his heart he knew that he was a fraud; but at least he could say to himself with truth that he had not now the shame of taking Dryfoos's money.

March and Fulkerson retrenched at several points where it had seemed indispensable to spend, as long as they were not spending their own: that was only human. Fulkerson absorbed Conrad's department into his, and March found that he could dispense with Kendricks in the place of assistant which he had lately filled since Fulkerson had decided that March was overworked. They reduced the number of illustrated articles, and they systematised the payment of contributors strictly according to the sales of each number, on their original plan of co-operation: they had got to paying rather lavishly for material without reference to the sales.

Fulkerson took a little time to get married, and went on his wedding journey out to Niagara, and down the St. Lawrence to Quebec over the line of travel that the Marches had taken in their wedding journey. He had the pleasure of going from Montreal to Quebec on the same boat on which he first met March.

They have continued very good friends, and their wives are almost without the rivalry that usually embitters the wives of partners. At first Mrs. March did not like Mrs. Fulkerson's speaking of her husband as the Ownah, and March as the Edito'; but it appeared that this was only a convenient method of recognising the predominant quality in each, and was meant neither to affirm nor to deny anything. Colonel Woodburn offered as his contribution to the celebration of the co-partnership, which Fulkerson could not be prevented from dedicating with a little dinner, the story of Fulkerson's magnanimous behaviour in regard to Dryfoos at that crucial moment when it was a question whether he should give up Dryfoos or give up March. Fulkerson winced at it; but Mrs. March told her husband that now, whatever happened, she should never have any misgivings of Fulkerson

       447

again; and she asked him if he did not think he ought to apologise to him for the doubts with which he had once inspired her. March said that he did not think so.

The Fulkersons spent the summer at a seaside hotel in easy reach of the city; but they returned early to Mrs. Leighton's, with whom they are to board till spring, when they are going to fit up Fulkerson's bachelor apartment for housekeeping. Mrs. March, with her Boston scruple, thinks it will be odd, living over the *Every Other Week* offices; but there will be a separate street entrance to the apartment; and besides, in New York you may do anything.

The future of the Leightons promises no immediate change. Kendricks goes there a good deal to see the Fulkersons, and Mrs. Fulkerson says he comes to see Alma. He has seemed taken with her ever since he first met her at Dryfoos's, the day of Lindau's funeral, and though Fulkerson objects to dating a fancy of that kind from an occasion of that kind, he justly argues with March that there can be no harm in it, and that we are liable to be struck by lightning any time. In the meanwhile there is no proof that Alma returns Kendricks' interest, if he feels any. She has got a little bit of colour into the fall exhibition; but the fall exhibition is never so good as the spring exhibition. Wetmore is rather sorry she has succeeded in this, though he promoted her success. He says her real hope is in black and white, and it is a pity for her to lose sight of her original aim of drawing for illustration.

News has come from Paris of the engagement of Christine Dryfoos. There the Dryfooses met with the success denied them in New York; many American plutocrats must await their apotheosis in Europe, where society has them, as it were, in a translation. Shortly after their arrival they were celebrated in the newspapers as the first millionaire American family of natural-gas extraction who had arrived in the capital of civilisation; and at a French watering-place Christine encountered her fate—a nobleman full of present debts and of duels in the past. Fulkerson says the old man can manage the debtor, and Christine can look out for the duellist. "They say those fellows generally whip their wives.

He'd better not try it with Christine, I reckon, unless he's practised with a panther."

One day, shortly after their return to town in the autumn from the brief summer outing they permitted themselves, the Marches met Margaret Vance. At first they did not know her in the dress of the sisterhood which she wore; but she smiled joyfully, almost gaily, on seeing them, and though she hurried by with the sister who accompanied her, and did not stay to speak, they felt that the peace that passeth understanding* had looked at them from her eyes.

"Well, she is at rest, there can't be any doubt of that," he said, as he glanced round at the drifting black robe which followed her free, nun-like walk.

"Yes, now she can do all the good she likes," sighed his wife. "I wonder—I wonder if she ever told his father about her talk with poor Conrad that day he was shot?"

"I don't know. I don't care. In any event it would be right. She did nothing wrong. If she unwittingly sent him to his death, she sent him to die for God's sake, for man's sake."

"Yes—yes. But still——"

"Well, we must trust that look of hers."

THE END

He'd have me or some other Christine, I reckon, unless he practised what he preached—"

. . . the developer who had an appointment down in the autumn upon the brief summer out ere they permitted themselves the Marches met Margaret Vance. At first they did not know her in the dress of the sisterhood which she wore; but she smiled joyfully, almost gayly, on seeing them, and though she hurried by unpacking her who accompanied her, and did not turn toward them, but the tired . . . of the impression that passed in their . . . standing, had looked at them from her eyes.

"Well, she is at rest now, and be any doubt of that," he said . . . and glanced round at the fluttering black robe which followed her free into the road.

"You mean she carried all the goodness that breathed his . . . I would . . . I asked if she ever told his father who . . . her; and with pure . . . assure that day he was shot."

"I don't know, I don't care, to any event it would be nothing. She did nothing wrong . . . is she who truly sent him to his death she sent him to die for God's sake, for man's sake."

"Yes—yes. But still——"

"And we must traighter look at him."

EXPLANATORY NOTES

A Hazard of New Fortunes: Howells's title is from *King John*, II. i. 71.

1 *March*: Basil and Isabel March are the main characters in the earlier Howells novel *Their Wedding Journey* (1871), which describes their honeymoon trip.
mucilage-bottle: containing adhesive gum.
since the morning stars sang together: echo of Job 38: 7.

3 *cotton to*: take a liking to, fasten on to.

5 *the newspaper syndicate business*: see p. 11, where Fulkerson explains the basic principle.

6 *chore-women*: charwomen.

9 *the Transcript*: the *Boston Daily Evening Transcript*, a newspaper representing the conservative New England tradition. In Eliot's poem 'The Boston Evening Transcript' it symbolizes the city's deadly dullness.

10 *cela va sans baiser*: Fr. that goes without kissing (as in '*cela va sans dire*'—'that goes without saying').

18 *his divided life was somewhat like Charles Lamb's*: the English essayist and poet (1775–1834) worked for 33 years as a clerk for the East India Company.

27 *Columbia*: Columbia University in New York, whereas Harvard University is in Cambridge, near Boston.

32 *never jam today*: slightly misquoting *Through the Looking-Glass*, Ch. 5.

33 *caciques*: tribal chiefs.

35 *sack*: a woman's loose coat, hanging down at the back; judging from the later passage in which it is mentioned (p. 134), Mrs March's sack has a form of cowl covering the head which can be thrown back.

38 *portier*: porter, door-keeper.
gimcrack: knick-knack.
portière: curtain hung over a door or doorway.

39 *tidies*: covers.
repoussé: with decorative work raised in relief.
spelter: zinc.

42 *the Herald and the World*: the *New York Herald*, a daily
paper with a very full news coverage, edited at this time by
James Gordon Bennett; and the *New York World*, another
daily which Joseph Pulitzer had made famous for its
crusading journalism.
horse-cars: street cars (trams) drawn by horses; they reached
the peak of their popularity in the 1870s, and were gradually
being replaced by other forms of transport by the mid-
1890s. The earlier omnibuses were also horse-drawn, but
had no rails laid down for them on the bumpy streets. They
have been called 'city stagecoaches'.

43 *Grace Church*: at Broadway and 10th Street; a Gothic
Revival church built in 1846, and used by the socially
prominent in 19th-century New York for their weddings,
christenings, and funerals.
Palmyra, Baalbec, Timour of the Desert: ruined ancient
cities.

44 *on our wedding journey*: see note to p. 1.
arrière pensée: Fr. behind thought; usually means 'hidden
motive', but as used here seems closer to 'underlying
suggestion'.
primo tenore: It. with the appearance of an operatic first
tenor. The Garibaldi statue was installed in 1888, so that
this is an important piece of evidence in attempting to
establish when the novel is set; although it should be noted
that in the *Harper's Weekly* serial version of the novel the
statue 'had not yet taken possession of the place'; subsequent editions have 'had already taken possession'.
Italian faces, French faces, Spanish faces: 5½ million immigrants arrived in the USA in the 1880s, and 4 million in
the 1890s. March's observations, here and later in the novel
(e.g. p. 162), reflect the changes in the pattern of im-
migration in these decades: the numbers of Irish and
Germans diminished, and the majority of those seeking
American citizenship were from Southern and Eastern
Europe—Italians, Jews, Russians, Greeks, etc.

45 *along the Park Street mall . . . out on Beacon*: celebrated streets in Boston.
écraser l'infâme: crush the vile thing; a phrase used by Voltaire.
Worth: Charles Worth (1825–95), an English-born fashion designer who came to dictate Parisian taste.

49 *kalsomining*: calcimining; a trade name for a white or coloured wash.

50 *L roads*: the 'el' or elevated transit line, consisting of tracks raised above the streets by a series of pillars. From 1871 onwards, the elevated network was extended throughout lower Manhattan; steam trains were used initially, with electric trains appearing in the last years of the century.

52 *coupé*: four-wheeled horse-drawn carriage, with two seats inside.

59 *the Hole in the Ground*: a popular play, first performed in 1887 by Charles Hoyt.

63 *Arachne*: in which the iron girders form a shape resembling a spider's web (in Greek myth, Arachne was changed into a spider by Athena).

69 *the natural gas country*: natural gas was discovered before the Civil War in Ohio, West Virginia, New York State, and Pennsylvania (Fulkerson's 'Pittsburg gas-fields'). Large-scale production got under way in the 1860s, and gas was often found alongside oil; hence Ohio, the hub of John D. Rockefeller's Standard Oil empire, was at the forefront of the new industry. Howells visited natural gas fields in Findlay, Ohio, during 1887.

70 *the cars*: railway train.
doggeries: cheap saloons.

73 *public-spirited as all get-out*: a slangy emphatic phrase; as public-spirited as he could possibly be.
the dads: his father's generation.
the Standard Oil Company: John D. Rockefeller's company was incorporated in 1870, eight years after he bought his first oil refinery in Cleveland, Ohio. By the end of the century it was responsible for four-fifths of the national oil output, and controlled iron, coal, shipping, and banking companies. The Standard Oil Trust Agreement of 1882,

forming a 'trust' or monopolistic corporation of corporations, became a prototype for those in other industries. Both politicians and the public were alarmed by this trend in big business, and Congress passed the Sherman Anti-trust Act in 1890, the year in which *A Hazard of New Fortunes* appeared, in an unsuccessful attempt to halt it. As is noted in the Introduction (p. xxvii), Howells had published an exposé of Standard Oil in 1881 as editor of the *Atlantic Monthly*.

75 *shade-trees*: any trees valued for the shade they provide.
the old Knickerbocker society: much of present-day New York State was settled by the Dutch in the early part of the 17th century, and a family called Knickerbocker arrived around 1674; however, the name was used as a general term for the New York Dutch after Irving's burlesque *Knickerbocker's History of New York* (1809).

76 *bunco business*: the trick of gaining a man's confidence; bunco or bunko, the name of a dice game, became used as a term for any form of cheating or swindling; Fulkerson facetiously overstates the amount of deception involved.
Bernhardt: Sarah Bernhardt (1844–1923), the great French actress, who made frequent appearances in America.

78 *Uhland*: Johann Uhland (1787–1862), the German lyric poet.

79 *the war—twenty years ago*: the American Civil War (1861–5), in which Lindau fought on the Union side. The figure of twenty years, and March's later remarks, suggest that the events of *A Hazard of New Fortunes* occur somewhere between 1883–5; much of the other detail in the novel, however, is in keeping with a later date.

80 *The anti-slavery battle ... in 1858*: three years before the War, when the issue was coming to dominate American political life. During 1858 Lincoln emerged as a major figure, alerting his audiences to the threat that slavery would become a nation-wide institution.
Berlin in 1848: during the Year of Revolutions there were riots in the city in March, which caused King Frederick William IV of Prussia to summon a Constituent Assembly. It sat until December, when he retracted his concessions.

89 *Pullman vestibuled train*: George Pullman developed his 'moving hotels', with sleeping-cars and dining-cars, in the 1860s, and they soon became very popular. The 'vestibule' was the part of a carriage connecting it to the next; in the 'vestibule train', which he patented in 1887, this cover-way was improved to eliminate danger and bumpiness as the passenger moved between carriages. (Like the references to the statue of Garibaldi on p. 44 and to the Statue of Liberty on p. 272, this detail suggests that the novel is set in the late 1880s.)

103 *siccative*: a drying agent.
  mop-board: skirting-board.
  scutcheoned: escutcheoned; with a heraldic shield, or shield-shaped decorations.

120 *duodecimo*: formed from sheets folded so as to make twelve leaves.

121 *those Tartarin books of Daudet's*: the French novelist, poet, and playwright Alphonse Daudet (1840–97), who achieved a great success with three novels featuring a blustering provincial simpleton, beginning with *Aventures prodigieuses de Tartarin de Tarascon* (1872); see the passage on the style of illustration proposed for *Every Other Week* on p. 123.
  a Daniel come to judgement: The Merchant of Venice, IV. i. 220.

124 *the ewig Weibliche*: Ger. the eternal feminine; alludes to the last line of Goethe's *Faust Part II* (1832), 'Das Ewig-Weibliche zieht uns hinan' (the eternal feminine draws us upward).

134 *sacque*: alternative spelling of 'sack'; see note to p. 35.

137 *train*: romp, carry on; a New England slang word.

139 *Dunkards*: also Dunkers; a German Baptist sect which first arrived in Pennsylvania in 1719, and acquired their nickname from the practice of baptism by triple immersion. Some of their characteristic beliefs are outlined on p. 221.
  Mennists: more usually Mennonites; a Dutch fundamentalist Protestant sect which emigrated to America in 1683, settling initially in Pennsylvania (Dryfoos's father was 'Pennsylvania Dutch') and then spreading to the Midwest

EXPLANATORY NOTES

and South. They also divided into several branches, including the Amish.

143 *some hydro-Mela*: a honey and water beverage; Fulkerson plays on the name 'Mela', just as he apparently puns on christen/Christine.

154 *the hobby*: a subject to which a person returns repeatedly and obsessively; literally, a strong, active horse.

157 *Tutt' altro!*: It. on the contrary!

158 *Bevans*: 'Neile Bevans', the pseudonym of Mrs Nellie Bingham van Slingerland, who wrote extravagant romances.

160 *the old Cornhill*: a literary magazine edited by Thackeray from 1860 to his death in 1863.

161 *congeries*: an aggregation of disparate things.

162 *Pelasgic*: Greeks; the name of the prehistoric inhabitants of Greece.
cue-filleted: presumably with a cue (plait) worn as a band around the head.

163 *Circassian*: the people of the western Caucasus.

164 *teams*: animals harnessed together, usually horses.
the end-man: the man at either end of the line in a minstrel show.

165 *shingle*: piece of wood (for hitting a naughty child).
the Chinese dwellers in Mott Street: Mott Street remains to this day the central thoroughfare of New York's Chinatown.

167 *Heine*: Heinrich Heine (1797–1856), the German poet and essayist, who travelled widely and became one of the leaders of the international democratic movement. His revolutionary sympathies doubtless contribute to the attraction of his work for Lindau. The quotation is from 'Die Heimkehr', LXIV, describing the poet as an upright man who provides his own sustenance (and hence has no need of patrons).

168 *crape*: black crêpe, signifying mourning.
Marmontel: Jean-François Marmontel (1723–99), a French author who came to Paris in 1745 on the advice of Voltaire. He wrote poems, plays, opera, and contributions to the *Encyclopédie* (the encyclopaedic dictionary edited by Diderot), some of which reflect liberal opinions. His best-

known works include *Contes moraux* (1761) and the political romance *Bélisaire* (1767).

169 *Greenwich Village*: in the final years of the 19th century, the Village was only just beginning to acquire its status, fully established after the First World War, as a literary and artistic colony. Lindau's goppler (cobbler) is a genuine, rather than a figurative, Bohemian.

there are fagots and fagots: Molière, *Le Médecin malgré lui* (1666), I. v: 'Il y a fagots et fagots'.

170 *the landlords and the merchant princes, the railroad kings and the coal barons*: the years after the Civil War saw the creation of the huge fortunes of such men as Andrew Carnegie, John D. Rockefeller, and Cornelius Vanderbilt, who became known collectively as the 'robber barons'.

the poet Rogers: Samuel Rogers (1763–1855), best known for his Byronic tribute *Italy* (1822–8) and his table-talk; he became head of his father's bank, and inherited his fortune.

the other Rogers, the martyr: John Rogers (c.1500–55), the first Protestant martyr in the reign of the Catholic Queen Mary, who was burned after preaching against Romanism.

172 *buncombe*: bunkum, humbug; the spelling reflects the origin of the word: a Congressman in the 1819–21 session defended a boring speech by saying that he was 'speaking for Buncombe (County)'.

Ruskin: in the years between 1860 and 1885 the English art critic John Ruskin (1819–1900) developed a social philosophy which combined aspects of Christianity and socialism. His ideas, like those of Tolstoy, contributed to the formation of Howells's socialist beliefs.

174 *Russian realism*: another important influence on Howells, who became the leading American spokesman of literary realism. Tolstoy was the major figure, but he also admired Dostoevsky, Turgenev, and Gogol, and published their work as editor of the *Atlantic Monthly*.

175 *the most inspired ass since Balaam's*: which speaks, rebuking its master, in Numbers 22: 22–35.

178 *like a mice*: (slang) with sudden energy.

jimmy: (slang) smart, neat.

dog: (slang) show, dash, display.

chromos: coloured chromium lithographs.

179 *divvy*: (slang) dividend.

188 *Mr. Depew*: Chauncey Depew (1834–1928), a railroad
lawyer, politician, and orator. He was a candidate for the
Republican Presidential nomination in 1888 (withdrawing
in favour of Harrison) and Senator for New York; in 1886
he was the main speaker at the ceremony of dedication of
the Statue of Liberty.

Mr. Evarts: William Evarts (1818–1901), a leading lawyer
who served as Secretary of State from 1877–81, and New
York Senator from 1885–91.

190 *Bismarck's shoes*: Otto von Bismarck (1815–98), the Prus-
sian statesman, who succeeded, over the course of three
decades, in establishing the German nation and then developing it into an empire with colonial ambitions. He finally
resigned his office as Chancellor in 1890.

195 *nipping*: catching (in order to obtain an advertisement).

Artemus Ward: the pseudonym of the humourist C. F.
Browne (1834–67), first used in 1857 in the Cleveland *Plain
Dealer*, for which he wrote a record of the imaginary
adventures of an itinerant showman. He achieved great
popularity on both sides of the Atlantic before his untimely
death.

196 *among those Rackensackens*: among other Dutch or German
inhabitants of the Midwest.

the Vanderbilts and the Astors: the Vanderbilt fortunes were
founded on **rail**road financing; those of the Astors on
control of the fur trade.

Castoria . . . Pearline: popular products; a medicine and a
laundry detergent, respectively.

grasshopper year: one in which grasshoppers destroy the
crops.

202 *shoomakes*: sumacs.

206 *'Piscopalians*: Episcopalian; the American institution of the
Anglican communion.

213 *the old Covenanter strain*: Covenant theology was a version
of New England Puritanism which involved a modification
of the Calvinist doctrine of predestination.

217 *Madame Geoffrin*: Marie Thérèse Geoffrin (1699–1777),
a rich widow who became an important patroness of

18th-century French literature, particularly the work of the *philosophes*.
Lady Barberina Lemon: the heroine of Henry James's story 'Lady Barberina' (1884).

221 *a point d'appui*: a point of leverage or support.

238 *Let your women keep silence in the churches*: 1 Corinthians 14: 34.

250 *San Luigi Gonzaga*: St Aloysius Gonzaga (1568–91).

254 *the patent outsides of the country press*: patent outsides (or insides) were sheets sold to editors of small newspapers; while one side would have miscellaneous matter printed on it, the other would be left blank for him to fill up as he chose.
l'appétit vient en mangeant: Fr. appetite comes with eating.

262 *the faith of Bunker Hill and Appomattox*: faith in the values of the American Revolution, and of the Union in the Civil War. Bunker Hill in Boston was the site of an honourable American defeat in 1775; the South surrendered to Grant at Appomattox in 1865.

265 *olla podrida*: a form of stew.
comptoir: Fr. cashier's booth.

266 *the University Building*: New York University (NYU).

268 *b'hoy*: (slang) thug.

271 *the Battery*: at the southern end of the island of Manhattan.

272 *the colossal lady on Bedlōe's Island*: the Statue of Liberty, which was dedicated on 28 October 1886.

279 *Saratoga*: a popular watering-place in upstate New York.

284 *an Abolitionist*: an activist in the anti-slavery cause.
the Anti-Nebraska party in '55: in 1854 Congress passed the Kansas–Nebraska Bill, allowing the two new states to determine for themselves whether they should permit slavery. This was seen as a victory for the South, raising the possibility of one or two new 'slave' states in the Union, and led to violent confrontations in the territories in question. The Republican Party was formed at this time in direct reaction to the Bill, and eventually attracted the future President Lincoln. Between 1854 and 1856 some anti-

slavery politicians called themselves Republicans, others anti-Nebraskans.

Fremont: John C. Frémont (1813–90), an explorer who became a Senator and the Republican candidate in the Presidential election, of 1856. He was defeated by the Democrat James Buchanan.

289 *old Pan-Electric himself*: possibly a reference to the inventor Thomas Edison (1847–1931), who had no taste for high society and never lost sight of his humble origins in Ohio. He revolutionized electric lighting in homes, workplaces, and streets, and established the first urban power-station in New York in 1882. This led to such tags as 'the Wizard of Menlo Park'. The *New York Times* writer George Jones, who defended the Pan-Electric Co. in a legal battle, has also been suggested.

298 *Stand not upon the order of your going*: Macbeth, III. iv. 119.
sack and sugar: *1 Henry IV*, II. iv. 516.

299 *Scott and Addison*: the novelist Walter Scott (1771–1832) was particularly admired in the Old South, and Joseph Addison (1672–1719), editor of the *Spectator*, was a model classical stylist. The French writers named by Beaton, on the other hand, would represent to someone like Woodburn a decadent combination of aestheticism and realism, especially in the treatment of sexual subjects.

Louis Napoleon: a descendant of Bonaparte who was elected President of France in late 1848. In 1851 he added to his powers by a *coup d'état*; in 1852 he took the title of Emperor Napoleon III, inaugurating the Second Empire, which lasted until the French defeat by Prussia in 1870. The poet and novelist Victor Hugo aligned himself with the republican opposition, and wrote *Napoléon le petit* in exile after the *coup d'état*.

301 *My substitute*: in *A People's History of the United States* (London: Longmans, 1980, p. 249), Howard Zinn notes that John D. Rockefeller, Andrew Carnegie, J. P. Morgan, Jay Gould, and James Mellon all paid substitutes, like Dryfoos, to take their place in the Civil War.

303 *monopolies—the Standard Oil Company, the Sugar Trust, the Rubber Trust*: see note to p. 73.
dry-goods: drapery and the like.

306 *Some of the men tried to form a union*: the 1880s saw workers in many industries attempting to organize themselves into unions, in the face of vigorous resistance from employers. 1886, in particular, became known as 'the year of the uprising of labour', with 1,400 strikes.

307 *Pinkertons*: in the 1870s and 1880s the detective agency formed by Allan Pinkerton before the Civil War became equally famous for its union-busting and strike-breaking services to employers. The methods used by Pinkertons men during the Homestead Strike (1892) caused particular outrage.

308 *the great railroad strike of '77*: unrest among railway workers was a frequent occurrence; there were several strikes in 1886, and a national strike in 1894.
the Battle of Dorking: part of a well-known fiction treating an invasion of England as 'something already accomplished'.

309 *conspiracy laws*: laws banning trade unions as a 'conspiracy' against employers, just as the Sherman Anti-trust Act of 1890 (see note to p. 73) declared trust agreements between corporations to be a 'conspiracy' restraining free trade.

315 *How hardly shall they that have riches . . .*: Luke 18: 24.

326 *Micky*: full of Irish.
the Old Homestead: a popular play first performed in 1887, by Denman Thompson.

330 *Bildad*: friend who only causes more pain; one of three 'Job's comforters' in the Book of Job.

331 *the man on horseback*: a hero.

332 *Bahyard*: a Bayard, or model of chivalric virtue; from the Chevalier de Bayard, a French knight known as *le chevalier sans peur et sans reproche*. Robert E. Lee was called 'the Bayard of the Confederate Army'.

347 '*As when a great thought . . .*': Tennyson, 'A Dream of Fair Women', ll. 43–4.

348 *We might adapt Kingsley*: Charles Kingsley, in 'A Farewell to C.E.G.', l. 9.

367 *Strike*: a rail strike occurred in New York, while Howells was writing *A Hazard of New Fortunes*, in early 1889.

369 *scare-heads*: newspaper headings intended to raise a scare.

370 *the roads*: (in this usage) the railway owners.

372 *De Foe's Plague of London style*: *A Journal of the Plague Year* (1722), by the novelist Daniel Defoe, reconstructs the course of the London plague epidemic of 1665—when the author was only a small child—using an imaginary eyewitness.

374 *the coup d'état*: see note to p. 299.

380 *set-bowl*: apparently a wash-basin; more usually a lavatory bowl.

399 *the marvel and the curse*: Browning, 'Gold Hair: A Story of Pornic', l. 140.

418 *a Scottish Seceder*: a member of the Secession Church, which originated when a body of Presbyterians left the Church of Scotland around 1733.

432 *'fated fairy prince'*: Tennyson, 'The Day-Dream: The Sleeping Palace', l. 56.

433 *Paul only went so far*: in 1 Corinthians 7.

440 *that a sparrow falls to the ground*: a reference to Matthew 10: 29.

441 *That if one rose from the dead it would not avail*: a reference to Luke 16: 31, Abraham's words concluding the parable of Dives and Lazarus.

443 *Jacqueminot*: a deep-red perpetual rose.

445 *"Spag at him like a wild-cat!"*: possibly misprint for 'sprang'.

449 *the peace that passeth understanding*: Philippians 4: 7.

THE WORLD'S CLASSICS

A Select List

SERGEI AKSAKOV: A Russian Gentleman
Translated by J. D. Duff
Edited by Edward Crankshaw

A Russian Schoolboy
Translated by J. D. Duff
Introduction by John Bayley

HANS ANDERSEN: Fairy Tales
Translated by L. W. Kingsland
Introduction by Naomi Lewis
Illustrated by Vilhelm Pedersen and Lorenz Frølich

ARTHUR J. ARBERRY (Transl.): The Koran

LUDOVICO ARIOSTO: Orlando Furioso
Translated by Guido Waldman

ARISTOTLE: The Nicomachean Ethics
Translated by David Ross

JANE AUSTEN: Emma
Edited by James Kinsley and David Lodge

Mansfield Park
Edited by James Kinsley and John Lucas

Persuasion
Edited by John Davie

ROBERT BAGE: Hermsprong
Edited by Peter Faulkner

WILLIAM BECKFORD: Vathek
Edited by Roger Lonsdale

R. D. BLACKMORE: Lorna Doone
Edited by Sally Shuttleworth

KEITH BOSLEY (Transl.): The Kalevala

JAMES BOSWELL: Life of Johnson
The Hill/Powell edition, revised by David Fleeman
Introduction by Pat Rogers

ANTHONY TROLLOPE: The American Senator
Edited by John Halperin

The Last Chronicle of Barset
Edited by Stephen Gill

IZAAK WALTON and CHARLES COTTON:
The Compleat Angler
Edited by John Buxton
Introduction by John Buchan

OSCAR WILDE: Complete Shorter Fiction
Edited by Isobel Murray

A complete list of Oxford Paperbacks, including The World's Classics, OPUS, Past Masters, Oxford Authors, Oxford Shakespeare, and Oxford Paperback Reference, is available in the UK from the Arts and Reference Publicity Department (RS), Oxford University Press, Walton Street, Oxford OX2 6DP.

In the USA, complete lists are available from the Paperbacks Marketing Manager, Oxford University Press, 200 Madison Avenue, New York, NY 10016.

Oxford Paperbacks are available from all good bookshops. In case of difficulty, customers in the UK can order direct from Oxford University Press Bookshop, Freepost, 116 High Street, Oxford, OX1 4BR, enclosing full payment. Please add 10 per cent of published price for postage and packing.